PRESIDENT
BARACK OBAMA
OF USA

The Atmosphere Of America & the Rest Of the World With Barack As America's CEO.

By

Dr. Festus S. A. Oguhebe-'Strongblood'
President, *Emancipation*USA

An Inspirational Gift

From:____

To:__________________________

On:__________________________

Comment:____

____

PRESIDENT
BARACK OBAMA
OF USA

The Atmosphere Of America & the Rest Of the World With Barack As America's CEO.

By

Dr. Festus S. A. Oguhebe-'Strongblood'
President, *Emancipation*USA

Credits:
Obama family pictures -- Obama Campaign
Obama at Capitol-- Barack Obama. Cortesy of Richmonddemocrat.blog spot.com
Other pictures—Wikipedia.
Cover Design—Festus S.A. Oguhebe.

Cover design---F.S.A.O. Strongblood

Paperback ISBN: **1-932110-21-6**
Hardcover ISBN: **1-932110-22-4**

Publisher Hebe's International Publishers
404 parks Road, Jackson, MS. 39212, USA.

DEDICATED

Primarily to Ann (Stanley) Dunham [Obama/Soetoro]—Barack's extra ordinary and loving mother, *Stanley Armour Dunham*—Barack's darling grandfather, and *Madelyn Payne Dunham*—Barack's heavenly grandmother. We appreciate all of you. May Ann's soul rest in peace. May grandpa's soul rest in peace. When God calls grandma home, may her soul rest in peace too. They have made many people happy.

Barack & mother

Barack's Grandparents

To Late President John F. Kennedy
May his soul rest in peace

To Late Robert F. Kennedy
May his soul rest in peace

To the Honorable Mrs. Ethel Kennedy
(The widow of Robert Kennedy)
May God bless you the way you desire to be blessed. Your husband did not die in vain. You have not suffered this widowhood in vain.

To the champion Senator, Edward (Ted) M. Kennedy
To the ever beautiful Caroline Kennedy
To Rep. Patrick Kennedy and to all of Kenney's family members.
You have sacrificed for the common man and for social justice.

To Senator John F. Kerry
You heard from God when you called on the Illionois State Senator, Barack Obama, to deliver the 2004 Democratic Convention major speech. I appreciate you.

And
To all Americans, whether you voted for Barack or not. You are beautiful and you ought to pat yourself on the back and shout,
"God Bless America!"

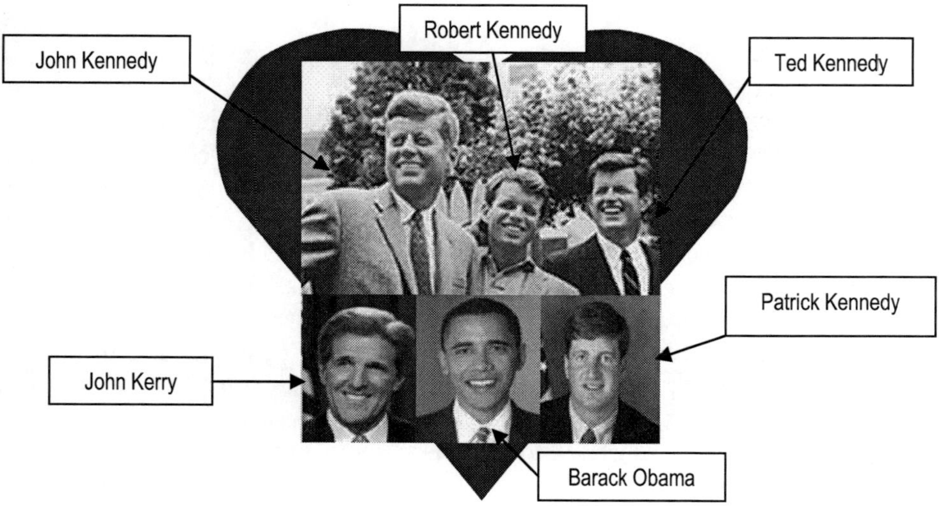

PREFACE

Besides recommending Barack Obama as the next president of the United States, this book teaches you how to make a wise decision in choosing a candidate for any political office. Besides, it does not matter whether you voted for Obama or not, this book will help you determine whether you have made a wise choice with your vote or not.

To today's Americans, it seems like they have been looking for change forever anytime they look at President George W. Bush policies, the policies they deem as very flawed, failed, and isolationist in character. Yet I do not share in all of the criticisms, for I know that President Bush may have also been appointed by God Himself to absorb the full weight of economic and political devastation of September 11, 2001 when Islamic fundamentalism and Al Qaeda bombed America with passenger airplanes, claiming over 3000 lives. Bush Jr. stabilized America during this tumultuous period.

Nevertheless, the ensuing economic and international relations woes and certain flaws in Bush administration's policy decisions have brought almost insurmountable pressures upon the population that cherishes freedom so much that they needed to be fielded in on any decision before it is taken. The biggest blunder seemed to be the very unpopular decision to switch from going after Al Qaeda in Afghanistan and Pakistan to going after Saddam Hussein and weapons of mass destruction in Iraq, causing the unpopular Iraq war. At least, according to investigations, it turned out that Iraq had no weapons of mass destruction and that the President may have tricked America into going for a wrong war, the war that a two-year US senator from Illinois, Mr. Barack Obama, opposed from the beginning before it was waged, while he was serving in the Illinois Senate.

This extremely unpopular war is claiming the lives of much more than expected U.S. soldiers, close to 4,200 as of July 17, 2008. The life and monetary costs are over 100 percent of Mr. President's original budget and expectations (see appendix 1). That's horrible management. It is sapping about $12 billion per month from American taxpayers, bleeding the economy to death and distracting policies and attention away from pressing domestic issues and other serious foreign and international concerns. America is literally dying economically, coupled with plunging relationship with the rest of the world. President Bush Jr. grossly miscalculated the costs and the interactive impacts of his war decisions.

The complicating problems ushered in a surprising newcomer and what seems to have slipped out of God's sleeves, Mr. Barack Hussein Obama. He is a two-three term U.S. Senator from Illinois, who happens to be black or biracial, with a black father from Kenya-Africa and a white mother from Kansas-USA. Propelled into the national scene by the excellent speech he gave at the Democratic national convention in 2004, U.S. Senator Barack Obama is on the move. With his strategic management acumen, the black Senator from Illinois, a unifier, the potential next American president for all people and races, is currently the 2008 Democratic Party's presumptive nominee for the president of the United States of America. He attained this mantle by, through his campaign operative, out-managing his opponents, defeating eight other Democratic candidates, including the powerhouse of the Clinton's political machine and the campaign of Senator Hillary Rodham Clinton, the wife of the former and still very popular President, William (Bill) Jefferson Clinton.

Barack Obama will be facing the Republicans' presumptive nominee, Senator John McCain, in the November 2008 US general election for the presidency of the United States of America. Although I am a staunch Christian conservative, this book tells you why you may have to vote for Senator Barack Obama, a labeled liberal, as the next president and CEO of USA. From this book, you will also learn how to choose a candidate in any presidential election. I hope you enjoy it..............*Dr. Festus S. A. Oguhebe-Strongblood*

1. Presidential hopeful Barack Obama, in 1979 gets a hug during his high school graduation in Hawaii from his maternal grandparents, Stanley Armour Dunham and Madelyn Payne, both natives of Kansas. (Photo courtesy Obama campaign).
2. Barack Obama plays on the beach with his grandfather on his mother's side, Stanley Armour Dunham. (Photo courtesy Obama campaign).

PRESIDENT BARACK OBAMA OF USA

TABLE OF CONTENTS

...By us, this change will not happen. Divided, we are bound to fail. But the life of a tall, gangly, self-made Springfield lawyer tells us that a different future is possible. He tells us that there is power in words. He tells us that there is power in conviction. That beneath all the differences of race and region, faith and station, we are one people. He tells us that there is power in hope. As Lincoln organized the forces arrayed against slavery, he was heard to say: "Of strange, discordant, and even hostile elements, we gathered from the four winds, and formed and fought to battle through." That is our purpose here today. That's why I'm in this race. Not just to hold an office, but to gather with you to transform a nation. I want to win that next battle – for justice and opportunity. I want to win that next battle – for better schools, and better jobs, and health care for all. I want us to take up the unfinished business of perfecting our union, and building a better America. And if you will join me in this improbable quest, if you feel destiny calling, and see as I see, a future of endless possibility stretching before us; if you sense, as I sense, that the time is now to shake off our slumber, and slough off our fear, and make good on the debt we owe past and future generations, then I'm ready to take up the cause, and march with you, and work with you. Together, starting today, let us finish the work that needs to be done, and usher in a new birth of freedom on this Earth. ....*Barack Obama. 2/7/07*

YES WE CAN!

CHAPTER 1

INTRODUCTION: WHO IS BARACK OBAMA?

When a child is born, one never knew what he would become. However, God knows. The contingencies that led to his birth are part of his life and are factored into the young person's life equation. Our job is to do all that God desires us to do for the youngster, and God does all the watering and the rest of the story. Are you inspired?

US Senator Barack Obama of Illinois. (barackobama.com)

Dear wonderful Americans of all colors, creed, classes, and age: change is a very hard thing. I am a conservative. [redacted] Who will build and blossom America's economy, strengthen the middle class, heal domestic social-cultural wounds, and develop strong international relations and solutions network? Who will truly deal with Russia and similar nations the way such nations may even be quite amazed and will actually listen to and work with the United States in a noncombatant fashion? The only choice and stand-alone answer you have in this election is Senator Barack Obama. Dear fellow Americans, develop the courage to vote for this man, Barack Obama, and then stand back and witness a great new image of USA, domestically and internationally. People, every action produces a reaction. Negative action (or in the form of reaction) produces negative and destructive reactions. Positive and loving action (or in the form of reactions) produce well-deserved POSITIVE reactions. Rowdy, tough, and rough-voice talks and gun-slinger attitude do not spell strength. America, Obama is your person! Don't make a serious, regrettable error again! Stop setting yourself up to be tricked in elections. Avoid "Had-I-known" disease! Weigh all factors. America, stop voting out of fear. Stop hindering your development. Obama is America's antidote against Russian threats and much more. He is the beginning of a new era, the healing and blossoming of USA! Give this man a chance to display what is already in him. America will be doubly blessed. Guaranteed!

To people like Dr. Jerome Corsi, with the inability to stand change, change is particularly very difficult. That was why Dr. Corsi spent his time to write a *fly-by-night* book called, *The Obama Nation*. Dr Corsi's perception or, should I say, 'pretended' perception of Obama is skewed, maimed, un-American and off. Besides, he is singing a wrong chorus that has been sung before. It is neither tasty nor interesting, except to those who enjoy being deceived. You do not need to read the book. It takes America backwards. I am a staunch Christian conservative, and that book does not speak for me or for the godly nation, the blessed United States of America. Dear fellow Americans: you are America not Corsi. You are too smart for Dr. Corsi and people like him. The more you read or hear lies and innuendos like that, the more you should send money to the Obama campaign to let such people know that you cannot be outsmarted by them any longer! It's high time they stopped such nonsense.

Enough is enough! You are true Americans who are not afraid of change, including having a strategic, loving, smart, one-wife, family-man and caring black person to be the next President of USA—the President for whites, blacks, Hispanics, rich, poor, Jews, gentiles, everyone, everyone, and especially for ONE-USA! I thank the Almighty God for all the wonderful white people of America—from south to north, east to west, and sea to shining sea who are not allowing themselves to be walloped by people like Jerome Corsi. May God reward them and bless this loving nation for their sakes. God bless America! God bless the USA!!!!!!! 

I certainly thank God for Stanley Dunham, Barack Obama's white grandfather, who took charge and be a father to his grandson, a son he had wanted from God. God saw fit to give him and his wife a no-nonsense son through their daughter, Stanley (Ann). If the veteran US soldier were alive right now, I strongly believe that he would tell Dr. Corsi and company to "*Shut Up and smell the right coffee*." The no-nonsense, loving, and exemplary white fellow would not let anyone slander his noble and down-to-earth grandson. Guess what—neither must we allow it. Let's do it for Stanley, Madelyn, Ann, and Obama Sr. Let's do it for America!

The 2008 presumptive nominee of the Democratic Party for President of the United States of America, Senator Barack Hussein Obama, was born on August 4, 1961 at Kapiolani Medical Center in Honolulu, Hawaii, USA. His father, Barack Obama Sr., was an African, a black man, from Kenya, East Africa; Barack's mother, Ann Dunham, was a white woman from Wichita, Kansas, USA. The parents met at the University of Hawaii, fell in love, and became married.

A marriage between a white woman and a black man during such a heated, racial period in the United States was a revolution in itself. That was enough to spell the extent of the brevity of Barack's mother and the nerve of his African daddy to dare engage in mix-race marriage when people were killed in the southern states for doing the same or ostracized in many parts of American society in the sixties. The black pigmentation of Barack makes him automatically 'black' or of a black race, and he is being treated likewise by the society and by all who see him or deal with him. Barack is a black man. However, he is one black fellow that is determined not to let 'blackism' be a hindrance but a blessing, just like anything God gives. He is a black man who is proud of his color and proud of other people's colors too.

Notice that I used the middle name too. Folks, the baby child (Barack) did not give himself the name. The parents did, and it might have come through God, Himself. God knew what he was doing when He decided to plot a good plan for America and the world, and to raise a man-child with controversial names, spanned many continents and religions, and yet he is a Jesus boy. Think about it. Do you think that it takes someone with tentacles in different continents and religions to help deal with the mess of today's America and the world? God may have dropped that middle name there to help make the Muslims and the Islamic world comfortable and more receptive to what American Obama will have to say.

You can do other extrapolations by yourself. What about his color and his biracial nature—the functions such nature will perform in America and in the world? Why did God choose to raise such a person through America--a nation that has been a champion in world charity and sacrifices, a nation whose motto is "*In God We Trust*," and a nation that has worked harder than any other nation on the face of the earth to promote love and human dignity? If you ask me, I will say, "That's an honor and recognition from above!" That's also an antidote for finally erasing a major sin of slavery that a loving nation of God had committed and had sincerely cried out to be forgiven. This is an opening door of a continuous blessing for the United States of America. In certain parts of Africa, USA was nicknamed, *"God's own country."* It is high time that America reclaimed this honor. I believe it is in the making through Barack Obama. Fellows, Barack embodies in himself the concern and love of Abraham Lincoln, the statesmanship of John F. Kennedy, the toughness of Ronald Reagan, and the unique strategic smartness and manner of approach of Barak Obama himself. If we miss electing this man the next President, we have missed TOO MUCH! Wake Up America! Go and put these words in the bank.

Declaration On Lincoln Steps

You cannot say that no one expected it because many did. Pundits and politicians cannot help but to expect that Senator Barack Obama will sooner, not latter, run for the presidency of the United States of America. This expectation was framed by a combination of events:

US Senator John F. Kerry of Massachusetts (Wikipedia)

(1) His excellent speech at 2004 Democratic convention, which thrust him into the national stage; thanks to Senator John Kerry, the 2004 presumptive Democratic nominee for the president of the United States, who chose Barack Obama to deliver the major speech.

(2) Obama's efforts in traveling and successfully campaigning for Democratic candidates in different parts of the United States.

Obama had been reported as saying, "No, no, no, no, absolutely not," in response to the question as to whether he was considering running for the presidency of the United States. President Bush Jr. noticed the man's popularity and warned Senator Obama, after Obama's US senate inaug-uration, that he be careful because people would be gunning for him for a slip. His popularity soared from 2004 all the way into the US senate. His activities led some people to tap him to run for the presidency of the United States of America.

Ethel Kennedy, the wife of Robert Kennedy, the assassinated presidential candidate in 1968, had prophesied on Obama's presidency in 2004 when she invited Barack Obama to speak on her husband's would have been 80th birthday. She introduced Obama as America's next president; she may have repeated the same prophecy in an interview two years ago, likening Barack to her husband, Robert F. Kennedy. (Zeleny and Hulse, January 28, 2008). In talking about Obama's candidacy, comparing her late husband's quest for social justice to Mr. Obama's, Ethel Kennedy said, "I think he feels it. He feels it just like Bobby did. He has the passion in his heart. He's not selling you. It's just him." (Zeleny and Hulse, January 28, 2008). This statement is more than a mouth full. On February 2, 2008, Ethel Kennedy formerly endorsed Obama as the next president of the United States. She said:

> Over these past few years, I've watched Senator Obama inspire Americans from all walks of life to believe in real change and a new sense of hope and possibility. He's a magnetic force, drawing the nation together for the common good and galvanizing us all to help shape our country's future. Barack is so like Bobby, who struggled for the rights of the poor in the Mississippi Delta and Appalachia, traveled to California to stand in solidarity with Cesar Chavez and farm workers, and fought to end another war that cost so many lives.
>
> Today, we crave a leader with vision who can help us regain our lost humanity and rekindle our inherent generosity. With courage, caring, and charisma, Senator Obama is leading us toward a kinder, gentler world. Senator Obama's candidacy sends out 'ripples of hope' that can build a 'current which can sweep down the mightiest walls of oppression and resistance.' I am proud to support Barack Obama, and look forward to him leading this country toward a brighter, more hopeful future. (BarackObama.com, February 2, 2008).

Ethel Kennedy
lbabuzz.com/politics

This is a very powerful endorsement. Unfortunately, the Illinois Senator and later, U.S. Senator, Barack Obama, did not see this coming 'too soon.' The presidential stuff may be in his heart but not quite in 2004 and before 2007. He had turned down the speculations about him running for president, a usually humble thing to do or he actually did not see it then. The turning down did not last after Martin Luther King Junior's '*fierce urgency of now*' kicked in and some fellow politicians kept urging US Senator Obama to get into the 2008 presidential race. That is what the man did. On the faithful day of Saturday, February 10, 2007, Barack Obama returned to Springfield Illinois, to the steps of the Old Capitol, where his hero, Abraham Lincoln, was a legislator, and he announced, "I am running for the President of the United States." The speech released by his 2008 campaign reads:

> Let me begin by saying thanks to all of you who've traveled, from far and wide, to brave the cold today. We all made this journey for a reason. It's humbling, but in my heart I know you didn't come here just for me, you came here because you believe in what this country can be. In the face of war, you believe there can be peace. In the face of despair, you believe there can be hope. In the face of a politics that's shut you out, that's told you to settle, that's divided us for too long, you believe we can be one people, reaching for what's possible, building that more perfect union.
>
> That's the journey we're on today. But let me tell you how I came to be here. As most of you know, I am not a native of this great state. I moved to Illinois over two decades ago. I was a young man then, just a year out of college; I knew no one in Chicago, was without money or family connections. But a group of churches had offered me a job as a community organizer for $13,000 a year. And I accepted the job, sight unseen, motivated then by a single, simple, powerful idea – that I might play a small part in building a better America.
>
> My work took me to some of Chicago's poorest neighborhoods. I joined with pastors and lay-people to deal with communities that had been ravaged by plant closings. I saw that the problems people faced weren't simply local in nature – that the decision to close a steel mill was made by distant executives; that the lack of textbooks and computers in schools could be traced to the skewed priorities of politicians a thousand miles away; and that when a child turns to violence, there's a hole in his heart no government could ever fill. It was in these neighborhoods that I received the best education I ever had, and where I learned the true meaning of my Christian faith.
>
> After three years of this work, I went to law school, because I wanted to understand how the law should work for those in need. I became a civil rights lawyer, and taught constitutional law, and after a time, I came to understand that our cherished rights of liberty and equality depend on the active participation of an awakened electorate. It was with these ideas in mind that I arrived in this capital city as a state Senator. It was here, in Springfield, where I saw all that is America converge – farmers and teachers, businessmen and laborers, all of them with a story to tell, all of them seeking a seat at the table, all of them clamoring to be heard.

I made lasting friendships here – friends that I see in the audience today. It was here we learned to disagree without being disagreeable – that it's possible to compromise so long as you know those principles that can never be compromised; and that so long as we're willing to listen to each other, we can assume the best in people instead of the worst.

That's why we were able to reform a death penalty system that was broken. That's why we were able to give health insurance to children in need. That's why we made the tax system more fair and just for working families, and that's why we passed ethics reforms that the cynics said could never, ever be passed. It was here, in Springfield, where North, South, East and West come together that I was reminded of the essential decency of the American people – where I came to believe that through this decency, we can build a more hopeful America. And that is why, in the shadow of the Old State Capitol, where Lincoln once called on a divided house to stand together, where common hopes and common dreams still, I stand before you today to announce my candidacy for President of the United States.

I recognize there is a certain presumptuousness – a certain audacity – to this announcement. I know I haven't spent a lot of time learning the ways of Washington. But I've been there long enough to know that the ways of Washington must change. The genius of our founders is that they designed a system of government that can be changed. And we should take heart, because we've changed this country before. In the face of tyranny, a band of patriots brought an Empire to its knees. In the face of secession, we unified a nation and set the captives free. In the face of Depression, we put people back to work and lifted millions out of poverty. We welcomed immigrants to our shores, we opened railroads to the west, we landed a man on the moon, and we heard a King's call to let justice roll down like water, and righteousness like a mighty stream.

Each and every time, a new generation has risen up and done what's needed to be done. Today we are called once more – and it is time for our generation to answer that call. For that is our unyielding faith – that in the face of impossible odds, people who love their country can change it. That's what Abraham Lincoln understood. He had his doubts. He had his defeats. He had his setbacks. But through his will and his words, he moved a nation and helped free a people. It is because of the millions who rallied to his cause that we are no longer divided, North and South, slave and free. It is because men and women of every race, from every walk of life, continued to march for freedom long after Lincoln was laid to rest, that today we have the chance to face the challenges of this millennium together, as one people – as Americans.

All of us know what those challenges are today – a war with no end, a dependence on oil that threatens our future, schools where too many children aren't learning, and families struggling paycheck to paycheck despite working as hard as they can. We know the challenges. We've heard them. We've talked about them for years. What's stopped us from meeting these challenges is not the absence of sound policies and sensible plans. What's stopped us is the failure of leadership, the smallness of our politics – the ease with which we're distracted by the petty and trivial, our chronic avoidance of tough decisions, and our preference for scoring cheap political points instead of rolling up our sleeves and building a working consensus to tackle big problems.

For the last six years we've been told that our mounting debts don't matter, we've been told that the anxiety Americans feel about rising health care costs and stagnant wages are an illusion, we've been told that climate change is a hoax, and that tough talk and an ill-conceived war can replace diplomacy, and strategy, and foresight. And when all else fails, when Katrina happens, or the death toll in Iraq mounts, we've been told that our crises are somebody else's fault. We're distracted from our real failures, and told to blame the other party, or gay people, or immigrants.

And as people have looked away in disillusionment and frustration, we know what's filled the void. The cynics, and the lobbyists, and the special interests who've turned our government into a game only they can afford to play. They write the checks and you get stuck with the bills, they get the access while you get to write a letter, they think they own this government, but we're here today to take it back. The time for that politics is over. It's time to turn the page. We've made some progress already. I was proud to help lead the fight in Congress that led to the most sweeping ethics reform since Watergate.

But Washington has a long way to go. And it won't be easy. That's why we'll have to set priorities. We'll have to make hard choices. And although government will play a crucial role in bringing about the changes we need, more money and programs alone will not get us where we need to go. Each of us, in our own lives, will have to accept responsibility – for instilling an ethic of achievement in our children, for adapting to a more competitive economy, for strengthening our communities, and sharing some measure of sacrifice. So let us begin. Let us begin this hard work together. Let us transform this nation.

Let us be the generation that reshapes our economy to compete in the digital age. Let's set high standards for our schools and give them the resources they need to succeed. Let's recruit a new army of teachers, and give them better pay and more support in exchange for more accountability. Let's make college more affordable, and let's invest in scientific research, and let's lay down broadband lines through the heart of inner cities and rural towns all across America.

And as our economy changes, let's be the generation that ensures our nation's workers are sharing in our prosperity. Let's protect the hard-earned benefits their companies have promised. Let's make it possible for hardworking Americans to save for retirement. And let's allow our unions and their organizers to lift up this country's middle class again. Let's be the generation that ends poverty in America. Every single person willing to work should be able to get job training that leads to a job, and earn a living wage that can pay the bills, and afford child care so their kids have a safe place to go when they work. Let's do this.

Let's be the generation that finally tackles our health care crisis. We can control costs by focusing on prevention, by providing better treatment to the chronically ill, and using technology to cut the bureaucracy. Let's be the generation that says right here, right now, that we will have universal health care in America by the end of the next president's first term.

Let's be the generation that finally frees America from the tyranny of oil. We can harness homegrown, alternative fuels like ethanol and spur the production of more fuel-efficient cars. We can set up a system for capping greenhouse gases. We can turn this crisis of global warming into a moment of opportunity for innovation, and job creation, and an incentive for businesses that will serve as a model for the world. Let's be the generation that makes future generations proud of what we did here. Most of all, let's be the generation that never forgets what happened on that September day and confront the terrorists with everything we've got. Politics doesn't have to divide us on this anymore – we can work together to keep our country safe. I've worked with Republican Senator Dick Lugar to pass a law that will secure and destroy some of the world's deadliest, unguarded weapons.

We can work together to track terrorists down with a stronger military, we can tighten the net around their finances, and we can improve our intelligence capabilities. But let us also understand that ultimate victory against our enemies will come only by rebuilding our alliances and exporting those ideals that bring hope and opportunity to millions around the globe. But all of this cannot come to pass until we bring an end to this war in Iraq. Most of you know I opposed this war from the start. I thought it was a tragic mistake. Today we grieve for the families who have lost loved ones, the hearts that have been broken, and the young lives that could have been. America, it's time to start bringing our troops home.

It's time to admit that no amount of American lives can resolve the political disagreement that lies at the heart of someone else's civil war. That's why I have a plan that will bring our combat troops home by March of 2008. Letting the Iraqis know that we will not be there forever is our last, best hope to pressure the Sunni and Shia to come to the table and find peace.

Finally, there is one other thing that is not too late to get right about this war – and that is the homecoming of the men and women – our veterans – who have sacrificed the most. Let us honor their valor by providing the care they need and rebuilding the military they love. Let us be the generation that begins this work. I know there are those who don't believe we can do all these things. I understand the skepticism. After all, every four years, candidates from both parties make similar promises, and I expect this year will be no different.

All of us running for president will travel around the country offering ten-point plans and making grand speeches; all of us will trumpet those qualities we believe make us uniquely qualified to lead the country. But too many times, after the election is over, and the confetti is swept away, all those promises fade from memory, and the lobbyists and the special interests move in, and people turn away, disappointed as before, left to struggle on their own.

That is why this campaign can't only be about me. It must be about us – it must be about what we can do together. This campaign must be the occasion, the vehicle, of your hopes, and your dreams. It will take your time, your energy, and your advice – to push us forward when we're doing right, and to let us know when we're not. This campaign has to be about reclaiming the meaning of citizenship, restoring our sense of common purpose, and realizing that few obstacles can withstand the power of millions of voices calling for change.

By us, this change will not happen. Divided, we are bound to fail. But the life of a tall, gangly, self-made Springfield lawyer tells us that a different future is possible. He tells us that there is power in words. He tells us that there is power in conviction. That beneath all the differences of race and region, faith and station, we are one people. He tells us that there is power in hope. As Lincoln organized the forces arrayed against slavery, he was heard to say: "Of strange, discordant,

> and even hostile elements, we gathered from the four winds, and formed and fought to battle through." That is our purpose here today. That's why I'm in this race. Not just to hold an office, but to gather with you to transform a nation. I want to win that next battle – for justice and opportunity. I want to win that next battle – for better schools, and better jobs, and health care for all. I want us to take up the unfinished business of perfecting our union, and building a better America. And if you will join me in this improbable quest, if you feel destiny calling, and see as I see, a future of endless possibility stretching before us; if you sense, as I sense, that the time is now to shake off our slumber, and slough off our fear, and make good on the debt we owe past and future generations, then I'm ready to take up the cause, and march with you, and work with you. Together, starting today, let us finish the work that needs to be done, and usher in a new birth of freedom on this Earth. (2008 Obama*for*America campaign).

I humbly pray that God should keep him and protect him for his family, for America and for the world. He did not get into this campaign for America's rescue for himself. He is doing it for the left-behinds of America and for the crying innocent ones of the rest of the world.

A Black Man and a Humble Beginning

In a society of signicant black minority and great racial tensions with whites, Barack has to strive or struggle to define himself, starting from as early as a baby. He happened to be colorfully different from all the children in her mother's circles and in schools. His mother, Ann Dunham, selected civil rights books and books on black race for Barack. He learned about his roots early from Mom, a very wise woman. Barack knew he was pigmented differently from most people around him. Events activated his senses very early in life to learn to diagnose situations and find a way to belong and to forge cross-barrier relationships. Whether he knows it now or not, his bipartisanship skill was part of an outgrowth of having to learn how to deal with his half-whites and his half-blacks. In his head, something lets him know that he is not just a black person, but black and white together. He represents his white mother and his black father. Long years of analyzing the good mix-up may have helped him internalize that all people are the same. America is not red, blue or green. America is "The United States of America,' and that he represents just that, *the USA*.

One may just have to call Barack, '*Mr. United Nation.*' When Barack was two years old, and after his father left him and his mother for further studies at Harvard University, the parents separated and later divorced. His mother married yet anther foreign man. This time the choice was not from an African continent, but from Indonesia, a nation in the continent of Asia. Indonesia is not just any kind of country. It is a nation that housed the largest population of Muslims in the world. Now Barack is from the continent of America, from the continent of Africa, from the continent of Asia, from the Muslim world, and he is a Christian, as we know him. Fellows, Barack is *Mr. United Nation*! He is *Mr.*

Foreign Policy put together by God who made the best out of a bad situation of divorces. Who knows if God had planned it that way for use in bringing a needed solution to a religious chaotic world years later. Today, the man does not have to learn foreign policy. He is relatively Mr. Foreign Policy.

Barack's mother, now Mrs. Ann Soetoro, took the 6-year old Barack and followed her new husband back to Indonesia in 1967. Barack attended local schools. Her mother also enrolled him in correspondent school for English. He certainly learned how to relate to people of different backgrounds, especially at a young age, the best time to learn anything. After his mother came back to Honolulu (USA) and later decided to get back to Indonesia for her doctoral research and possibly work, mostly with the poor, the young Barack decided to remain in Honolulu Hawaii with his white grandparents.

Barack attended Punahou School from fifth grade until his graduation with a High School Certificate. The poor Barack, in search of his identity, just may have played a lot of basketball to prove that he is black. Jaymes Sung of Associate Press stated that Obama found refuge and identity in basketball (Song 2008). One of his teachers had stated that Barack lived Basketball in Hawaii, becoming part of his school's state championship team. Attesting to his work ethic in striving to make the team and to stay on the team, Song wrote, "Obama could often be seen carrying books in one hand and dribbling a basketball in the other. He eventually earned a spot on the heralded varsity team. 'He'd be the first one to practice, and after practice, he'd go to the park and play more,' said McLachlin, [Obama's coach]. 'So his passion for the game is unmatched by most of the players I've ever had.'"(Song 2008).

As those who know him believed, Barack used basketball sport to connect with the father he longed to know. After eight years of absence, living in Kenya, Barack Obama Sr. returned to America for a brief Christmas visit and handed a gift of an orange basketball to Junior. You can imagine how that feels

In this 1977 file photo provided by the The Oahuan, yearbook of Punahou School, Barack Obama, second row center, is seen with is junior varsity basketball team in this 1977 yearbook class photo in Honolulu. Obama loved basketball and as a forward dubbed "Barry O'Bomber," he favored a left-handed double pump shot. During his senior year, the varsity team captured the state championship. (Panahou School "Oahuan" yearbook photo)

for a young child who longed to see his daddy. You can also imagine that the basketball actually represented a place of comfort for his dear father who lived in far away land, but did not have enough money to visit as he wanted. African fathers love their children a lot, and they particularly work extra hard to influence their sons.

Barack Sr. may not have visited America as much as he wanted due to lack of finance, and he may not want Barack Junior to come and reside in Kenya due to poor infrastructures that usually overwhelm most African nations. Therefore, the orange basketball is much bigger than the ball itself. The ball is more like Mr. Barack Obama Sr. As Barack's sister, Maya Soetoro-Ng, stated, "Obviously, that visit meant a lot to Barack and had a profound impact. After all, that was the only real image he had of his father that he experienced firsthand. You can imagine a boy coming of age; such an encounter would be of vital importance." (Song 2008).

Barack's father, Obama Sr., was very educated. He studied at the University of Hawaii with a USA scholarship offered to select African foreigners. He had a Doctor of Philosophy degree in Economics from Harvard. In the quest to help his country and to be with the family (African wife and son) in Kenya-Africa, he went back to Africa after graduation. He worked in Kenya and criticized the government through his writings concerning economic reforms and land problems. It was a good thing to note the criticism because almost all African governments now and worse then usually hated to be challenged. Land dispute and killings associated with it have always been a nightmare in Kenya. Obama Sr. actually fought for Kenyan people in his writings. Besides, instead of remaining in the United States with all of her relatively perfect infrastructures of roads, hospitals, 24/7 electricity, clean water, the economy, and goodies of everything else, Barack Obama Senior decided to head back home to Africa to live and to fight, politically.

That is the mentality of the average African male. Most African males you find outside their home nations are usually in those nations just to make money and help their extended families in home-nations. African males are addictively family and native-oriented. They are never comfortable outside of their home nations and they miss their children beyond any non-African's imagination. Barack Obama Junior, therefore, should know that his father, although he was not there for many years, was addictively and perennially thinking about him and crying to God for his success almost on a continual basis. That is the African man! I know what I am talking about because I am African from head to toe in the area of family system. In fact, Obama Senior's thoughts and prayers have everything to do with Barack's divine guidance then and now!

What God embedded in the heart and mind of a concerned father about his child is impeccably spiritual. It is the spiritual ammunition that actually gets the job done. Any physical behavior from the immediate parent or supervisor that is not spiritually founded or grown does not have much impact upon a child. Sometimes a teacher, who may not outwardly know how to convey his point across, may actually wish knowledge into his students through his intensive desire for that to happen. However, most good teachers usually end up training and accumulating appropriate method of imparting needed skills

Did the African man, Barack Obama Sr., have everything to do with today's Barack Obama Junior? Yes! God honored his heart for his son through his days and nights of tearful prayers. Commitments in Africa precluded Obama Sr. from executing his desire to be with Obama Jr. in America. Nevertheless, through divine impartation, forced by his father's intense love and wishes for him, Obama Junior of today is the result. As the father cried and wished, God did the job through the beautiful Ann (Obama's mother) and the wonderful white grandparents, who, together, also wished all goodies for Barack Hussein Obama Junior. Barack Obama Junior has in him an unmatched Caucasian-American love of charity in general and an unmatched African love of family. It is great! He is African-American divine-proper. Value system is the person, not the look of the person. An individual is a collection of values, beliefs, attitudes, intentions, and behavior. That was what I inferred in my analysis, the Oguhebe's Human Being (Oguhebe 2002).

Barack Sr. died at the age of 46 in 1982 due to injuries from auto accident. Outside marrying and divorcing, or just having children anywhere, which is very un-African, Barack Obama Sr. certainly cherished his children. He had married two wives in addition to the original wife in Kenya. He stayed with Kezia, the first wife, until his death. Others divorced him. Kezia now lives in Britain. All of Barack Obama Senior's children are successful. Thanks to his hardworking wives. Although he deeply cared for his children, I am tempted to give him a 'D-' grade for value system--for marrying anyhow without a thorough-thought of taking care of these women and living with them. In fact, I still give him the "D" for such foolishness. Thank God for His intervention and for the educated wives who were able to find jobs and helped take care of their children. Obama Senior was not religious. He started with being a mild Muslim, and finally became atheist. During his time, and in some African nations, men may marry more than one wife.

Barack Obama Junior's mother was a single parent of two children, Barack Obama and Maya Soetoro-Ng, his sister. She later divorced her second husband, Lolo Soetoro of Indonesia. The woman was doubtless very hardworking and independent. Ann Dunham was born in Kansas USA to Stanley and Madelyn Dunham in November of 1942. Her parents named her Stanley, for her father had expected a son. Ann was the only child. She was born while Stanley was fighting in World War. Stanley got to be called Ann later. Ann was educated. She studied at the University of Hawaii, earning a Doctoral degree in Anthropology.

Having spent sometime in Indonesia and understanding the needs there, she decided to go back to the country as she wrote her doctoral dissertation, titled *Peasant Blacksmithing in Indonesia: Surviving and Thriving Against All Odds.* This topic will let you know how much this beautiful woman desired deep in her heart to help people and how she was touched by people's sufferings and wanted to do something about it. One can tell that Barack Junior internalized this endowment from her mother. After her doctorate, Dunham pursued a career in rural development, championing women's work and dealing with world's poor; she worked with Indonesia's oldest bank, the United States Agency for

International Development, the Ford Foundation, Women's World Banking, and as a consultant in Pakistan. She mingled with leaders from organizations, supporting Indonesian human rights, women's rights, and grass-roots development.

This one woman is not afraid to try new things and to swim into uncharted territories. She certainly believed that she could deal with anyone and anybody at any place and still come out with success for all. This kind of character cannot be founded without first possessing good, ulterior motive for all others. One can see this quality in the actions of Barack Obama Junior today. Many Republicans and Americans seem to be shocked when Barack indicated that he would not mind talking directly with America's enemies without precondition. Ladies and gentlemen, the man instinctively made that statement because he can really handle it and it will be successful.

Just because the meetings failed to yield good results with others does not mean they will not succeed with Barack. It is a matter of faith and a matter of the atmospheric value system, which the leader or top negotiator brings to the other people. Some people will show up in a room and cause demons to act out of other people to the destruction of the talk-purpose and the meeting. Others will show up in the same room, filled with the same people, but with different results. Goodies! What happened? The demons of strife and ego left the room and freed the other people to talk sensibly and reach godly accords; that's what happened.

Obama is in the second category. This skill came from God to him through his Mama and general upbringing. Understanding the plight of the poor and needy and having an unquenchable desire to work to help them also came from the honorable, Mother Ann Dunham Obama-Soetoro. She died of cancer in Hawaii in1995; her two children, Barack and Maya, scattered her ashes on the Pacific Ocean.

Barack's grandfather (mother's side) was actually, physically and spiritually, the father of Barack Obama Junior. Barack is the son his grandfather had wanted in 'Stanley that turned out to be Ann.' The man, who had decided to go off to world war after Pearl Harbor was bombed, got his wish in a black boy through a loving daughter. Barack's biological father was another continent away from being there for Barack. Clearly, the ultimate father, both physically and spiritually, was Mr. Stanley Dunham, Barack's grandfather. Ultimately, the hand of God was there.

While Stanley was at war, other contingencies had forced his wife, Madelyn, to leave Kansas and finally ended up in Seattle, Washington. The thirteen-year old Ann attended a new High School that taught her the importance of challenging societal norms and questioning authority. Later, she certainly did, marrying a black man, and here comes Barack Obama Junior--the man that may have been manufactured by God for use in a difficult time in American and world history. I usually do not like to say it as many people do, "*God works in mysterious ways*." It is mysterious because we do not understand it or cannot figure it out. If Ann was in Kansas, which is in the southern United States, she may dream of marrying a black man, but it can only be a dream, and there would be no Barack Junior today. The beautiful grandmother, Madelyn, worked hard to protect and nurture her grandson while Ann was away at school or at work in a foreign land.

All these people and conditions define Mr. Barack Obama's bedrock and diverse value-system. He cannot forget the poor because he knows what it is to be poor, to struggle, and to fight to be accepted. I have no doubt that Barack Obama of today is one of the best friends of working people and poor people while appreciating the contributions and efforts of the rich. He became a true American and a lover of America. One serious mistake that anyone will make is to try to make a decision one-way or the other because of the man's pigmentation only. We must look at the man's make up. He is Mr. USA! He is Mr. United Nation! He is a true embodiment of American engineering.

A True American

Barack Obama delights in hard work not handouts. He knows and believes that if you want it, then you have to work for it. He believes in American volunteerism. He also believes in one other thing that makes him super American. This is it--He does not believe that the color of his skin is a hindrance to him achieving his goal. Fellows, although he does not say it, that's where his faith in God comes in. That's where he applies his Christian belief. For as long as you are committed to doing right, "If God be for you, who can be against you?" (Romans 8:31). Abraham, against all odds of him and his wife being close to 100 years old, believed in God and did not waver that he would be the father of many nations; the Bible described it as, "who against hope believed in hope that he might be the father of many nations' (Romans 4:18). Abraham did have a child by Sarah, his wife, at the old ages.

Faith and hope keep you moving and never giving up! Barack internalized it and it's working for him. It should work for all. It will work for others who can summon the courage to believe God, other things being equal.

Barack was well schooled. The mother prepared him well as a child, being an example to him, and challenging him with schoolwork and correspondence activities. He finished High School in Hawaii and pursued a B.A. degree in International Relations at Columbia University, New York. Afterwards he worked for Business International Corporation and New York Public Interest Research Group. At this point, I am beginning to feel that Barack had wanted to be a politician for a long time just to be able to serve people, to correct what he sees as errors in government dealings with the people, and to ease burdens in the society. He therefore carefully picked jobs that will steer him toward this ultimate goal.

I strongly believe that he had thought at this time about one day running for the top job in the country, the presidency of the United States of America. I believe that God had flashed the calling in his heart, and early in life.

This drive was not for personal power and achievement; it was to fulfill an inner cry and torture to help a divided country in need. This kind of fulfillment cannot be obtained by making millions of dollars; it comes by getting down in the gutter, working with the people, crying to God, and allowing God to help resurrect and push this innermost desire to the forefront. It is a desire that no money can buy except just enough to effect changes within and among the suffering people of America and the rest of the world. It is the kind of need that can only be dented through policy changes and the presidency of the United States.

After four years in New York City, Obama moved to Chicago to work as a community organizer for three years--from June 1985 to May 1988 as director of DCP, the Developing Communities Project. This is a church-based community organization originally comprising eight Cath-olic parishes in Greater Roseland Chicago South Side, one of the major slump areas in the United States. According to a report, Obama's DCP directorship produced an increase in staff by 1200 percent (1-13) and annual budget by over 471 percent ($70,000 - $400,000) in just three years (Wikipadia 2008-06-18). He helped set up a job training program, a college preparatory tutoring program, and a tenants' rights organization in Altgeld Gardens Chicago. He worked as a consultant and an instructor for the Gamaliel Foundation, a community organizing institute. From another reading, Barack had also worked for a civil rights law firm in the city of Chicago.

Folks, Obama's work at those times in Chicago marked a huge managerial accomplishment. As a Professor of Management for several years, a consultant, an uncompromising Minister of Jesus Gospel, and President of *Emancipation*USA, I can tell you that the man (Barack Obama Junior) merits an A+ in this regard, after considering all necessary forces. It is not how long one worked or has been on a job that blossoms the resume. It is the nature of achievement per unit of time spent on the job that measures the acumen or the anointing behind the job; that's the real strength of a resume. The young man, while on the job, created an atmosphere of "can-do spirit" and "faith-in-oneself-to-achieve" among many people of *bruised* and *un-bruised* minds and backgrounds.

He literally gave them hope and became a source of hope and inspiration for these people who then found new reasons to believe again, to live again, and to fight again. Instead of maintaining any iota of attitude that leads to throwing-in the towel, many people learned from this young man that life could be better if we work together and fight evil together in love. Without a can-do spirit, you just can't do! Therefore, Dear people, remember that the young man, Barack Obama, was doing this job by faith in God, hoping that it will lead him to something greater than just getting a job in a big company and making six figures. His heart cry was and still is "to help people."

Once again, and whatever it is, "Yes We Can!" Whatever it is —"Yes We Can!" These are not just words. They are powerhouse, divine-laden words. We can do all things in Christ who strengthens us (Philippians 4:13). What is

Christ? *Answer: Love for fellow man.* That's what Jesus is all about. If you are for Jesus, then you must love and avoid sin. If you do sin, then you had better repent. Love for fellow man is the principal thing. That's the wisdom of God. Love one another. Do to people what you will like people to do to you – not to a select people, but to all people. Jesus equals unselfishness, holiness, and righteousness. It all begins with loving one another. That's what the young Barack became part of in Chicago, driven by the values instilled in him by God through his mother. One can talk Jesus, but if talk is not followed by work, then the talk is just a tinkling cymbal or a sounding gong. Action speaks louder than words.

Later, Barack visited Europe and then Africa (Kenya) for the first time in 1988. In Kenya, his father's home, Barack visited with his relatives and the Africans. This part of Barack is not a learned foreign-policy attribute. He is the foreign policy attribute in relative terms. From child to adult, even without visiting any outside world, the man's blood and all of his thought-processes (from childhood to adulthood) nurture and rehears the nature and structure of world's cultures and their interactive impacts on America and world's economic, political technological, educational and whatever outcomes.

I have not talked to Barack, but he cannot help but to confirm what I just stated. It is in the blood to know about outsiders once you are related to any outside nation or continent, especially being a concerned citizen of a civilized and relatively loving nation like the United States. The visiting certainly magnified this intrinsic, foreign-policy calculating instinct and his desire to strengthen America and help the world in some unspeakable terms. Barack already knows that without the USA and the country's love in establishing student foreign aid, his father would not have been able to make it to America for his education. Without Barack Obama Sr. being in America, there would be no Barack Obama Jr. He owes everything to his nation and has a special and inner patriotic drive to overhaul and to cause America to be blessed better than before. This is not a man after money. This is a man driven by a search for the best way to repay his nation and to help the downtrodden and the middle class of this great nation. He wants to help these people massively so the nation can rise again and take a salute from the world once again.

Later, Barack went to Harvard Law School, arguably the best in the nation or in the world. He graduated with *magna cum laude* not "*Thank you lorde.*" It means he graduated with great praise, as one who spent time to study and learned what is expected of him, not some barely-making-it degree. At this great University, probably regarded as the best in the world, he became an editor of the all-acclaimed *Harvard Law Review* just at the end of his first year. In his second year, he was elected as the first black president of the Review, supervising 80 editors, a volunteer position. You do not become elected to this kind of executive position in a reputable school like Harvard University if you do not extensively know what you are doing. Barack knows how to manage people and how to bring the best out of people. I drew this inference as I monitored his presidential primary campaigns. I even sent my hard-earned money to him, the first time I ever donated to a campaign.

The University of Chicago attracted Barack Obama Jr. to teach constitutional law for several years up to 2004. They did it by providing him with a fellowship, a teaching contract, and an office to work on his first book contract, *Dreams From My Father; A Story of Race Relations and Inheritance*, which was published in 1995 by Three Rivers Press, a Crown Publishing Company/Random House Publishers. In 1992, Obama directed a Project-Vote in Illinois which reached its goal of registering 140,000 of 400,000 unregistered African African-Americans in the state, causing *Crain's Chicago Business* to name Obama to its 1993 list of "40 under Forty" powers to be. This massive registration effort in seven months may have caused Illinois to turn democratic for Bill Clinton.

What we have been reading is about a man who is indeed nonstop, action-oriented person, willing to achieve for a common purpose and for common good. That's the kind of heart God admires and rewards. One thing about it is that regardless of what religion one claims to be, what race, what business, what "whatever," as long as your heart is right toward another human being (not being selfish), you will always be rewarded by a divine touch on what you do and on the people around you. I know because all my selfish efforts have become total wastes, even though I talked and sang Jesus a lot. What Jesus wants is mostly action. Barack is action not talk. I am learning from him too. Hard work, going to school, volunteerism, and love of people make Barack a true American.

Marriage and the Family

There will not be a strong Barack as we know him now without a good wife cheering him on. Barack made a good choice in a spouse called *Darling* Michelle Obama. God gave her the beautiful 'lady' who acknowledges him as the head of the home and who helps put more inspiration into the man that is already inspired. Barack, in turn, inspires 'the heck' out of the *lovely* Michelle. Selfish and contentious women can destroy or ruin good men. Those men, with their good ideas, are languishing in pains and sorrows now.

Many of them die daily of heart attacks and other ailments. This has been a major problem among countless, successful black men, who made terrible mistakes of marrying destructors, contentious, bulldozer women for a wife. Such horrible choices have cut their lives into many pieces. Many of these men are sleeping-crying daily. Contentious women and the American courts have kicked out these men from their homes. Many are sorrowing today and living in limbo right now. They have neither mouth nor money to defend themselves

Michelle and Barack Obama on their wedding day in 1992. (Photo: Family Photo)/CBS

against such wives who have milked them to death or half-dead.

Barack should therefore be thanking the Almighty God for Michelle. I know he does. I just love the way he looks at her and appreciates her; it is all real, not a fake. The only exception is that the next time he plans to pat her on the 'behind' in public, I must have to close my eyes. That is, if they let me know when it is going to take place. Did you see that fist bump and how Michelle had always initiated some nice and spontaneous moves? I like all that, including the little pat on the butt too. They are husband and wife, and they are already exhibiting to America that the nation has a choice of a real, loving, and united family to lead her.

Love extends from the home to the rest of the nation. That's the right way, and that should be the American way. You cannot put into the White House some fly-by-night person who deals double-standard on his wife and vise versa. You should not grace the top home in the nation with a couple who will use the house as a boxing ring. Barack and Michelle seem to be ordained for such a time as this in the American and world's political arena. The DEMS made a perfect choice in the 2008 primary. Other choices are good, but the Obama brand is better.

Well, Michelle did not start by being Michelle Obama. She was once Michelle LaVayghn Robinson, born on January 17, 1964. She was born and raised in the Southside of Chicago, Illinois. She also graduated with honors at Harvard University Law School with a JD degree in 1988. She met Barack at Sidley Austin Law Firm in Chicago and she was assigned to mentor him. Uuuuuuh! Some mentoring! Aaaaaah! I think God just used the 'poor' *Sidley Austin* to do His thing. Barack and Michelle were the only two African Americans in the law firm and he was a summer associate. Do you see how God works? Keep your hands and soul clean, and God will bring the right person to youe door even if He has to bring someone from another continent to help manufacture a spouse for you.

He may drag your future spouse from Hawaii to Indonesia and back to Hawaii, then to New York, then to Chicago, then to Harvard where you once went, and back to Chicago, and into your laps, while you are busy behaving right, not fooling around! That's how God works! That is how He plots rescue mission for a group of people or a nation. He can see the future state of a nation and start early to build a leader, like Barack Obama, whom He can use to help America of today.

By October 1992, Michelle Robinson became Michelle Obama, and Barack has a full permission from the Almighty God to treat Michelle as his wife, including giving her a little public pat on the butt, being a godly example in the home, and being there for her always. They now have two girls, Malia Ann, born in 1998, and Natasha (called Sasha), born in 2001. Michelle has held various job positions—in Chicago mayor's office, at a major law firm, as Executive Director for the Chicago office of Public Allies, the Associate Dean of

Student Services at the University of Chicago, and currently as Vice President for Community and External Affairs for Chicago Hospitals.

We pray that she continues to be a good wife to Barack Obama and an example to girls and women everywhere. I wish her the opportunity to use the podium of the White House to serve the Almighty God, being example to the nation and to the rest of the world. Let her mind stay firm on the Lord as she intercedes for her famuly. Let Barack take care of her and his love for her grow daily until death do them part at very old ages. In Jesus'name we pray. Aaaaaaamen.

Government for the People

I believe Barack Obama became a politician in order to work for the people and for helping America this time. He did not desire to be a politician for popularity purposes or to grab personal power. He first became an Illinois State Senator, representing Chicago South side area. He was elected to the Illinois Senate in 1996, reelected in 1998, and 2002. In 2000 he had run and for the U.S. House of Representatives and lost a Democratic primary to the then incumbent Bobby Rush. Besides an atmosphere of bipartisanship, which he provided at the Illinois Senate, some of Obama's accomplishments at the Illinois government are as follows:

a) Legislation reforming ethics and healthcare laws
b) He sponsored a law that increased tax credits for low-income workers
c) Negotiated welfare reform and promoted increased subsidies for childcare
d) As co-chairman of the bipartisan Joint Committee on Admini strative Rules, he backed then Republican governor and passed payday loan regulations and predatory mortgage lending regu lations aimed at preventing home foreclosures.
e) He sponsored and led a unanimous, bipartisan passage of legislation to monitor racial profiling by requiring police to record the race of drivers they detained and a legislation that requires videotaping of homicide interrogations. State of Illinois became the first state in the union to adopt this type of interrogation.
f) In 2003, he became chair of the Illinois Senate's Health and Human Services Committee.
g) In July 2004, he wrote and delivered a keynote address at the 2004 Democratic National Convention. Senator John Kerry, the then Democratic nominee for President, chose him for the speech. Barack Obama delivered an excellent speech, criticizing President Bush on the Iraq war, drawing attention to the need to treat our Soldiers right, and to the fact that America cannot continue to act divided and look divided as liberal or conservative, red state and blue state, etc. America should be and is "the United States of America."

This speech threw him on the national scene and certainly helped his senate run. Obama had already won the Democratic primary before the speech; he emerged as a top candidate from a pool of about 15 Democratic and republican candidates. In November 2004, Obama won the U.S. senate election against the republican, Alan Keys, with 70 percent of the votes. This became the largest margin of victory ever recorded in a statewide-office election in Illinois. Obama's U.S. senate accompli-shments are as follows:

a) Despite being a new comer to the House of Senate, Obama recruited and hired a tea of established, high-level advisers devoted to broad themes that exceeded the usual requirements of an incoming first-term senator. This will let you all know that this man is not an average politician. He wants to work and to do things right. His staff consists of--Chief of staff – Pete Rouse, a 30-year veteran of national politics and former chief of staff to Senate Democratic Leader Tom Daschle. Policy Director – Economist Karen Kornbluh, former deputy chief of staff to Secretary of the Treasury Robert Rubin. Foreign Policy Advisers – Samantha Power, author on human rights and genocide, and former Clinton administration officials Anthony Lake and Susan Rice as foreign policy advisers.
b) Obama is considered as the fifth African American Senator in U.S. history by *Senate Historian* and the third to have been popularly elected. Barack is the only Senate member of the Con-gressional Black Caucus.
c) Obama sponsored successful bills associated with energy, immi-gration reform and protecting the borders. Other bills he sponsored include weapons reduction, Government Transparency Acts (one of them establishes *USAspending.gov*), fighting radio-active leaks, Democratic Republic of the Congo Relief, Security, and Democracy Promotion Act," (marks the first federal legislation to be enacted with Obama as its primary sponsor), eliminating lobbyists and their gifts in *Honest Leadership and Open Government Act*, Iraq War De-Escalation Act of 2007, Defense Authorization Act adding safeguards for personality disorder military discharges, and calling for an official review following reports that the procedure had been used inappro-priately to reduce government costs, Iran Sanctions Enabling Act" supporting divestment of state pension funds from Iran's oil and gas industry, State-Foreign Operations appropriations bill, etc.
d) Current or former member of Foreign Relations, Environment and Public Works, Veterans' Affairs, Health, Education, Labor and Pensions and Homeland Security and Governmental Affairs, Chairman of the Senate's subcommittee on European Affairs.
e) Travels as a member of foreign relations committee took him to Eastern Europe, the Middle East, and Africa. In August 2005, Obama

traveled to Russia, Ukraine, and Azerbaijan. The trip focused on strategies to control the world's supply of conven-tional weapons, biological weapons, and weapons of mass destruction as a first defense against terrorist attacks. After meetings with U.S. military in Kuwait and Iraq in January 2006, Obama visited Jordan, Israel, and the Palestinian territories.

At one meeting with Palestinian students two weeks before Hamas won the legislative election, Obama warned that "the U.S. will never recognize winning Hamas candidates unless the group renounces its fundamental mission to eliminate Israel." [that's straight-talk] On his third official trip in August 2006, he traveled to South Africa, Kenya, Djibouti, Ethiopia and Chad. He practically told the Kenyan leaders what they did not want to hear concerning political corruption and ethnic rivalries.

What is listed in this little section about Obama's government activities at Illinois and the U.S. senate can always be found in the Obama's Senate web site, the Wikipadia, or any other government source. I listed these so we can be able to diagnose who the man really is and what he is made of. The accomplishments listed above under the U.S. senate are just under 2 years (2005 and 2006). He became consumed with the presidential election starting from January 2007 up to now. In fact, becoming the presumptive nominee of the Democratic Party may be the greatest achievement of all and for America because it proves that he is speaking for the people of the nation as a whole in whatever he stands for.

Dear people, we not only have a man for the people, but a man who is a quick learner, not afraid to be different, willing to share his views, and has ability to get opponents to see his sometimes out-of-space, but necessary approach to solving problems. Take a close look at the bills he sponsored and promoted in the Illinois senate and the U.S. Senate. You may need to read about those bills in detail to be able to understand what the man did. The impression is that he does his best to fight for the common person. He strives to fight for those who seem to have no mouth to fight for themselves. He believes in truth and ethics, and his tough stance on this speaks volumes for him. You do not have many government officials calling for transparency in government and seriously refusing lobbyists' money. That is a big fight against serious, special interest group. However, the man tries to stand the heat as he vows to do right.

Barack has the ability to work across the isles. Most of the bills he sponsored or promoted were bipartisan. He travels enough, he is educated enough, and he reads enough to be able to understand and articulate foreign policy positions and their impact on domestic activities. We have an institutional leadership champion in Barack Obama. Some people may visit nations tens of times and still not be able to understand the mathematical impacts of events and their causes. For Barack Obama and his background, one or two travels may be more than enough, especially when he has access to news media as the rest of us do. A quick learner and hard working person like Barack can grow at a geometric performance-pace and become much, much better than slow learners and self-servers who fill up today's most political offices. Pinching myself against calling some names, I can tell you that Barack has more than enough foreign policy experience to be the President of the United States of America. He is much better than many who compete with him.

Some people claim that they cannot vote for Obama as President at this time due to lack of experience. Many of these people may have a different reason; lack of experience will not be one of them. For those of you who are serious about the experience card, it is important that you understand that longevity on a job does not equate experience. It is your accomplishment per unit of time spent on that job. Furthermore, there are some experience that is not worth having; being a lame-dock, a yes-man, and special-interest pleaser in the Senate or House of Representatives are some of them. In other words, the kind of things some people actually call experience that Barack needs to have are not necessary.

The man has more than the required experience besides having a good dose of ability and motivation to gain whatever skill that may be lacking. He possesses super-high and positive learning curve effect and the knack to surround himself with smart juggernauts that can help him tackle problems. He has demonstrated this acumen in his Senate staff-hiring decisions and all races he has run, especially the 2008 presidential primary election. He improves rapidly almost on a daily basis. This skill of a person is what America needs in this age of stiff international competition at all levels and many troubles at home. Barack Obama is far above his challenger, the Honorable Senator John McCain, in the 2008 national presidential election when it comes to needed presidential skills to help America domestically and internationally.

Barack Obama understands the American people. He is more than a typical American as one can read from his life story. He knows what it is to suffer, to be small, to be looked down, to have no father but needed a father, to be different, to have little, to have a lot, to be white, to be black, to be educated, to be uneducated, and so on. These are the things that tugged the man into politics—to find a way to wipe his tears by serving and dying for the common man. I feel the man although I do not agree with him on one or two cultural issues. I know because I find most of myself in the man. I want to help people so much that I often become tearfully overwhelmed when I do not foresee the quick opportunity for me to do so.

People are suffering beyond measure, and the primary reason is lack of solid and uncompromised leadership and love from the top. This man will rather see himself die than not work for the common good of this beautiful nation and the world in need of love. He loves the rich, the middle class, and the poor. However, he understands the fact that economic building and long-run sustenance is not of a trickle-down phenomenon as previous governments tend to believe and act on. Sound business-economic principle is a function of trickle from all angles, not just from the top. I will discuss this further. He understands that the rich needs to contribute their fair share and not be functioning to the detriment of the middle and lower classes.

The man understands the American people and their needs. He dreams and embodies them for years. When money cannot buy a man and lust for women cannot stop a man, then the man is serious. Barack is serious about helping the United States of America. He wants to repay his debts and he wants others to receive all the blessings of USA as he did. I see a man who will continue to fight for the common people of America and the little folks of the world until he dies. He cannot help it! Again, he understands America. As part of his writing on why Barack Obama should be President of the United States, Josh Muphy, probably a student from *The* University of Tampa Florida wrote:

> If someone wants to mention experience as a prerequisite for being president, the current administration carries with it decades of military, political, and D.C. experience, and look where we are today. It is time for a new America, one that can endure the trials and tribulations of tomorrow with the grace and intelligence that is needed today. We have major problems facing this country ranging from health care, immigration, terrorism, education reform, social security, etc. We are literally facing a turning point in the history of America and truly, the world. Our generation will bear the main burden of these issues if we do not elect *a leader who can understand us, understand our pains, understand our problems, and understand our need to survive.* It takes a deep understanding of the average American and the issues we face in our daily lives, and how we can come together, no matter our race, creed, or income, to make this nation what it should be, which should be a new and shining hope for our generation and our future kids. I therefore challenge you: take a stand, fight for your rights and beliefs, because if you do not, no one else will! (The Minaret Online Edition, May 22, 2008).

As a dedicated Christian conservative, I may disagree with Barack on one or two issues, but I must agree with Josh that Americans need to rise up at this time for the common man and for love that this man, Barack Obama, represents. An intelligent man, not easily provoked, a quiet demeanor, but a man that cannot be messed with—these attributes describe a foreign-policy image that the world needs from America at this time and that America really wants to project to the world at this time. The man America needs now for the unraveling and solution of her domestic issues is a man who understands suffering, a man for the poor, a man for the working class, and a man who understands the rich. He must be a man of education, a man who understands the unread, a man for black, a man for white, a man for green and blue, a man for all; he must be a man that can't be bought, a man for equal love. That man is Barack Obama. Elect him, pray for him, and stand by him and then watch America blossom.

The rest of the book will prove what I have already stated—Barack Obama is the right person at this time to serve as the next president of the United States. Barack Obama candidacy will be rated on several dimen-sions that must be used to evaluate and qualify a leader. The exercise will help you answer the following questions now or after the Presidential election of November 2008:

1) Whom will I vote for or have I voted for a wrong person in the 2008 USA presidential primary election and November presidential election? [Before and after November 2008]
2) Will my vote count or did my vote count for good or bad? [Before and after November 2008]
3) Will I vote rightly or did I vote rightly? What must I learn about casting my vote rightly?
4) What will influence you to vote for or against Barack Obama or influenced you to vote as you did? [Before and after November 2008]
5) Will I consider all issues before I vote or Did I consider all issues before I voted? [Before and after November 2008]
6) How will I vote patriotically or did I vote patriotically?

Understanding Barack From Barack's Private Prayer In Israel

This section is actually one of the last to be written in this book. I am extremely impressed to have God continuing to confirm to me that Barack Obama is and has been a humble person the best way he knows how. Barack Obama's visit to Israel in July 2008 caused him to go and pray at the Wall of Prayer. After he posted his prayer and gone, a Hebrew seminarian sneaked up and took it. Now some Newspaper from Israel got hold of it and the piece of paper has been circulating. Although he did not sign the paper, I strongly believe that was Obama's prayer that day. This is the prayer:

> 'Lord — Protect my family and Forgive me my sins, and help me guard against pride and despair. Give me the wisdom to do what is right and just. And make me an instrument of your will.' (Yahoo News/AP, July 25, 2008).

Fellows, this is exactly the way Jesus Christ taught us to pray (Holy Bible, Matthew 5-7). Lord: He recognized Jesus as the Lord and the receiver of all prayers. Protect my family: that's a prayer of wise head of household. Barack is always on the road and he lets us know that family is number one. He has to ask God to protect his family; they need him, he was not there with them; he must therefore call on the Lord who is everywhere at the same time to help. Forgiveness of sin and help in dealing with pride constitute man's intense need from God; such prayer is a sign of humility. Asking God for wisdom and for Him to use us as His instruments is the heart of God for every human being on this earth.

According to Associates Press, the image of Obama's prayer was released or published by Maariv, an Israeli newspaper, on Friday July 25, 2008. The paper and the seminarian attributed the note to Senator Barack Obama, the Democratic presidential contender. The newspaper says Obama wrote the prayer and left it in the stones (cracks) of the Western Wall, Judaism's holiest site, during a visit early Thursday, July 25, 2008. The Israeli newspaper's decision to make the note public drew criticism and some anger. The rabbi in charge of the Western Wall, Shmuel Rabinovitz, said that removing and publishing the prayer intruded in Obama's relationship with God. According to Associates Press, "Many visitors to the 2,000-year-old Western Wall leave notes bearing requests and prayers. Obama did so during a pre-dawn visit there, Thursday, following a day he spent meeting with Israeli and Palestinian leaders." (Yahoo News/AP, July 25, 2008).

Although I was not happy about the seminarian and the newspaper tampering with the private and secret prayer, the release has given America a beautiful opportunity to see who Barack Obama really is. Thanks to the Lord, Jesus Christ. Above all, the Lord blessed my soul by letting me see it, confirming what I had seen and known in prayers all along. If you really understand the Lord, if you are a committed Christian, or if you are just someone who understands righteousness in Christ and God's commandments and directives to us through His Holy Bible, you will know that this is a perfect prayer that we can pray. To have just a slight clue of what I am talking about, you may read Matthew chapters 5 and 6 of the Holy Bible. Asking God to use you for His will tickles God more than anything. He loves it and He honors it.

Jesus taught us to always pray to God and to present ourselves before Him to help us eradicate pride, to have our our sins forgiven, and to receive strength to be able to love and serve others. Only Christ can give one the strength to do so, but you must ask (John 15:1-7). It's all about God's will and no other. I have been knowing this about Barack Obama. When I was in prison, which the Lord saw fit to send me, I prayed hard for the United States of America. After I came out, He got me attached to this man, Barack.

Dear America, charity begins at home. In line with that, Barack recognizes that blessings and protection for him and his family are not of the security agents and from the people but from the Lord. He recognizes that our pride and lack of faith in Him (the Lord) are major reasons for our downfall and for never accomplishing our callings in life. Barack asked the Lord Jesus to help him guard against pride and despair (hopelessness). When we are humble before the Lord and pray as He directed us, God functions. When God functions, then all will be well!

I have known that this man is a moderate America Christian, intrinsically loving, and that his loving ability is of the Lord. The only thing is that Barack does not want to be sounding the trumpet about him being a Christian so he can be able to accommodate all people. It has to be by example—that's his belief and that's fine. Nevertheless, after they continued to lie against him, I had to write and urge him (and I am sure some did) to start talking about the Lord he knows. His opponents forced him to talk about the Lord openly.

The prayer the Presidential candidate prayed is more like the prayer of King Solomon who succeeded King David. God told Solomon to ask anything and he would grant the request to the young Solomon. Solomon asked the Lord for the wisdom to lead his people. The motto in my house has been, "*Education Without Jesus is Devil to the Highest Degree*." The people who are ruining this world are not those who did not go to school. They are people who have gone to all kinds of schools but do not have enough sense to fear God and exhibit love and righteousness (Jesus). America, Barack Obama is your choice to lead you at such a time as this in America. I dare you to do the right thing.

I have been trying to avoid a testimony that I am about to give simply because my 'pride' is twitching about what people might say. I have suffered a lot. I have been in the valleys a lot. My caring for people in general, especially for millions and millions of crying children, subdued women, and the abuse of few good men in Africa and few other places has overwhelmed me, causing me to cry a lot, for I feel helpless for them. I have suffered numerous betrayals from people I trust and I have suffered because of my errors too. I therefore could not even remember when I am not crying and looking to the Lord for help. I strive to please the Lord, making many mistakes as I do.

In the midst of all these, and during a seven-day fasting period in my home, a message came to me and to my son at the same time in a dream. Read it on the next page and draw your own conclusion. Let me tell you, dear people, to work for God is not easy at all, especially because our flesh is often in the way. I knew that rescuing America is part of my calling. Sometimes it makes people angry because of the way I speak. Nevertheless, I cannot help it at all.

I believe the vision may help you to believe this book a little bit more. I believe that America must be healed and be blessed beyond measure again. I believe that one day Americans will come to their senses and get serious with being the example that God has called the nation to be in the eyes of the world—not evil of example but a good one. America is a critical nation in God's plan of events. Those that love her need to really wake up to please God that created her. We really need to live right to permit this God to remain by our side. We need to take our motto seriously. "*In God We Trust*" is the best motto in heaven and on earth. Let's get back to this motto and enjoy the awsomeness of America's God again.

I don't know about you, but when two people see similar visions at one time, that's a serious message. It is a serious way of confirming something true. The bible is filled with examples like that. In fact, God hardly does a thing without confirming it.

Guess what. Just about 20 days after this vision, the devil really tricked me into disciplining my other son too hard. I spanked him out of anger. The next

THIS IS THE VISION OF MY 15-YEAR OLD SON (FESTUS JR.) AS HE TOLD IT AND DREW IT BY HIMSELF IN HIS SUNDAY SCHOOL NOTEBOOK DURING PRAYER TIME ON THE EARLY MORNING (about 6:00 a.m.) OF MAY 22, 2004, during our Saturday marathon praise/prayer. (Reported verbatim). I was about to give a testimony, but he quickly interrupted me, yelling, "Daddy, Daddy, I had a dream or vision." he joyously told the vision as pictured here.

HE SAW AND DESCRIBES TO US:—

[#1] AMERICA IS FACING UPSIDE DOWN AND MOVING IN THE WRONG DIRECTION. Everyone is walking upside down, very sad and in fear.

To correct this, God sent His Angels to administer antidote. Then he asked me, "Daddy, guess what is inside the syringe or what the antidote is?" Non of us responded. He jubilantly said, "It's you daddy!" (that's me, *Festus Sunday Akaolisa Oguhebe-Strongblood). "You are to be injected* into the United States of America through the State of Mississippi. The devil hates to see this happen and desired to kill daddy (that's me). The devil (the big-huge-vicious snake, covering across the USA) sent out demons to destroy Daddy and company (the antidote). Serious battle broke out. The angels of God started fighting with the devil (the vicious snake and his demons).

[#2] DADDY (That's Me) IS INJECTED INTO AMERICA THROUGH THE STATE OF MISSISSIPPI.

The Angels killed few demons and then injected the antidote daddy (that's me) into the United States through the state of Mississippi. The antidote begins to work immediately.

[#3] AMERICA IS HEALED BY GOD WITH THE ANTIDOTE DADDY (FESTUS AND COMPANY)

The United States of America turned upward and heading in the right direction. Everyone in America is jubilating and smiling again. "Festus, you are finished," God said. >>>My son concluded. [I copied this from Festus Jr.'s 36" x 48"poster, transferred from his Sunday School notebook]

NOW GUESS WHAT MY TESTIMONY WAS TO BE?

Most spectacular! — Almost exactly the same vision or message was given to me independently on the same day (same night/morning). I had a dream where God's Spirit told me, "I have sent you to kill the Prince of America." Suddenly Daniel chapter 10, which dealt with the demon prince of country Persia came to my mind. The same chapter talked about the demon prince of Greece. These princes fought the angels that came to deliver answers. What does that tell you about USA? God showed my son "Vicious Snake," but He showed me "Prince of America." **DO THE MATH!** Do you want to know what the Prince of America is?

VISION CAME DURING A FASTING/PRAYER PERIOD

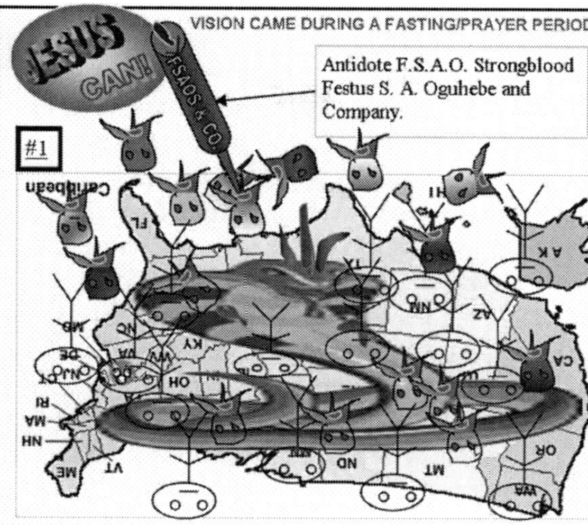

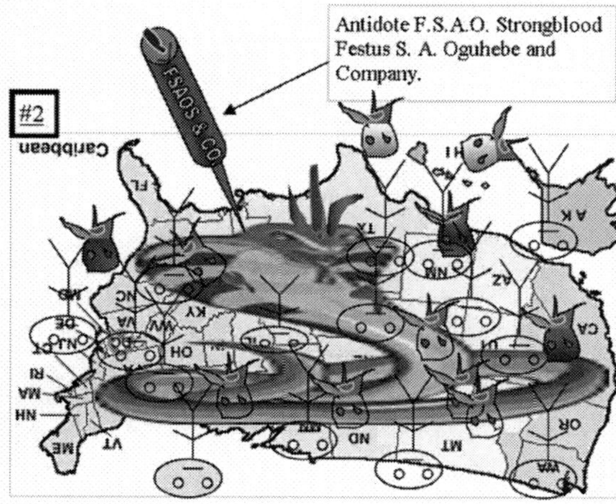

#3 HALLELUJAH!!! America is healed. Jubilation time!!!

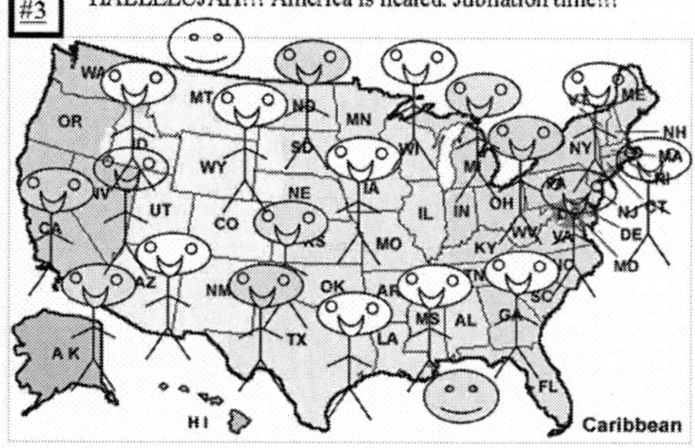

thing you know was an accusation of child abuse by the State of Mississippi, the children were taken away from me, and I was sent to prison. Truly, the way everything happened was very funny, hard to explain. As the accusation was going on, the Spirit of God let me know that God Himself has a plan in it. Soon I remembered the vision above. I could not believe it. The devil actually came after me in a big way to destroy me and my family. However, God put His feet down and did not let me defend myself or to get out of it. He (God) wanted me to go to jail. I didn't like it at all. I fasted for 40 days, eating nothing but drank water in the last 21 days and ate a slice of watermelon per day in the first 19 days. After the fast, I gathered strength, called the Mississippi Hinds County Attorney's office, the trial was done, and I was sent to prison. You will hear more about this as you read.

Nevertheless, my dear Americans, we need to fight to rescue America. Only God can do it. Which God? The only God we know—the God of the universe, the God of America, the ONE in Whom America used to trust like "*In God We Trust*." Can we do it?

Festus Sr. and Jr.

YES WE CAN!

AMERICA, A CHERISHED NATION OF THE LORD, HAD BETTER WAKE UP OR ...

That's right--Yes We Can!

With all love from—

Dr. Festus Sunday AkaOlisa Oguhebe- 'Strongblood'
As you read, you will find out the meaning of these names and how they came about.

"IN GOD WE TRUST"

In God we trust. The motto we hail.
The great USA motto
For El Pluribus Unum
Not in weapons, they all must fail
Not in dollars, powerless they are
Depend on none but God of all
The great God of the Holy Bible
For El Pluribus Unum
In God we trust.

In God we trust. The motto of mottos
Forgotten for the dollar
Forgotten for the sex
The devil is rejoicing
For the foolish USA
Depend on none but God of all
The great God of the Holy Bible
For El Pluribus Unum
In God you must trust.

I came from Africa for this very news
Dollar is nothing. Weapons are nothing
Immoral sex is nothing.
Great troubles they are.
Broken-home troubles. Wasted children
Messed-up people. Messed-up nation
Depend on none but God of all
The great God of the Holy Bible
For El Pluribus Unum
In God you must trust.

It started right. It must end right.
The nation made by her God
Has turned to serve tables
Anything-goes America
Is never God's cup of tea
Think, America, run to your God
The great God of the Holy Bible
For El Pluribus Unum
In God we must trust.

CHAPTER 2

2008: BARACK OBAMA, JOHN McCAIN AND HILLARY RODHAM CLINTON

A race or competition of anytime is the survival of the fittest. Preparation and execution are part of the fitting package or else... Are you fired up and ready to go?If not, one or more unanticipated stumbling block may stop your move. But the Lord...

Barack walks along Waikiki Beach shortly before he and his mother moved from Hawaii to Indonesia to live with her second husband, Lolo Soetoro, in 1967. (Photo courtesy of Maya Soetoro-Ng)

The Republican and Democratic 2008 primaries began with a large field of candidates for each party. Senator John McCain of Arizona beat the Republican crowd and clinched the nomination in March of 2008. He defeated Rudy Giuliani, former mayor of New York, Senator Sam Brownback of Kansas, Representative Duncan Hunter of California, Governor Mike Huckabee of Arkansas, Representative Ron Paul of Texas, Mitt Romney, former Governor of Massachusetts, Representative Tom Tancredo of Colorado, Fred Thompson, former Senator of Tennessee, and Tommy Thompson, former Governor of Wisconsin. Most of these candidates pulled out after they discovered that Senator McCain had overwhelming lead.

The Democratic primary was a different ball game. It went all the way to the wire, till the last primary vote was counted in Montana on June 3, 2008. It was an epic primary race for the Democrats, spanning all 50 states. It was so because the originally presumed and inevitable favorite and frontrunner, with the big name and money behind her, the Honorable Senator Hillary Rodham Clinton, suddenly found herself in the ropes after the first primary election in the state of Iowa. She came in third place there because of campaign mismanagement; the ultimate underdog, Barack Obama, won the state out of the seven Democratic contenders:

US Senator Joe Biden, State of Delaware
US Senator Hillary Clinton, State of New York
US Senator Chris Dodd, State of Connecticut
Former US Senator John Edwards, State of North Carolina

Former US Senator Mike Gravel, State of Alaska
US Senator Barack Obama, State of Illinois
Governor Bill Richardson, State of New Mexico

Eventually the rest dropped out, leaving Barack Obama and Senator Hillary Clinton. The former first lady, Mrs. Clinton, the wife of former President, William (Bill) Jefferson Clinton, fought tooth and nail, and gained many delegates. However, the late charge was not enough to catch Senator Barack Obama, who did a perfect primary mathematics and homework, and implemented basic management strategies that got him to win majority of the states on super Tuesday (February 5, 2008) and eleven more state victories in a row afterwards, giving him an insurmountable lead in pledged delegates.

Although Hillary, as everyone calls her, (for she is well known), did not win the primary battle, she is included in this chapter because of her formidability, contribution to the race, and the general leadership acumen she helped stimulate out of Senator Barack Obama during the primary race. Her formidability and challenge trained and actually prepared Barack Obama for the general election against the maverick, John McCain, and the Republican party. The party has a good history of dirty and gutter campaigns against any Democratic presidential nominee.

Summary of Democratic Party's Primary Contest

The Democratic primary race is a race for delegates. Each state's pledged delegates are usually divided among the candidates according to the proportion of the votes they secured from the state's primary voters and/or caucuses. A contestant can get a share of the pledged delegates for as long he or she gets 15 percent of the votes cast. At the onset of the race, there were 4,049 total delegates (without Michigan and Florida), including about 850 super delegates. Super delegates' number can change anytime depending on deaths and winning/losing elections. A significant number of the super delegates had pledged for the most popular and financially sound candidate, former First Lady, Senator Clinton.

At the beginning of the primary season, Senator Hillary Clinton was seen as the indomitable favorite, leading overwhelmingly in super-delegates (party officials' endorsements) and in popularity, being a well-known wife of a former, very popular president. She was leading in the national polls with 42% of likely voters, over Obama 23%, Edwards 16%, and the rest of the pack shared the remainder. On January 3 2008, Obama surprisingly won the Iowa caucuses by 38 percent, Edwards 30 percent, Clinton 29 percent, and the rest shared the remainder. This victory in Iowa, with 91 percent Caucasians, boosted Obama popularity throughout the nation. The Democratic race really became a race and the first lady certainly became nervous and shaken. Other contenders began to drop out at this point.

On January 8, Obama very narrowly lost the New Hampshire primary to Clinton after being the favorite there. He went ahead to win Nevada caucuses on January 18, and a huge win in south Carolina on January 26 by a little over 2 to 1 against Clinton who came in second there. At this point, there was a hidden uproar in the Clinton camp and a shaking going on. A statement by former President Clinton that sounded like Barack Obama won the state because many blacks voted for him or that he was a black candidate offended Senator Edward Kennedy, causing the Senator to endorse Obama openly.

That was significant to say the least. Senator Kennedy is not just anybody. He is one of few American icons and a super heavyweight in the Democratic Party. The only rival to him would be the former President, Bill Clinton, who of course, was triple-busy supporting and campaigning for his wife, Hillary Clinton. The campaign was something to watch; it consisted of a huge drama after drama that I'm sure will make an excellent Hollywood movie someday. It was a spectacle that certainly caused most people to miss their regular assignments and glued to the TV or internet. This is not the place to describe all that happened.

Millions of people who have never been interested in politics were feverishly into it, both young and old, most of them attracted to Barack Obama's change and hope message and the nature of his person. A huge majority of black people everywhere, with tears in their eyes and liberation in their hearts, could not wait to get to the polls to vote for Obama after they saw that THIS THING could be possible as indicated by white-Iowa's votes for the black man. One can imagine, and confirmed through my observations, the usually saddened hearts of the majority of blacks all of a sudden beginning to lift up in love for white people and all people. The blogs are still filled by black people, young and old, who just do not know how to pen down their admiration for those who voted for Barack, who will vote for Barack, and who will not vote for Barack. I can see the demonic feeling of discrimination or dislike for any white person (whether good or bad) beginning to leave many or most black people after they saw Obama's victory in Iowa. They are beginning to believe that whites may not be prejudicial and that they reward hard work and performance and not skin pigmentation. The rest of the excited folks, mostly women, arose to support Hillary Clinton who had a chance to become the first female President of the United States. Hillary invoked gender and called on women to rise up after she missed Iowa and got to New Hampshire. Suddenly, women who went for Obama started rushing for Clinton.

Against the rules and regulations of the Democratic Party, States of Michigan and Florida moved their primary dates in front of February 5 to January 15 and 29, 2008, respectively. They voted on those days despite the fact that the Democratic Party ruled that those votes would not count and all the candidates agreed to it. The candidates did not campaign in the states. Many of them actually withdrew their names from the ballot. In fact, thousands of voters did not even go to the polls, some switched to the Republican primary side after they discovered that their votes would not count. Clinton did not remove her name, although she agreed and also stated that the votes would not count since both states violated the rule.

On Super Tuesday, February 5, 2008, Obama won 13 out of the 23 contests. Clinton won 10. From February 9 to 19, Obama racked up eleven more wins, including the Democrats abroad. Without Michigan and Florida, the number of delegates needed to win was 2024. Obama now had 1,192 pledged delegates to Clinton's 1,035. Clinton was still leading in super-delegates, 250 to 192. This lead had started to narrow down as some un-pledged super delegates began to go more toward Obama than toward Clinton. Obama's lead in total delegates had become insurmountable.

Clinton must have to win almost all the other contests by huge margins of about 80 percent average for her to surpass Barack Obama. This was particularly difficult for at least four reasons: (1) Barack Obama had long overtaken her by 2 to 1 in fundraising through the internet, made up of over 1,500,000 highly inspired, small donors. (2) Obama's team is very shrewd and they work well together, knowing exactly what to do or not to do. (3) The proportional, delegate-sharing Democratic Party rule guaranteed Obama almost a third of the delegates just for showing up in a state. Obama drew not large crowd but large-crowd squired. At one point in Oregon, he drew about 75,000 people. (4) Serious endorsements had started coming to Obama from almost every works of life.

To say the least, the honorable Senator Hillary Clinton and his team kicked, cried, misspoke countless number of times, used every kitchen-sink strategy, yelled and tossed around. However, none of the thunders shook the calmness and quiet strategy of Barack Obama and company. Hillary racked up wins in Texas, Pennsylvania, and Ohio, which started causing the atmosphere to change. It now came to Indiana and North Carolina where Barack was heavily favored in the former and very slightly in the latter. Almost everyone tended to believe that had Senator Clinton clinched North Carolina and Indiana, most of the super-delegates would have rushed to her side regardless of Obama's lead in pledged delegates at that point. Clinton and her surrogates had overwhelmingly argued that Barack Obama was not winning big states and white states. Although a flawed argument, people were beginning to believe her. Barack has come to be known as master of calmness, but the 'poor fellow' and his strategis, David Axelrod, must have gone to the bathroom twice in every two minutes with the way things were looking then in both states, especially when one poll showed that North Carolina race had narrowed almost "too much."

In Obama's heart, he must have jumped a wall without a poll after he saw the results on the faithful night of May 6, 2008. Barack was quick to say and yell that he won North Carolina, "A BIG STATE." I am laughing and crying as I write this portion, for I could imagine his feelings and those of millions of young people (white and black) and those old black folks who were watching, crying, and praying for him. They love Hillary but they want Barack to win. To them, it is a personal business. Barack Obama does not really own himself now.

The people believe they own him. They campaign for him, and they are deadly serious with it and with their $5 regular donations. There is no room for Barack to fool around after God, through these tearful, "helpless birds," gets him into the office of president of the United States of America. Well, Barack became the Democratic Party's presumptive nominee after the last primary in Montana on June 3, 2008. Most superdelegates endorsed him and many of Clinton's superdelegates had switched sides. That's democracy, and may God keep blessing America!

A Quick Match-Up and the Issues

What happened in the primary sheds light on the type of person that America should be voting for in this 2008 presidential election. I will be referring to it as we go through chapters 3 to the end. Let us use chapter 2 to summarize select critical issues and note some more things that arose during the primary.

Barack Obama and Hillary had constantly stated that John McCain is running for President George W. Bush Junior's third term. Some people may think that those words are just politics, but you ought to spend time to look at what they said and which Barack is now constantly echoing. On the Iraq war, McCain is certainly going to continue the Bush policy there if the Iraqi leaders continue to fool around with internal sectarian conflicts and squandering US dollars. A poor understanding of the Islamic world and values has caused the United States to commit many blunders in dealing with the Middle East. The best way to deal with Islamic factions when you have a serious problem with one of the leaders is not to get the leader and stay in the nation. It is to get the leader and simply leave the nation and let Muslims deal with the rest of the issues, especially when you are considered the worst of the infidels. Since a mistake has been made in not planning the war right, the next best thing is to seriously warn the Iraqi government that America must pull out on so date, and that "you better get your acts together." Barack is perfectly right in advocating for a timetable and the need to pull out quickly. The Iraqi's must continue to milk the dollars of the United States and never do anything serious unless they know that someone like Barack is coming.

That's exactly what is happening now! If you have been monitoring what is going on in Iraq in recent days, you must discover that since the Iraqi people recognized that Barack is serious, they started to hustle, taking matters into their own hands and getting serious jobs done. They began serious offensive against the Shiite *Al Sadr* militia and they were winning. That is a credit to Barack Obama's heart-talk and serious talk to the Bush administration and to the Iraqi's. Bush and McCain may be planning to use Iraq as a base to invade Iran, but that will be another foreign policy mistake in itself. Iraqis will hate it, and it will be perceived as a trick to the irqi people who will always fight against it.

Barack Obama has a much better understanding of foreign issues than Senator John McCain does. You see, Senator John McCain might know the tough talk, the weapons, and how to use them, he may even know the *superficial* aspects of human and international relationships, but he lacks in ciritcal areas relaive to Barack Obama. Obama knows how to put brains to the weapons so the weapons become smart instruments that cannot move until the brain finishes the nuances of the necessary calculations and the subtle and system-oriented maneuverings required to get problems solved without the killer-weapons. Such maneuverings require some intrinsic understanding of the value system of the people you are dealing with, your genuine love for them, and your clear conscience toward them.

Obama is by far better qualified than McCain in keeping America and Israel safe without causing America lots of headaches, heartaches, bellyaches, political aches, economic aches, and world hatred. He can also help minimize the troubles of the Muslim world by telling them the truth and offering them serious solutions. They will trust him, and they will also respect his words that he will fight back and hard if they sidetrack him or try to terrorize USA interests. Note this, Obama is more like Ronald Reagan with a lot of brain. To learn more about the ratings of Barack Obama, Hillary Clinton, and John McCain on several dimensions of presidential leadership, please get my book, audio-book, or video titled, *WHITE HOUSE 101: How to Choose Whom To Vote for As President Or CEO of USA [Now who Is More Qualified—Hillary Clinton, Barack Obama, or John McCain]–(*EmancipationUSA.org).

The economic issue sounds more like Barack has something and John McCain really has nothing. I like John McCain and I love President George W. Bush. If you do not believe that I love my President George W., all you need to do is to visit EmancipationUSA.org or Champion-Society.com and get a record album that I made for him during the time when everyone was bashing him. We need to be careful about judging President Bush Jr. harshly. I felt like protecting my President when almost everyone was using derogatory language against him. Besides, not everyone might have been able to stabilize a huge ship in the middle of Pacific Ocean after it has been hit by the worst, unexpected tide, and oceanic earthquake. That was what happened on September 11, 2001, and the *honorable* President George W. Bush managed to steady this ship called the USA. It would have been much worse. You "guys" had better give him some credit before God gets angry.

Nevertheless, what I am writing here is not about my brother George W.; it's about who is more qualified to be elected President of the United States of America for such a time as this period in American and world situation. The answer is Barack Obama when it also comes to economic issues. Barrack understands the tears and sorrows of common people. He feels the heartbeat of the working men and women of America far better than McCain and our current President, George W. Bush Jr. do. Believe it or not, my dear people, it is not just trickle-up, it is trickle from all sides that builds a nation. America has misused trickle-down theory that she forgets that the rich people at the top are self-interested human beings like everyone else. They do not let much trickle-down. Many of them trickle the wealth outside the country. Furthermore, boosting the working (not idle) lower and middle class helps them in many ways as they still spend that money to purchase the goods and services of the upper class and the top-rich people. Bottom-up economic policy is "the real policy" for today's wobbling American economy. Prove me by placing Barack Obama into office and give him eight years with America, ceteris paribus. America will blossom again.

The unwritten domestic issue of inspiration is hardly discussed during the campaigns, but it is hugely important. This is an issue that only Barack Obama has right now. The American public needs inspiring right now. Without inspiration, forget motivation. Without motivation, forget performance. Beautiful America, please listen to me. One may have all kinds of good plans, but if the people who are supposed to help implement such plans are not inspired, they cannot have the needed motivation to help, to perform, and to achieve. The plan becomes a lame-dock, just on-paper activity. It has to take the spirit of the people, not just the few leaders, to get the job done. I have no money at all. I have so many people to take care of. I am in the worst monetary crunch of my life, yet I find myself looking for where to get some money so I can send to Barack Obama after I received a video indicating that he opted out of the public financing system. I felt so sad that I have no money that I paused and prayed to God to please bless me and bless others to send him money. That was one of the most humble, heart-rending, 3-minute prayer that I have ever prayed. That is what inspiration will do to you. It causes you to move. From "move", you get "motivation." You are not motivated until you start acting. Inspiration produces motivation. It will take mass inspiration of America's population for America to rise again.

Millions of people are overwhelmingly inspired in the United States right now. How can you explain the overflowing gatherings at Obama's meetings—10,000; 15,000; 20,000; …75,000? How can you explain all the flowing tears from the eyes of people of all races? This is not just hype! When you get the ultimate grassroots inspired, then you are really an inspirer. Young people are the ultimate grassroots. They are the future. Those who never get interested in the affairs of the nation are the missing links. They are the grassroots. To America right now, Barack is not white, black, or green. The man is Mr. USA. He is *Mr. The People.* The joy is that it will not get to his head. He will work for the people or die trying!

So dear fellows, do not quench the light that is shining in these young people and bunch of other people right now. It is the light of God. It is the light of love. It is the light of healing. It is the light of great reconciliation. It is the light of unity. It is the light of one accord. It is the light of performance and solving problems. It is the great light of the UNITED STATES OF AMERICA coming back again! America is about to blossom again. Relatively speaking,

America deserves it. Why? It is because for so many years this nation has sacrificed her money and blood to serve the world in many ways.

America blesses so many nations through her unmatched charities by their wonderful majority race. She protects the little "guys" within and without; yet many people and nations are criticizing her unfairly. She permits many people to come from other countries to learn and to work toward bettering themselves, their loved ones, and their respective nations. She educates most of the uncivilized world, especially their leaders, to behave and to take care of one another. She uses her tax money to bless foes and friends alike, yet the foes and even some so-called friends do not even know how to say "*Thank You.*" It's heartbreaking! Some even want to destroy her.

Yes, America is faltering and she continues to mess up in many areas, especially in her family system, but she is still the most loving nation on the face of the earth. "God, please bless America again, and help her citizens get back to you! Have mercy on all of them. Bless her with leaders that can be examples to them." My tears never stopped flowing. I believe that this man, Barack, is part of God's blessing to America. Something is in God's sleeves for USA, and it is something good!

Culture, Religion, and the Issues

This year I really become ashamed of being called a conservative in the company of those so-called conservatives who do some deplorable things against God that some of them profess to serve. A serious conservative is supposed to be one who stands for what is right and just. Looking at the foundation and founders of the United States of America, the Holy Bible speaks volumes about how a conservative is supposed to act. Lying and cheating in order to win are not some of them. Check it out and you will discover that all the wrong rumors being spread all over the internet originated from the so-called one or more conservatives who also claimed to be Christians and lovers of fellow human being. Such behavior is not American. Such behavior is not Jesus-like. I am not a Democrat or Republican, but I know how I have voted for a long time. The GOP is kicking folks like me out. Serious Christians do not like to win by cheating, by lying, or by false smearing.

Barack Obama is a Christian. He is not a Muslim. He said it. The issue of Rev. Jeremiah Wright certainly helped expose the fact that the man is truly a Christian. The only people who may not believe it are those who, for one reason or the other, will never vote for Obama in the first place. Now there are people who genuinely believe that he is a Muslim mainly because of his middle name, Hussein, his associations, and especially after the United States just finished ousting Saddam Hussein of Iraq. Isn't it mystical? Isn't it funny? Especially to the funny part, I am almost sure somebody said, "Heck no! I need some explanation!"

Well, we know Barack's wife is very educated, and has a mind of her own. That woman is not the kind that will marry a Muslim if she is a Christian, and she is. I can tell you one thing for sure. Barack is not a Muslim at all. He is what some people might call a moderate Christian, not liberal. He is moderate in the sense that he espouses deep Christian values but he is not interested in actively preaching to anyone to choose Christianity. Furthermore, from what I can infer from his speeches and nonverbal behavior, he certainly hates gay lifestyle but he leaves it to those fellows to realize some day that the life is not right and it is against God's way. He is not the kind that will overtly tell someone about gay or abortion being wrong. That is where I disagree with him BIG TIME! That is where I agree with McCain.

Before I go further, it is important at this juncture to let our lovely Muslim friends understand why Americans, though they love Barack, but are terribly scared of him being a Muslim, and why the campaign spends a lot of time to let people know that he is not. Since the people who bombed the world trade center and other places in the world were Muslims, Americans have the right to be scared off their pants. All Muslims may not be like those violent ones. However, imagine yourself being a non-Muslim American and you always read the news or watch the TV broadcasts about Muslims killing some people or killing each other daily?

So dear wonderful Muslims and great Americans: I hope you understand why Americans are scared about voting for a Muslim into a very sensitive office like the Presidency of the United States. Years of tumults in the Islamic nations or between Islam and other people have created serious Islam-phobia. In northern Nigeria and many other places, there have been horrible riots and killings of Christians by Muslims, all in the name of religion. Almost on a weekly or monthly basis, you hear about some Muslim slaughtering other people or themselves, with no regard to human right. That kind of behavior, constantly associated with a particular religion, scares the bottom out of people.

Getting people to be scared of you is not good. Eventually, the same people may summon the courage to fight back and become your enemies. It is important to treat others as you would like to be treated. How will you like people of other religions to kill you and kill your family just because you are a Muslim? I am sure it is not right, and I am sure Muslims will not like it. If I see anyone killing a Muslim for such a reason or for most reasons, my God will require me to tell the authorities after I try to save him or her. I really hope that wonderful Muslim people all over the world will take the steps to market Islam as a peaceful religion. Let your lifestyle force people to become part of you not by the use of force or scare tactic.

I share with Islam some of the conservative practices such as strong family and discipline, modesty, and dislike of promiscuity. Promiscuous lifestyle is destroying America and that is one major reason many Islamic and African nations just do not appreciate America well. Nations want democracy, but they do not want America to bring democracy and then bring family destructions and immoral sexuality with it. This is one issue that no Presidential candidate in America ever addresses for one of two reasons—they are afraid to be unpopular or they are part of the evil lifestyle. To fully understand the true audacity of hope for rebuilding a lasting America, please get my book, audio-book, or video titled, *THE ULTIMATE AUDACITY OF HOPE FOR TODAY'S USA: Emancipating America and Her Dreams* (*Emancipation*USA.Org or ChampioSociety.Com).

I know that Barack Obama supports abortion rights. However, abortion is tied to premarital intercourse. The Muslims, African, and Asian nations vehemently discourage fornication and promiscuous lifestyles. Such lifestyles result to unwanted pregnancy, which leads to the temptation to commit abortion and murder. Fornication or premarital sex is not right for a man or woman. God hates it, and America drinks it like water. Even a spouse can plot to divorce his or her mate so she and the children can have freedom to commit fornication as much as they like without the interference of the Christian parent. It happens. No right-minded man desires to marry a woman that has been used. Neither a serious girl will desire to marry some man that has slept with other women. People who engage in premarital intercourse are people who are more likely to commit adultery, most of the time with their former fornication-partners. Fornication is what leads to unwanted pregnancy. If a child messes up in disobedience and then gets pregnant, she is supposed to give birth to that child. What would have happened if Barack's mother decides to abort Barack? Barack or someone else may argue – it is because she wanted to have Barack, and besides she was married. Now think about it. The little Barack or John or Jane is in the womb, living, breathing, and helpless on his or her own, but totally trusting on his or her mother to protect her. Next thing you know, the mother makes a decision to kill him or her because---

(1) The baby does not own the mother's body. The mother's body belongs to the mother. This is a lie. The baby owns that body because the baby did not ask to be put in there. The mother made the choice that led to the baby being there. The baby belongs to God, to the pregnant woman, the male culprit, and to the society.

(2) The baby is the "it" not he or she. Lie again. It is like destroying a watermelon plant that is just one day old or one week old or two weeks old and refused to call it a watermelon plant. Everything about watermelon is in that plant. Once you kill that baby, you just killed a human being and his or her descendants that God planned through him or her. If you make a mistake, as some people may say, you should keep the baby instead of adding salt to injury or gasoline to fire. You pay in the end.

(3) No one wants to have his baby girl punished with a baby if she makes a mistake. That is the only thing that sounds dumb that I have heard

Obama said. You must not love a child too much that God's law will be violated. Disobedience emits serious and lasting consequences in the end. Nevertheless, that's tight. It is a mistake or disobedience of God that she chose to make. She or he must learn from that mistake and not by making the mistake worse than what it is already. If a person cannot help it, the acceptable choice in the sight of God is to get married. That is why it is good to surround oneself with a group of people who desire the same kind of righteousness, reinforcing one another in the Lord who they love and fear. Feeding on immoral television shows and hanging with wrong company promote immoral sexuality very easily.

Now, why should a person like me who opposes abortion and gay marriage find myself supporting Obama? Well, it is not very easy but it is clear. You must choose the better of two evils or the better of two goodies, whichever is the case. I want people to know that I think John McCain is a decent man, and what I am going to say next is not necessarily against McCain. I am referring to leaders and election candidates in general. One problem with voters most of the time is that they waste their votes based on a simple look at one attribute instead of the whole field of attributes. One may argue that racism slaughters more people than abortion. In fact, racism is a form of ethnic cleansing technique, except that it kills the millions of people very slowly as it destroys their dignity and crucify them psychologically. The worst is that racism destroys both the giver and the receiver in the end. It ruins the society beyond every imagination. It is a nuclear bomb that kills slowly.

Sometimes we vote for a womanizer and adulterer just because the person opposes gay marriage or abortion. We never stopped to think that adultery and womanizing by a leader trickles down to the people he leads. He is not only the ultimate role model, but he is like the covering for the whole nation and her citizens. If he is morally filthy, everybody else suffers in both the short and the long run. This is the perfect, proven truth. Spiritually, the immoral behavior or lifestyle of the top person will transmit to anyone who is not spiritually protected. Millions of children and adults will be affected. They will be attacked by immoral sex demons and the results are bunch of unwanted pregnancies, innumerable abortions, broken homes, single parenting, child abuse, psychological problems, thousands of all crimes, and the rest of the stories. Now recall that we voted for this person or persons because they oppose abortion or one thing we really hate. However, you have seen whom he really is, a catastrophic juggernaut.

Fellows, we must always look at the total picture. The election of Barack will rebuild millions of lives and provide hope and the mind-set for people to look to God again because of God's goodness. People are hurting very badly now. Sometimes God chooses some one among us to accomplish His will despite the one's weaknesses in one part. One thing that God looks at when He wants to bless a nation or a group of people is the extent or magnitude of institutional love that the person has. Institutional love is that love that a leader or potential leader has for the people, causing him to be willing to sacrifice himself for the benefit of those he leads while possessing the ability to offer and implement necessary solutions that fits the contingencies of the time. Obama is more of this type of leader for the United States and the world at this time than the most Honorable, Senator John McCain. McCain is good, but Obama is better. In fact, I look forward for Obama to have McCain in his cabinet when he wins, and vice versa. McCain has a beautiful spirit.

Real Issue and *The* Ultimate Audacity of Hope

This section is a hard-hit on Barack Obama and his book, *The Audacity of Hope*. I am going to write this section directly addressing Senator Barack Obama. It addresses some things that America never gives attention in their presidential and other campaigns. If they do, it is partially and usually brought up by some ungodly conservatives who also may lack love for everybody else. Dear Barack Obama, since you seem to have love for everyone, I am going to address you directly simply because you wrote a popular book called, *The Audacity of Hope*. The problem is that the real hope is not in that book or at least I have not heard you, Senator McCain, or any presidential campaigner talk about it. It is the issue of strong family based on the fear of the Almighty God not on Darwinism or anything-goes.

Please look at Figure 1 very closely, a general model of societal building or societal destruction. This figure will appear about two more times in this book. It is critical that we understand it. Any hope that is not founded on this rock called the family, with strong father and mother adhering to the principles of morality and righteousness, is no hope. Such rebellious hope is dangeous. It represents empty hope. You may know what you are saying, but you seem to be missing the foundation or are shy to talk about it. The moral base of America is completely gone. America has become the United States of Anything-goes, and you must not want to contribute to make it worse than what it is already. The foundation and the
ultimate place to begin are the family and the American God, the God of the Holy Bible!

- Why do you think we have run-away divorces in America?
- Why do you think we have run-away fornications and adulteries at all levels in America?
- Why do you think we have run-away teenage pregnancies in America?
- Why do you think we have run-away single parenting in America?
- Why do you think we have run-away gang violence and troubles in America?

•

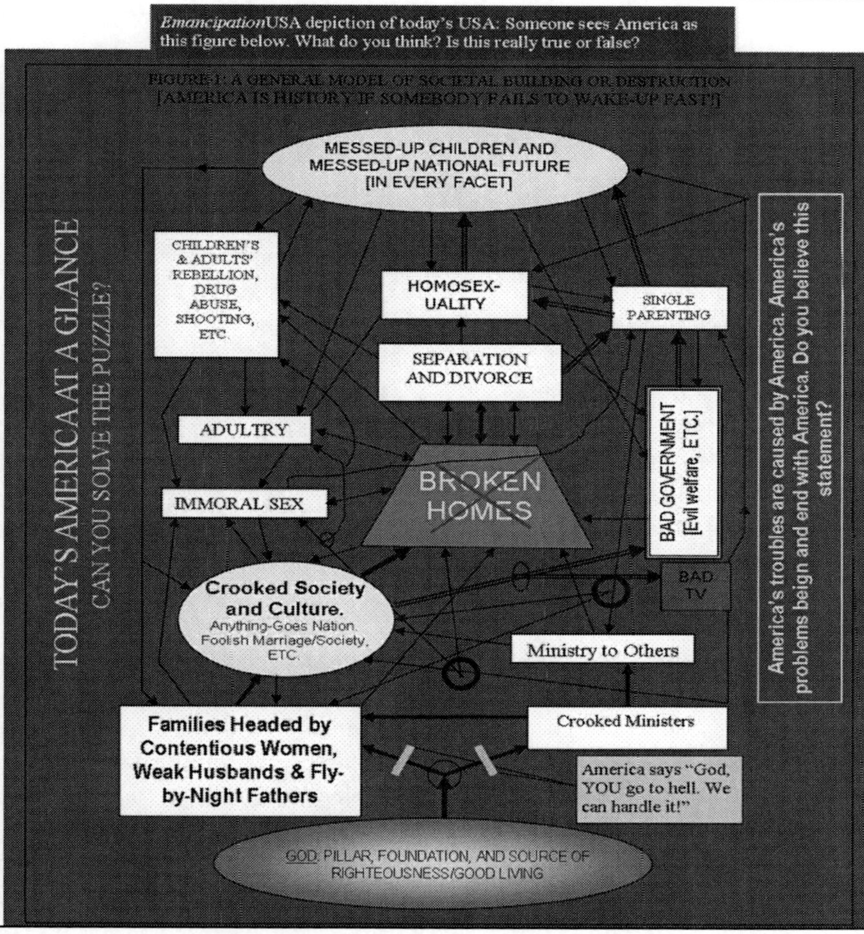

Any hope for America begins and ends with the understanding depicted in this model. Every American leader needs to understand this model. Dear so-called conservatives: even though you may share this value, your knowing it cannot cause "the it" to be manifested to the benefit of the society unless you first have love within you. You can know, do, or say anything, but if you don't have love, you are nothing (1 Corinthians 13). That's the problem with most conservative leaders. Let's try to possess and communicate love first. To liberals: love that ignores the God of righteousness and adopts anything-goes is making your flesh God, and that is wickedness to the highest degree. The flesh never wants discipline. The flesh never wants anything that makes it hurt. The flesh loves immorality. The flesh hates authority. Without authority, nothing works!!! Divine authority is "the Authority." America already has his model in the Holy Bible.

- Why do you think we have run-away horrible school performance in America?
- Why do you think we have run-away fornication-laden American children in America?
- Why do you think we have run-away homemade terrorists in America?
- Why do you think we have over 80 percent of black race subdued in America's welfare?
- Why do you think we have that millions of teens in America have no remorse to get pregnant and have children before it is time?
- Why do you think we have run-away children's and adult disobedience in America?
- Why do you think we have America that is plunging down toward becoming worse than the so-called third worlds?
- Why do you think we have the prisons and jails in America constantly overpopulating?
- Why do you think we have children running their parents in America and everything is going haywire?
- Why do you think we have sexual immoralities of untold proportions in America?
- Why do you think we have run-away gay lifestyles in America?

Did you read about some 17 teenage white girls that made a pact to become pregnant? Have you noticed that such heavy-duty immorality is taking place in Massachusetts, one of the most liberal states in the USA? Does that tell you something about being liberal to a point of disobeying God's moral standards? Do you read and hear about the passing of sex condoms in schools? Were you part of the bunch that permitted that kind of stupidity and wickedness or do you support it? What does such approval tell our children? Do you see it as a license for them to go and enjoy the so-called sex or do you see it as helping them? Do you see it as violating God's moral code or do you see it as going by your own fleshly law—whatever pleases the flesh?

Sir, your *Audacity of Hope* is a perfect piece of problem if it is not grounded upon sound moral principle, governed by divine righteousness. There is a huge limit on how far one can go or endure just believing in himself or herself if himself or herself is not grounded on divine value system. The founding fathers recognized it .It is the Holy Bible. You MUST therefore use your platform to address this matter seriously as stated here, otherwise I MUST DOUBT YOUR LOVE AND CARE for these young people and many folks who love you and are voting for you.

Please listen to me Sir: Since they will listen to you, you must strive not to give them empty hope but hope that lasts. That hope is hope in the higher power, which must guide their values, beliefs, attitudes, intentions, and behavior.

What Jesus Christ represents, the values, beliefs, and life-style that Jesus Christ represents are healthy; they are the moral standard of life for Americans. Since Americans forsook this moral principle in Jesus for the ease of doing what they like, what is easy, what pleases the flesh, including consuming adulteries and fornication, hells are breaking loose in America's so-called homes; children and so-called adults are in shambles. Troubles everywhere! America has become not the United States of America but the United States of Anything-goes. The bedrock of America is the America's God, the God of the Holy Bible, the God of righteousness, the God of holy living, the God of morality and chastity not immorality and anything-goes! Sir, you must find a way to cry out to the American adults and children on this issue of STRONG FAMILY based on the word of God that America knows.

Another huge destructive tool is America's welfare system as it is now. It encourages broken homes, single-parenting, teenage pregnancies, and other atrocities. Millions of black people (and now expanding to other races) have special love for welfare and to their own fatal detriment. This welfare menace affects the whole society and the rest of the world. The seventeen white teens that became pregnant are depending on the USA government to be their husbands and the father of their children. That is exactly what is killing America today! A serious audacity of hope will seek to stop it, not to assist parents like that. Real Audacity of hope will fine these girls and their sexual partners and/or throw them into prison for such crimes against the children and the society! Their parents must also be questioned. Unfortunately, the American government, as it is set up now, is the sponsor of these evil pregnancies, the children that follow, and most of the crimes that ensue afterwards. America is almost dead, and you must work hard not to contribute to it or I must cry to the Almighty God of heaven and earth to deal with you and discipline you. It is high time that American leaders woke up to real seriousness and solve problems the right way whether the way is popular or not.

You must use your position now to cry out. A messed-up family system spells messed-up children. Messed-up children spell messed-up adults. Messed-up adults spell messed-up culture. Messed-up culture spells messed-up political system. Messed-up political system and the other messed-ups spell a nation going down into the Bermuda Triangle for her burial! America is going down to her death! Figure 1 shows you what is happening to America, anation that I truly care for. See if you can figure the mess. The figure represents America's condition right now. America is dying fast. The only hope for revival is to get America back to her God through the families. The Figure is also shown in my website, *Emancipation*USA.Org. While you are there, you may want to consult my presentation titled, *THE ULTIMATE AUDACITY OF HOPE FOR TODAY'S USA: Emancipating America and Her Dreams*.

Barack must work on the issue discussed here. Since he has head enough to reason, he can see the urgency and he will know that Reverend Martin Luther King's *"Fierce urgency of Now"* begins and ends with the bedrock I just presented. Dr. King was able to stay the course and die for the righteousness of what he believed and accomplished. Therefore, my dear Senator Barack Obama, I really trust that you can seriously tap into the bedrock that guided Rev. Martin Luther King Jr. and speak with "real" authority and audacity toward building America's family system again to reflect the desires of this bedrock as depicted in Figure 1. Politics without truth or principle spells sweet talk that bears no lasting fruit. The flesh hates standards. America needs value standards again. America has strayed TOO FAR AWAY from her God, and that is why (once again) hells are breaking loose. America's enemies are not completely Muslims or Osama bin Laden. America's enemy is America! She has forgotten and forsaken her first love, her God of righteousness, the God that she used to trust.

By us, this change will not happen. Divided, we are bound to fail. But the life of a tall, gangly, self-made Springfield lawyer tells us that a different future is possible. He tells us that there is power in words. He tells us that there is power in conviction. That beneath all the differences of race and region, faith and station, we are one people. He tells us that there is power in hope. As Lincoln organized the forces arrayed against slavery, he was heard to say: "Of strange, discordant, and even hostile elements, we gathered from the four winds, and formed and fought to battle through." That is our purpose here today. That's why I'm in this race. Not just to hold an office, but to gather with you to transform a nation. I want to win that next battle – for justice and opportunity. I want to win that next battle – for better schools, and better jobs, and health care for all. I want us to take up the unfinished business of perfecting our union, and building a better America. And if you will join me in this improbable quest, if you feel destiny calling, and see as I see, a future of endless possibility stretching before us; if you sense, as I sense, that the time is now to shake off our slumber, and slough off our fear, and make good on the debt we owe past and future generations, then I'm ready to take up the cause, and march with you, and work with you. Together, starting today, let us finish the work that needs to be done, and usher in a new birth of freedom on this Earth. ....Barack Obama. 2/7/07

YES WE CAN!

CHAPTER 3

QUALIFIED TO BE PRESIDENT: THE LINCOLN FACTOR

Love is the antenna in a man by which God knows His choice and through which God does a job to the blessing of a people. The man with that love is always guaranteed to be the divine choice for national emancipation and jjjhealing.

Abraham Lincoln and his wife, Mary

Barack Obama Loves People

Abraham Lincoln was the man of America in the 1860's. Barack Obama is the man for today's United States of America. During the time of Abraham Lincoln, America was in the hell of hatred, division, and other sinful acts against one another. The issue of slavery was such a money-maker and economic backbone of millions of people that no one dared to speak up and face the wrath of the slave owners and their states. Evil was going on in the United States, sapping the moral fabric of the great nation. The evil of human rights violation was a hidden cancer that was eating up America's image and constitution both before America's God and the whole world. One man dared to teach himself law and jumped into politics to fight and to die for the RIGHT thing, even when it was not popular at all. The "truth" Abe or Abraham Lincoln, a two-term US House Repre-sentative from Illinois, said to himself that 'enough is enough.'

Love of people and nation drove the skinny, tall man into the arena of politics to help stop man's indignity to man and to restore what was supposed to be a Christian nation back to her God and to her motto, "*In God We Trust*." It started with him eloquently arguing the evils of slavery and the ruining of the United States because of it. God gave him the nomination for the presidency of his nation through his then party, the Republican. Although he may have promised the southern slave owners about not abolishing slavery, God knew the heart of the man and what he would do once elected. Even the southerners feared that Lincoln would abolish slavery; that was why they opposed his candidacy, for they knew Lincoln's record of accomplishment and moral standard. Lincoln fought for the common people. He got into the presidential race to make America a slavery-free nation—to rescue the voiceless. Against Kansas-Nebraska Act of 1854 which permitted people to have the right to decide whether or not to allow slavery in their territory rather than have such a decision imposed on them by Congress, Lincoln decried:

> [The Act has a] *declared* indifference, but as I must think, covert *real* zeal for the spread of slavery, I cannot but hate it. I hate it because of the monstrous injustice of slavery itself. I hate it because it deprives our republican example of its just influence in the world — enables the enemies of free institutions, with plausibility, to taunt us as hypocrites — causes the real friends of freedom to doubt our sincerity, and especially because it forces so many really good men amongst ourselves into an open war with the very fundamental principles of civil liberty — criticizing the Declaration of Independence, and insisting that there is no right principle of action but *self-interest*. (Abraham Lincoln,Wikipedia).

Standing on righteous principle, and shunning politically correct positions, his heart cried against slavery, he ran for the stoppage of such inhumane behavior, and won the presidency of the United States of America. Abraham Lincoln wisely fought the civil war that resulted because of his stand, defeated the confederate southern army, formulated and freed the slaves in his Emancipation Proclamation of September 22, 1862, and then united the states with love into one union, with little or no punishment of the captured confederate army and the secessionists. America's dignity before God and man came back. He was assassinated in April 15, 1865 for his love of people and his stand for righteousness and against evil. The plotters gained nothing but purchased straight tickets into hell-fire where they continue to wail and gnash their teeth today.

Although Abraham Lincoln was dubbed inexperienced, God knew that he was fully experienced for the job He and Abe Lincoln would do. Two year's in the House of representative was just enough. He was chosen for such a time like that period in the life of America. He was chosen because of the condition of his heart for all people. Dubbed to be inexperienced, he was a quick learner and an intelligent strategist. He was not a soldier but he had the "head" to study the war situations and made wise decisions. Love is the ultimate qualification that is needed for use in leading people and accomplishing divine-mandated objectives. That was Abraham Lincoln.

Everyone has a calling on his or her life and that calling is something good not evil. The key is to preposition yourself so you do not miss the fulfillment of such a calling. Barack Obama is at that stage right now. I am urging America to let it happen. Don't fight it or smear it. Glory is to God!

Barack On *Lincoln Balance Scale*

Things are becoming a little mystified because I am beginning to see Barack Obama as Abraham Lincoln image for today's America and yet possesses the Kennedy, the Reagan, and the Barack for all-round blossom of USA. Instead of the 'truth Abe,' we now have the "truth Barack." He clearly and categorically stands for the common person and the helpless as Abraham Lincoln stood during his time. Being of black race and touting against special interests and lobbyists in Washington create huge odds against him. However, like Abraham Lincoln, God is also with Barack. Who can ever imagine that he would be able to discover and to raise the money that amerced without special interests? Who could have ever imagined that Barack Obama, the heavy underdog (culturally, politically, and economically) would beat the other candidates, including the once inevitable front-runner, first lady Hillary Rodham Clinton, to win the Democratic nomination? Who could have predicted that Iowa and significant number of white people in America would vote for a black man? Most black people did not believe it and they are still living in astonishment and awe. It is nothing but God, the "fierce urgency of now" hatched by God for use with His chosen one. God can use anyone. He only looks in the heart.

You have read his announcement to run for the presidency of the United States. Everything he stated there came from the heart, and Lincoln would have stood for every one of them. In fact, the agenda is a continuation of the Lincoln agenda—to make more perfect the union called *The United States of America.* In search of this more perfect union was the purposeful platform of Lincoln in fighting injustices and human rights violations to the blessing of USA. From birth to now, and after seeing the cries and prayers of many in the United States of America and 'even' the world, God started manufacturing a man, a black man, a biracial man, for use in placing a soaring, sealed stamp in what Lincoln had done. It is about restoring America again through the forgiveness of America's slavery-related sins, and to set America up for the next blossoming, domestically and internationally!

Something is definitely in the air, and I hope that we will not mess it up. Today's America is certainly divided and has been doing business divided. Washington and all levels of governments can attest to it. Social relationship among races has progressed but Lincoln and Martin Luther King would have suggested a new phase of revolution to move America into the next God's stage of blessings. The Joshua generation is today's Obama bandwagon. It was not a surprise to me at all that Rev. Jeremiah Wright's issue came up. It was not even a huge surprise that the white Catholic Reverend, Michael Pfleger, made the comments he made afterwards. These Reverends were not completely in control of those statements. Years of harboring these thoughts and frustrations, coupled with some working of God caused them to say what they said. The statements were part of God's convoluted map toward the cleansing and blessing of America again. It is hard for most people to understand, but the way God works is far deeper and opposite man's ways and thoughts.

On Lincoln scale, it seems like Barack is one side and Lincoln is on the other, and the scale is balanced. What is happening now in America is a balanced mathematical equation of blessing through inventions and innovations—something new and challenging to the people. America desperately needed a new direction during the so-called inexperienced Abraham Lincoln, truth-speaking Abraham Lincoln. Today's America certainly needs change, hope, and new direction. She has to go from *cowboy* diplomacy to *love and direct-communication* diplomacy, from trickle-down economic theory to bottom-up and middle class economic empowerment and management, from the country of the few haves to the country of every hardworking citizen, from a nation of health for the wealthy to universal healthcare, from a nation of divisive politics and leadership to *The United States of America*. That's innovation! That's a new vision! That's Lincoln, and that's Barack Obama.

Besides, and just like Lincoln, Barack happens to be a lawyer, intelligent, quick learner, and a good strategist who loves people and his nation. Just like Lincoln, Barack served two terms in the Illinois legislature and two terms at the federal level before running for the president of the United States. Just like Lincoln, Barack Obama was tall and skinny while their wives have a little more flesh and broad faces. As Lincoln was assassinated, we pray, in the name of Jesus, that no American will be so hateful of a bold change of electing a qualified black person into America's presidency that he or she would like to see Barack dead or hurt in any manner. We pray that God protects Barack and transforms the heart of any one who may hate him that bad. Amen. Vote for Lincoln--Vote for Obama. Let us cap up what Lincoln boldly did and release blessings for America and the rest of the world. Let's complete the job.

> *...I want us to take up the unfinished business of perfecting our union, and building a better America. And if you will join me in this improbable quest, if you feel destiny calling, and see as I see, a future of endless possibility stretching before us; if you sense, as I sense, that the time is now to shake off our slumber, and slough off our fear, and make good on the debt we owe past and future generations, then I'm ready to take up the cause, and march with you, and work with you. Together, starting today, let us finish the work that needs to be done, and usher in a new birth of freedom on this Earth.* ....*Barack Obama. 2/7/07*

YES WE CAN!

CHAPTER 4

QUALIFIED TO BE PRESIDENT: THE MANAGEMENT PROCESS

Management is the process of working with people, through those people, and with other organizational resources toward achieving organizational goals. A leader must know how to manage.

Presidential hopeful Barack Obama, in 1979 gets a hug during his high school graduation in Hawaii from his maternal grandparents, Stanley Armour Dunham and Madelyn Payne, both natives of Kansas. We're very proud of them. (Photo courtesy Obama campaign)

Briefly, this section will examine Barack Obama and rate him on the identified elements of management called the management process. Many a time, the problem with the electorate is voting for potential leaders without weighing them on these important dimensions. People vote on silly things like relationship to them, beauty and physical features, race, one-issue, etc. If the person you voted for can't manage, then he can't lead. It will be catastrophic. Based on what we have seen Barack Obama do so far, we will try to rate him on the processes of management --planning, organizing, staffing, directing, and controlling.

Barack In Planning

Planning is the process of setting goals and determining how to achieve the goals. Throughout Barack Obama's life before and during politics, we see a man who has proven that he can set wise goals and pursue such goals within set strategies. He went to school for a political science and law degrees with a certain purpose at heart—to equip himself to be able to come back and help a community and finally a nation in need. Working with the common people as a community organizer gave him a sense of urgency that there is more to this thing than just working at that level. The fight to help the community and the nation should go through the Illinois state government and the USA capitol. The man came back from law school, picked up where he left off in the state of Illinois, and making it into the Illinois senate few years later.

The most beautiful display of Obama's understanding of leadership's planning function happened before our eyes during the 2008 Democratic primary. Coming as a sure underdog, being of black race and certainly not much money compared to the then inevitable frontrunner, *First Lady* Hillary Clinton, Barack Obama set a goal of winning the Democratic nomination for the presidency of the United States. He foresaw, adopted and implemented a delegate race-strategy, trusting in his acumen that money and other things would flow into his campaign as he analyzed and judged. He studied and mastered the rules of the game and determined that he could win the nomination through both caucus and primary election strategies. He understands the difference between the two elections and the 'factor' that the Democratic Party awards pledged delegates by proportion. That is part of the reason why he won the primary, beating the more experienced and entrenched candidates. Judgment surpasses experience.

Democratic primary gives us a glimpse of what Barack Obama will govern as president of the United States of America. He will not be a cock-and-shoot type of leader that is hampered by myopic values or skill. Barack Obama will set America's goals and determine how to achieve those goals based on thorough analysis of all necessary domestic, foreign, and international forces that will influence such a decision or decisions. We can trust him to deal with and compete with foreign leaders and nations toward achieving healthy victories for USA. He is already a man that is established in weighing his options and analyzing contingencies typifying a particular situation before making a decision associated with that situation. We can trust his decision because we know he is good in identifying and choosing the right process to making a right, competitive, and winning decision.

Barack In Organizing and Staffing

Once Barack Obama decided in the privacy of his own mind and home that he would be running for the President of the United States, he moved forward to organize toward achieving such a goal. He first needed to win the Democratic primary. He put together a campaign organization that still marvels his competitors and the nation. Again, this is a man that does not want to make too many mistakes. He studied previous campaigns, learned something about their successes and failures, and weighed the contingencies of the present and future America. Based on this knowledge, Obama created his own campaign organization. He recognizes the importance of having such job units as the generally known structure of campaign manager, lead strategist, fundraising department, economic advisers, foreign-policy advisers, and the rest of them.

Everyone that runs a campaign or an organization should be expected to know the basic departments. However, Barack Obama not only has this knowledge but he implemented it well and better than his competitors did. He infused into his structure an atmosphere of fluid relationship. His campaign departments, although they are separate and should perform separate functions, have an inherent no-choice value system to have to depend on one another for each and everyone's success and victory. In other words, the structure is more of a good-family house instead of the regular classical, rigid atmosphere. Every department exists and works for other departments in a very friendly and exciting atmos-phere. Although there is clear authority relationship, flat and fluidity of structure naturally psychologically exist, eliminating unnecessary mental bureaucratic ills and anxiety-producing elements.

Barack's view of the type of structure he desires caused him to put together some of the best people that can work in such a campaign. Many political pundits and the media have lauded such successful staffing approach. Taking cues from Barack Obama and his top employees, David Plouffe (the shrewd campaign manager) and David Axelrod (the wise strategist), the rest of the staff naturally blends with Barack and his vision for the nation and the immediate goal of winning the Democratic primary according to set strategies. Barack Obama envisioned a structure that must joyfully be one and functions as one. That is what happened. He and his top staff brought the right people together to help foster such atmosphere. For this reason, we did not hear any bickering and frustration in the Obama camp while the other campaigns suffered internally and poured outwardly. Newsweek alluded to Obama's staffing benefit as follows:

> Obama has been fortunate in his senior advisers. Obama's chief strategist, David Axelrod, combines big-picture idealism and Chicago School politics of hard knocks. Plouffe is sure and steady. Having managed the successful campaign to get the mercurial Bob Torricelli elected in New Jersey to the Senate in 1996, Plouffe impressed Democratic political gurus. In 1997, Steve Elmendorf, chief of staff to former House Democratic leader Richard Gephardt, hired Plouffe as his deputy. "There are a lot of people in politics who are good strategists and there are a lot of people who are good managers," says Elmendorf. "There are not a lot of people who can do both, and David can do both." The genius of Axelrod and Plouffe was to combine astonishing (even to them) fund-raising potential on the Internet with grass roots organizing. While Clinton was aiming for a knockout by sweeping Super Tuesday, Axelrod and Plouffe were methodically organizing a state-by-state, district-by-district strategy—including states that most political experts ignored. For example, Idaho: Obama won by 60 points and netted more delegates than Clinton took out of either Ohio or Pennsylvania. (Wolffe and Thomas, May 19, 2008).

The internet fundraising department and its staffers cannot be overemphasized when talking about Obama's organizing and staffing IQ. He raised more money than any primary candidate ever did, all from about 1.7 million little donors ($5 and more) and mostly through the internet. Because of these little, low-income donors, Obama was able to even make a decision to skip $85 million from the public financing system for the general election, the first candidate to ever do so.

There is so much to infer about Barack's campaign organizing and staffing. In general, he created an adaptable, semi-organic campaign structure, filled the positions with intrinsically and highly motivated people. This hybrid structural system is just perfect for the situation. It is serving him well now; it served him perfectly well during the primary season. Every member of the system loves what he or she is doing in relation to Barack Obama and to one another. Barack Obama and the top leaders maintain minor classical grip on the way information is licked to the public.

Fellows, we can trust Barack Obama's IQ to do the same for America as he has done for his campaign organization. In fact, he will do much better because he will then have an endless stream of support and people that can help make it happen. He believes in using the best people for the right positions and toward the attainment of specific goals. He is a group leader and an achiever. Barack Obama loves to achieve by helping people achieve. He cannot cut corners in the process of creating the right atmosphere that will enable him and his team to do something meaningful and rewarding for the United States of America. In other words, the man will do a perfect job in organizing and staffing America toward achieving his campaign's platform for America. Obama will also be ready to handle any contingency; he continues to show that he is smart enough to handle unexpectedness like maneuvering to avoid a deer that suddenly emerged from a bush and on his partway. He knows when not to try to avoid the deer and hurt the nation; he knows when to avoid it for as long as the nation is safe. The right judgment depends on the decision's contribution to the security of and other benefits to the United States of America.

Barack In Directing

Directing is the process of leading, motivating, and communicating with people toward the attainment of organizational goals. From the observation of Barack Obama's primary election management, we can say something about his directing skills. Beyond the shadow of a doubt, no one will argue that Barack has not done an excellent job in mobilizing his staff toward achieving the democratic nomination for president. He has definitely inspired both paid and unpaid staff members to work very hard and joyously in his campaign for president of the United States. He actually paid his average employee less than the competitor did, yet his employees are much more motivated to perform. Some competitors paid too much, and found themselves in debt and hurt water. This kind of success in motivating workers stems from first doing a good job of staffing—recruiting and employing the right people.

Verbally and nonverbally, Barack Obama is able to communicate to all employees and donors that the ship belongs to *"all of us, together."* The underlying and frequently spoken theme is that "this is your campaign." Employees, volunteers, and donors took it very personal, and they work for Barack's campaign for President as if it is their own, and it is. Barack makes sure that the people see it that way by making sure that he hides nothing and that he is transparent. People that work for him and donate to him trust him. Trust and honesty produce great motivation from a leader's coworkers and subordinates. Obama achieved that status right from the beginning and it has been carrying him up to now toward the general election.

To throw some light on Barack Obama's directing approach to management, read an excerpt on part of Obama's campaign strategy as titled by Newsweek in "*Sit Back, Relax, Get Ready to Rumble.*" Cate-gorically stating that Barack seems to be taking everything in stride, Wolffe and Thomas wrote on how team-Obama will handle the GOP onslaught toward the November 2008 general election:

> How do you know if Barrack Obama is unhappy with what you are saying— or not saying? At meetings of his closest advisers, he likes to lean back, put his feet on the table and close his eyes. If he doesn't like how the conversation is going, he will lean forward, put his feet on the floor and "adjust his socks, kind of start tugging at them," says Michael Strautmanis, a counselor to the campaign. Obama wants people to talk, but he doesn't want to intimidate them. "If you haven't said anything, he'll call on you," says Strautmanis. "He's never said it, but he usually thinks if somebody is very quiet it's because they disagree with what everybody is saying … so Barack will call on you and say, 'You've been awfully quiet'." There are no screamers on Team Obama; one senior Obama aide says he's heard him yell only twice in four years. Obama was explicit from the beginning: there was to be "no drama," he told his aides. "I don't want elbowing or finger-pointing. We're going to rise or fall together." Obama wanted steady, calm, focused leadership; he wanted to keep out the grandstanders and make sure the quiet dissenters spoke up-- good formula for running a campaign—or a presidency.
>
> It worked against Hillary Clinton, whose own campaign has been rent by squabbling aides and turf battles. While Clinton veered between playing Queen Elizabeth I and Norma Rae, Obama and his team chugged along with a superior 50-state campaign strategy, racking up the delegates. If the candidate seemed weary and peevish or a little slow to respond at times, he never lost his cool. But the real test is yet to come. The Republican Party has been successfully scaring voters since 1968, when Richard Nixon built a Silent Majority out of lower- and middle-class folks frightened or disturbed by hippies and student radicals and blacks rioting in the inner cities. The 2008 race may turn on which party will win the lower- and middle-class whites in industrial and border states—the Democrats' base from the New Deal to the 1960s, but "Reagan Democrats" in most presidential elections since then. It is a sure bet that the GOP will try to paint Obama as "the other"—as a haughty black intellectual who has Muslim roots (Obama is a Christian) and hangs around with America-haters.
>
> Obama says he's ready for the onslaught. "Yes, we know what's coming," he told a cheering crowd as he won the North Carolina primary last week. "We've seen it already … the attempts to play on our fears and exploit our differences to turn us against each other for pure political gain—to slice and dice this country into Red States and Blue States; blue-collar and white-collar; white,

> black, brown." Hillary Clinton was not above playing on those fears. Refusing to concede defeat last week, she cited an Associated Press poll "that found how Senator Obama's support among working, hardworking Americans, white Americans, is weakening again." As Washington Post columnist, Eugene Robinson wrote: "Here's what she's really saying to party leaders: *There's no way that white people are going to vote for the black guy. Come November, you'll be sorry.*" (in News Week, May 19, 2008).

When you have a leader that integrates himself among his staff and communicates with them at an honest, friendly, and interdependent level, the organization cannot help but operate as a team of lovers. Such a team can withstand any outside attack. You may have heard Jesus' statement in the Holy Bible, which says, "*a house divided against itself cannot stand.*" A team that is truly together always wins. A husband and wife whose house is fret with contentions and strife never make it. Such a home usually becomes a victim to societal onslaughts of immoral attacks and anything-goes until the home breaks up. The home cracks because it is not held together by that very-important directing function or because some-body may have made a serious error in planning, organizing, and/or staffing.

Therefore, the Obama team is ready for the Republicans because of the faith the team has on one another and on the leadership of their presidential candidate, Barack Obama. The NewsWeek magazine said that the strategy worked against Hillary Clinton and company and why not against the Republicans. Even the former GOP Vice President, Dan Quayle, admitted the force of the Obama management factor. According to an Associates Press interview:

> Former Vice President Dan Quayle said Tuesday he respects Democrat Barack Obama "because he beat the Clintons" and fears Republican John McCain has an "uphill battle" to defeat Obama in November's presidential election. Quayle also acknowledged that he expected Democrat Hillary Rodham Clinton and Republican Mitt Romney would meet in the general election. "I don't think anyone saw, including myself, the Barack Obama movement" coming, he said. "I have a lot of grudging respect for what he did because he beat the Clintons, something we couldn't do in 1992," said Quayle, a former GOP senator from Indiana who served under President George H.W. Bush. "The Clintons were very convincing in the campaign they ran. So I thought she would be the candidate. "I think she made obviously some very tactical mistakes," Quayle continued. "One, underestimating Obama. And, two, the whole inevitability that `I am entitled to the nomination' ended up hurting her quite dramatically." (Sonner July 1, 2008).

It is good to know the opposition's mistakes or shortcomings. It is also good to have the right plan, the organization, and the right staff in place to be able to deal with the opposition. If the leader fails to direct the staff appropriately according to proven management tactics, plans cannot be implemented, opposition's errors cannot be exploited, and the enemy's strategies cannot be withstood or defeated. Barack Obama understands the directing function. He understands his staff, leads them, communicates with them, and motivates them toward goal-achievement with a sense that they are all equal and into it together. If one hurts, everyone hurts, and one rejoices, everyone rejoices, no finger pointing. Such is Barack Obama's campaign character. He leads by example and remains strong for others.

Barack In Controlling

Controlling involves measuring performance, comparing it with the standard, and taking any corrective action. Barack Obama is also good at controlling outcomes. He won Iowa and narrowly lost New Hampshire. He retooled and bounced back to the winning of the nomination. Look at the way he handled the gaffes, especially the Jeremiah Write controversy. Spontaneously and intuitively, he knew that he had to do what he had to do—challenge the race issue head on. He succeeded with a perfect speech that stunned all competitors and the nation. At first, he did not abandon the Reverend Jeremiah Wright, a very wise and loving move. He was finally forced to denounce the man after Reverend Wright messed up the second time. Reverend Wright had behaved as if Obama was not serious about his speech on race and about denouncing the racially, divisive, and incendiary comment the Reverend had made. Obama bounced back from the very-serious problem; he has so far turned it to his advantage. At least Reverend Wright's issue helped people see that Barack is really a Christian, not a Muslim. The campaign capitalized on it directly and indirectly.

The small-town gaffe also forced Barack Obama and his campaign to get down and actually let the people know that Obama was and still is at their level. The gaffe and the commotion forced Barack to learn the language of the average American folk and to talk about the family and kitchen-table issues that people are worried about. In fact, I believe that the small-town gaffe helped and is still helping Barack Obama in his campaign for the presidency of the United States.

What about the Muslim accusation? Barack Obama is now using the opportunity to showcase his Christian belief openly and without hindrance or criticism. Usually politicians do not raise religious affiliation or make too much ado about religion during campaigns. Nonetheless, some conservatives' sinister and back-door attacks on Obama and the Muslim issue have given the candidate a huge hand in displaying his Christian faith all over the United States, stealing away some conservative Christians from GOP. Those were good controlling moves.

Barack Obama's recent move to compete in almost all states, taking advantage of the 50-state marathon Democratic primary, is another wise controlling and intuitional strategy and skill. While deploying staff in all the 50 states, he is paying special attention to about 14 or 18 states that formerly went for GOP. The intense Democratic primary has created constituencies in these states that Barack Obama wants to take advantage of toward widening the battlegrounds for the Democrats. Again, this is the first time such strategy has been attempted. Besides, he is coordinating thousands of meetings in all the states to bring together his supporters and those of defeated Democratic candidates, preparing for a heavy-duty campaign for the November general election.

Have you ever wondered how Barack Obama dealt with the loss in Texas and Ohio, a failed chance to put away the nomination? Look at Newsweek's report to help you understand Obama's controlling strategy, which is supposed to rightly merge with the directing function as discussed above:

> Obama "doesn't micromanage," Axelrod tells NEWSWEEK. But, he adds, "there's never a doubt who the alpha dog is." The day after his big defeat in Ohio and his popular-vote loss in Texas, Obama traveled to the large corporate offices in Chicago that serve as his campaign headquarters. The mood was grim; they had, after all, blown their third chance to end the primary season early—after the shock of New Hampshire and the muddled results of Super Tuesday. Obama toured the office, visiting every desk to thank his mostly young staffers for their efforts and urging them to keep their chins up. Then he walked into a conference room for a far tougher two-hour conversation with his senior staff. "We rise or fall together," he started out. "I'm not pointing fingers at any single person because we all share responsibility." He talked through his own mistakes as a candidate and went around the table asking people for their input in the postmortem. Speaking calmly but intensely, he then took control to explain how he saw it. He worked his way through a detailed, handwritten list of what went right and wrong—including how they misspent time and money, how they relied too much on impersonal rallies and how the schedule was flawed.
>
> At the end of the meeting, Obama stood up and began to walk out of the room, before wheeling around to say one more thing to his somber staff: "I'm not yelling at you and I'm not screaming. Although for $20 million for two primaries and the results we got, I could," he said, laughing. "But I'm not." Obama's almost preternatural equanimity has helped keep his campaign on an even keel. Although he can seem slightly humorless on TV, as he is fencing with an inquiring anchorperson or debating an opponent, he has a light touch in the office, and he can laugh off adversity. Obama has shown signs of exhaustion, and he has appeared increasingly gaunt. Mocked for not finishing his waffles, he has made a joke about his newfound willingness to drink beer in blue-collar bars and sop up the gravy at working-class diners. After he lost the Pennsylvania primary to a beer-swilling, whisky-downing Hillary, Obama mordantly announced to his staff, "OK, now I'll eat anything."
>
> Some candidates are feared and respected by their staffs, but they are very rarely liked after a few grueling months on the campaign trail. Obama seems to have retained the affection of his. As the crucial North Carolina and Indiana primaries approached, Axelrod pulled a series of all-nighters to try to close the deal. After the campaign plane landed at one brief stop in Charlotte, N.C., Obama asked how Axelrod was doing. "I'm really tired," Axelrod said.

> Obama put his hand on his shoulder and said, "Why don't you stay here and have a nap?" Axelrod reluctantly agreed: "You know, I think I will." To those around, it spoke to the unconventional and close partnership between the candidate and his *consigliore.*
>
> On the night before Indiana and North Carolina, Axelrod appeared unusually grim and gloomy. The final night of internal polling showed Obama 12 points down in Indiana against Clinton—a disastrous collapse after two or three days of closing the gap. The campaign's pollsters cautioned that the last night's sample seemed weird and they should rely instead on the three-day rolling average of 2 points. But Axelrod feared the worst, that Wright had sunk the campaign in Indiana and possibly in North Carolina, too.
>
> The next day, after visiting some polling stations, Obama arrived back at his hotel and stopped by the coffee shop, where he urged some curious bystanders to vote for him. When a NEWSWEEK reporter asked him about Axelrod's gloomy prognosis, Obama shrugged and said: "It is what it is. We've had a month, two months of bad stuff. It's been hard to change the storyline." He smiled and walked out to get ready for his now traditional Election Day game of basketball. If he was at all worried, as his senior staff was, he hid his concerns successfully from the outside world. (Wolffe and Thomas May 19, 2008 Issue).

What you just read is a controlling function in action. Undesired results have been received and everyone was naturally feeling bad. The leader must undertake necessary evaluation and adopt remedying strategy. That was what Obama did in this case and report. Some would have handled it differently, but Barack Obama handled it right. The 'bad girl' Hillary Clinton had forced the modest Obama into deciding to eat anything or drink anything if that's what it was going to take to win the next primaries against the daunting, whisky-downing Hillary. Look at the level of paternal strictness of the meeting, moderated by love, behavioral concern, and togetherness. America will be blessed when this kind of management practice matches into the White House. We will talk more about this practice and this meeting in the next section. Unity is strength. A house with people who understand each other and guided by the right leadership always wins.

The Man Is Mr. President On The *Management-Process Balance Scale*

People, a candidate like Barack Obama is rare. He is almost all-round smart, and he is what the United States of America needs at this time in American and world history. He certainly understands the principles of management necessary for any leader to be any good. The fact is that Obama is not going to be any kind of leader because, according to the *Management Process Balance Scale*, Obama is very balanced at a 95 or higher percentile. The fact is that America has had former Presidents who may not even reach a 50 percentile on this scale and they did fairly well. Understanding this principle is a critical experiential force for being a good leader. I think Obama, based on this factor, will be an excellent President of the United States of today, ceteris paribus. He is better than the competitors on this scale. Again, to see my evaluations of Obama, Hillary Clinton, and John McCain on this dimension, you may consult my audio-presentation titled, *WHITE HOUSE 101: How To Choose Whom To Vote for As President Or CEO of USA* (EmancipationUSA.Org or ChampionSociety.Com).

CHAPTER 5

QUALIFIED TO BE PRESIDENT: APPROACHES TO MANAGEMENT

One may really need something for use in meeting his objective. That something belongs to Mr. X. To get the something from Mr. X requires a good manner of approach. My father has scolded me for not using good manner of approach sometimes.

Barack Obama poses with his grand-mother during his first trip to Africa to visit the family of his father, Barack Obama Sr. (Photo coutesy Maya Soetoro-Ng)

Some people may work with others and fail. Different people may work with the same others and succeed. The difference is in approach. Some leaders can make a set of working staff good or better. Another leader may make the same staff bad or worse. The difference is not in planning, organizing, staffing, directing, and controlling. The difference is how you plan, how you organize, how you staff, and how you control. The way Barack Obama has approached the management of his campaign made a huge difference in him winning the primary against formidable opponents. This skill is already making a remarkable difference in the way Obama's opponent and others see the team Obama in the coming general election. The competing party is openly worried, considering whom McCain is running against in the general election:

> Four months have passed since John McCain effectively captured the party nomination, and the insiders are getting restless. Top GOP officials, frustrated by what they view as inconsistent messaging, sluggish fundraising and an organization that is too slow to take shape, are growing increasingly uneasy about the direction of the McCain presidential campaign. While the practice of second-guessing presidential campaign decisions is a quadrennial routine, interviews with 16 Republican strategists and state party chairmen — few of whom would agree to talk on the record — reveal a striking level of discord and mounting criticism about the McCain operation. "It's not just message or not having just one single meta-theme to compete with Obama," said a veteran Republican strategist with close ties to McCain's top advisers. "It's not just fundraising, which is mediocre. And it's not even just organization, which is [just] starting or nonexistent in many states."
>
> "McCain's campaign seems not to have a game plan. I don't see a consistent message," said Ed Rollins, a veteran of Republican presidential campaigns. "As someone who has run campaigns, this campaign is not running

> smoothly. But none of this matters if they get their act together." Indeed, some Republican officials who spoke to Politico noted that there is still time for the campaign to find its footing and that no campaign is without its detractors.
>
> But the bulk of those interviewed expressed serious concern about what has appeared to be an aimless campaign so far, one that has failed to take advantage of a four-month head start on Democrats and has showed little sign of gaining traction…"What's the political strategy when you allow your opponent, who has just had a grueling four months, time to catch their breath, regroup, fundraise and start to define himself?" asked a Republican strategist who helped lead a past presidential campaign. "It's politics 101." (Kuhn July 1, 2008, Politico).

Comments like this are all over the tabloids. The funny thing about it is that I cannot recall anytime in recent presidential elections when the Republicans have been this worried about a Democratic nominee until this time with Barack Obama and what seems like a tough year for GOP. The primary reason is that the Republicans know they are going against a Democratic candidate who has done his homework, knows how to fight back attacks, and knows how to introduce his agenda to American voters, using the right approach in relation to the voters and to his campaign staff.

Good people can be mismanaged and so are good citizens. The right approach is always needed to get the best out of people or whatever one purports to manage. Good things, good economy, good political system and good culture can be wounded or made worse by a poor manager. Over the years, we have seen good economies suddenly flopped just because of wrong leaders who brought bad atmosphere. We have seen cultures and political systems that have gone from tolerance to tearing down of oppositions and stifling democracy. Senator McCain is a good man, but he is and will be a lower-case manager in the White House relative to Senator Barack Obama. Obama is more relaxed and global in character in his approach to doing things. It means Obama will see better and farther than Senator McCain will.

McCain will be more rigid in order to avoid complications in his mind or he will be too aloof and excessively dependent on the advice of other people for the same reason. His age may not help the matter. Today's American presidency needs a person that can tackle complicated problems and still be healthy.

Summarizing Managerial Approaches and Mr. Leader

Leadership is the ability to mobilize a group of people toward achieving a goal. A leader shows the people he leads the path toward the goal that should be achieved. How the candidates manage their campaigns say very much what they can do with the country, especially with Barack Obama in this 2008 election process. The man is a huge inspiration for people; he represents a model for going from scratch to supreme! All one needs is the brain, and he or she will outman the competition that seems to be indomitable. Barack Obama is a capable leader, much better than Senator Hillary Clinton, his major competitor in the Democratic primary, and Senator John McCain, his competitor in the 2008 general election. In the management literature, the approaches to management are listed as classical, behavioral, contingency, systems, and management science. We will focus mainly on the first four. The last one, Management science approach, simply recommends that managers consider the use of numbers and figures in managerial decision processes.

The first of any way of doing something has mostly been referred to as classical. Classical approach to management proposes that the leader should be strict with his subordinates, provide clear line of authority and job description, and supervise employees closely. You can tell that the approach assumes that subordinates or employees are lazy, immature, untrustworthy, dislike work, have little or no interest in the organization, do not have the experience needed to do the jobs, or that urgency or emergency calls for such an approach. In general, this style of leadership has been labeled boss-oriented and dictatorial. However, there is nothing wrong with being dictatorial if the situation calls for it. Unfortunately, it is in the best interest of the manager or leader to create an atmosphere that will require less supervision of those who work with him so he can devote more time to exceptions.

Behavioral approach, on the other hand, calls for a leader to be opposite of what I showed for classical approach. The assumption is that employees or workers are trustworthy, industrious, and mature, have the best interest of the organization at heart, and are capable to deal with the situation. This sounds good. Nevertheless, the criticism has been that some leaders are just classically oriented regardless of the situation, and some are behaviorally oriented regardless of the situation. There is a time that calls for a leader to be strict and be closely watchful of the people who work with him. There is also a time to be behavioral in nature. That is why the best style has been generally regarded as the *Contingency* approach in the managerial literature.

Contingency principle requires a leader to know when to apply classical skills and when to apply behavioral depending on the organizational values, beliefs, attitudes, intentions, behavior of the employees and other impacting forces. If the conditions that support a classical approach are in existence, then the leader will elicit a better performance employing classical techniques. If the conditions favor behavioral approach, a leader needs to switch to behavioral techniques for better performance.

What is the catch here? The reason good companies hire good CEOs or top manager is so there will not be damaging surprises to the companies. A chief executive manager is supposed to analyze conditions, and then make choices (decisions) that will equalize (make the best use of) such conditions. No Surprises and dramas! In fact, the Obama campaign has been known for just that name, *No Drama*! That is the theme the candidate and leader Obama put forward at the outset of the campaign. That was his goal when he started putting together his campaign staff. It is therefore the responsibility of the leader to bring together qualified people who will fit the use of a style of leadership that will give the leader ample time to do something else.

The next management approach is labeled systems. A system may be defined as a set of interdependent parts, functioning together, to achieve a common goal. System's approach, as I have formulated it to be, simply tells the leader or manager never to accept any decision as the right decision until that decision weighs favorably on other parts of the system. In other words, a leader does not want to choose a decision that will take away instead of adding to the progress of the total system and its various parts. Such decision-making process or managerial approach is a reco-gnition that every part is important to the survival and growth of the system or organization.

This is where most politicians, leaders, husbands, wives, thieves, adulterers, fornicators, rapists, drug dealers, and the rest blow it. When we understand that we belong to a system called our nation, our state, our neighborhood, or our family, it will be very hard for any of us to willfully engage into anything that will harm somebody else regardless of how far away such a person tends to be from us, physically, biologically, and racially. As a system, we are interdependent. We are depending on one another. One falls, all fall! One makes it, all make it!

Obama's approach to management is soundly behavioral in nature within a contingency format, with a good understanding of system's principle. He can afford to use behavioral approach with a tiny element of classical flavor because he put together a staff that loves what they do, knows what they are doing, and demands little supervision. Such atmosphere gives the candidate ample time to concentrate on campaigning and doing other things that the staff cannot handle. That is why the Obama team is very effective. Now read the quote below once again:

> How do you know if Barrack Obama is unhappy with what you're saying— or not saying? At meetings of his closest advisers, he likes to lean back, put his feet on the table and close his eyes. If he doesn't like how the conversation is going, he will lean forward, put his feet on the floor and "adjust his socks, kind of start tugging at them," says Michael Strautmanis, a counselor to the campaign. Obama wants people to talk, but he doesn't want to intimidate them. "If you haven't said anything, he'll call on you," says Strautmanis. "He's never said it, but he usually thinks if somebody is very quiet it's because they disagree with what everybody is saying … so Barack will call on you and say, 'You've been awfully quiet'."
>
> There are no screamers on Team Obama; one senior Obama aide says he's heard him yell only twice in four years. Obama was explicit from the beginning: there was to be "no drama," he told his aides. "I don't want elbowing or finger-pointing. We're going to rise or fall together." Obama wanted steady, calm, focused leadership; he wanted to keep out the grandstanders and make sure the quiet dissenters spoke up--good formula for running a campaign—or a presidency…

Obama "doesn't micromanage," Axelrod tells News Week. But, he adds, "there's never a doubt who the alpha dog is." The day after his big defeat in Ohio and his popular-vote loss in Texas, Obama traveled to the large corporate offices in Chicago that serve as his campaign headquarters. The mood was grim; they had, after all, blown their third chance to end the primary season early—after the shock of New Hampshire and the muddled results of Super Tuesday. Obama toured the office, visiting every desk to thank his mostly young staffers for their efforts and urging them to keep their chins up. Then he walked into a conference room for a far tougher two-hour conversation with his senior staff. "We rise or fall together," he started out. "I'm not pointing fingers at any single person because we all share responsibility." He talked through his own mistakes as a candidate and went around the table asking people for their input in the postmortem. Speaking calmly but intensely, he then took control to explain how he saw it. He worked his way through a detailed, handwritten list of what went right and wrong—including how they misspent time and money, how they relied too much on impersonal rallies and how the schedule was flawed.

At the end of the meeting, Obama stood up and began to walk out of the room, before wheeling around to say one more thing to his somber staff: "I'm not yelling at you and I'm not screaming. Although for $20 million for two primaries and the results we got, I could," he said, laughing. "But I'm not." Obama's almost preternatural equanimity has helped keep his campaign on an even keel. Although he can seem slightly humorless on TV, as he is fencing with an inquiring anchorperson or debating an opponent, he has a light touch in the office, and he can laugh off adversity. Obama has shown signs of exhaustion, and he has appeared increasingly gaunt. Mocked for not finishing his waffles, he has made a joke about his newfound willingness to drink beer in blue-collar bars and sop up the gravy at working-class diners. After he lost the Pennsylvania primary to a beer-swilling, whisky-downing Hillary, Obama mordantly announced to his staff, "OK, now I'll eat anything."

Some candidates are feared and respected by their staffs, but they are very rarely liked after a few grueling months on the campaign trail. Obama seems to have retained the affection of his. As the crucial North Carolina and Indiana primaries approached, Axelrod pulled a series of all-nighters to try to close the deal. After the campaign plane landed at one brief stop in Charlotte, N.C., Obama asked how Axelrod was doing. "I'm really tired," Axelrod said. Obama put his hand on his shoulder and said, "Why don't you stay here and have a nap?" Axelrod reluctantly agreed: "You know, I think I will." To those around, it spoke to the unconventional and close partnership between the candidate and his *consigliore.*

On the night before Indiana and North Carolina, Axelrod appeared unusually grim and gloomy. The final night of internal polling showed Obama 12 points down in Indiana against Clinton—a disastrous collapse after two or three days of closing the gap. The campaign's pollsters cautioned that the last night's sample seemed weird and they should rely instead on the three-day rolling average of 2 points. But Axelrod feared the worst, that Wright had sunk the campaign in Indiana and possibly in North Carolina, too.

The next day, after visiting some polling stations, Obama arrived back at his hotel and stopped by the coffee shop, where he urged some curious bystanders to vote for him. When a NEWSWEEK reporter asked him about Axelrod's gloomy prognosis, Obama shrugged and said: "It is what it is. We've had a month, two months of bad stuff. It's been hard to change the storyline." He smiled and walked out to get ready for his now traditional Election Day game of basketball. If he was at all worried, as his senior staff was, he hid his concerns successfully from the outside world. (Wolffe and Thomas, Newsweek May 19, 2008).

Barack Obama On ATM Balance Scale

How can we rate Barack Obama on ATM (Approaches To Management) balance scale? From the Newsweek excerpt above and from other things we have learned so far about the man, Barack Obama, we can state the following characteristics about his leadership style:

1. He does not micro-manage yet everyone knows who the top dog is.
2. He is preternaturally unemotional and possesses high equanimity. It means that Obama has self-control beyond what comes natural to people, given circumstances. He is a very calm person, causing the people around him also to be calm in dealing with situations.
3. He loves open discussion and demands everyone's participation in solving problems.
4. He loves his staff and cares for them
5. He plants and encourages teamwork. No elbowing or finger pointing. Everyone shares the responsibility. Everyone is accountable. 'We win together or we lose together' attitude.
6. Team-oriented, Achievement-oriented, highly motivated leader.

Based on the above characteristics, the following conclusion can easily be drawn. Barack Obama is not using behavioral style just for its sake. He knows and fully believes that his staff is capable of intrinsically working toward achieving any goal they collectively set for the campaign. A leader cannot feel comfortable in employing the above characteristics if the members of his organization are less-than-committed and intrinsically motivated to work for the success of the campaign. A leader will find it difficult to consider the emotions or view points of someone who has proven to be at odds with the goals of the system.

What has clearly taken place here is that Barack Obama took the time to populate his organization with people who love the job, care for him, and do not require too much push in order to get them moving. Obama employs behavioral tactics because he trusts the people that work for him and with him. He is a contingency-approach type of leader who clearly understands the critical importance of strategic staffing in the management function of directing. He knows that everyone is important to the campaign's success and no one must be ignored. I will give the man 98 percent on ATM scale. I strongly believe that this skill will carry over to the White House when he wins the November 2008 election. Notice that I said 'when' not 'if' he wins because I believe that he will win given his strategic leadership ability and the team behind him, other things being equal.

CHAPTER 6

QUALIFIED TO BE PRESIDENT: THE PRODUCTION PROCESS

The outcome of any process, whether good or bad, right or evil, is really the product of that process. Good process causes good to happen or grow, and bad process causes bad to happen or grow. The producer is the one who is instrumental to that outcome. Deal with the producer to deal with the process and to influence the outcome.

Barack's mother, Ann. Barack's grandparents, Stanley and Madelyn. Barack's father, Barack Obama Sr. Photos courtesy of Barackobama.com, Maya Soetoro-Ng (Obama's sister)

Understanding Production-Process System

A good way of evaluating or understanding a presidential candi-date is whether he understands the production process. We can learn such understanding from the answers they give to appropriate questions that voters and the media asked them. It is therefore critical that campaigns dwell on debates about the issues not about anything else that has little or noting to do with the candidate's contribution to the nation. Based on what we know about Barack Obama and Senator John McCain, I will try to show in this section that the production-process principle will recommend Obama as the next President of the United States.

Take a look at Figure 1, *The Simple Production Process Model.* Successful businesses understand that in order to compete effectively, they must understand both their internal and external environments to see how both can influence the goods or services they plan to produce and sell in a competitive industry or world system. Such aware companies, under any given circumstances, engage the best resources, turn these resources into work-in

FIGURE 1: SIMPLE PRODUCTION PROCESS MODEL

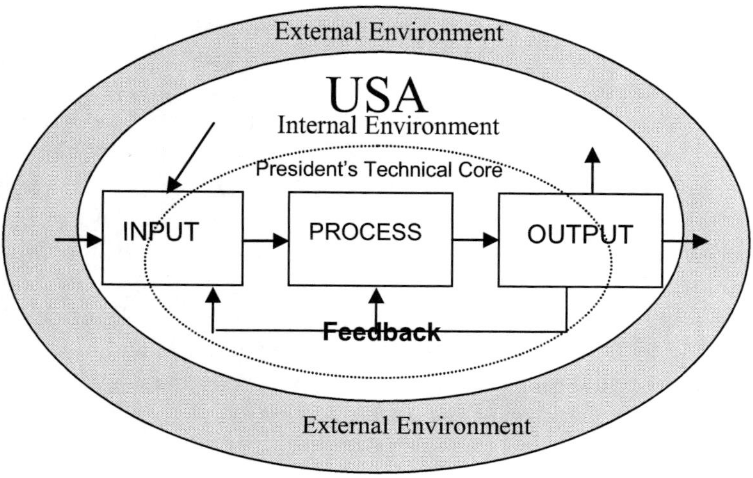

Presidential candidates need to understand that the nation they are aspiring to lead is a system within a bigger system called the world, with bunch of other nations, characterized by different values, beliefs, attitudes, intentions, and behaviors. These candidates need to know that they are actually vying to be CEO of a huge company called the USA or whatever nation. Their products are the qualities of the citizens and sustainable life-facilities that they leave behind after their administrations expire. The resources (people and things) or inputs they use to build their citizens come from both within the nation (internal environment) and the rest of the world (external environment). The process system is supposed to use the best of the crops of the society to produce high quality citizens who become outputs into the internal and external environments. Can you now see what will and must happen when you have some stupid fellow to lead a nation? Can you also see what will happen when you have some good fellow to lead a nation? Can you see why it is critical to go to the voting booths and cast that vote?

The best scenario for making a good product out of a nation's citizen is when everyone realizes that he or she has a very significant part in it regardless of how big or small one is. It therefore takes a n inspirational and sometimes a transformational leadership to usher in this kind of atmaosphere. America seems to have this gift in Barack obama.

process using the best technological system, and finally delivering the finished products to the external environment. The better their products the more the company is needed or recognized by its employees and the rest of the nation and the world. The poorer the product the less recognized the company and the closer the company draws to its demise.

This is a more serious thing when it comes to nation building and destruction. A look around the world will show you good leaders and terrible leaders. Good leaders will produce their kinds. Unfortunately, I do not have a really good one that I can cite as example for now. In general, a good one will love his nation and all his fellow citizens with a good understanding that he is in that post to live or to die toward making the lives of his people better and sustainable. Selfishness is out of the window! This leader will be an example that fellow citizens will love to imitate. In other words, the leader will leave office with the cultural, educational, political, economic, and technological forces of the nation being significantly better than when he or she took office. A bad and foolish leader, like Robert Mugabe of Zimbabwe, and many other nations, not only worsens the cultural, educational, political, economic, and technological forces of the nation, he also has given birth to a mess of citizens who will sustain the mess of evils that he has created until a serious revolution takes place with a loving leadership.

For the United States of America, the candidates need to understand that they are actually campaigning to have an opportunity to rebuild American citizens for the better and not for worse! Almost all the candidates seeking for any kind of political office do not really know this. That is why they get into offices and behave any-how, producing worse citizens than the nation reflected when they took office. The production process system for USA shows that the leader must understand the relationship between the outside world (external environment) and the internal environment (the USA), and between those environments and the technical core. Here, the technical core is the President's management machine of operation in decisions associated with inputs, process, and outputs.

This presidential machine includes his creation of, influence, and/or relationship with the three branches of the USA government (executive, legislative, and the judiciary), and other government agencies associated with family, education, work, values, and other aspects of American life. Through the presidential machine, the president can hire great minds, work with great minds, and influence the technical core into creating or making great citizens. This creation process, like using clear water and cleansing agent, involves: (1) sifting and re-sifting through the population (the USA) in the continuous process of getting rid of debris or dirt (ignorance, bad values, beliefs, attitudes, intentions, behaviors) out of people. (2) Imparting standing, nation-building characteristics (wisdom, good values, beliefs, attitudes, intentions, and behaviors) into the same people, producing better and better population.

A good president must lead by example. As good and aware people (products) are being produced, they (the products) will help the President and his great minds to continue the sifting and resifting of the population to make people like them and better. Yes, the population gets better and better as good people, intrinsically motivated to improve themselves, and under the direction of a great leader, work on one another. "Good begat good and evil begat evil." The big boss is critical to a nation's grass-root and every-root healing, growth, and development.

All people must be inspired and motivated for a nation to be ready to catch a golden fire that will burn through all the fabrics of the nation for better tomorrows. Something good and great can happen to and for America and through Americans if this man, Barack Obama, can listen and take the cue from God. I believe he will. I prayed for this loving nation for many years. I also had to enjoy myself in 2007 prison term, for I had enough time to dedicate myself to prayer on many things, including the leadership of USA. Do you know why the United States is in a mess today? I had gone to prison for child-abuse; I spanked my boy too hard. Do you know why America of today has become *The* United States of Anything-Goes instead of *The* United States of America? The answer can be found in the years of *half-good half-evil* leadership, years of divisive leadership, years of immoral-welfare system and traditional-family-destruction leadership, years of fornication and adultery-laden leadership, years of selfish leadership instead of love leadership, and years of "*America's God go to hell and we don't need you*" leadership.

What do you get for these years of horrible leaders? The answer is today's America of numerous family ruins, divorce and more divorce, single-parenting, crimes and more crimes, over-populated prisons, anxiety-laden children and adults, time-bomb children and adults, lazy children and adults, weaker and weaker school system and school pupils, and America that is slowly lagging in technology and education. America is driving at thousands of miles per hour toward suicide in the Bermuda Triangle. Today's America is filled with weak girls and their mothers who dress naked and spread their legs wide open to every Dick and Harry and still claim to be beautiful and to love their husbands. The nation is populated with weak boys and so-called men who cheat on their wives, mess up weak-minded females, and still claim to be real boys and men instead of impostors, misfits, and national-demonic juggernauts. America is all about anything-goes, anything-goes, and anything-goes! Something has to be done.

Who can bail this stinking cat? It must begin with the boss-man! It must begin with the top person in the land crying, "Foul!" and doing something serious about it. Wake-up America or else! If you really want to know how America can dig herself out of this rattlesnake-filled hole and how you can help, just visit audio, video, and books from *Emancipation*USA.org or championSociety.com. America needs overhaul now or she must die.

Barack On *PP-Balance Scale*

How does Obama weigh on the Production-Process Balance Scale? Not so good, it may be a rating of about 70 percent for now. However, why must I recommend him for President of the United States with this kind of performance on this scale? It is simply because, and relatively speaking, he has genuine love for all people (both rich and poor) and is suited to help stabilize America for such a time as this in the American history, domestically, internationally, and economically. America's head is about to go under water. Barack Obama seems to be the one that God can use at this time to lift America about half-way out of drowning. God will then wait

(1) To see if he (Barack Obama) and America can open their eyes and see the light, and then move toward the light.

(2) To see if America can unstuffy their noses and smell the good coffee, and then move to possess it.

(3) To see if America can wake out of deep sleep of immorality and seize the moment toward new USA, the America of truly "*In God We Trust*," the America of strong family system and child-rearing.

In fact, the man, Barack Obama, seems to be called at this time mainly to bring life, dignity, and a feeling of love to those that have been left out for many years by the American ship of under the banner of trickle-down theory and the injustices of race and poverty. The working class is about to have real say in the American dream, not just the rich. The poor and the downtrodden, who have felt truly forgotten and without say over the years, are getting hope and faith to live and to believe that God truly is.

The people who have been maimed psychologically, physically, morally, and economically because of the schemes of slavery and tortures of racism are about *TO BE REALLY FREED* to forgive, to love, and to thrive again, knowing that God is, and that all things are possible to those who believe and who will work hard in the USA. The majority race, which has felt guilty because of the slavery days and has prayed for God's forgiveness through its loving members, is about to be relieved, to be blessed, and to experience great love from all people and from her God.

Fellows, Barack's election into the office of Presidency of the United States is all it will take for God to do what He wants to do and then turn the office to someone else for the next phase of rebuilding America. It is not necessarily about what Barack Obama promised to do or not to do. God will take over as this man gets into office; again, something good will be massively triggered only because Barack Hussein Obama is in the White House! The man is a special 'manufacture' of God, a black man, a biracial man, with all the strange names (including *Hussein*, out of millions of other names that would have been chosen by his parents). You may add to this mystery the fact that the United States just toppled another Hussein out of office, and God's hand may be in the toppling. All these mysteries, coupled with Obama's friendly ties and upbringing, will let you know that only God can muster such a person into the presidential scene of USA. To many people, it may have been easier for Obama to think about burying himself alive than to venture into seeking the highest office of the United States of America given all these clearly seen obstacles. Fellows, that's exactly the way God works!

America is about to be blessed, and Barack Obama himself is about to be transformed into a fanatic lover of Jesus Christ. The primary reason why he is chosen is that God prepared him in "*love business*." He is in the love-business of God to help the downtrodden. What the poor man does not know is that he is in for something much, much grander than he can imagine. Once again, I want the reader to know that I have never spoken to Barack Obama or anyone who knows him. I can tell you right now that Barack Obama is not really as liberal as it is usually understood in the USA demagoguery.

He is slightly an above-average American Christian in value system who happens to be passionately drawn to the mission of rescuing those he felt are suffering or are less fortunate. His is not about politics; it is about love for the less fortunate. He is deeply concerned! He is on a journey, but God, the God of the Holy Bible, is the driver. The man is the best person the working class can ask for at this time in American history. In this period, he is also the best, available candidate for America's president and for America's restoration in the international arena.

> *By us, this change will not happen. Divided, we are bound to fail. But the life of a tall, gangly, self-made Springfield lawyer tells us that a different future is possible. He tells us that there is power in words. He tells us that there is power in conviction. That beneath all the differences of race and region, faith and station, we are one people. He tells us that there is power in hope. As Lincoln organized the forces arrayed against slavery, he was heard to say: "Of strange, discordant, and even hostile elements, we gathered from the four winds, and formed and fought to battle through." That is our purpose here today. That's why I'm in this race. Not just to hold an office, but to gather with you to transform a nation. I want to win that next battle – for justice and opportunity. I want to win that next battle – for better schools, and better jobs, and health care for all. I want us to take up the unfinished business of perfecting our union, and building a better America. And if you will join me in this improbable quest, if you feel destiny calling, and see as I see, a future of endless possibility stretching before us; if you sense, as I sense, that the time is now to shake off our slumber, and slough off our fear, and make good on the debt we owe past and future generations, then I'm ready to take up the cause, and march with you, and work with you. Together, starting today, let us finish the work that needs to be done, and usher in a new birth of freedom on this Earth. ....Barack Obama. 2/7/07*

YES WE CAN!

CHAPTER 7

QUALIFIED TO BE PRESIDENT: THE MARKETING FACTOR

The ultimate attractiveness, salability, and demand of what you have depend on the perceptions associated with what you have and the positioning of what you have.

Barack with grandparents, Stanley and Madelyn. Family Photo

At this time, the American brand is being trashed both within the USA and in the the world. I am not talking about USA products such as automobiles, wheat, beef, information, and the rest. I am talking about what America represents to all Americans and to the outside world. The world likes the American dollar but not America! In fact, some people pf the world are beginning to reject anything USA for fear of contamination of "something" they consider deadly.

When it comes to the point where what you have cannot be explained or can only be explained negatively or poorly, then something is terribly wrong with what you have and people will not like to rush to it. America is in that position right now, domestically and internationally. America is looking for a true, straight-talk leader who can truly tell America "what the heck is siphoning America out of the United States of America. The beef is going, going, and about to be gone from the Big Mac called America and people are seeing and eating just the white bread. There is a serious need to redefine America, take away what has been eating the beef, replace the beef, dress the Big Mac, and go selling and sailing again. Once the product attribute is bad, you can only fool the buyer once. He will not come again and he may even seriously demand his money back.
Let me give you a true straight-talk. American culture spells America, and most nations are scared of having the USA as neighbor at this time. The real attraction, the America's God, is far away from America because America left her God. The American culture of immoral sexuality, promiscuity, and traditional-family breakdown constitute the foundation of all other problems that America is having today. They produce messed-up children and adults who run and ruin the American society aground and underground! *Getting the family back on track*

will bring America back in-step with her God, and the rest is history. Guaranteed!

The 4Ps and Today's America

Having exposed to you that the beef in America's burger is America's God in America's family system, let me now discuss the four Ps of today's America and later try to choose a candidate that can help at this time. Marketers are smart folks. Their livelihood and continuous success depend on selling the products or goods that they have. The consumers or buyers are getting smarter and smarter, so the selling process has actually become a marketing technique. In other words, it is no longer a matter of putting together anything and forcing it down the throat of a buyer through pressure or sleek selling process. It is now a matter of having the right product attributes as defined by the eyes and cognitive processes of the buyer who then gets to choose based on whether the marketer pleased him (the buyer) or not.

Marketing can be defined as the process of getting the right **P**roduct at the right **P**rice, with the right **P**romotion, and at the right **P**lace or time. Product, price, promotion, and placement are referred to as the 4P's of marketing. In other words, if you do your job right in these four areas, you will be rich because customers will beat a path to your door, requesting and buying the products. Your product is in high demand. A marketer solves problems. If a marketer has a product that solves a chosen people's problems, then the people will choose the marketer's product instead of the competition. A good marketing model must then begin with the formulation of a product by first studying the potential customers' values, beliefs, attitudes, intentions, and behavior, understanding competitors' offerings, and then creating a product that fits those customers' characteristics better than those of competitors. Such product must sell. It's a great product.

Unfortunately, the product may not sell at all or sell as it should have if it comes at too high a price. If the customers cannot afford the product, only few of it may get to be sold and the problem that the product is supposed to solve goes significantly untouched. So, there is a great requirement to have the right product associated with the right price. Customers need to be able to afford what you are selling for you to sell it.

Unfortunately again, you may not sell the product as much as you should if people do not know about it. That's where promotion comes in. You just need to find the right way to let people know that you have what they need to solve their problem or problems. You must send your product messages to the right people through the media that reach those people. The right people represent your target market. The process of you reaching them is called product targeting. Through promotion, you will position in people's minds that your brand is the right solution for the problem or problems they are looking to solve.

Now they have seen your ads and promotion and they are excited. They now want to be able to get their hands on the product. That's where placement comes in. You must get the product where all the people who want it can get it. This means that you may certainly have the right product, at the right price, with the right promotion, and will still remain broke or worse if you do not have vendors and retailers to get the product to where your market can get to it easily. When you satisfy the requirements of the 4P's of marketing, the theoretical assumption is that you've got it made. You're the winner!

This concept of marketing gives us great insight on how to analyze and choose candidates for political or any office. Every politician should see himself or herself as a product that must help the citizens solve their problems. If a candidate is a misfit product, that candidate must be rejected. If he is better than the competition, then he must be accepted for the solution of the problem or problems. How can this phenomenon help us choose the next President of the United States of America? How does Barack Obama weigh on the Marketing Forces Balance Scale?

Barack On *MF Balance Scale*

Dear voters, you just learned a little lesson. You do not waste your vote and expect your problems to go away. If you vote for Barack Obama because he is black, he looks like a rock star, or he is tall or short, then you have a serious problem. Very serious problem! Such attributes cannot help you! If you vote against Barack Obama because he is black, not white, his names are silly, or he is not from your hometown, then you have just committed suicide and even helped to murder few folks, for problems remain unsolved. You can only vote for a candidate because he or she represents a product package that will solve your problems after you buy and use the package. Always look at each candidate as a product and then take a hard look at your many problems. Then ask yourself, "Which candidate represents the right medicine that I must buy and swallow to help cure my serious problems?"

Think about this. Assume that you have aids or a deadly cancer disease, and you have a black-colored medicine and a white-colored medicine. Are you going to reject the black-colored medicine and drink the white-colored medicine even when you know that the black tablet will cure your disease and let you live? This decision will certainly separate an ignorant person from the rest. You see, the choice must always be based on who will solve your problems the best given existing and incoming contingencies.

As you watch the campaigns, you should be able to know which candidates are trying to show you their real product attributes and which ones are trying to deceive you and distract you. Anyone that tries to distract you by employing non-attribute related ploys must be rejected. That candidate is not serious about proving himself or herself as a problem-solving product to you! On the other hand, if a candidate focuses on trying to show you what he can do about solving your problems, you had better go with that candidate.

A good candidate must first help you by defining what the problem is. In politics and the nation, sometimes the citizens and the voters may not even know what their problems are. Candidly, it will take a no-nonsense candidate to let the people know, "THIS IS YOUR PROBLEM AND THIS IS HOW IT MUST BE SOLVED!" Sometimes the exposure may not be what the people may like and sometimes it may. This is where communication and explanation come in as the inventor or candidate explains to the people (through questions and answers) what the product can really do. People are becoming very smart. People are hurting. If the real problem is pinpointed and serious solution offered, the people may reject the solution one time or two but will be forced to accept it the next round. For one reason or the other, I just love to eat rice and my kind of stew everyday when I feel hungry. However, after I noticed that it is causing a swelling or pain on my knees and elbows, it does not take NASA to fly a shuttle to the planet Mass to convince me to say, "Bye to rice and Hello to greens and beans." Do you get it?

You, the voters, must be smart to know who is telling you the truth and who is simply looking to be in the office at any cost or reason. The keys for getting your vote must always be "understanding the problems and understanding the solutions." A candidate can change his mind if he believes that somebody else's proposal is better than his. However, you must also be able to gauge and know when one is grossly Mr. or Ms Flip Flop. Excessive flip-flopping is an indication of lack of originality and managerial thoughtfulness.

On the root of problem-definition for the United States of America, I'm yet to see a national candidate that will truthfully and convincingly let the American people know that their caner of all cancers lie in their family system and child-rearing strategies. Most candidates, including Senators John McCain and Barack Obama, are heavily joking to my perception. They do not have it at all. They may know it but they are not saying it just because it is not popular to say it. This is where I will almost love to dislike Barack Obama if I do not care about Christ. He seems to know that the decaying American traditional family system and *fly-by-night* child-rearing strategy are sinking America, yet he is not yelling at the top of his voice and using his linguistic ability to let the people know. However, God has consistently convinced me that Obama will change after he listens, and that he is not afraid to listen to reason.

I am not even recommending him because of this potential change. I am rooting for him because of what I have presented earlier in addition to the other points you will read below. The problem is that the electorate has yet to have a perfect or near-perfect candidate when it comes to my definition of America's core problem. "*I don't want my baby to be punished with a child if she makes a mistake*" is one of the silliest and almost atheistic statements that I have never expected to hear from a person like Barack Obama who is supposed to be a Christian and a societal problem-solver. This continually lets me know that God in-deed is incredible in the way he functions relative to our narrow understanding and perception. That reason or statement given by Obama in his defense of abortion-right certainly sounded, "*sorry squared*" in the ears of God, yet God Himself knows why He is using Barack at such a time in the American history. The man Barack is far from being perfect and so I am. According to the Holy Bible, we must all strive toward perfection, imitating Jesus Christ.

Senator McCain, although he is against abortion, is not significantly different from Obama in the extent of their belief in strong family values. In fact, Obama seems to talk about strong family much, much better than McCain although some people may question what he (Barack Obama) is calling strong family values—Adam and Steve or Adam and Eve? I know what he means any way. Unfortunately for Barack, it is in this abortion and gay issues that I tend to see that he may be hiding his true values for Democrat votes. Even though there is a serious flaw in him with regard to abortion and traditional family issues, Obama is getting large votes right now because of the immediate need to remember and to equalize the poor and the working classes of America. The poor and the working class need empowerment through economic rebuilding. Obama's common love for all and the crucial need to bring healing to the whole USA through divine intervention in amending the divisive atmosphere of America are part of his vote getters at this time.

The so-called Christian conservatives and Ministers may seem to be lamenting that Obama is supporting abortion and gay rights, but the same Ministers, out of their gruesome selfishness, have done extremely very little to mitigate the problems of America's poor, the working class, and the racial atmosphere despite the many years God has allowed them to do so. In fact, the most racial group of people may be found among so-called God's Ministers. No wonder Sundays have been labeled the most segregated times in America. You can yell, preach, quote all kinds of scriptures, give your body to be burned, give all your money to the poor, but if you do not have love, you are actually Mr. or Ms Demon, working for the devil (1 Corinthians 13). Too many American so-called preachers actually work for the devil. You may have to get my book called *Pulpit In Hell Fire: Are God's Ministers Thieves Or Tricksters* or just check out the many audios and videos on the site, including anyone that addresses God's Ministers As Destroyers of America (*Emancipation*USA.org, *Champion* Society.com). Real Christian conservatives must operate out of love FOR ALL! God can never be fooled! Action speaks louder than words.

Discounting the family issue, Senator Obama equates well with the other aspects of the 4P's of today's America compared to Senator McCain. The troubled brand of America around the world, the trickle-down economic theory that is not working for all Americans, the crucial need for universal healthcare, and the need to include Americans more in running the affairs of the country are helping to define "Obama for America." The need to mitigate the influence of lobbyists in hijacking Washington and controlling national-government decision processes is helping to define "Obama for America." The overwhelming desire for all Americans' can-do spirits to be inspired toward action again is helping to define "Obama for America." The candidate Senator Obama has defined himself better than the candidate Senator McCain has done for himself. Although Barack Obama may not understand the word of God as some of us (the so-called Christian conservatives) do, the Senator is actually applying the little he knows into what he does. People like it and so does God Himself. Again, love is everything!

In marketing his brand to the voters, and especially under the attack about him being a Muslim, Barack got serious with parading his Christian belief. A serious accusation requires a serious response until the voters internalize the truth. Noticing that he is being too reluctant about injecting religion into the campaigning, but continues to entertain subtle bombardments on the Islamic accusation, I was forced to write him to wake up or lose the election through swift-boating lies:

June 12, 2008
RE: YOUR RESPONSE TO BEING A MUSLIM

Dear Senator Barack Obama:

If you cannot happily and joyfully defend the fact and your belief that you are a Christian while enjoying it at the same time, then you certainly deserve to lose, and I won't feel bad if you lose because of it. Sir, actually, God is giving you a chance to use your position to talk about Jesus Christ and MEAN IT! If you read the Bible at home, if you have Bible study times with your family, if you have scriptures from the Bible TO QUOTE that guides your life, if you have a value system that stems from God's commandments and the life of Christ, etc.---

THIS IS THE TIME TO SPEAK UP FOR JESUS NOT FOR YOU

Sir, God is giving you this opportunity to represent Him and Him alone. Don't mess it up! Most people do not get this kind of opportunity. It has to come from your heart and belly! If you are 'wishy-washy', it will be exposed!

Rise up to the occasion and speak for God or be burned! Your head did not get you where you are now. The hand of God has been at work since you were little, preparing you for America's rescue mission and for delivering some lessons to both Americans and the rest of the world. God's hand is in this! – your campaign! When you speak for God, you're speaking for everyone's wellbeing. You should apply Dr. King's "*Fierce Urgency of Now*" in this controversy, which is really a good controversy. In fact, God (not the devil) is stirring it up so He can use it to help you win. I have been an ardent Minister of the Gospel of Christ for many years. I know what I am talking about. Listen to my advice on this and you will be blessed.

Sincerely,
Dr. Festus S. A. Oguhebe (Strongblood), Evangelist
Body of Christ Evangelism

The Obama brand is unique and serious to solving some major problems; may be not all. Like I said before, I have never given a penny to any presidential campaign, but I certainly gave to Barack Obama's campaign because I am heavily inspired, just like millions of others. Besides, I consider myself a Jesus fanatic. I am not alone. Ben Smith of Politico reported on Stephen Mansfield, the conservative Evangelical biographer of George W. Bush and Tom DeLay, who wrote of Barack Obama:

> "Young Evangelicals are saying, 'Look, I'm pro-life but I'm looking at a guy who's first of all black-and they love that; two, who's a Christian; and three who believes faith should bear on public policy," … "They disagree with him on abortion, but they agree with him on poverty, on the war." "For Obama, faith is not simply political garb, something a focus group told him he ought to try. Instead, religion to him is transforming, lifelong, and real," Mansfield writes, going on to compare Obama favorably to Christian Democratic presidents Jimmy Carter and Bill Clinton, who he says erected a "wall of separation" between their religion and their governance. By contrast, "Obama's faith infuses his public policy, so that his faith is not just limited to the personal realms of his life, it also informs his leadership," Mansfield writes….
>
> Mansfield writes that Obama "is unapologetically Christian and unapologetically liberal." But he writes that in substance and in style, Obama holds an appeal to Evangelicals that Senator John McCain may lack….In his Fathers Day speech at a Chicago church Sunday, Obama again spoke explicitly of his personal Christianity: "We do what we can to build our house upon the sturdiest rock, and for me that means building that house on the foundation of Jesus Christ." Mansfield's book validates Obama's attempt-which began in earnest in his 2004 speech to the Democratic National Convention–to provide a compelling public face to the nascent "Religious Left." In that speech, he proclaimed that "we worship an awesome God in the blue states," and Mansfield tracks his continuing attempts to contest the Republican hold on white Evangelical voters.
>
> One notable moment came in 2006 when Obama appeared at Reverend Rick Warren's mega church beside GOP Senator Sam Brownback. "Welcome to my house," Brownback told Obama on stage. "This is my house too," Obama responded. "This is God's house." Obama, Mansfield writes, "made it clear to all that he [will] not be moved from his rightful place in the Christian fold." Obama's Christianity, however, has been under attack on two fronts this campaign season. The first is from a false, but widely held, belief that he is a Muslim. Mansfield dismisses that charge… (Politico, Monday 2008, June 16).

Now this is what is called promoting a brand to a target market (the Christian conservatives) who is still vacillating whether or not Barack is a Muslim. Some conservatives do understand. Many liberals are already happy. However, several conservatives still need convincing. Obama has no choice but to talk about the Lord Jesus. Mansfield stated that he would vote against Obama in November for a single reason and quote, "Because I'm pro-life." What Mr. Mansfield does not understand is:

1] Poverty kills more people than abortion. Obama is here to deal with poverty.

2] Inability to pay for healthcare by the hardworking poor and working class of this nation causes millions of useless deaths per year (worse than abortion). Obama is here to save those lives.

3] Millions of people of all races (the Appalachian and the rest) have really been cheated out of the American dream. The train has left most people behind. Barack Obama is being used by God to reverse the almost irreversible train to go and pick up our brothers and sisters of the United States of America, restoring lives and dignity.

4] Unnecessary wars or poor foreign policy spells millions and millions of deaths, catastrophes, and psychological damages. Obama is here to save people from such traumas.

5] Racism and lack of love among races and divisive politics claim millions of lives per year, physically and psychologically. Barack Obama is currently God's answer to these problems.

6] Special interests have stolen Washington and have silenced the electorate regardless of the people's votes over many years. This has destroyed millions of lives over those years and counting. Is it not good to have someone dare to speak against such interests and be serious on doing something about them?

7] Selective love in foreign policy that winks at murder and genocide in one area but gets serious with the other area is as good as the sin of abortion or even worse.

Dear Mr. Mansfield, I love you. However, you should know better to be voting against your conscience or just on one issue. Make sure to take a hard look at the other seven areas just outlined. You are not being a good Christian conservative after reading this explanation and still plan to vote as you stated. In fact, be a man. Tell us what you will really do in that voting booth! You are voting for Barack or you have your conscience to fight you for many years until you repent. I myself do not agree with Barack on abortion and gay marriage. In fact, let me speak like most Americans when they get angry, "Barack *pieces* me off and really makes me *mad* on his stand on those." However, Brother Mansfield, Barack has true love for all people and he stands for other things much greater than abortion. I also believe that if someone will sit down regularly and engage in serious discussions with Mr. Obama, he may change his mind on abortion and gay marriage, especially using tax-payers' money to support the horrors. Based on his stand on other areas, I have no choice but to vote for him.

Barack Obama as President of the United States will really provide major solutions to major problems facing this nation domestically and internationally. His presence in the oval office is enough to market this nation globally and trust her far up to the roof of love and liking, the place she use to be or even better. One conservative Indiana attorney, a prominent Republican, former Deputy Attorney General William D. Ruckelhaus who served under GOP President Nixon's number two in the Justice Department, endorsed Obama by saying, "Senator Obama's ability to attract not only Democrats, but also Republicans and Independents, makes him uniquely qualified to build the broad coalitions needed to address our nation's challenges." (Our Republic, April 17, 2008). The challenges represent the problems that must be solved, and this prominent attorney from an opposing party declared that Obama is the best solution among the available alternatives.

Another prominent Republican attorney, a staunch conservative, Douglas W. Kmiec, endorsed the Obama brand as the real deal for today's America. Mr. Kmiec is Caruso Family Chair and Professor of Consti-tutional Law, at Pepperdine University. He served as head of the Office of Legal Counsel (U.S. Assistant Attorney General) for Presidents Ronald Reagan and George H.W. Bush. He is the former Dean of the law school at The Catholic University of America. He was a member of the law faculty at the University of Notre Dame for nearly two decades. Mr. Kmiec risked it all and had no other choice but to endorse Barack Obama as the next President of the United States of America. He said:

> Today I endorse Barack Obama for president of the United States. I believe him to be a person of integrity, intelligence, and genuine good will. I take him at his word that he wants to move the nation beyond its religious and racial divides and that he wants to return the United States to that company of nations committed to human rights. I do not know if his earlier life experience is sufficient for the challenges of the presidency that lie ahead. I doubt we know this about any of the men or women we might select. It likely depends upon the serendipity of the events that cannot be foreseen. I do have confidence that the senator will cast his net widely in search of men and women of diverse, open-minded views and of superior intellectual qualities to assist him in the wide range of responsi-bilities that he must superintend.
>
> As a Republican, I strongly wish to preserve traditional marriage not as a suspicion or denigration of my homosexual friends but as recognition of the significance of the procreative family as a building block of society. As a Republican and as a Catholic, I believe life begins at conception, and it is important for every life to be given sustenance and encouragement. As a Republican, I strongly believe that the Supreme Court of the United States must be fully dedicated to the rule of law and to the employ of a consistent method of interpretation that keeps the court within its limited judicial

> role. As a Republican, I believe problems are best resolved closest to their source and that we should never arrogate to a higher level of government that which can be more effectively and efficiently resolved below. As a Republican and a constitutional lawyer, I believe religious freedom does not mean religious separation or mindless exclusion from the public square.
>
> In various ways, Sen. Barack Obama and I may disagree on aspects of these important fundamentals, but I am convinced, based upon his public pronouncements and his personal writing, that on each of these questions he is not closed to understanding opposing points of view and, as best as it is humanly possible, he will respect and accommodate them.
>
> No doubt, some of my friends will see this as a matter of party or intellectual treachery. I regret that, and I respect their disagreement. But they will readily agree that as Republicans, we are first Americans. As Americans, we must voice our concerns for the well-being of our nation without partisanship when decisions that have been made endanger the body politic. Our president has involved our nation in a military engagement without sufficient justification or a clear objective. In so doing, he has incurred both tragic loss of life and extraordinary debt jeopardizing the economy and the well-being of the average American citizen. In pursuit of these fatally flawed purposes, the office of the presidency, which it was once my privilege to defend in public office formally, has been distorted beyond its constitutional assignment. Today, I do no more than raise the defense of that important office anew, but as private citizen.
>
> Sept. 11 and the radical Islamic ideology that it represents is a continuing threat to our safety, and the next president must have the honesty to recognize that it, as author Paul Berman has written, "draws on totalitarian inspirations from 20th-century Europe and with its double roots, religious and modern, perversely intertwined. ... wields a lot more power, intellectually speaking, then naïve observers might suppose." Sen. Obama needs to address this extremist movement with the same clarity and honesty with which he has addressed the topic of race in America.
>
> Effective criticism of the incumbent for diverting us from this task is a good start, but it is incomplete without a forthright outline of a commitment to undertake, with international partners, the formation of a worldwide entity that will track, detain, prosecute, convict, punish, and thereby stem radical Islam's threat to civil order. I await Sen. Obama's more extended thinking upon this vital subject as he accepts the nomination of his party and engages Sen. McCain in the general campaign discussion to come. (Kmiec, in *The Slate*, Easter Sunday, March 23, 2008).

The Obama phenomenon is not something written in the wind, ready to be blown away. This is a reality. America has serious problems and the better solution is the Obama brand. The candidate and his campaign are doing excellent job of disseminating the information about the candidate and dispelling the efforts of competitors to block him. However, some element of racism is hurting the candidate subtly, and it is sad that some people will risk to nuclear-bomb this beautiful country just because the better presidential choice is a black person. Where is patriotism?

Barack Obama is the right product at the right price. There is little risk associated with him relative to John McCain. Obama is doing a good job to show the country that his schooling, any experience, and mostly his judgment are more than enough to handle the affairs of the presidency. He has shown the country in many ways that his judgment is superior to those of his competitors. Besides his judgment on Iraq war and other areas, just take an objective look at his insurmountable judgments in running his campaign. It is an evidence of high-powered CEO for a price that the nation can afford—low risk, no-drama, no-chaotic management. It is like night and day when compared to Senator McCain and others who have dropped out of the race. Forget about him being a Muslim smear. He is not. The benefits from Obama brand highly outweigh the swift-baoting risk or the Republican smear.

Former Vice President, Mr. Dan Quayle, rightly criticized the McCain organization by saying that McCain needs to communicate a "clear vision of what he wants to do as president. When 80 percent of the people think we are on the wrong track, you need to do that. It needs to be strategic. That's not been done yet. They may be waiting for the convention, but that needs to be done." (Scott 2008, Associates Press). Many notable republicans, including a very popular and former house speaker, Newt Gingrich, had recently complained that the McCain campaign was inconsistent in its messages and that the organization failed to take advantage of its head start since McCain seized the GOP nomination four months ago. Just as majority of the U.S. population and most pundits believe, Wolffe and Thomas stated that Obama team has "always out-strategize the opposition." (Newsweek May 19, 2008).

Fellows, Barack Obama passes the 4-P test at a 75 percentile. That's the highest he can get after considering the abortion and the gay issues. The man is the best product brand that America can get at this time for solving America's problems. It comes at virtually no price except the presidential salary and benefits. The man will make informed decisions after thorough consultation with great minds that will surround him. Guess what? Like he usually does a good job in hiring his Senate and campaign staff, hates to compromise on knowledge, and knows how to inspire and lead them, he will surround himself with the right people as the President of the United States of America and will guide them toward achieving USA goals without much drama. I have a feeling that he will use the *Honorable* Senator John McCain as a member of his cabinet, for both have a bipartisan nature. Besides, John is a good man. I like him.

CHAPTER 8

QUALIFIED TO BE PRESIDENT: STRATEGIC MANAGEMENT IMPERATIVE!

High conceptual skill defines a good CEO. Understanding how to break it down into policies, procedures and rules make a great one. Your plan and action today define your place and achievement tomorrow. You can do it if Barack can! Just get started! Will you?

Democratic presidential hopeful Barack Obama in New York City during the 1980s while a student at Columbia University. Obama received his B.A degree in political science in 1983 from Columbia. (Photo courtesy Obama campaign)

Like Senator Hillary Clinton clearly told the people at the campaign trail during the grueling Democratic primary, voters must look at voting for a candidate in the office of Presidency as hiring a Chief Executive Officer of the nation. Can you trust such a one? Can you go to bed and sleep comfortably knowing that the nation is in good hands? Here you will see that I have done some good job for you in answering such questions. Forget ALL-STATE Insurance Company and its good hands that are wide open for your dollars and your business. Try Barack Obama brand at this time in America.

I am for All–State. I do business with the company too. However, you are truly in good hands with the *All-States'* candidate and all people's next President, called *President* Barack Obama of *The* United States of America. Barack Obama has the eyes of a capable CEO. He has the nose to smell like a proactive CEO. He has the ears to hear and listen like a wise and awesome CEO. He has the mouth to communicate sensibly and institutionally like a loving and a high achieving CEO. He has the head that connects all these living machineries together while supplying them with appropriate dose of well-cooked information or reasoning that stands the test of necessary contingencies. Finally, he has the heart and the spinal cord that provide steady hands and shock absorbers necessary for the rest of the citizens to remain calm and know that all is well. That is what America needs in this period of her history. She needs a man who is not afraid to handle responsibility by doing all the mathematics involved before making a decision.

Summarizing SM Imperative

Strategic management can be defined as those set of decisions and actions required for planning and implementing plans toward achieving the long-term goals of an organization or system. It marks the ability of a leader to see far in the future and to study all necessary forces that will affect the system or a particular undertaking, and then make decisions regarding the long-term goals and the strategies to achieve such goals. In a theoretical concept, it involves:

1. Analysis of all environments surrounding the nation
2. Determining the purpose and goals of the system or nation
3. Determining the long term strategies required for achieving such purposes and goals
4. Determining implementation plans and actually implementing the strategies
5. Undertaking appropriate evaluation and controlling measures.

For one to manage a system like a nation strategically requires a good dose of conceptual skills. Conceptual skill is the intuitive ability to understand what is going on in the nation as a whole and possesses a general knowledge of necessary intervention mechanisms. It is being able to have a feel of where the nation is and where it is going without too much of sitting down and doing calculations. In fact, the body of the Chief Executive Officer will be like an automatic clock or gauge that determines such level of system development. It is having the right nose to smell the coffee before everyone else smells it, the right eyes to see what is happening and what is coming before everyone else sees it, the right ears to hear the tornado or hurricane coming before everyone else hears it. That's my best way to explain conceptual skill.

The Almighty God is the end of the line for conceptual skill and all wisdom. People that are highly disciplined, filled with love, well trained in broad analysis of situations, and faced with various pieces of decision-laden experience have great chance to gain high conceptual skill. People who dedicate their lives to living right, loving people like they love themselves, and pray a lot have great chances of divinely acquiring high conceptual skills. A national position like the Presidency of the United States demands high doses of conceptual skill.

Equally important in seeing and understanding what is going on and what is coming at a glance is having the ability to plan, organize, staff, direct, and control to prepare and deal with the threats, minimize the impact of nation's weaknesses, while taking advantage of the oppor-tunities through the optimal application the nation's strengths. You are not employing a CEO to create and be engaging in crisis management. You are employing a CEO that is proactive in nature; he should be able to see the future and plot today how to deal with that future while providing stability for the ship in troubled waters at the same time.

Think about it for a moment. Any kind of person can never be a CEO. The person must be a multiple problem-solver on a consistent basis and for a long time, ready to handle any kind of stress that comes with the job, and be ready to work nights and weekends, physically and psychologically to the fullest extent of the throttle, and still be able to provide an even keel to the ship or nation.

I cannot help but to point out that the choices we have now for the November 2008 general election for the presidency of the United States cause this model to swing more toward Obama than toward McCain. Senator Obama will perform significantly better as President than Senator McCain according to this inevitable analysis. More cost or risk is associated with John McCain than with Senator Barack Obama. If you want to know how Senator Hillary Clinton, Senator McCain, and Senator Obama squired up, go to Emancipation USA.org and grab the audio titled, *White House 101: How to Know Whom to Vote For As President and CEO of USA.*

A top leader of any nation, and certainly that of the United States, must pass *Strategic Management Imperative (SMI) index test.* The raw problem is that voters just do not know how to vote or do not know the characteristics they need to base their votes. The media and those who ought to help the voters decide have many a time forgotten their jobs by not asking the right questions but dwelling on sensationalism instead of on problem solving.

The political pundits and news media may be failing the electorate for not taking their job seriously or by not knowing the nuances that must characterize a nation's CEO and his or her helpers. The nation must lovingly provide a mechanism that will assure that the best available pool of candidates are presented to voters, otherwise the one that makes the most noise or the richest candidate, or the one with the most popular name may end up into the White House. If he or she is a mess on SMI, the nation and everyone else are in limbo, heading into hellish oblivion.

Barack On *SMI Scale*

A blogger wrote, "The thing about Obama that has impressed me the most is his superior strategic decision making ability with his ability to understand that our polarization is the biggest internal threat we face. His vote on Iraq, understanding that Chinese economic dominance and expansion constitute our challenge this century, knowing that mandatory health care would be doomed in the Senate, taking the high road on the bogus gas tax holiday, and especially the strategic way he ran his campaign show that he could be a good president for America. I know Hillary tried to make a point that the Obama's team said they would win Indiana and he fell just short. But Obama's team said that May 6th would be the date he secured the nomination and they were absolutely right."

I cited this comment because the humble blogger continues to use the word 'strategic' and seems to understand that strategic personality is critical in the life of a President or presidential candidate. The blogger also used several examples to show that Barack Obama is strategically oriented. He went from a strategic vision to action in trying to qualify Barack Obama. He pointed out that Barack is a visionary in being able to foresee the threats and the troubles the nation really faces and the major causes for some of the troubles. Citing Barack's campaign management success, the blogger believes that the presidential candidate can actually set long-term, medium-term, and short-term goals and strategically achieve them. People, one may claim to have all the experience in the world, but if that experience fails to translate into correct strategic judgments, then you need to trash the experience as null and void or worse. As Senator Jim Webb wrote in his book, *A Time To Fight*–"What It Means To Be a Leader"—

> Just before we graduated, a tough but insightful lieutenant colonel who had fought in World War II, Korea and Vietnam gave us a speech, a warning that echoes in my memory almost every day. He recounted a story of a fight in Korea that went incredibly bad—where, for all his experience, he made an error in judgment.
>
> "I had the enemy pinned down on a ridge," he said. "I set up a base of fire and sent 13 Marines into the tree line in order to envelop the enemy. Thirteen Marines went into the tree line, and all 13 were killed. And, gentlemen, there is not a day that goes by when I don't think of that."...
>
> *What, then, must we do?* In one form or another, this question is asked daily in every community and in almost every household around the world. In authoritarian societies, it's whispered; in others, it is debated. In America, we quite frankly find ourselves doing a little of both. Our challenges lie in improving the way we've been selecting our leaders. To the American voters, I offer this advice: Be as shrewd and ruthless in your demands on our leaders as the wizards running campaigns are in their strategies to get your vote. Do your part to send to Washington people who truly want to solve the problems of this country from the bottom up.
>
> You won't regret it. You will benefit from it. And the stakes could not be higher. Sometimes the business of politics seems silly. It can also be infuriating. But you must stay in the game, because you and your grandchildren will be the inheritors of both our successes and flaws. (Webb, May 18, 2008; Parade.Com)

I certainly agree with this blogger's assessment of Barack Obama. I see what Senator Webb of Virginia is teaching. Fellows, this is Barack Obama. Some opponents accuse Obama of not having the experience, but Obama has outwitted them and proven to them over and over again that he is Mr. President. Judgment is the key. In addition, right judgment never comes unless you possess the right eyes, the right nose, the right ears, the right brain, the right heart, and the right spinal cord. One may come to a right inference, but he will come short of openly drawing such inference because he does not have enough strength in his engine (the heart) and his spinal cord/brain (the transmission) to make the conclusion. Forget this man's color and other prejudice or half-analysis you may have. Barack Obama is the best choice for the next President of today's United States.

1. The man has the necessary love for all people. This love provides the basis for divine help in diagnosing America's situation and coming up with great prognosis for USA to the betterment of all.

2. He possesses the visionary ability of a true CEO and comes up with innovative ways for healing a sick nation, including freeing Washington from the influence of lobbyists, working class empowerment, universal healthcare, and his all–inclusive and exciting grassroots approach to problem solving.

3. He has the muscle, knowledge, and of a perfect age to challenge and withstand (while enjoying it at the same time) the rigors of today's American presidency. He not only has great conceptual skill, he has the mouth, the brain, the heart, and the spinal cord muscles to deal with the nuances of mobilizing and supervising great minds that will work with him. Together, he and his staff will involve in: (a) Analyzing all environments surrounding the nation. (b) Deter-mining appropriate purpose and goals for various national branches or subsystems of government. (c) Determining the long term, medium-term, and short-range strategies required for achieving such purposes and goals, (d) Determining implementation plans and actually implementing the strategies, and (e) Undertaking appropriate evaluation and controlling measures.

4. He possesses within him the critical diversity, training, and knowledge to make appropriate corrections to USA foreign policy, to lift America to higher heights in international relations, and to actually reason with the Muslim world and getting them to be people of peace and love for a change, both among themselves and between them and the rest of the world. Israel will see that Barack Obama is one of the best friends they have been wishing to have. The Muslim world will also see him as a good friend. The nations of the world will also see him as a friend. Just think about it. When your heart is right, peace usually follows.

   Does this mean that Barack Obama will not be tough enough to engage in a war to protect America's interest? No. It means that the man may be the toughest or one of the toughest Presidents America has been graced with. He must not engage in any war unless it is necessary and that all options are fully exhausted. He will actually have the backing of most people, domestically and internationally, if he ever decides to fight any nation. Will Iran have any chance of getting a nuclear weapon under Mr. President Obama? It will not happen! The man is quietly serious and dangerous to bad or troublesome people. Love and humility constitute the greatest strength you can ever ask for. Muscle, ugly face, and rash talk are not. God always stands behind love and humility. In addition, when God is with you, who will be against you?

5. Finally, the man has the guts to depend on his God instead of on America's military weapons for anything. Some people do not know this. He can only embark on those weapons only if it is absolutely necessary that even God himself may mandate it. The military weapons will be used wisely.

Why do you ever think that many serious conservatives are backing Obama's bid for President? Why do you think that serious people and heavy-duty businesspersons like Warren Buffet of all people (the richest man in the world) and Rupert Murdoch of all people (owner of Fox News to say the least) are openly supporting Barack Obama? We know that these people are not stupid by a long shot! According the blogs in Newsweek online, May 23, 2008:

> Today, Fox News owner Rupert Murdoch endorsed Obama. Murdoch says that even though he is a Republican and an arch-conservative, he can't possibly vote for McCain, since McCain is "very weak on the economy.
>
> In related news, Warren Buffet, Chairman of Berkshire Hathaway and the richest man in the world, came out in support of Obama recently. Mr. Buffet said that although he admires Hillary Clinton and has supported her in the past, he feels that Senator Obama will do the most good for America, and positively charge the economy.

Wait a minute. Do you think these people are supporting Barack Obama just based on the economy? Think again. I challenge someone to approach them and ask this question. The men are global thinkers, not narrow minded; besides, they have CEO heads attached to their necks. They might let you in to a few secrets why they are supporting Obama besides the economic prognosis. They cannot lend their support openly to someone whom they have not seen as the best alternative for correcting America's current problems domestically and internationally.

Plotting To Win November 2008 General Election

What management strategy is at stake for the general election in November between Senator Barack Obama and Senator John McCain? By the capable lead of Barack Obama, his campaign has been studying McCain, studying the states, and weighing all states according to their respective responses to the Democratic primary, to the previous presidential elections. The campaign is analyzing the demography of the nation, the electorate's perception of the current GOP president, and the current events facing the nation. Obama's campaign has mapped out its goal and strategy for winning 2008 presidential election. They understand what happened to previous democratic candidates and how they narrowly lost several states to the GOP just because they had gotten accustomed to ceding the so-called red states to the Republican Party. Obama is making sure that he fights tooth and nail in all states, especially in those states where the 2000 and 2004 Democratic nominees lost by narrow margins. What is the campaign letting people know right now?

1. The Obama campaign has already studied and mastered what factors contribute to winning 270 electoral votes that anoint a candidate the next president of the United States of America. They know how many votes come from each state. Then, and for the first time, the campaign unearthed for people like me that there are at least two states that actually award electoral votes some other way besides winner takes all. The campaign is determined to grab any electoral vote where it can get it. In addition, the campaign devices different ways to reach the goal of 270, not just one way. The one-way strategy had denied past Democratic campaigns the presi-dency. In fact, Obama campaign is teaching both the Democrats and the Republicans new things on how to set goals, formulate strategies, and implement strategies.

2. Although Obama narrowly leads McCain in national preference polls, nothing is taken for granted. There is no guarantee of any win yet. The broad strategy is to fight Senator McCain and the GOP in a wide playing field, including many states that went Republican four years ago. The Republicans have never expe-rienced this kind of fight before. GOP is really scared.

3. To reach the strategic goal of 270 electoral votes, the plan is to make sure the campaign wins all the 19 states won by Senator John Kerry, and then wrest away one or more states from the GOP. John Kerry, the last defeated Democratic presidential candidate in 2004, received 252 electoral votes to the current President, George W. Bush's 286 electoral votes from 31 states.

4. Currently, the campaign strategically mapped out the 50 states according to the following categories of action: *strong Obama* (11 states with 165 electoral votes and the District of Columbia with 3 three electoral votes—states are California, Connecticut, Delaware, Hawaii, Illinois, Maryland, Massachusetts, New Jersey, New York, Rhode Island and

Vermont. They strongly voted for John Kerry in 2004), *strong McCain* (10 states/87 electoral votes – Alabama, Idaho, Kansas, Nebraska, Oklahoma, South Dakota, Tennessee, Texas, Utah and Wyoming. Voted super heavily for Bush in 2004 and had voted Republican in presidential elections going back many years), *lean Obama* (4 states/32 electoral votes – Maine, Minnesota, Oregon and Washington. All voted for John Kerry in 2004), *lean McCain* (7 states/52 electoral votes – Arkansas, Kentucky, Louisiana, Mississippi, South Carolina and West Virginia, but some of these are potentially competitive now), battle-ground states or most competitive states (18 states/199 electoral votes – are Alaska, Colorado, Florida, Georgia, Indiana, Iowa, Michigan, Missouri, Montana, Nevada, New Hampshire, New Mexico, North Carolina, North Dakota, Ohio, Pennsylvania, Virginia and Wisconsin).

5. The campaign has started airing introductory advertisement in the 18 battleground states. The campaign also stated that they will work to snatch at least 1 electoral vote from Nebraska out of its 5. David Plouffe, Obama's campaign manager, believed that the campaign might win 1 electoral vote from the Omaha-centered 2nd District, which is more politically competitive than the other two Nebraska districts. Nebraska is one of two states that awards one electoral vote per congressional district and then two to the overall winner of the statewide. The campaign also looks to snatch some votes from the state of Main, the other state that does not use winner take-all rule, although she is yet to split her votes between two parties. Her second district is leaning Democratic.

6. The campaign is sponsoring and encouraging thousands of volunteers in all the 50 states to get together and strategize as directed by the campaign. These sessions include all (especially Senator Clinton's) supporters, Obama supporters, and all people (including Republicans and independents). This strategy, in addition to Obama's courting of Senator Hillary Clinton, is helping to unify the Democratic base as well as reaching out to others. Obama and Clinton campaigning together, which kicked off in Unity, New Hampshire, was a perfect strategic and symbolic decision by the Obama campaign. During the Democratic primary, Unity, New Hampshire gave Obama and Hillary 107 votes each. In another strange outcome, each also received one write-in vote in another party's (the Republican primary). The tiny city of about 1700 people became a perfect place to start a unity campaign for the Democratic Party following a bruised primary that left many feelings hurt, especially on the part of Hillary's supporters who just couldn't stomach her defeat, for she really seemed unbeatable as we stated earlier.

7. Obama campaign plans to respond to the GOP attack machine by responding fast to any attack. The campaign will make use of the already established identifiers of attacks and smears, and take it directly to Senator McCain, especially if the attack is negative since McCain had once been at the receiving end of such smear and negative campaigning. Obama campaign knows that GOP camp had no choice but to use negative attacks, including all kinds of race cards and smears about his associations. If GOP can lie to derail John Kerry through the famous swift-boat campaign, GOP can do it to Obama five times over as someone suggested.

    Republicans feel they are in a bad shape in this election and strongly feel like they have no choice but to use any kind of negative tactics to try to win. I really think negative tactics will backfire because of the kind of Democratic candidate they will be attacking this time and the elevated intelligence of the electorate. The Obama team is very smart; the electorate has suffered too much to be deceived this time. Barack Obama has been quite successful in preparing the electorate on what the GOP will do, letting them know that the negative attacks are for dividing the nation, planting fear, and taking us back. He constantly lets the people know that the GOP employs such dirty and negative tactics because they have nothing good to say about their performance or their platform. The dirty campaign had already failed to reclaim GOP seats in three republican strongholds of Louisiana, North Carolina, and Mississippi. The voters did not buy it.

What can we say about Obama's presidency following the revealed portion of his campaign's national election strategy summarized above? In fact, Obama campaign is teaching both the Democrats and the Republicans new things on how to set goals, formulate strategies, and implement strategies. The campaign knows how to mobilize public opinion. The candidate is not just charismatic; he is smart, articulate, and a quick learner. He is an educated strategist and a team player who brings the best out of people that work for him and with him. The man is a manager and a leader. He is a visionary who is not afraid to arrive at an innovative decision and moves quickly to implement the decision even when such a choice has never been made in current and previous years by anybody in similar situations. That's a perfect characteristic of a good and solid strategist. That is a characteristic of anyone that should be president of any nation, especially that of today's United States of America.

Adding some meat to what we have already discussed and in awe of the Obama's team and the 50-state strategy, Eleanor Clift reported:

> …for now he (Plouffe) epitomizes the "no-drama Obama" candidate and his campaign. … Plouffe put up a series of electoral maps and with surgical precision illustrated a variety of ways Obama could reach the 270 electoral

votes needed to win the presidency. "We're not going to wake up on November 4th with our campaign worrying about one state," he said, harking back to Florida in 2000 and Ohio in 2004. "We will have a lot of states in play … a lot of ways to get to 270." Were he any other partisan strategist, I would discount 50 percent for spin. But Plouffe is convincing, and here's why: He ran a brilliant primary campaign, and Obama will have the money and the technology to pursue every last vote he thinks might be his.

…"If Obama holds all the Kerry states, he's at 252. Add Iowa for 259. Add a win in Virginia or North Carolina, "and it's game, set, match," says Plouffe. Or add Colorado and New Mexico, Republican states where Obama now leads, to reach 270. The campaign last week put up a biographical ad in 18 states, including Alaska and Montana, historically Republican states. It looked like Obama was just trying to taunt McCain, lure him into spending money in states where he shouldn't. But Plouffe insists "there's not a head fake in the bunch." Alaska's octogenarian Sen. Ted Stephens, under investigation for corruption and the sponsor of the infamous "bridge to nowhere," is in a tight race for reelection. Montana, which Bill Clinton won in '92, has a Democratic governor and senator.

… There's Georgia, a state that hasn't gone Democratic since 1976, but the presence of former Georgia Rep. Bob Barr, who's running for a third party—Libertarian—could drain 2 to 4 percent from McCain and put the state within reach for Obama. "Indiana is another place where I would ask you to reorder your thinking," Plouffe said with clinical certainty, adding it to his list of states "behaving" more Democratic. "Our goal is to adjust the electorate more to our liking," he said, explaining how registering a record number of African-Americans and young people under 40 could swell Democratic turnout and swing Republican-leaning states to Obama.

Plouffe made several references to a "persuasion army" of Obamacons deployed everywhere and turning the campaign's 50-state strategy into reality... This year, if you're in any demographic that might possibly vote Democratic, the Obamacons will find you.

The "enthusiasm gap" between Obama and John McCain is huge; only 13 percent of Republicans are very enthusiastic about McCain, while Obama can fill stadiums with people who swoon when he blows his nose. For all the consternation about whether Obama could win over Hillary Clinton's core constituencies—women and Hispanics—Obama enjoys a healthy gender gap, leading McCain among women by anywhere from 12 to 21 points (Kerry won women by 3 points; Gore by 11, and Clinton by 16 points over Bob Dole in 1996). Public polls also show Obama winning Hispanics over McCain with a margin of between 21 and 29 points (Kerry won Hispanics by 9 points; Gore by 27). [News Week, June 27, 2008]

After reading the 50-state strategy and its explanation, one blogger, Alvin Ernest, most probably raised in Europe (because of the way he writes or spells some words) wrote:

So, I am convinced that *Americans will vote for Obama... that is the map to victory*. No one who is honest about modern America will do otherwise. He is *the only candidate that has ever presented truth and enlightenment to the people*. He has not stood up for race or money; he stands only for principle...and deep down inside, we all know this!

The realisation that the Appalachian American (mainly white) has been poor for 200 years proves that there is no grand racist conspiracy; it proves that even if you are white, black or blue, if you were not considered economically mobile, you were forgotten and left on the scrap heap. I believe that both white and black Americans are realising this, especially as people from these groups become more educated... Appalachia can no longer be appeased by the notion that they are racially superior when the reality is that they have been at the bottom of the economic ladder along with blacks for 200 years; blacks no longer believe that they are inferior. They have seen that power comes from organising and focusing their power of consumption. All Americans realise that history has been all about economics. Nobody has really cared until you showed him or her money. *A new politics is needed to ensure that everyone* is enlightened and empowered to deliver what they can for their country and for their families, no matter who they are because nothing else matters.

The *appeal of the Obama campaign is its meekness and humility*. They are humble enough to ask all Americans for support; *they are not reliant on old systems and structures that have failed America*. The Appalachian American, the Black American, and the Native American have been poor and ignored for 200 years. That is the reality of American political history. *The Obama campaign is the common ground that is bringing Americans together*. The well-educated and privileged Americans are also turning away from the status quo, because they too recognise that there is a lot that is wrong with American politics, a lot that has gone astray from the path set out by the founding fathers of America. Moreover, they understand the *increasing importance of real democrac*y to business and economic prosperity. (Posted by: alvinernest 06/28/2008)

Need I say more? That is how millions of people feel about Barack Obama. In the above citation, you can see description of Obama as having love, humility, and caring for the people, standing for truth, bringing America together, the answer for the forgotten, a new politics, etc. These have been the general terms or phrases used to characterize Barack Obama and his campaign. America cannot go bad choosing this man as her next President.

CHAPTER 9

QUALIFIED TO BE PRESIDENT: ALL-SOURCE TRICKLING ECONOMIC POLICY

In every family, if the head gets right, the rest gets right. Can this work for a nation? It depends on who the head or heads are. This is a serious principle. Being head is not easy. Being head is being an example. Are you up to it?Barack is up to it for today's USA. Charity begins at home!

Barack with wife, Michelle, and daughters—Malia and Sasha.

Courtesy--ObamaCampaign

If you poor water on the head, it naturally flows down to the rest of the body. If that head has some kind of a selfish, big bocked on it, the water collects in the bocket while the rest of the body stagnates. After this stagnation, the head also dies. If you understand this analogy, you will understand what has happened to America's economic system and her trickle-down theory.

Millions of American homes are factories for producing mindless, authority-averse, drug-heads and super-rebellious children who, in turn, become wicked and crime-laden adults, ruining America in cyclical strangleholds. One can trace the primary reason for such bad human factories to who is heading the families. In many cases, the heads of the families are the useless, immoral men, who spend most of their ceremonial headship disregarding God's commandments, scared of their wives, scared of their children, and scared of the government. In other cases, they are the so-called American strong women who are also immoral, hopping from man to man, super-materialistic, welfare-loving, super-rebellious, and contentious to God's face.

The result is *the United States of Anything-Goes*. That is where America is today. Most of the so-called heads of the homes have little or nothing meaningful to offer the children, the same children they are supposed to raise into champion adults and role models of the society. If the head is messed up, most of the time the rest of the body is messed up or highly short-circuited in life. How does this scenario apply to choosing a President and building our economy? Remember, a nation is a collection of families. Families or homes make up the state, make up the nation, and make up the world. The way a good family functions must be the way a good nation functions in order for that nation to have real success. If you have an unloving person at the top, the rest of the USA body will be stagnated.

The Trickle-Down Theory

Human beings, without a firm grip of biblical modesty and golden-rule principle, are grossly of self-interest and self-worship. To put it another way, the slogan for people of the world is "*Me First, then, if I feel like it, I may consider others or they may just go to hell.*" What can *Trickle-Down Theory* to economic building do with people like these? Little or nothing or worse can be expected and achieved. Today's hard-hit American working people and anxiety-filled lower and middle-income families and their children spell the end-results of this theory that has been practiced for years in this blessed nation, the USA.

Trickle-Down Theory proposes the strengthening of the top economic class of the society and their businesses with the hope that the riches of this top class will trickle down to other classes of the society. The expectation is that as the top class grows and gets better and better, their wealth will trickle down to the middle and lower classes or to the rest of the society. The theory assumes that as the rich gets richer, opens businesses, they will then employ other people, reducing employment and boosting standard of living for all.

This wrong theory has led to continuous tax-cuts and tax-breaks for the rich at the expense of the rest of the society. This is a half-thought, crappy theory. It chooses 'wrong heads,' self-interested heads, and trusts them with feeding and nurturing the rest of the society. The theory forgot who the average human being really is. It forgot that the average person is a mass of *Mr. or Ms. Selfishness* who looks after himself and probably his family interest. Instead of helping to distribute the nation's wealth and dreams across-the-board, the theory simply makes the rich richer, the poor poorer, and forcing most members of the society to always go from hand to mouth, waiting for the next paycheck. They do all these as they struggle to send their children to school.

How can this be happening in America that is so blessed? Wrong heads have been at the helms of America's leadership and worsening. To heal America, America must deal with and discipline the executive branch, the legislative branch, and the judiciary branch of America. The most important of all of them is the person with the biggest pulpit, Mr. or Madam President. Abolish this theory and adopt what I call the *All-Source Trickling Economic theory* to economic and social stimulation. The theory recognizes that development and growth of any system is a function of maintainance and improvement activities in every part of a system especially in a world of human selfishness and *me-alone* motivation.

All-Source Trickling Economic Policy

Part of the reason we have serious grudges or bickering among the middle class, the lower class, the very poor folks, and among the races can be traced to people's economic state and their perceptions of how they are treated in the distribution of the American blessings. Millions of working class folks rightly feel embarrassed and in psychological space after they continue to see nothing following their hard work and sacrifices. They continually ask themselves, "What's happening?" 'Am I part of the great USA?" "Where is the dream?" Nevertheless, they do not seem to know or grab hold of the answer. Reinforcement for economic survival has been grossly one-sided. There should be some tilting but it has been in the wrong direction. The tilt has been to the filthy rich, who really do not need it, except the always-wanting greedy ones who do not really understand that their greed is unpatriotic.

How can a good father with hard-working children give all his wealth to one child and hope that the child will trickle it down to the rest of the bunch? It is very possible that the good child will do it or can even give more to the rest. It has happened before. However, think about a society where the top rich people do not see the rest of the population as members of their families. The rest of the population becomes like a dog that picks up the crumbs that happen to fall from his master's table.

The answer to the cries of America's working class and all truly patriotic people is the *All-Source Trickle Economic Theory*. The theory states that economic stimulation policy should stem from charging up and jumpimg up all classes of the society, with special emphasis to the lagging corner of the economic system. One may call it *a family approach to economic management*. The all-source theory has the following assumptions or principles:

1) *The Principle of National Family*--The nation belongs to her children called citizens, and the manager of the nation and his assistants are responsible for equitably distributing national wealth among citizens according to citizens' positive efforts in building the nation while lovingly nurturing the weak to rise up to the occasion of nation-building.
2) *The Principle of System and Body Function*--recognizes that a nation is like a bodily system where all parts are interdependent and the glory of one part spells the glory of the rest, the hurting of one part spells the hurting of the rest, causing all parts to have to work to nurture and heal any hurting part.
3) *The Golden- Rule Principle*--extending selfish love to other people by treating people as you will like to be treated.

What is the implication of what we just presented for USA economic policy? We know that the working class, the great majority of the nation, has been working really hard to make ends meet. We know that the Appalachian parts of the nation and many others who have also been working hard have actually been left behind by the American train because of the trickle-down nonsense. We also know that there are lazy members of the society who do not like to work, but they love to still eat as they commit crimes and fill prison houses. We know that there are thousands of people in prisons who have been left behind and they are really locked up because of the mistakes of their so-called parents and many years of blind American government. What you will read below is an ideal *all-source trickle theory* to economic stimulation that takes advantage of the principles and situation stated above:

1] Tax breaks should be given to rich people and companies that obey the above principles by remembering that their workers are members of the family. If they are shipping jobs overseas, they need to find a way to help their workers with money and employment elsewhere. They should be happy that these workers have helped them to build fortunes.

2] International cooperation in trades must take into consideration the well being of the workers not just the solely monetary self-interest of the company owners. In fact, the company owners, the governments, and the lobbyists should know that the workers who actually worked hard over the years to build or maintain the companies are psychologically part owners of such companies. Enough is enough! These owners should gladly work for the workers' interest too.

3] The American government must really learn to help companies compete overseas who are also treating their workers as family members. If other countries like Japan and the rest are indirectly helping their companies to win bids or in any other way (less regulation, etc.), America should find a way to also help her companies to be able to compete internationally without unila-terally punishing the American companies. It is time for America to fight for America. Charity begins at home. You cannot help outsiders that much if you are getting weaker and weaker.

4] Workers' compensation may have to be subsidized through huge tax-breaks or through the companies they work for in order to help companies compete with international opponents and still maintain major work offices in the USA. Millions of people of the middle and lower classes need boost from the government in the form of large subsidies or tax breaks. They need it badly. Remember that most of that money is quickly spent by these groups back into the hands of the rich. Major stimulus should be tilted toward the hardworking poor and middle class people.

5] Lazy people must not receive one penny from the govern-ment. If they commit crimes, they must be severely punished. Today's American prison is not for correction but for destruct-tion. Most prisons are places where criminals go to live and eat free three meals per day. This is horrible and destructive. *This is not love but hate*!!! You are not showing love to those prisoners by locking them up and feeding them without hard, hard labor! Most of them got to prison because they are LAZY! A lot of them got there because they were rebellious to their parents and authorities. They must be made to work hard in the farms at least 8 hours per day, do schoolwork, attend church services, and watch no television except some Christian videos. We are still talking about *All-Source Trickle Economic Policy 101*.

6] Stupid marriages, divorce, and single parenting must be stopped cold by all necessary means. These catastrophic marriage issues are bleeding America to death, culturally, politically, education-ally, technologically, and competitively. America's child-rearing strategy is a mess, producing children and adults that cannot stand pressures but have turned into time-bomb folks. To understand what I am talking about fully, please consult *EmancipationUSA.org or ChampionSociety.com* and check out some of the audio or video presentations. You will educate yourself on why people, such as Britney Spears, have been suffering, why smart children and adults have been going on a shooting rampage, etc. Fellows, we are still talking about *All-Source Trickle Economic Policy 101*. The worst economic waste of any society comes because of useless marriages, divorce, and poor child rearing.

7] Finally, the top, rich rcih people, who simply make huge millions of dollars per year should be taxed appropriated for the help of the rest of the society. These rich people should be happy to pay the tax, for without the rest of the society buying what they have, they will be just like the rest of the society or worse. They should patriotically love to give back.

The Economics of Divorce and Single-Parenting

As reported by David Crary of the Associate Press through the *Institute for American Values*, a sponsored academic research by Georgia State University economist Ben Scafidi produced the following results about divorce and unwed childbearing:

1] Divorce and out-of-wedlock childbearing cost U.S. taxpayers more than $112 billion a year, according to a study commi-ssioned by four groups advocating more government action to bolster marriages. Sponsors say the study is the first of its kind and hope it will prompt lawmakers to invest more money in programs aimed at strengthening marriages.

2] "The study documents for the first time that divorce and unwed childbearing — besides being bad for children — are costing taxpayers a ton of money," said David Blankenhorn, president of the Institute for American Values. "We keep hearing this from state legislators, 'Explain to me why this is any of my business? Aren't these private matters?'" Blankenhorn said. "Take a look at these numbers and tell us if you still have any doubt."

3] Scafidi's calculations were based on the assumption that house-holds headed by a single female have relatively high poverty rates, leading to higher spending on welfare, health care, criminal justice and education for those raised in the disadvan-taged homes. The $112 billion estimate includes the cost of federal, state and local government programs, and lost tax revenue at all levels of government. Reducing these costs, Scafidi said, "is a legitimate concern of government, policy-makers and legislators." While the study does not offer formal recommendations, it does suggest that state and federal law-makers consider investing more money in programs intended to bolster marriages. Such a program has been in place in Oklahoma since 2001; Texas last year earmarked about $15 million in federal funds for marriage education. "Because of the very large taxpayer costs associated with high rates of divorce and unwed childbearing, and the modest price tags associated with most marriage-strengthening initiatives ... programs even with very modest success rates will be cost-effective," the study says. (Scafidi, 2008, Associates Press, April 15).

Before I comment, let me show you the criticisms to the study and its recommendation. According to David Crary of the Associate Press:

> Two experts not connected to the study said such programs are of dubious merit and suggested that other investments — notably job creation — would be more effective in aiding all types of needy families.
>
> Tim Smeeding, an economics professor at the Maxwell School of Syracuse University, who was not involved in the study, said he's seen no convincing evidence that the marriage-strengthening programs work. "I have nothing against marriage — relationship-building is great," he said. "But alone it's not going to do the job. A full-employment economy would probably be the best thing — decent, stable jobs." He also noted the distinctive problems arising in black urban areas where the rate of single-mother households is highest. "A high number of African-American men have been in prison — that limits their future earning potential and makes them bad marriage partners, regardless of what kind of person they are," Smeeding said. "A marriage program doesn't address that problem at all."
>
> Another expert not connected to the study, University of Michigan sociologist Pamela Smock, suggested that bigger investments in education would pay long-term dividends — improving economic prospects even for children from fragmented, disadvantaged families. "Providing a global number doesn't

> give us anything to go on," said Smock, who was skeptical of the study's $112 billion estimate. "We're now nearing 40 percent of kids in America born out of wedlock," she said. "I can't fathom that those marriage programs, even with increased investment, are going to reduce that." Blankenhorn said it was "fair criticism" to note that the study made multiple references to marriage-strengthening programs while not proposing other strategies for reducing the cost of family fragmentation. "Maybe we should have been more ecumenical," he said. "Let everybody have their say. Let's try things out. (Scafidi, 2008, Associates Press, April 15).

Dear reader, this is the problem. First, you need to know that I am educated with a BS in Management and Economics, MBA in Business Administration, and DBA in Management with minors in Marketing and Economics. I know exactly what these "experts" are talking about. I also know that many of these experts have been good at running away from the real solution because they themselves do not like or are not able to abide by the real solution. Anything that tries to discipline the flesh and tries to limit the freedom of the flesh to do what it pleases scares many of these so-called experts. I'm not saying that the fellows here are "so-called." I'm saying that many academicians are.

Number one, a careful observation of the direct and indirect impacts and costs of divorce and unwed parenting will not only exceed $112 billion per year but may include many costs that can't be measured. Innumerable deaths and catastrophes result from divorce and single parenting. Cost of fighting healthcare/mental problems, street crimes, home crimes, and terrorisms associated with divorce and single parenting are bankrupting the United States of America financially, educationally, technologically, politically, and competitively. Trillion dollars per year cannot touch it! America is sinking into the Bermuda Triangle and she must be ready to embark on real and true solution for her problems. Take another look at Figure 1, *a general model of societal building or destruction.* See how family issues represent the center of all troubles, the source of all remedial expenditures in a nation. It will help you understand the nature of America's broken homes and their impacts, including limitless amount of dollars.

You can create all kinds of jobs and make them available to all the people, but if the people's basic value systems are immoral and against traditional values, you will have the same problems and may even become worse. They now have some money to buy sex, produce more children out-of wedlock, or do some other evils that money can permit. Job creation will help one place food on the table but it is not solving the problem we are talking about; it just creates new problems if the person's moral base is shaky!

*Emancipation*USA depiction of today's USA: Someone sees America as this figure below. What do you think? Is this really true or false?

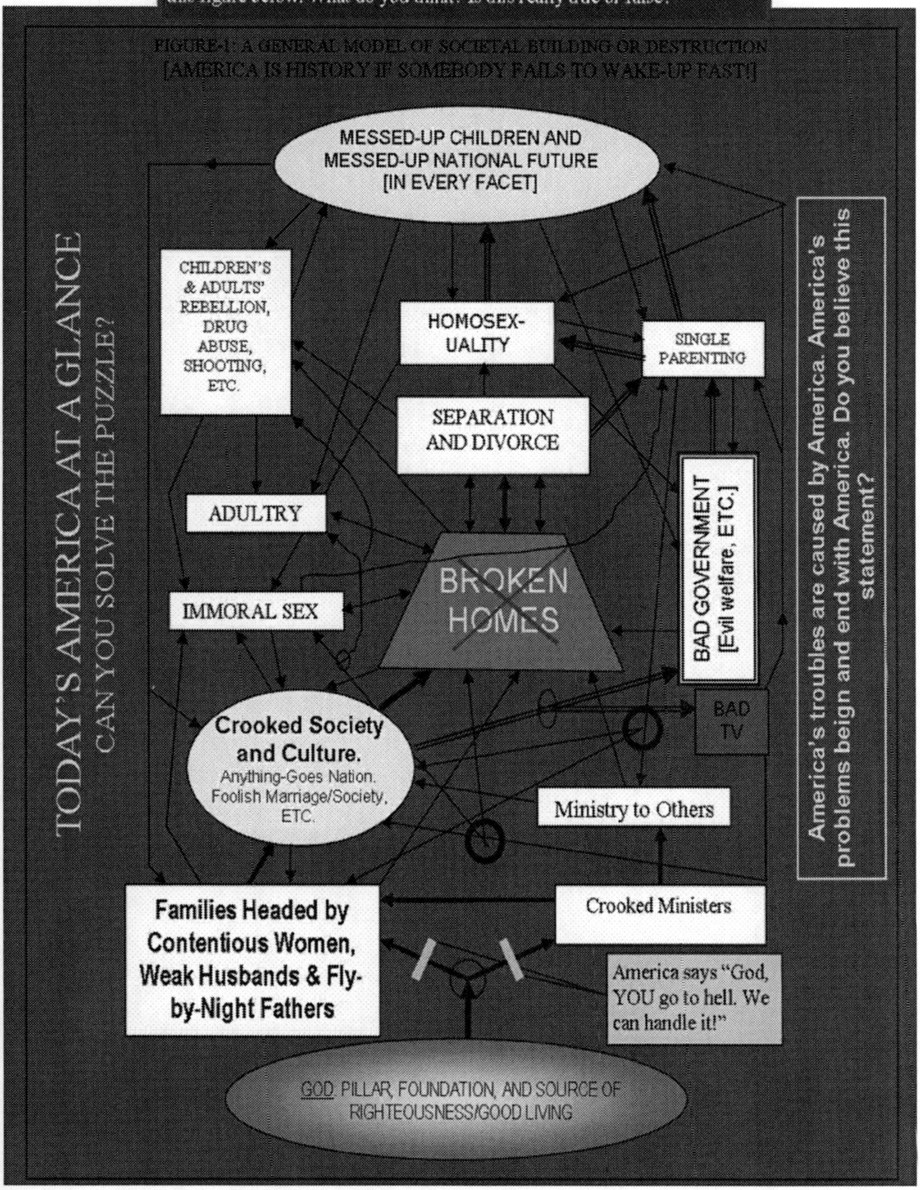

Any nation that rejects the righteousness of God, which spells strong morale values, will fail. Only time will tell. America, get back to your God!

A huge number of African-American men being in prison spell exactly a *70 percent or higher* of the product of marriage/family breakdowns. A strong family withstands tough situations, including injustice, etc. When people are man-raised instead of hen-raised, as ordained by God under the full family system of father and mother, those people are morally and emotionally strong to tackle situations. Why is it so? It is because the system and the process is being handled the way God commanded. Once you do it God's way, then God becomes a partner in it, and the rest is history. Others, the hen-raised bunch and government-fathered, are significantly much more morally decadent and much more likely to get into all kinds of troubles for themselves and for others without serious biological fathers in their lives. Their condition wastes billions of economic resources that should be used to solve problems somewhere else. Serious parents must strive to come to one conclusion—"remain together for the sake of God and for the children or die trying!" When you make up your mind like this, and commit to praying to God for help, then God shows up. As long as one of the parents has one leg in and the other out, God is far away unless the other partner is a dedicated, prayerful, and holy-living person.

Check it out thoroughly because I have taught and researched it by myself for over 17 years. Children and adults (black and all races) who are raised in families with strong fathers (with mothers who honor those men) have consistently been found to be super smarter and emotionally stronger than other children. Even in families where mother and father are just together but not as spiritually bonded as in the first example, heavy-duty, smart and emotionally strong children have been the result when compared to those of single and divorced parents.

The key is having father and mother that love the Lord according to the Holy Bible. Even when the parents are not Christians, the key becomes having a serious and well-defined family structure. Somebody must be the head. Somebody must have the final say in cases of confusion. Why do you think some companies perform better than others? They have good CEOs and great VPs who direct the affairs of planning, organizing, staffing, directing, and controlling the companies under different circumstances. There is no confusion as to who have the final say.

The CEO and trusted immediate subordinates provide stability for the ship (the company) and provides emotional and loving support for the total employees as he maneuvers the system through the company's industry. This CEO causes the company to compete and excel. The family is just like that. Guess what. That is exactly the way God of the Holy Bible, our God, provides it (see Genesis 3, 1 Corinthians 11:3, Ephesians 5). Those who truly follow God's commandments do excel. Those who rebel always experience problems and all kinds of confusions. Therefore, marriage program is fine. The question is, "what type of marriage program"—real deal or fly-by-night?

Today's America's economic problem and most of the other problems are the products of America's failing family. Solving such problems takes a holistic approach as I outlined in *Emancipation*USA chart (see Figure 2). Once the homes are messed-up, so goes the children, the adults, and the heads required to solve the problems. Why? The people themselves have become the problems. Total overhaul in value system and re-education are needed. The few people who see the light must speak up and save the rest.

Dear Mr. President Barack Obama:

You now know, and I strongly believe that you have known, that divorce and single parenting are huge menace to the American society, economically, culturally, and politically. What must you do about these catastrophes? Will you try to appease the lovers of divorce and single parenting or will you try to do right? I believe that you love the Lord and you must do something here to explain this problem to millions of loving folks who love you and vote for you. Many of them do not understand the math. Millions of them have not been raised to understand such a math. Open your mouth with love (as usual) and they will listen to you. If you humbly employ your voice and intellect to explain to them the problem and the solution, many of them might hear and take serious heed. The ultimate grass-root approach to nation building is to begin and end with the ultimate grass-root, the family. You must use the biggest pulpit in the world, the USA presidency, to yell this thing out and to expose it to the core.

Some people may not like you for yelling the right thing and offering concrete solution to the real American problems, but God will like it and your conscience will not kill you. That's what matters. In the long or short-run God will look at your sacrifice and then help the people in this mother-of-all-problems area. They will then remember you and thank God for giving you the guts to speak up and to offer the needed solution. I wish I can speak like you or have some opportunity to yell. I must yell because people are suffering and dying in droves, yet they want to window-dress their true problems and the ultimate solution. A seriously sick patient may hate the needle but he or she had better accept the injection if he or she wants to be well. Many a time, the injection may have to be mildly forced for the good of the whole society. America is in deep trouble. Act!

--------*Your friend, Festus S. A. Oguhebe (Strongblood).*
July 5, 2008.

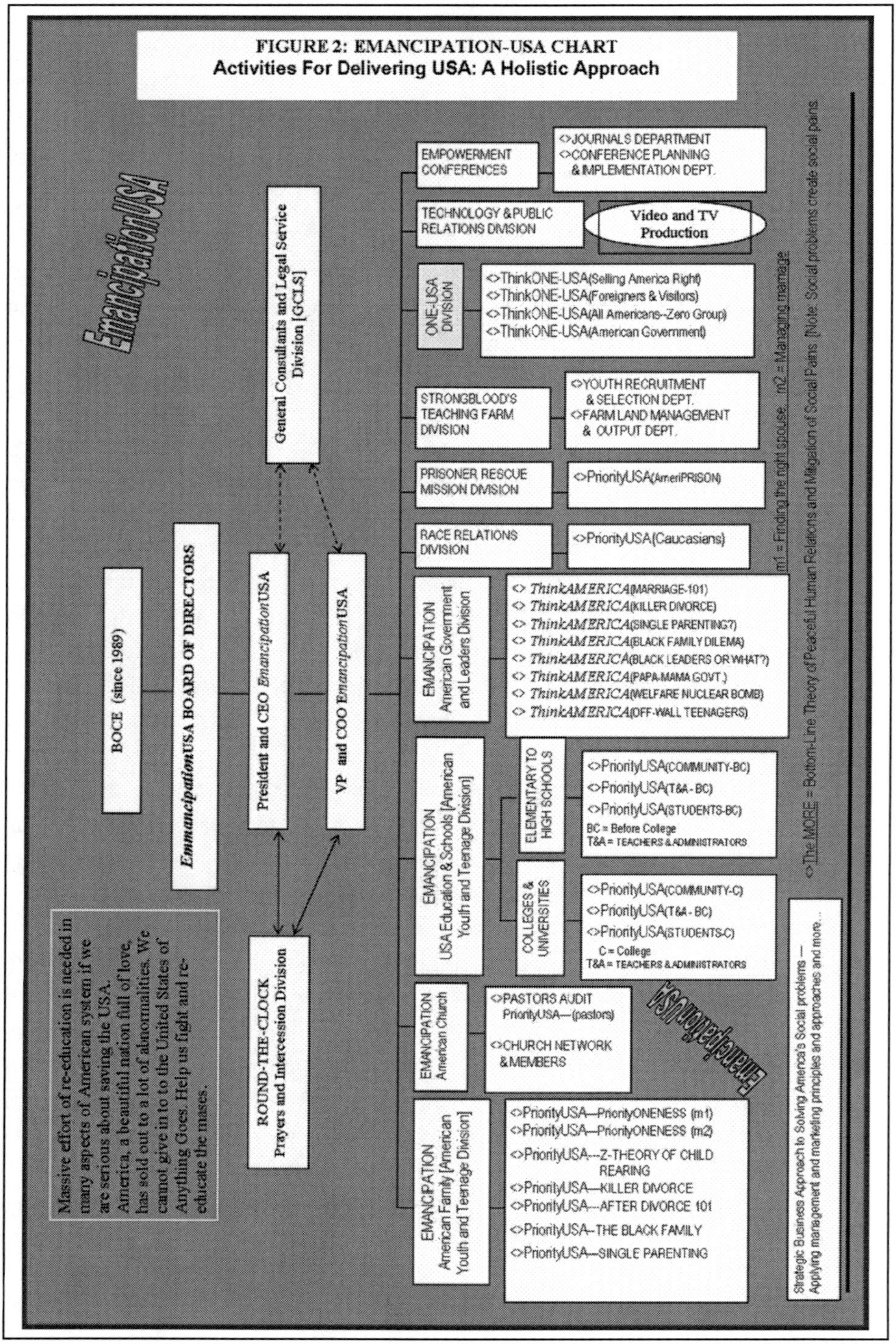

FIGURE 2: EMANCIPATION-USA CHART
Activities For Delivering USA: A Holistic Approach

The Economic Factor and Choosing President Obama

Barack Obama may be labeled liberal, but I think he is following a conviction that may be actually pleasing God by not being pushy about the things I talked about regarding traditional marriage, divorce, single-parent and the economy of the nation. I also believe that he is the kind of person that likes reasoning and can therefore change his mind if he discovers that his understanding is wrong. We have made a serious argument here; it is left to him to listen.

With regard to the other tentacles of the *All-Source Trickle Economic Theory*, his paraded platform speaks for itself. He is much closer to the principles of this theory than Senator John McCain is. Barack Obama's tax system that will relieve the working class and lower, his position on taxing companies that ship job overseas, the $4000 education support, universal healthcare, fighting lobbyists and wanting to renegotiate NAFTA are part of the theory. In trying to tackle the current housing crises, you often hear the GOP and Senator McCain state and quote, "No help for those people who had bad credits at the time when they signed their mortgages. Help can only go to those who have good credits to bail them out of foreclosures." Now the same GOP government bailed out banks that made wrong decisions with billions of dollars. This is discrimination and wrong, always making the rich richer. If you helped the bankers who made wrong decisions, why can't you help the consumers who made wrong decisions too? That has been Obama's argument.

That's why Barack Obama stated that significant number of mortgage holders needs help out of foreclosures. If the few and top businesspersons can receive billions of dollars worth of assistance from the government, the average mortgage holder should qualify for govern-ment help out of foreclosures. Can you imagine the physical and psycho-logical catastrophes that befall millions of people who lose their homes? Most of them are of the lower and middle classes? Can you imagine the psychological impact on the nation as a whole? The GOP needs serious lesson in golden rule and the system concept. I believe Barack Obama will do more and will get much better at it when he assumes office and engage with his advisers. Boosting the lower and middle classes and helping the opening and maintenance of small businesses represent the major keys of economic stimulation. Many educated people and serious businesspersons like Warren Buffet and Rupert Murdoch knew that Obama could handle the economy before they endorsed him. Voters—be smart!

CHAPTER 10

QUALIFIED TO BE PRESIDENT: HE IS MR. FOREIGN POLICY

Blood is thicker than water. A person born in a nation and is 25 years old knows the nation much better than the visitor who have been in the nation for 25 years and is 50 years old. A child who visits nations and has acquaintances in different nations has intrinsic or built-in experience than someone who visits many nations at older age. Have you ever wondered why children learn faster than adults do? You've gotten it now. God took the time to put Barack together for bringing healing to today's America.

The 50-year old person came to the nation when he was 25 years and he is 50 years now. The other person is born in the nation and he is 25 years now. Every culture or nation has its own atmosphere. Even the Holy Bible suggests that every nation seems to have a particular prince of the devil that is in-charge of that nation (Daniel 10:1-20), that is working against whatever good God wants to do for the nation. The values, beliefs, attitudes, intentions, and behaviors of people of a society form spiritual atmosphere that govern or influence that nation. That's why when one shows up at a particular culture, your body tells you that something is different and you begin to find a way to adjust.

The same scenario applies to various homes. In the United States, there are parents or heads of families who vowed that the average American culture would never govern their homes. A serious Christian may cultivate a no-nonsense life of holiness and makes sure that his family follows the Lord and the rules of the Holy Bible uncompromisingly. When you find yourself into homes like that, you will immediately notice an atmosphere different from the wind that is blowing outside. If you use to dress half-naked and looking for an adulterous or fornication partner, you automatically decide to put the attitude on hold until you get out of the house.

What about a woman who married a committed Christian man but still wants to keep running after other men? The young woman was used to fornicating all her life although the man did not know it when he married her. The woman lived with the man for a long time, but she was always miserable. She wanted to live a life of promiscuity even when she was married. She resorted to hiding and fornicating or at least wished to do so. Her husband is just a serious Christian when it comes to fooling with strange women. The man hates to do such a thing because it offends his God. The woman actually tried to get the man to chess other women so she could justify her infidelity. The man rebuked her. Not so long the wife concocted a reason and left the husband. What really happened? The atmosphere of the house, which this Christian man cultivated, continued to fight the woman's spirit of infidelity to the point where she could no longer handle it.

Can you really now see how to raise champion children? Can you now see how homes produce in the children the dominant atmosphere that exists in the homes? Can you now see why the American society continues to produce the same kind of rebellious and sex-sensitized children and adults? Can you see how Barack Obama's upbringing can produce in him *'a natural'* in foreign policy?

Foreign Policy and Mr. United Nations

Barack Obama's presence in America's oval office will auto-matically change the atmosphere of foreign policy in the globe and favorable to the USA. Let's look at Figure 1, the Making of Mr. United Nation. One major characteristic of the average foreigner in the United States is an intrinsic interest in foreign affairs. Foreigners watch news, listen to news, and read news. The average foreigner knows what is happening in other nations much better than Americans are. It is hard to explain, but one reason might be because they are foreigners and they are naturally interested in what is going on in other nations, including their home countries. America's political progress and economic environment have been long-time benchmarks upon which foreigners assess what is happening in their own nations and around the world in order to find out how to help in their countries.

Barack Obama, a son of a black man from Kenya-Africa and white mother from Kansas-USA/America, with a step father and sister from Indonesia-Asia, have spent childhood periods in America, Indonesia, and the international (unique cultural) state of Hawaii, and has a middle name of Hussein--is *Mr. United Nation*, *Mr. Reconciliation*, *Mr. Foreign Policy*. The man cannot help it but to develop and nurture intrinsic desire to learn all there is to know about other cultures. He is of a mixed culture and race. He is graced with the love and charity of the United States and the deep values of America. His attachment to the rest of the world and being deeply married to his mother's innate desire to work and help in foreign lands do multiply this locomotive desire in Barack to dream and learn about foreign cultures from childhood. When you learned something at childhood, you have learned that thing.

FIGURE 1: THE MAKING OF MR. UNITED NATION

Photos: Courtesy of Obama Campaign—Barackobama.com

I can tell you that there is no day that passed in which Barack Obama does not think about the world and how it can be helped. He has to think this way because he is a product of many world cultures—the American continent, the African continent, the Asian continent, and the Middle East sentiment. He cannot help it but to find himself meditating on foreign cultures from a very young age. He also has no choice but to listen to news, read news and books, and watch news, all with a different level of intensity and analysis when compared to people who are not familiarly attached to world cultures. The fact that his middle name is Hussein may cause him to learn and to pay more attention to the issues of Islamic religion and the Middle East. He may have meditated hard on how to approach the problems surrounding the region. He is not a Muslim, but Muslims can trust him when he talks. This is a blessing to America and the world.

From interviews, we learned that Barack Obama decided to major on International Relations at Columbia University after his high School. What influenced him to major in such a foreign policy-related discipline? His interviews gave the clue. Besides the previous forces, the Obama we know today is a function of multiple international forces. They are Barack's mother of USA, Barack's growth in the international state of Hawaii, Barack's international experiences in moving from Hawaii to Indonesia at very young age, the conscripting and sending of his stepfather to Guinea by Indonesian government, his Kenya-African biological father, and his multinational mother who worked with the United Nations. These forces made a foreign-policy man out of Barack Obama Junior. The Senator actually said the same thing on his interview by Fareed Zakaria in CNN, Zakaria's **"GPS."** (July 13, 2008). He started cultivating the nuances of foreign relations from a toddler level. Obama loves international relations and he is intrinsically and familiarly motivated to learn about other nations.

One may travel to foreign lands as many as he wants, but it is not a guarantee that the person will understand the cultural nuances of the places he has visited and how he can formulate policies associated with those places. Motivation to learn those cultures is the ultimate key to great foreign policy. Barack Obama has actually internalized the culture of Africa, Middle East, America, and many parts of the world because of his world nature. This knowledge started building in him from childhood. He is a citizen of the United States and a citizen of the world. He understands that strong foreign policy begins with first strengthening the home, the USA. Charity begins at home! Since he is a product of several world cultures, Barack will relate to people of different cultures much easier than Senator McCain. He will formulate and adopt a more loving foreign policy approach than his competitor, Senator John McCain and the GOP.

Fellows, Barack Obama's world nature and years of diagnosing people's sufferings as experienced by himself, his mother, extended families, and interactions with different classes of people caused him to have deep compassion for all. I dare to say once again that possessing a good dose of love and compassion for all people causes God to become your cheerleader. Such characteristic can be seen in Obama's listed foreign policy plan (ObamaforAmerica.Com). After reading the policy, you have a sense of balance, a sense that all men are regarded equal. You will smell an atmosphere of bringing quarreling factions together and actually forcing them to iron out their problems in love. You will also smell the wind that cannot tolerate murderers and oppressors of their citizens. You have a serious sense that Obama will act to not only protect the United States but to seriously speak out and be ready to do more for little people and little nations.

I can see African leaders struggling to get their acts together? Let me tell you one serious truth. What someone who cares does not write down is usually more than what you read. Love and compassion are very deep and hard to express. It only unfolds as life goes by. That's what is going to happen with Barack Obama. America will be cherished again, and the world will have an addition in its arsenal a loving, peaceful, but a lion-heart leader, one that cannot be fooled or taking for granted.

Now do you trust that he will do what he stated? I strongly believe that he will. Remember, he has all the intellectual, spiritual, world-culture muscles to do the job. Do not forget our conclusion on Barack Obama's SMI scale. It's worth reading again because what he has stated in his foreign policy plan is critical and requires able-bodied, wholesome man to tackle the challenges. We stated that Barack Obama is the best choice for the next President of the United States in this period of American and world history because:

1. The man has the necessary love for all that provides the basis for divine help in diagnosing America's situation and coming up with

   great prognosis for USA to the betterment of all.

2. Obama possesses the visionary ability of a true CEO and comes up with innovative ways for healing a sick nation, including freeing Washington from the influence of lobbyists, working class empowerment, legislating universal healthcare, and his all–inclusive and exciting grassroots approach to problem-solving.

3. He has the muscle, knowledge, and of a perfect age to challenge and withstand (while enjoying it at the same time) the rigors of today's American presidency. He not only has great conceptual skill, he also has the mouth, the brain, the heart, and the spinal cord muscles to deal with the nuances of mobilizing and supervising great minds that will work with him. Together, they will work brilliantly (a) to analyze all environments surrounding the nation, (b) to determine appropriate purpose and goals for various national branches or subsystems of government, (c) to determine the long term, medium-term, and short-range strategies required for achieving such purposes and goals, (d) to determine implementation plans and actually implement the strategies, and (e) to undertake appropriate evaluation and controlling measures of whatever he does.

   Obama will do this much better than McCain will. The problem is that even in an area where Senator McCain may have a better proposal than Obama, poor management of the proposal may cause it not to bear expected fruits. It will be a wise thing for Barack Obama to use Senator McCain in his cabinet and tap on some of McCain's proposals if analysis favors such a decision.

4. Obama possesses within him the needed and critical diversity, training, and knowledge to make appropriate corrections to USA foreign policy, to lift America to higher heights in international relations, and to actually reason with the Muslim world and getting them to be people of peace and love for a change. We really need some kind of peace, of at least a yearlong, among the Muslims and between them and the rest of the world. Israel will see that Barack is the best friend they have been wishing to have. The Muslim world will also see him as a good friend. The nations of the world will also see him as a friend. Just think about it. Fellows, when your heart is right, peace usually follows.

   Does this mean that Barack Obama will not be tough enough to engage in a war to protect America's interest? No. It means that Obama may be the toughest or one of the toughest Presidents America has been graced with. He must not engage in any war unless it is necessary and that all options are exhausted fully. He will actually have the backing of most people, domestically and internationally, if he ever decides to fight any nation. Will Iran have any chance of getting a nuclear weapon under Mr. President Obama? It will not happen! The man is quietly serious and dangerous to bad or troublesome people. Folks: love and humility constitute the greatest strength you can ever ask for. Muscle, ugly face, and rash talk are not. God always stands behind love and humility. Moreover, when God is with you, who will be against you?

5. Finally, the man has the guts to depend on his God instead of on America's military weapons for anything. Some people do not know this. He can only embark on those weapons only if it is absolutely necessary; even God Himself may mandate it. The military weapons will be used wisely. When the world sees that a leader is not trigger-happy, a wise troublemaker in the same world will respond to diplomacy or face the military might of the humble leader with the full support of the rest of the world. The humble leader will pounce decisively and achieve the victory. Why? God is also with him!

Iraqi Government Responds To Obama

In differentiating Barack Obama from Hillary Clinton, Betsy Reed stated "In (Obama's) rhetoric and his stance toward the world outside our borders, Obama does appear to offer a way out of the testosterone-addled GOP framework. As he said after losing Pennsylvania, 'We can be a party that thinks the only way to look tough on national security is to talk, and act, and vote like

George Bush and John McCain. We can use fear as a tactic and the threat of terrorism to scare up votes. Or we can decide that real strength is asking the tough questions before we send our troops to fight.'" (Reed 2008, *The Nation* May 3).

Reed's statement is strictly an endorsement for Obama's foreign-policy/Iraq strategy. For those of you who may not know what "testosterone" means in this case, I might help. It is that kind of hormone that says, "I am a man and I rather die fighting in this thing than take the shame of calling it quits, sometimes whether I am at fault or not." Unfortunately, this is not even a matter of testosterone; it is a matter of the right strategy given the culture of the region and the general political and economic condition of USA now and worsening. It is high time America started taking care of herself, taking care of all her citizens, and stopping these horrible wastes of resources elsewhere. Creating a military base in Iraq is useless and does not benefit *The* United States or Israel when all factors are considered.

The base can never be used to defend Israel because the country and her Muslims must never permit it to happen. Majority of the Arab Muslims have natural hatred for Israel! If America defies this cultural norm and tries to use Iraq in any manner to defend Israel, almost all the Iraqi population will pounce on the US base and wipe out the soldiers with whatever weapons they can grab. Furthermore, the members of the indigenous government that allowed the USA to maintain the base will not only be ousted; they will most likely be beheaded or terrorized to death. Guaranteed! Besides, significant number of the country's citizens will be attacking the United States on a daily basis any chance they get whether America does anything or not. Arab Muslims consider America as the chief infidel. Fellows, America needs to use all the billions of dollars she has been burying in Iraq to rebuild herself. America needs to pick up millions of Americans who have been left behind by the big ship called *The American Dream.* Barack Obama understands this urgent need much, much better than Senator John McCain does. Wake up America and start putting your money where your mouth really is.

Why do you think that the Iraqi government all of a sudden got serious in fighting Al-Queda in Iraq, the Shiite Al-Sadr militia, and other insurgents? Remember that the Iraqi leaders have been very quiet for months or years, enjoying their infightings, power struggles, sectarian hatred, and the billions of US dollars per month as they let the Al Sadr militia, Al-Queda, and the rest slaughter their own people and everyone else. Forget the so-called surge of U.S. soldiers into Iraq. If the indigenous government refuses to do a thing, you can add 400,000 American soldiers in Iraq and the situation would have remained exactly the same or worse. The Iraqi leaders woke up. After hearing Barack Obama's continuous sounding of the trumpet about his plan to bring the troops home within a year or sixteen months, and believing that the man will get the Democratic nomination for president, and understanding that this unwavering, quiet-strength Barack might win the USA presidency, the Iraqi leaders woke up.

They quickly put together a serious plan (*BY THEMSELVES*) and went after the insurgents, the Al-Queda, and the Al-Sadr warriors. The Iraqi government won and the leaders are becoming more and more serious in handling their own affairs. Listen carefully. The US army surge of 2007 did not do it. The willingness of the Iraqi leaders, of the Sunnis and the Shiite's leaders to come together and fight the spoilers did the job. Guess who the catalyst is. Barack Obama's campaign is the catalyst; it is a major whip behind the Iraqi leaders to wake up and behave. Don't be surprise if you later discovered that the Bush administration actually used Barack Obama's campaign promises and potential administration to urge the Iraqi leaders to better wake up, reconcile their internal rifts, and fight the insurgents.

Fellows, that's foreign policy! That's being able to understand the people you are dealing with! The Middle Eastern nations cannot fool Barack Obama at all. They cannot sap billions of dollars from Barack Obama and the USA and not account for it as they have been sucking from my loving brother and friend, President George W. Bush Jr. and previous American leaders. Fellows, nations and leaders like the Middle Easterners have certainly tricked the United States into pouring billions of dollars towards them, money that can hardly be accounted for. Many of these leaders have been made filthy rich with little or nothing achieved! Senator John Kerry may be very right in criticizing John McCain:

> "John McCain ... has proven that he has been wrong about every judgment he's made about the war. Wrong about the Iraqis paying for the reconstruction, wrong about whether or not the oil would pay for it, wrong about Sunni and Shia violence through the years, wrong about the willingness of the Iraqis to stand up for themselves," Kerry, who supports Democratic presidential candidate Barack Obama, said on CBS' "Face the Nation." (Yen 2008, Associates Press July 6).

Obama is more right on Iraq and the Muslim culture's impact on policy relationship with the Middle East than Senator McCain and many other presidential candidates in 2008 primary elections. You cannot win a sectarian war in Iraq. You simply need to set a goal that must always be less than staying there for a long time. '*Get in and get out*' type of strategy! Trying to set up a military base in a nation that has significant Sunni Muslims and Shiite Muslims will always stimulate militia attacks and suicide bombings as one sect tries to win the sentiment of the population, claiming to be fighting off the chief infidel, the United States of America.

After removing Saddam Hussein, many unaware people might think that the Shiite's will love the Americans and America. Unfortunately, they like Americans removing Saddam but they said "Thank You" by killing more American soldiers than the war that captured Saddam Hussein. This is not anything against the Shiites. It is about getting the American government to know how to analyze the situation before jumping, especially when it involves addiction to religion of any kind. Barack Obama will do a good job. Finally, America needs to know when and how to really take care of her lagging citizens. Wrongly pouring billions of war dollars in a nation like Iraq is a very poor strategy when millions of Americans are not stabilized, stifling, or even begging bread. Iraq's oil is supposed to be used as part of Iraq war and her reconstruction.

Now can you guess who is taking Barack Obama very seriously? Iran is getting the hint. Talk is not tough. Iran knows very well that when Barack Obama finally opened his mouth and said that he will "do everything in his power to stop Iran from having nuclear weapon, everything…everything," they took him very serious. Ahmadnejad knows that something very bitter will take place now or soon if he and his supporters continue to scare people with tough talks and dangerous weapons. Iran is therefore quick to respond to President Bush's shift in strategy of having a member of USA government be present during nuclear disarmament negotiation. Obama has long been talking about face-to-face meetings with any enemy. That way you will know that all options are truly exhausted before involving the big guns. Now the Iranians will know that the move may be the last diplomatic step by the Bush administration before military action. The agreement between the Bush administration and Barack Obama's policy of direct-talk with the enemy did the trick and looks like it may accomplish something. America, your next Commander In Chief should be Barack Obama. He is Mr. Foreign Policy.

Comfort and Workability of a Policy

If you watched Barack Obama's one-week trip overseas in July 2008, you will not help but to see a person who is very comfortable with people, regardless of whom they are and where he finds himself. The foreign leaders also felt very comfortable around him. That's Obama's nature. He intrinsically and naturally initiates a friendly atmosphere and the leaders would find themselves chatting and holding hands as if they have known each other for years. Without comfort in a system, any solution-talk is coming out of stressed minds. Such talks do not solve problems but make them worse. Barack Obama brings calm and unique intelligence to the world scene of leaders.

America should expect many problems to be solved diplomatically and more peacefully during Barack Obama's tenure as USA president than America has seen in years. America, you really do not want to miss this opportunity. This man, Barack Obama Jr., is not just smart. I believe he is gifted. God manufactured him for use during this time in America and world conditions. He is God's gift to today's USA.

Dear America, it is one thing to have a good sounding policy. It is another thing to employ it. In international relations, comfort is heavily required for workability in a policy. Nations are becoming more and more nationalistic. They are not as dependent on America as before. The arena needs a new, loving, and strategic player to harness the nuances of negotiations and reach agreement, with every leader still feeling good. America, your choice for today's USA is Barrack Obama. Those of you who may fail to vote for this man only because of his color need to know that you may be worse enemy to this Untied States than thousands of Osama bin Ladens and other haters of America put together. You must know that you are a huge cog in the wheel of progress of this loving nation. Wake up and smell the coffee. Put your money where your mouth really is.

CHAPTER 11

WHAT THE WORLD WILL GAIN WITH BARACK AS PRESIDENT OF USA

Two heads have always been said to be better than one. Unfortunately, it will be a bad news if any of the heads is a bad head. I don't think they mean any two heads. Barack is a good head. We need someone in the world scene that will not mind devising a methodical, face-to-face talk with a world troublemaker to help the leader mend his ways.

Obama's mother Ann, center, being held by her parents Madelyn ("Toot") and Stanley Dunham. (Photo: Family Photo)?CBS
Obama campaign site

The tumult in today's world does not need any additional trouble from major playing nations like the United States of America. There is confusion in just about every continent. World Islamic extremism and bombings, the selfish and criminal attitudes of select African leaders, the genocide and slaughtering of human lives in many parts of the world, the food crises, issues of global warming, modern-day slavery in different parts of the world -- all require the next President of the United Stated States that is capable to help.

America's choice in the next addition should be a person who is truly capable, educationally, compassionately, deliberatively, and action-ably. The troubles of today's world do not require a regular politician as we know it. The mess demands heads that are serious about solving problems, not power grabbers and selfish name-seekers. Senator Barack Obama will be a serious and major brainy addition to the world leadership scene. It is the best contribution that America can make to the world at this crying time. America will benefit immensely and the world will have a light heart in working with America toward solving world's problems and securing American interests abroad.

Atmosphere of Non-Condescending Attitude

Years of American leadership of the world, especially by Republican Presidents, seem to show scenes of condescending attitude toward other nations' views, cultures, or even leaders. These nations and their leaders need to feel that they are independent nations with no indirect or direct pressures from a perceived external boss or feelings of smallness in relation to the United States of America. When the United States is seen as domineering in a wrong way, one must expect resentments from nations that feel highly nationalistic in character. America wants to lead by brains and reason not by intimidation or portraying a message of superiority, which we have seen during President George W. Bush Jr. presidency. What do you think the President of Iran meant in the following statement as reported by The Associates Press?

> "the next U.S. administration would need at least 30 years in order to compensate, renovate the damages done by Mr. Bush." Today, the government of the United States is on the threshold of bankruptcy — from political to economic," "The greatest threat in the Middle East and the whole world ... is the United States' intervention in other countries," Ahmadinejad said. He urged Washington to heal its image by "relying on (the) basis of justice, humanitarian acts and respect for human beings." (Joshi 2008, Associates Press July 8).

This is a chilly assessment of the United States. It is also humbling, coming from Ahmadinejad of all people, offering a serious advice to a crumbling nation. Unbelievably, America will crumble if Americans do not wake up the right way. America is certainly crumbling politically and economically and this man, Barack Obama, is the beginning of the real answer or solution. Truly, America may not help it but to become bankrupt, forcing her to wake up and recognize that her family system is killing her. I just needed to refer to the family issue again because it is the foundation of all problems or successes. Ahmadnejad is referring to America's political and economic bankruptcy. However, I am reminding the nation that traditional-family bankruptcy is the beginning of all bankruptcies.

Nevertheless, part of what Ahmadinejad is referring to is how America degradedly treats other leaders; he is feeling it. He is talking about respect for human beings by USA. Although I do not see him as having any respect for human beings when he constantly calls for the decimation of Israel, his lamentation is partly referring to America's disregard of other people's views or acting superior to other foreign leaders. I must continue to support America's intervention in nations where wicked leaders maltreat their citicizens. Without America, many citizens of the world would be zipped forever.

Let us get back to Ahmadnejad's credible concern. Did you notice how Barack Obama acted when the media asked him and Hillary Clinton about what they would do if Iran throws a nuclear bomb on Israel? Senator Clinton furiously stated that America would annihilate and decimate Iran. Obama, on the hand, played it cool, indicating that you do not make statements like that, especially when you still have opportunity to deal diplomatically with such so-called unfriendly leaders like Ahmanejad of Iran. Erratic statements or answers like

Senator Clinton's do not really show strength and leadership but weakness for a leader and tension and defensiveness in the world. God does not favor characters like that, and world leaders will be scared to be led by such people. Cowboy-talk or gunslinger-diplomacy is not welcome in world scene of proud and independent nations. Nations may feel degraded at statements of superiority. Quiet reasoning, quiet strength, and quiet love will do the charm of solving world problems. Do not ever be seen as putting out the guns first!

Barack Obama is a calm and intelligent man that the world desperately needs now. World leaders will respect him highly because he will treat everyone as equals, allowing every leader of every nation to feel comfortable around him and to voice their opinions without fear of anything. That's the man's nature. That's the nature that will lift America up again in the world scene.

Mighty Dove International Relations

Jesus told His followers to be as wise as serpents but as harmless as doves (The Holy Bible 10:16). This is already in Barack Obama's nature. He has been described consistently as a calm or cool person, not easily angered or startled. Such a characteristic is a function of the inner harmony; coming into agreement with your God often creates such nature or character. The way this personality has influenced Barack's campaign is the way that it will influence his presidency. It is the way that it will influence world leaders and the associations that they share with Barack.

Obama will make sure there will be no drama as much as possible. There will be no war unless it is necessary. The world will breathe easy at that. Obama will be an instrument to talk with any troublemaker in a way that he or she will actually understand; he may even get the troublemaker to apologize to the world. Don't be surprise if Ahamadnejad and Obama Obama become good friends because of the way Obama will relate to him, talk to him, and love him as Jesus commanded us to do. Love can destroy any evil intention. Don't be surprise if Ahmadnejad and the Iranians quickly agreed to dismantle all pursuit of nuclear ambition just because Barack Obama lovingly and non-condescendingly talks with Ahmadnejad and the clerics. Don't be surprise if Israel experiences the best peace that they have ever had in their lives because of the love-diplomacy that Barack Obama will exhibit in the Middle East. Don't be surprise!

Israel will see Barack Obama as her best friend. The Middle East, Arab and non-Arab nations, will surprisingly see Obama as their best friend too, even when Obama is helping Israel decisively. The key is love for all. The two sides, especially the Muslims, will clearly see that Barack Obama loves them and does not intend harm for them in any way. At the same time, they will be highly convinced that Obama will be more like Ronald Reagan (or better) in defending and protecting America's interest when provoked. This is the best position that America wants to be. God has something good up in His sleeves for America and the rest of the world with Barack as the next President of USA.

African citizens and African leaders will wake up. African leaders, especially the tyrants and the dubious ones, will not like to see Barack Obama elected as the next President of America. They won't see any white man or white woman to blame when Barack Obama falls on their backs and holding them squarely responsible for their atrocities. The wicked and selfish man of Zimbabwe, Robert Mugabe, will be shut up in his foolish rhetoric of always blaming the white man as he annihilates his own people. Barack Obama's emotional attachment to the world and to Africa will cause him to go after these kinds of wicked African leaders with all necessary means until they learn to establish true democracy in the continent.

The best of all is that the presence of Barack Obama as the President of America will challenge the African citizens to rise up and help in their respective nations with the attitude, "If Barack can do it then I can do it too." In addition to this attitude, they will feel that they have a brother as the President of the most powerful nation in the world, offering them motivation to stand up against injustices, corruption, and murders in the land of Africa. They will be inspired to love fellow citizens and to be patriotic in-deed. Barack's election as President of USA will be a firecracker of inspiration around the world for all people and races, especially for the poor, the less fortunate, and the oppressed, which usually have excuses for not making it.

Can you now see how the good leaders of the world nations can benefit directly and indirectly by having Barack as the next President of America? No good leader will not like to have every faction of his or her citizens inspired and intrinsically motivated to believe that he or she can make it and excel if he or she can work hard like Barack Obama with some help from families and the government. Wise leaders can use Barack's position as a motivational tool for boosting the morale of their citizens, especially those who have lost hope. Let's get Barack in the oval office and reap the rewards. It will be the beginning of a great blessing for the loving and the ever-sacrificing United States of America.

America's True Democracy

The election of a black man, Barack Obama, as the next President of America will flash a message all over the world that America is indeed a nation of true democracy. The message of democracy that America has been trumpeting to every corner of the world and giving their lives for it will come to life in America and in the world in such a special way. It will show-case America that does not care about the color of a candidate but about his or her qualification to lead the nation. It will display America that is far past the times of slavery and racism. It will show America of true love for all, *The* United States of America not the United *Section* of America. It will put a cap to what the honorable, Abraham Lincoln stated, fought for, and died for. Against Kansas-Nebraska Act of 1854 which permitted people to have the right to decide whether or not to allow slavery in their territory rather than have such a decision imposed on them by Congress, Lincoln decried:

> [The Act has a] *declared* indifference, but as I must think, covert *real* zeal for the spread of slavery, I cannot but hate it. I hate it because of the monstrous injustice of slavery itself. I hate it because it deprives our republican example of its just influence in the world — enables the enemies of free institutions, with plausibility, to taunt us as hypocrites — causes the real friends of freedom to doubt our sincerity, and especially because it forces so many really good men amongst ourselves into an open war with the very fundamental principles of civil liberty — criticizing the Declaration of Independence, and insisting that there is no right principle of action but *self-interest*. (Abraham Lincoln,Wikipedia).

Can you see what I am seeing? Can you see the handwriting of blessings and honor for the USA on walls of the world and of heaven? Can you see the thrill of all members of America crying at the top of their voices, "We are the United States of America" not Hispanic American, African-American, Italian American, English American, or whatever American. Can you truly hear all black people crying, "We are truly free at last?" This is the beginning of a great progress in America, one that has never been imagined. If America can truly come together as one, America will notice that she has been enjoying only a speck of what her blessings should have be. Electing Obama will usher in this psychological and enduring feeling of unity. "If Barack, a black man, can make it in America by being her No. 1 person, the man from the most denigrated race in the nation over many years, then I must be anything that I can be, and all races are just equal as stated in the USA constitution." The windows of heaven shall burst open for America. The world would have learned a great lesson as it helps to stop hate and genocide. The world will see America as a true constitutional democracy in deed! May God bless and sustain America again.

Can you see the message such an election can send to nations and leaders that practice racism and hate all over the world? Can you see the message and life such an election can send to minorities all over the world? Can you see the power that such an election can give to the United States in combating genocide and human rights violation all over the world? Can you see the respect that the USA can attract to herself until Jesus comes? I leave you to answer the questions. As one smart endorser of Barack Obama clearly stated--Barack Obama being in the White House come January 2009 is all the foreign relations and image building that America needs in the world (Los Angeles Times 2008).

A Stronger America

The world needs stronger America than the one that is quickly collapsing before our eyes. For years, the world regards the United States of America as a safe-haven for foreign investments, whose currency can be trusted anytime without iota of fear. Today, years of mismanagement has put America in severe trouble of losing her top safe-having status as most notable foreign nations, leaders, and investors see alternatives in other places, especially the EU. In fact, since September 11, 2001 some people are beginning to see the USA as being no different from other nations.

Dear Americans, this is not a good perception. It is destructive for America's reputation. Since September 11, 2001, the US dollar has been falling in value like a rock. This phenomenon is causing speculators to start re-evaluating the dollar and giving serious consideration to using other currencies as their central reserve assets or units of trade. Although President George W. Bush did a good job in holding this nation from utterly collapsing because of the attack of September 11, the Iraq war and its mismanagement were definitely a huge source of trouble in weakening the US economy.

Barack Obama understands it very well. The man will literally have to reverse the course that President Bush is taking in the economy and in the war. Blind application of trickle-down theory is a mistake. America must get down to empowering its middle class and relieving its poor. These people have suffered enough. By reversing the course in Iraq and strengthening the economy through *all-source trickle* as I presented earlier, America will rise again and provide the world a cushion that she once was and still partially is.

The death of America will be a fatal blow to most little folks and little nations. Tyrants and wicked leaders will run amuck. Hitlers will be everywhere. China, Russia, and any other nation may not do a thing to help, but may even worsen the situation as China has been doing with the Darfur genocide. The world needs America badly. To understand why America is still the best nation in the world, go to *Emancipation*USA.org or ChampionSociety.com and get my books titled *God Bless America* and *God Bless the USA*. Numerous wicked leaders of the world are not exercising some of their wicked powers because America still alive. Robert Mugabe of Zimbabwe would not have agreed to discuss ways to share power with the opposition if the United States was not around. This is why good people must continue to pray and fight for the long-lasting of America as a dominant world power. Unfortunately, this status cannot last with America kicking her God on the butt anywhere you look.

CHAPTER 12

WHAT AMERICA WILL GAIN WITH BARACK AS PRESIDENT OF USA

Like a good invention spells riches to the inventor so is a hard, but desired change to a nation that summoned the courage to make it.

An American, Thomas Alva Edison, invented the phonograph (gramophone) and the long-lasting light bulb. It takes hard work to achieve. It takes boldness to take a step further into the next move of things. Like he said, "*Genius is one percent inspiration, ninety-nine percent perspiration.*" Voting for a black man Obama can be much perspiration for many white people, but his presidency will be great and profitable invention to them and for America.

It was very difficult and sweaty. It took many faithful trials and sometimes heartbreaks before Thomas Edison finally invented the electric bulb. Now look where we are. If he had given up at one of those trial stages, where shall we be today without good electricity? Everyone is enjoying it now, but they didn't know how much sweat it cost the invent-tor, Thomas Edison. Edison himself said, "*Genius is one percent inspira-tion, ninety-nine percent perspiration.*" (Thomas Alva Edison, Harper's Monthly, September 1932).

Many people have prayed for better America. Many members of the white race and all races have prayed to God for Him to bless America and to do great and mighty things for USA. Now the test has come. To many people, this test is just too hard. How can I vote for a black man while I hate blacks or I just want them to remain at a distance? These voters go to church daily but they can't seem to pass this hurdle. It is too hard. Even if he is the best choice, I rather die and let my family members die, or even let America perish instead of voting for a black person. That's how hard it can be. Perspiration squared!

It is bravery to note that many of the people who feel as stated above are actually forcing themselves to vote for Barack Obama. Many others (like the Iowans and the rest) who are just angels are also voting for Obama. These are the Thomas Edisons! They are about to make great invention. They are about to light up America and the rest of the world. The devil is crying now. He is not happy at all. America is about to really blossom. To all people of different color who are voting for Barack Obama regardless of his race,, I say, "Congratulations!" You are being example to me and to the whole world; you will be blessed highly. As the electric bulb is to America and the world, so will Barack's election into the highest office of America be to America and the rest of the world.

Overall Impact On Culture and Sociology

Culture can be defined as a set of values, beliefs, attitudes, intentions, and behaviors that typify a group of people or nation. Sociology can be defined as the nature of relationship among people. The argument here is that Barack Obama's election into the presidency of the United States will certainly improve the culture and social relations of the United States of America. The mere fact that Barack Obama is succeeding and mainly because of the support of whites has cleansed so many hearts, eased so many minds, and blessed so many souls. As Melissa Harris-Lacewell, a professor of Politics and African-American studies at Princeton and an Obama volunteer stated:

> Iowa was an astonishing moment. Watching Barack win the caucus felt like Reconstruction. There was something powerful about feeling as though you were a full citizen. In democracy the ruled and rulers are supposed to be the same people. The idea that black folks could be engaged in the process of being rulers over not just black folks but over the nation as a whole struck me as very powerful. (Reed 2008, The Nation may 3).

People are rejoicing. Black people are breathing life and hope in the United States of America. To see a black man succeeding and receiving the white votes as Barack is getting is forcing tears of joy out of many black people's eyes (Figure 1). It is a cry of joy. It is a cry of liberation. It is a cry of "*thank you to the Lord*" for receiving affirmation form the majority race. It is a healing cry. It is a cry that sooths the soul as it clears all the pains of oppression and racism and replacing all with love. It is a cry of forgiveness and love. It is a cry of finally beginning to accept the majority race. It is a cry that only black people and those who have been through rejections and oppressions would understand. It is a cry of release. It is a healing cry.

It is a feeling like one is really a citizen of USA, no longer being pushed to the corner or trampled under the feet of society. It is a cry that says, "I think I am beginning to live now." It constitues Abraham Lincoln and the Kennedy's cries. This is a healing that no doctor in the world can ever offer except God Himself through the process that is just about to create the first black President of the United States of America, ruling all races in the USA. Please vote for Barack Obama. Take time to meditate on the following cultural benefits to America:

1.

FIGURE 1: THEY ARE CRYING AS BARACK OBAMA SPEAKS

1. The black race of America will be psychologically healed from head to toe, believing that they can work hard and accomplish anything. There will be much less thought and talks about white racism or that racism. Emphasis will shift to hard work and to be like Obama in any person's area of endeavor. Even if some black person feels discriminated against at a place, he or she might actually ignore it but works hard to overcome it by trying to be a positive example to his or her perceived oppressor.

2. The white race and other races of America will begin to witness a new kind of behavior and attitude from the average black person. Instead of that of white skepticism, it will be white love and open-arm acceptance of all white people. There will be a lot of trust in relationship between white race and all races in the USA with the belief that the majority race will reward one for what one can offer and will not reward one if one don't measure up through hardwork. Again, there will be much less talk about discrimination and more emphasis on hardwork. Pygmalion effect or what we know as self-fulfilling prophecy will cease in the relationship between whites and blacks. Don't you know that many black people have actually become self-destructed because they simply believed (before they try) that the white people hated them? That belief had led some to perform poorly by themselves without the white teacher or employer doing anything to cause it.

3. The majority race and all those who have prayed and voted according to their good conscience will feel very proud of themselves that they have indeed transcended racism and continued to add on their resume as the best white people in the world as far as I'm concerned. I have said it before and I'm saying it again for God's benefit, "On the average, the white folks of America are the best set of people in the world." Their charity and love are unmatched.

4. Since their hearts and minds are healed, the black race will be able to focus (without worry) on education and possess the faith that they are indeed part of the nation called USA. They will believe that their educational efforts will be rewarded. Confidence in oneself is a great medicine! For years the black people of America have directly and indirectly sought to be approved by the majority race. Electing Obama President of the United States is a great approval. It is an approval that says, "black, white and everybody else are equal in the United States, as stated in the Holy Bible and in the constitution of the United States. It will give emotional and psychological boost to the black race to want to work hard and contribute with joy to the growth of USA. They can now fight

and die in the wars with great joy. The relationship among various races in the US army will significantly improve.

5. What about other minorities in the USA? If Barack Hussein Obama can do it, I can do it too; only live right. That will be the attitude. Every home that usually under-performs or does not perform will find hope and inspiration to wake up and fight the spirit of intimidation, poverty, or laziness. "I-can-make-it" attitude will fill the air.

6. The greatest blessing will be divine intervention in handling the affairs of America. God Himself will become America's sheriff and re-warder. Any person that tries to take advantage of America's love for the purpose of harming the nation will be exterminated by the Almighty God whether they believe there is that God or not. The same God that America trusts in the great motto, "*In God We Trust,*" will be activated to take care of some serious America's businesses on a continual basis.

Overall Impact On Politics and the Economy

Once the culture of a nation is overhauled rightly, everything else falls in line. Culture determines the state of everything else. Bad culture produces bad politics and bad economy. A culture of love produces politicians and leaders of love and creates an atmosphere where everyone is somebody as everyone works boldly to help himself or herself, moving the country toward excellence. Like a family of strife and fights, which leads to anxieties, sicknesses, divorce, single-parenting, and all kinds of poor performances among affected children and parents, a nation of strife produces citizens that are troublesome, full of anxieties, poor perform-ances in schools, jobs, politics, and everything else, costing the nation immeasurable amounts of dollars yearly. Remember the costs of divorce and single parenting that you read earlier.

Election of Obama as America's CEO will start something very good in the political and economic systems of USA. We will expect to experience the following blessings:

1. Black leaders or potential black leaders (on the average), who have consistently and unfortunately shown to be performing very poorly and selfishly in representing their constituencies, will wake up, feel challenged, or stand to be insulted with disdain. Enough is enough! Barack Obama will become a reasonable yardstick of measure-ment. Useless excuses and white-blame mentality can no longer be welcome as much.

2. With time, welfare-dependency will decrease as people get serious with their lives and wanting to contribute to the nation instead of sucking the nation as parasites. Hardwork and more productivity by the average person will boost the economy.

3. Crime-reduction and ensuing economic and political atmosphere of love will promote trust in America by outsiders, increasing USA safe-haven status back to almost a 90 percentile that it used to be. Foreign investments will rise as investors work to possess USA dollar. As of now, the status is tumbling between 50percent and 55 percent by my estimate.

   America's balance of payment equilibrium has consistently been poor. America used to excel in everything. Now the nation is trying to balance the account with exports of services. Unfortunately, other nations are offering formidable competition in the area. America's children and the adults that are coming out of such children are poorly trained and challenged to compete. Serious leadership and a no-nonsense focus on traditional family and child rearing systems will do the job. For now, and to some extent, the inspiration pouring from Barack Obama will help fire-up millions of people to rise up and work for themselves and for the common good. This kind of inspiration will affect every facet of American life.

Embracing America Again

It is critical that America pays attention here. It is right that foreigners or outsiders do not vote in America's or any nation's election. However, it is critical that America pays attention to the cries and yearning of the world if America still believes in leading the world and in using the world to achieve America's interests or goals. Those who consistently refuse to listen to Barack Obama because of his race needs to ask themselves whether they really care for America. Closed-mindedness can be worse than genocide and equivalent to Hitler's lifestyle if it continues to undermine right judgments that will propel the nation to higher heights. Such people are actually nation-destroyers instead of builders.

There is a general cry in America about the nation connecting to the world again and leading world's trust in accomplishing necessary goals that face the United Nations and NATO. There is a cry in America about the nation becoming one instead of remaining divided and accomplishing relatively very little. There is a cry in America for a true 'uniter' and lover of all people to help America domestically and internationally. God has sent that person. His name is Barack Obama. For some people not to vote for him because of his color is atrocious, considering the need of someone like that in America and in the world today.

In Afghanistan, in Iraq, in Jordan, in Israel, in Germany, in France, and in London, this man has a knack of making people feel comfortable with him, and he clearly shows love and a sense of comfort with the leaders and people that he talks with. His visits to these nations in July 2008 ought to tell any racist something. Look at how he is loved both by white, black, yellow, and green people! Look at how they are ready to help him help America excel again! Robin Oakley, CNN's European political editor said that Obama enjoyed widespread popularity in Europe,

> "He is one of those politicians who reach parts other politicians don't reach… After the unpopularity of George W. Bush, the world is waiting to love America again, and many see in Obama, with his youth and his optimism, somebody who can bring that about." (Johnson 2008, CNN).

This statement is heartfelt, and many Americans are yearning for it. Such embrace will positively affect America's economic and political systems. In Berlin, Germany, Obama spoke before about 200,000 Germans and other foreigners. Read the speech and witness a candidate that is truly strong on national security and possesses the management acumen, the mathematical brain and strategic understanding to get the job done. He is a candidate that will have no choice but to stand and fight for the common person. Read:

Thank you to the citizens of Berlin and to the people of Germany. Let me thank Chancellor Merkel and Foreign Minister Steinmeier for welcoming me earlier today. Thank you Mayor Wowereit, the Berlin Senate, the police, and most of all thank you for this welcome.

I come to Berlin as so many of my countrymen have come before. Tonight, I speak to you not as a candidate for President, but as a citizen - a proud citizen of the United States, and a fellow citizen of the world.

I know that I don't look like the Americans who've previously spoken in this great city. The journey that led me here is improbable. My mother was born in the heartland of America, but my father grew up herding goats in Kenya. His father - my grandfather - was a cook, a domestic servant to the British.

At the height of the Cold War, my father decided, like so many others in the forgotten corners of the world, that his yearning - his dream - required the freedom and opportunity promised by the West. And so he wrote letter after letter to universities all across America until somebody, somewhere answered his prayer for a better life.

That is why I'm here. And you are here because you too know that yearning. This city, of all cities, knows the dream of freedom. And you know that the only reason we stand here tonight is because men and women from both of our nations came together to work, and struggle, and sacrifice for that better life.

Ours is a partnership that truly began sixty years ago this summer, on the day when the first American plane touched down at Templehof.

On that day, much of this continent still lay in ruin. The rubble of this city had yet to be built into a wall. The Soviet shadow had swept across Eastern Europe, while in the West, America, Britain, and France took stock of their losses, and pondered how the world might be remade.

This is where the two sides met. And on the twenty-fourth of June, 1948, the Communists chose to blockade the western part of the city. They cut off food and supplies to more than two million Germans in an effort to extinguish the last flame of freedom in Berlin.

The size of our forces was no match for the much larger Soviet Army. And yet retreat would have allowed Communism to march across Europe. Where the last war had ended, another World War could have easily begun. All that stood in the way was Berlin.

And that's when the airlift began - when the largest and most unlikely rescue in history brought food and hope to the people of this city.
The odds were stacked against success. In the winter, a heavy fog filled the sky above, and many planes were forced to turn back without dropping off the needed supplies. The streets where we stand were filled with hungry families who had no comfort from the cold.

But in the darkest hours, the people of Berlin kept the flame of hope burning. The people of Berlin refused to give up. And on one fall day, hundreds of thousands of Berliners came here, to the Tiergarten, and heard the city's mayor implore the world not to give up on freedom. "There is only one possibility," he said. "For us to stand together united until this battle is won...The people of Berlin have spoken. We have done our duty, and we will keep on doing our duty. People of the world: now do your duty...People of the world, look at Berlin!"

People of the world - look at Berlin! Look at Berlin, where Germans and Americans learned to work together and trust each other less than three years after facing each other on the field of battle.

Look at Berlin, where the determination of a people met the generosity of the Marshall Plan and created a German miracle; where a victory over tyranny gave rise to NATO, the greatest alliance ever formed to defend our common security. Look at Berlin, where the bullet holes in the buildings and the somber stones and pillars near the Brandenburg Gate insist that we never forget our common humanity.

People of the world - look at Berlin, where a wall came down, a continent came together, and history proved that there is no challenge too great for a world that stands as one.

Sixty years after the airlift, we are called upon again. History has led us to a new crossroad, with new promise and new peril. When you, the German people, tore down that wall - a wall that divided East and West; freedom and tyranny; fear and hope - walls came tumbling down around the world. From Kiev to Cape Town, prison camps were closed, and the doors of democracy were opened. Markets opened too, and the spread of information and technology reduced barriers to opportunity and prosperity. While the 20th century taught us that we share a common destiny, the 21st has revealed a world more intertwined than at any time in human history.

The fall of the Berlin Wall brought new hope. But that very closeness has given rise to new dangers - dangers that cannot be contained within the borders of a country or by the distance of an ocean.

The terrorists of September 11th plotted in Hamburg and trained in Kandahar and Karachi before killing thousands from all over the globe on American soil. As we speak, cars in Boston and factories in Beijing are melting the ice caps in the Arctic, shrinking coastlines in the Atlantic, and bringing drought to farms from Kansas to Kenya.

Poorly secured nuclear material in the former Soviet Union, or secrets from a scientist in Pakistan could help build a bomb that detonates in Paris. The poppies in Afghanistan become the heroin in Berlin. The poverty and violence in Somalia breeds the terror of tomorrow. The genocide in Darfur shames the conscience of us all.

In this new world, such dangerous currents have swept along faster than our efforts to contain them. That is why we cannot afford to be divided. No one nation, no matter how large or powerful, can defeat such challenges alone. None of us can deny these threats, or escape responsibility in meeting them. Yet, in the absence of Soviet tanks and a terrible wall, it has become easy to forget this truth. And if we're honest with each other, we know that sometimes, on both sides of the Atlantic, we have drifted apart, and forgotten our shared destiny.

In Europe, the view that America is part of what has gone wrong in our world, rather than a force to help make it right, has become all too common. In America, there are voices that deride and deny the importance of Europe's role in our security and our future. Both views miss the truth - that Europeans today are bearing new burdens and taking more responsibility in critical parts of the world; and that just as American bases built in the last century still help to defend the security of this continent, so does our country still sacrifice greatly for freedom around the globe.

Yes, there have been differences between America and Europe. No doubt, there will be differences in the future. But the burdens of global citizenship continue to bind us together. A change of leadership in Washington will not lift this burden. In this new century, Americans and Europeans alike will be required to do more - not less. Partnership and cooperation among nations is not a choice; it is the one way, the only way, to protect our common security and advance our common humanity.

That is why the greatest danger of all is to allow new walls to divide us from one another.

The walls between old allies on either side of the Atlantic cannot stand. The walls between the countries with the most and those with the least cannot stand. The walls between races and tribes; natives and immigrants; Christian and Muslim and Jew cannot stand. These now are the walls we must tear down.

We know they have fallen before. After centuries of strife, the people of Europe have formed a Union of promise and prosperity. Here, at the base of a column built to mark victory in war, we meet in the center of a Europe at peace. Not only have walls come down in Berlin, but they have come down in Belfast, where Protestant and Catholic found a way to live together; in the Balkans, where our Atlantic alliance ended wars and brought savage war criminals to justice; and in South Africa, where the struggle of a courageous people defeated apartheid.

So history reminds us that walls can be torn down. But the task is never easy. True partnership and true progress requires constant work and sustained sacrifice. They require sharing the burdens of development and diplomacy; of progress and peace. They require allies who will listen to each other, learn from each other and, most of all, trust each other.

That is why America cannot turn inward. That is why Europe cannot turn inward. America has no better partner than Europe. Now is the time to build new bridges across the globe as strong as the one that bound us across the Atlantic. Now is the time to join together, through constant cooperation, strong institutions, shared sacrifice, and a global commitment to progress, to meet the challenges of the 21st century. It was this spirit that led airlift planes to appear in the sky above our heads, and people to assemble where we stand today. And this is the moment when our nations - and all nations - must summon that spirit anew.

This is the moment when we must defeat terror and dry up the well of extremism that supports it. This threat is real and we cannot shrink from our responsibility to combat it. If we could create NATO to face down the Soviet Union, we can join in a new and global partnership to dismantle the networks that have struck in Madrid and Amman; in London and Bali; in Washington and New York. If we could win a battle of ideas against the communists, we can stand with the vast majority of Muslims who reject the extremism that leads to hate instead of hope.

This is the moment when we must renew our resolve to rout the terrorists who threaten our security in Afghanistan, and the traffickers who sell drugs on your streets. No one welcomes war. I recognize the enormous difficulties in Afghanistan. But my country and yours have a stake in seeing that NATO's first mission beyond Europe's borders is a success. For the people of Afghanistan, and for our shared security, the work must be done. America cannot do this alone. The Afghan people need our troops and your troops; our support and your support to defeat the Taliban and al Qaeda, to develop their economy, and to help them rebuild their nation. We have too much at stake to turn back now.

This is the moment when we must renew the goal of a world without nuclear weapons. The two superpowers that faced each other across the wall of this city came too close too often to destroying all we have built and all that we love. With that wall gone, we need not stand idly by and watch the further spread of the deadly atom. It is time to secure all loose nuclear materials; to stop the spread of nuclear weapons; and to reduce the arsenals from another era. This is the moment to begin the work of seeking the peace of a world without nuclear weapons.

This is the moment when every nation in Europe must have the chance to choose its own tomorrow free from the shadows of yesterday. In this century, we need a strong European Union that deepens the security and prosperity of this continent, while extending a hand abroad. In this century - in this city of all cities - we must reject the Cold War mind-set of the past, and resolve to work with Russia when we can, to stand up for our values when we must, and to seek a partnership that extends across this entire continent.

This is the moment when we must build on the wealth that open markets have created, and share its benefits more equitably. Trade has been a cornerstone of our growth and global development. But we will not be able to sustain this growth if it favors the few, and not the many. Together, we must forge trade that truly rewards the work that creates wealth, with meaningful protections for our people and our planet. This is the moment for trade that is free and fair for all.

This is the moment we must help answer the call for a new dawn in the Middle East. My country must stand with yours and with Europe in sending a direct message to Iran that it must abandon its nuclear ambitions. We must support the Lebanese who have marched and bled for democracy, and the Israelis and Palestinians who seek a secure and lasting peace. And despite past differences, this is the moment when the world should support the millions of Iraqis who seek to rebuild their lives, even as we pass responsibility to the Iraqi government and finally bring this war to a close.

This is the moment when we must come together to save this planet. Let us resolve that we will not leave our children a world where the oceans rise and famine spreads and terrible storms devastate our lands. Let us resolve that all nations - including my own - will act with the same seriousness of purpose as has your nation, and reduce the carbon we send into our atmosphere. This is the moment to give our children back their future. This is the moment to stand as one.

And this is the moment when we must give hope to those left behind in a globalized world. We must remember that the Cold War born in this city was not a battle for land or treasure. Sixty years ago, the planes that flew over Berlin did not drop bombs; instead they delivered food, and coal, and candy to grateful children. And in that show of solidarity, those pilots won more than a military victory. They won hearts and minds; love and loyalty and trust - not just from the people in this city, but from all those who heard the story of what they did here.

Now the world will watch and remember what we do here - what we do with this moment. Will we extend our hand to the people in the forgotten corners of this world who yearn for lives marked by dignity and opportunity; by security and justice? Will we lift the child in Bangladesh from poverty, shelter the refugee in Chad, and banish the scourge of AIDS in our time?

Will we stand for the human rights of the dissident in Burma, the blogger in Iran, or the voter in Zimbabwe? Will we give meaning to the words "never again" in Darfur?

Will we acknowledge that there is no more powerful example than the one each of our nations projects to the world? Will we reject torture and stand for the rule of law? Will we welcome immigrants from different lands, and shun discrimination against those who don't look like us or worship like we do, and keep the promise of equality and opportunity for all of our people?

People of Berlin - people of the world - this is our moment. This is our time. I know my country has not perfected itself. At times, we've struggled to keep the promise of liberty and equality for all of our people. We've made our share of mistakes, and there are times when our actions around the world have not lived up to our best intentions.

But I also know how much I love America. I know that for more than two centuries, we have strived - at great cost and great sacrifice - to form a more perfect union; to seek, with other nations, a more hopeful world. Our allegiance has never been to any particular tribe or kingdom - indeed, every language is spoken in our country; every culture has left its imprint on ours; every point of view is expressed in our public squares. What has always united us - what has always driven our people; what drew my father to America's shores - is a set of ideals that speak to aspirations shared by all people: that we can live free from fear and free from want; that we can speak our minds and assemble with whomever we choose and worship as we please.

Those are the aspirations that joined the fates of all nations in this city. Those aspirations are bigger than anything that drives us apart. It is because of those aspirations that the airlift began. It is because of those aspirations that all free people - everywhere - became citizens of Berlin. It is in pursuit of those aspirations that a new generation - our generation - must make our mark on history.

People of Berlin - and people of the world - the scale of our challenge is great. The road ahead will be long. But I come before you to say that we are heirs to a struggle for freedom. We are a people of improbable hope. Let us build on our common history, and seize our common destiny, and once again engage in that noble struggle to bring justice and peace to our world. (CNN/ObamaCampaign).

What do you get from the above gathering and speech? The cynics and the fear-mongers will see negatives. Even some shortsighted people see a common celebrity instead of God's gift to America and to the world of today. However, you and I do see a man that can relate to many people and cultures and be able to get things done. Successful solution of world problems requires that the world be part of solving such problems. For the world to have the ability to unify and solve its problems, the world needs a rallying point and a rallying, non-condescending leader. The man is Barack Obama at a relatively 99 percentile, not John McCain at all.

Senator McCain, though a good person, cannot handle it at all or as well as Barack Obama. America, let us be wise to choose right. Do not let the color of this good man to cheat you of your God's blessing for this nation. If you really want to have a breath of fresh air, peace, and prosperity, then vote for Barack Obama. If you want troubles as usual and mechanic-workshop-laden foreign and domestic policies, then go ahead and vote for the beloved John McCain. But remember—"Don't complain in the future and don't start cursing and insulting the leader you helped elect." Please let us be smart this time. Do not be derailed by liars and deceivers. The whole world is a system and America is part of the world and a major leader. Place a loving and peaceful man into the office and witness real peace and prosperity for a change, ceteris paribus.

How Conservatives Can Use Obama

Fast and pray. Something good and great will happen to Obama in the presidential office. So, the first way to use Obama is to love him, then fast and pray for him. Again, something good and great will happen to him in office and he will be used to truly usher in a new day and years in the United States of America. Obama has said many times that he is open to dialogue. Christian conservatives need to choose some educated, humble conservative to spend sometime with Barack Obama or even be one of Obama's advisers. This individual will be able to explain the word of God to Obama with power and authority not just words!

People are atheists or half-believers in the real God because they haven't seen the power yet. What we have today are bunch of so-called conservatives and preachers who talk the talk but hate to walk the walk or work the work. They hate abortion and fight against it but they are monstrous racists, which kill a lot more people than abortion, psychologically and physically. To convince intellectuals like Barack Obama to understand the fullness of the gospel requires action not talk. It requires real faith not fake belief.

As I may have stated before, Obama is really conservative or middle of the road when it comes to family system. He is not liberal. He just elected not to interfere in whatever the liberals and anybody else want to believe and practice. What he does not know or may really know but tries to suppress it is that the word of God condemns supporting evil in any manner. Using the federal money to support gay life style and abortion is adding salt to injury in the site of God.

Many black people and many loving folks like Obama will love to register GOP and vote GOP but they are scared away by anti small-folks, lack of compassion, and sometimes by the racist behaviors that tend to characterize the Republican Party. Republican Party is fully supported by the so-called conservative Christians. However, these Christians do nothing to correct the mess and attract the right people to the party. If Christians consider GOP as the party of Christians, a significant percentage of the citizens need to see the love, universal love coming from the party. Jesus said, "by this they will know that you are of me — if you have love one for another (Holy Bible, John 13:35), must love your neighbor as yourself (Holy Bible, Matthew 19:19), and love must be without dissimulation (Holy Bible, Romans 12:9)." What can you say about a Christian church whose name is *The Open Church*, but they do not accept blacks? This actually happened. It happened to the amazement of a new black family in the area who wanted to join the church. The pastor secretly told the family that the white members would not like it.

This is one perception that GOP needs to clean up. Many GOP spokespersons may be like the members of such an open, but closed church. The GOP agenda may look as good as God. However, if it is sponsored by the devil and implemented by the devil—just for the few, then it is of the devil. The Democrats, on the other hand, may already be bunch of liberals and demon-worshippers who succumb to whatever feels good to their flesh. Nevertheless, they apply whatever it is to everyone else without dissimulation. They actually believe they are doing good. Which one do you think God will accept? Who do you think God will punish the more?

Dear fellow conservative Christians, let's be conservatives by example—in word and in deed. We can influence many people that way. We need someone with power and love to work with and explain the scriptures to Barack Obama, the next President of the United States. Much of what Obama says in defense of his support for gay marriage and abortion is more of excuse and poor understanding of the scriptures than anything else.

A Message To White Supremacists

I saw on the television where a self-proclaimed white supremacist indicated that they would vote for Obama in order to help wake up racism and hate in the nation and a campaign against minorities. I want to encourage them by saying that God is in control. God is in control of America. He will never let America that they love be ruined for as long as we humbly obey. In fact, enough has already been done for God to continue to uphold and fight for this nation as He continues to sound His trumpets of repentance.

To all members of the white race who think that electing Barack Obama or any black person the President of the Untied States is a bad thing, I want you to know that it is not. It will be a great blessing for you and for all Americans. I know you really love America, but I wish that you will love every person too. Watch and see how God will use the election of Barack to bless all white people in general because of those Caucasians who did not consider color in voting in this election—whether they voted for McCain or for Obama. If God puts it in your heart that Obama is the better candidate, please force yourself to vote for him. You will be surprised how God will reward America because you defied what Satan is trying to make you do and decided to obey your Maker, the Almighty God.

If Barack Obama (the black candidate) is the right choice in your heart, vote for him. If John McCain (the white candidate) is the right choice, then vote for him. Please do not deny Obama your vote just because he is black. Do whatever it is just to please your God and watch out for blessings to open up again for this great nation called the USA. You can do it! YES YOU CAN! Give Satan the black eye because you are children of the living God. You are indeed! God Bless *The* USA!

CHAPTER 13

DEALING WITH CRITICISMS

Criticism is not bad if one knows how to use it to one's advantage. Mama would have helped her son very much at this time but "All Is Well."

The 1960 high school yearbook photo of Stanley Ann Dunham, Barack Obama's mother. She attended Mercer Island High School in Washington. (Mercer Island High School)
Courtesy Chicago Tribune

We may call these criticisms the flaws of Barack Obama as some people, mostly his opponents, see it. Some of the criticisms levied on Obama are: Obama is a Muslim, Obama has criminal associations, Obama used drug, Obama is elitist, Obama is a gaffe machine, Obama has no experience, Obama is liberal and now tending toward the center, Obama is a flip-flopper, the press favors Obama, Obama is misinterpreting the Bible, and Obama is weak on security.

The Muslim Thing and the African Attire

Call your attention to the New Yorker Magazine's back cover, which portrayed Barack Obama and Michelle, his wife, as terrorists. They claimed the drawing was just a show or some satire. Definitely, it was and still is ridiculous. The New Yorker magazine, representing American conservatives, knows very well the implication of what they have done. For donkey years, the black man and the black race have been dubbed all kinds of things that it is hard to even remember any positive thing to associate with the race in America. Thanks to years of racism and the negative labels. Now the nation happens to have a humble and a smart black person running for the top office of the land and the New Yorker magazine and too many static conservatives like Dr. Jerome Corsi, who are averse to such a dramatic change, cannot stand it. Some do not really want to stand it at all, regardless of how many times they know that such a change would beautify America tremendously in the sight of God.

Therefore, wonderful voters and the great Caucasians who have been color blind—Just do It! Do not be derailed. You should be smart to know that the negative drawing, comparing one to an Islamic terrorist and burning the American flag, is not a joke at all. It is aimed to derail the movement of a wise campaign. I urge you in the name of the Lord Jesus to gather the courage and elect this man Barrack as the President of the United States. It will be overwhelmingly beneficial to America and to everybody. It's a lifesaver in-deed; it will bear great fruits for America both in the short and the long-run. Do not be scared or be deceived by the people who cannot stand serious change, love, and the invention of super-blessed USA. Many of them know the benefits, but it is too hard for them to adjust for this great invention. You, the bold voters, must do it for them. They will love it at last.

Wise American voters must know that these fiatrics by poople like Dr. Corsi (in the Obama Nation) and the negative advertisements are designed to scare them; they can never save the econmy, rebuild America's political system, heal internal social relations problems, and provide food on their tables of the working class Americans. For years, the Republicans have employed negative tactics like these in winning elections. Not this time! That is the GOP style-attack and the so-called 'swift boating' in process. It is upsetting, potentially hateful, and divisive? Actually, the New Yorker picture and Dr. Corsi's book may have contributed to derailing Senator McCain's campaign. I responded in one of the blogs concerning the New Yorker satire artwork:

> This job by the GOP and the New Yorker Magazine has helped derail McCain campaign. McCain will lose the November election. The people driving GOP need to embrace love (JESUS) and still be tough on planting and nurturing righteousness in the nation. Then God will buy it. You cannot serve God and the devil at the same time.
>
> I am more of a GOP than of any party. I am not a Democrat. I am disappointed that a party that I can call mine is doing this. I must say that the so-called Christians in the Republican Party better rise up and be speaking against evils like this drawing which take away discussions from issues and then guzzle votes by fear, producing leaders that keep leading America into the ditch, without God's backing. The so-called Christian conservatives are keeping quiet again, yet they continue to wonder why the younger Christians are frustrated. Hate-mongering, excessive dislike, cheating and Jesus do not mix. True love and Jesus work together.
>
> When shall the GOP have faith enough to just hold on to GOD alone and win an election fairly and squarely so God can help America again? I say this because people like me and majority of Christians tend to see GOP as the alternative party for serious Christians. GOP is driving away real Christians by this type of divisiveness and insults on people and the nation. This is not politics. This is excessive-dislike mongering, lying, or cheating. McCain is a good man. However, I'm afraid that his campaign is derailed!

In a certain town, a white woman found her Obama signs painted with human feces even though the signs were stationed in her property. One may hypothesize that the type of folks who did such a mess to the signs may have something to do with the divisive picture on the New Yorker magazine. I am a serious Christian conservative, and the magazine is not speaking for me.

Obama is not a Muslim. He is a Christian. He was a member of Trinity United Church of Christ, a predominantly black congregation within a predominantly white denomination. Rev. Jeremiah Wright pastored the church for all the 20 or so years that Barack and his family were members. A white clergyman is the head of The Trinity Church of Christ denomination. Obama really got some serious breaks with the Reverend Wright's controversial sermon, which caused the nation to focus on Obama's 'Christian' church not Muslim church. Largely, the church, which is really a Christian church, helped bury the internet lies that Obama was a Muslim.

Dear fellows: what I have learned in America is that any lie can be told against a candidate by his or her opponent just to win votes. I also learned that the Clintons could indeed do anything in order to win. They are just as vicious as the Republicans. In fact, I tend to believe that they actually withheld some armor against Obama just because he is a fellow Democrat or that the party will not like excessive dirt. I strongly believe that the Clinton campaign, a supporter of the Clinton candidacy, or the old GOP put the smear rumors in the internet in an effort to derail Obama's campaign. Throughout the primary, the Obama campaign was fighting against heavy duty, master politicians:

- Hillary Rodham Clinton. Somebody said, "When Hillary speaks, men listen." I personally like her because of her ability to endure the impacts of her husband's infidelity.
- William Jefferson Clinton known as Bill Clinton, husband to Hillary. Has been known to be ruthless in campaigns and did certainly pull off some serious negative attacks, including the race-card deal against Obama.
- Chelsea Clinton, the Clinton's daughter and only child. She stumped everywhere for her mother. She did a very nice job. I hope she doesn't learn the bad tricks. The parents are grooming her for something. We know that.
- The GOP: I know for sure that the conservatives and GOP pundits did everything they can to get Hillary to win—ranging from lies in the internet and the blogs against Obama to Rush Limbaugh actually using his radio show to get Republicans to switch parties temporarily and vote for Hillary Clinton. This man and his *Operation Chaos*, as he called it, actually caused Barack to lose the state of Indiana narrowly to Hillary Clinton. Republicans see Hillary as an easier target than Obama in the November 2008 general election against their candidate, Senator John McCain. A presidential candidate, Mrs. Clinton would have helped to inspire the uninspired conservative base who is not really enthused by McCain's GOP nomination.

What do you then expect under the above circumstances? You will expect the allegations of Muslim association and worse. When the GOP and the Clintons go against you, you are certainly in a slammer-hammer. Only a combination of a shrewd candidate and God Almighty can get out of it. The Obama campaign launched e-mail campaigns, asking people to copy and mail "The truth" to their friends and acquaintances to help stop any kind of lie against

Obama. John Kerry, who may have lost the 2004 presidential election because of the GOP's famous swift-boating lies against his military accomplishment, said, "If lies can be spread virally, let's prove to the cynics that the truth can be every bit as persuasive as it is powerful." (Stirland 2008, Wired January 24, 2008).

This is how to treat lies harshly, especially coming from America's political opponents. When one of the lies can be proven, then the rest that cannot be proven may be lies too. Look at the following lies about Obama, which may have come from racists, doubters, political opponents, or their supporters:

- One of the e-mails charges that Obama is a radical Muslim who refuses to recite the Pledge of Allegiance Obama. Wrong after verification by pundits. Go to Obama's site and watch the video where he was leading the pledge of allegiance in the senate.
- Obama is secretly a Muslim who attended a radical Islamic school in Indonesia. Wrong after verification by pundits. Check out CNN.
- Another e-mail claims that he was sworn into the Senate using a copy of the Quran. Wrong after verification by pundits. Just call the US government.
- Obama loves the Hamas and hates Israel. Wrong! Just check out his voting records and statements. In fact, he will be one of the best friends Israel ever had in the White House.

First, you need to know that the above lies have been investigated by TV stations like The CNN and other pundits and have been found to be totally untrue (Stirland 2008, Wired January 24, 2008). If you are even remotely doubtful, then go to my.barackobama.com to see the answers for yourself and to witness Obama on video, leading the Senate on the pledge of allegiance. That picture is worth more than a thousand words.

Again, why is the fear about a presidential candidate being a Muslim or not being a Muslim? Why must being Muslim and seeking the highest office in the land scare Americans? Well ask yourself the questions: Will you make your enemy or potential enemy your Commander In Chief? Will you make one of the September 11, 2001 attackers your boss? Your answer will show you how most Americans feel. Put it another way: Will Iranians, Saudi Arabians, or Syrians make a known Israeli or a staunch Christian their Commander In Chief? Most Arab Muslims hate Israel and anyone who is helping the Israelis. They also abhor a Christian being the leader of nations like Saudi Arabia, Iran, and Syria.

The average American is mightily scared 'to death' about anyone or anything associated with Islam in any manner. I strongly suggest that Muslims engage in serious marketing campaign to prove to the world or those who are fearful of Islam that the religion is not dangerous or something to be feared. This might be a very tall order given the violence that usually involves Muslims in different parts of the world almost on a daily basis. We have to find a way to live in peace without forcing anyone to be part of a religion. Serious Christians and

Muslims generally agree on strong family system and are against immodesty and sexual promiscuity. I wish we could be one in these areas without forcing anyone to switch religion. Religious allegiance should be a choice not by force. The general perception is that Islam forces people to become members or else! Christianity, on the other hand, leaves it to people's choice.

Now, what about the Kenya-African traditional attire that caused a minor uproar? Do you remember the picture of Barack Obama in a traditional Somali-African wear that the Clinton campaign released in the internet to smear Obama as being a Muslim? Hillary Clinton, President Bill Clinton, and President George W. Bush Jr. had all dressed in some foreign attire in order to relate to the people they were visiting.

Hillary and her daughter, Chelsea, were once in a truly Muslim nation and were wearing the Muslim women's attire, from head to toe. You may go to Clintonlibrary.gov to check out Hillary in Islamic attire. Does the attire make Hillary and her daughter a Muslim? The answer is 'No.' At this point, I must advise the Obama campaign to understand that part of the reason the fear exists concerning him is because Obama has not been around in the public scene as long as Hillary Clinton and John McCain have. Obama must therefore continue to talk about Jesus and his belief from pulpit to pulpit, and from one campaign stop to another until people believe him.

Wearing foreign attires is a serious form of good diplomacy in foreign lands. It helps a leader break through some cultural barriers before trying to make some type of deal with foreign cultures. In America, it is always business before pleasure. A meeting set at 8:00 o'clock must start at 8:00 o'clock; not so in places like Africa and some nonwestern cultures. At 8:00 o'clock, people may begin to arrive, and you must relax to ask questions and answer questions about your spouse, children, and relatives. You may even have to eat some good meals, do some serious charting, and some other things before you get into your business meeting. Cultural closeness precedes every other thing if you want to win favors in most foreign cultures regardless of how smart or how good your product or other diplomatic skills may be. Obama's Somali attire does not make him a Muslim. It makes him a smart diplomat.

Obama's So-Called Associations

A 46-year old man had had many reputable jobs with reputable, law-abiding organizations. In those jobs, the man had coworkers. The association the man had with those workers is now labeled as something bad. What do you think about that? I do not think there is any 46-year old person in this world who had jobs like community organizing, practicing law, teaching in a university, serving in a board of directors of a major organization, ran state senate campaigns, and ran US senate campaigns that has not come in the company of one or more former criminals, people with different political opinions, or some really bad person. If the individual is really loving and friendly, he would attract all kinds of people toward him for friendship and inspirational purposes.

Barack Obama fits the above scenario perfectly. He is the kind of person that will not turn anybody away, but at the same time, you cannot plot with him to do evil and he will help change you for the better. Smart, loving, and friendly people do not run away from people that desire their atmosphere. However, they help to improve people that come around them through life examples. Now look at the Obama's associations of interest:

1] Antoin (Tony) Rezko is a businessman from Chicago, a Middle-Eastern, who has raised funds for Obama in his senate campaigns, lived next door to Obama, and has helped Obama purchase some residential property. Rezko has also helped other Illinois political candidates in fundraising. Any money donated to Obama or raised by Rezko for Obama's presidential campaign has been donated to charity by the Obama campaign. Problem: Rezko is recently convicted on 16 of 24 counts involving mail fraud, wire fraud, money laundering and aiding and abetting bribery of public officials.

2] Mr. William Ayers is a member of the faculty at the University of Chicago. That was where Obama met him, also as a professor at the same University. Mr. Ayers had one time held a meet-the-candidate meeting for Obama in his home. Obama and Ayers served at the same time on the board of a Chicago charity organization and were co-panelists or discussants on academic panel discussions. Problem: 40 years ago Mr. William Ayers was a member of the Weather Underground, a radical group that claimed responsibility for a series of bombings, including at the Pentagon and U.S. Capitol. Obama was 6 years old then. He never saw or knew Ayers until at the University as colleagues.

3] Emil Jones Jr. is the President of the Illinois State Senate. He assisted Barack Obama to be elected to the US Senate. When Obama was a member of the Illinois state senate, Emil Jones assigned Obama to handle high-profile legislations. Problem: Washington Times claimed that Mr. Jones has been known to steer state money to favored institutions, including those that employ Mr. Jones' relatives. His relatives have gotten state jobs, and his wife's government salary jumped 60 percent after Mr. Jones became Senate president. He played important role in blocking Illinois ethics legislation (Washington Times, June 8, 2008).

4] Mr. Khalidi, a friend of Obama, is a Palestinian scholar and author on Middle Eastern affairs who has called Israel a racist state bent on creating "an apartheid system." Khalid and his wife hosted a political fundraising for Obama's 2000 Illinois senate race. While Obama served on Wood's Fund Charity board, the charity gave some donation to the Arab-American Action Network run by Mrs. Khalid. Mr. Khalid likes Obama's compassion to the Palestinians and his willingness to hold talks with the President of Iran.

5] The Reverend Jeremiah Wright and Father Michael Pfleger, the clergies in Obama's life. Rev. Wright was Obama's pastor for over 20 years. He preached one or more sermons accusing the United States of causing September 11, 2001, ruling by racism, and killing blacks with aids. Father Pfleger, the white pastor of a mostly black Catholic parish in Chicago, has been protesting against gun shops. Mr. Obama has referred to Pfleger as a spiritual adviser. Pfleger had visited the Trinity United Church of Christ and preached a sermon that mocked Senator Hillary Clinton's refusal to cede the Democratic primary contest to Barack Obama.

Considering the fact that Obama is running against the GOP, this looks tough. This association is what happened when you are overly friendly and loving like Barack Obama. He is the kind of fellow that will welcome all people who are rejected by everyone else. That's what love and compassion do to a person. I can tell you that Obama's association with these people are for good and not for evil as his opponents will want you to believe. I know myself for instance. I am always attracted to people that are rejected, sometimes the worst kinds of people. How can they be helped if everyone runs away from them?

I believe Barack Obama's friendly and inspirational nature and his desire to know and associate with people of any culture are characteristics that bring numerous people to him as friends. He is not rude to turn anyone away unless current unethical act warrants it. He is not the kind that likes to remember the evils that one did. He is the kind that forgives and looks to the future. The good thing about Barack is that although he has this association with all people, he cannot be deceived in serious matters. He will be methodical. Being generally friendly is what happens when you have the United Nations' spirit in you. Barack will be fair to all, without ulterior motive. He will be a perfect mediator of peace. Remember how cautiously and lovingly he handled the Jeremiah Wright's issue. That's how much love he has for people in general. He does not shove you under the bus unless it is critically necessary.

On the part of Obama's accusation concerning Jeremiah Wright, Ronald Kessler wonders why Barack continues to go to the "racist church" if he rejects the Rev. Wright's warped view of America. He wrote:

> Imagine if Mitt Romney's church proclaimed on its website that it is "unashamedly white." The media would pounce, and Romney's presidential candidacy would be over. Yet that is exactly what Barack Obama's church says on its web site — except in reverse. "We are a congregation which is

> unashamedly black and unapologetically Christian," says the Trinity United Church of Christ's website in Chicago. "We are an African people and remain true to our native land, the mother continent, the cradle of civilization." That's just the beginning. The church has a "non-negotiable commitment to Africa," according to its website, and its pastor, the Rev. Jeremiah A. Wright, Jr. subscribes to what is called the Black Value System.
>
> While the Black Value System includes such items as commitment to God, education, and self-discipline, it refers to "our racist competitive society" and includes the disavowal of the pursuit of "middle-classness" and a pledge of allegiance to "all black leadership who espouses and embraces the Black Value System." It defines "middle-classness" as a way for American society to "snare" blacks rather than "killing them off directly" or "placing them in concentration camps," just as the country structures "an economic environment that induces captive youth to fill the jails and prisons."
>
> In sermons and interviews, Dr. Wright has equated Zionism with racism and Israel with South Africa under its previous policy of apartheid. On the Sunday after 9/11, Wright said the attacks were a consequence of violent American policies. Four years later, Wright suggested that the attacks were retribution for America's racism. "In the 21st century, white America got a wake-up call after 9/11/01," Wright wrote in a church-affiliated magazine. "White America and the western world came to realize that people of color had not gone away, faded into the woodwork or just 'disappeared' as the Great White West kept on its merry way of ignoring black concerns."
>
> In one of his sermons, Wright said, "Racism is how this country was founded and how this country is still run!...We [in the U.S.] believe in white supremacy and black inferiority and believe it more than we believe in God." As for Israel, "The Israelis have illegally occupied Palestinian territories for over 40 years now," Wright has said. "Divestment has now hit the table again as a strategy to wake the business community and wake up Americans concerning the injustice and the racism under which the Palestinians have lived because of Zionism." (Kessler 2008, Newsmax.com).

In addition to the above Wright's statements, the Reverend has also been quoted as saying, "America invented AIDS virus for use in killing blacks," "God damn America," etc. Now you can see how tough this is. That is what happened to people like Wright after one has suffered deep oppression and being ignored for too many years. Does Rev. Wright love America? My answer is categorically YES! Does he love Israel? My answer is categorically YES! Why is he then vomiting the above statements? Once again, that's what happened when one has so much love for a nation, for himself, for where he came from, but has been oppressed and suppressed for what may seem as countless number of years. That's what happened after one has so much love for a nation, for himself, for where he came from, but has witnessed his race oppressed, suppressed, and losing their African heritage for what may seem as countless number of years.

Look beyond those statements and notice that the man is literally crying for black people and for all those he think are oppressed in any manner. Are some of the statements wrong and gross—may be yes! It may be important to interview him and let him explain a lot more. However, it is important that you see a very angry man in Rev. Wright. Many blacks are deeply angry and always in sorrowful tears, especially the concerned leaders like Rev. Wright. Seriously, concerned leaders can be carried away in mental anguish that they come to a point of saying anything out of total frustration. Any white person who may humble himself or herself and empathize with the black situation over the years will actually have his or her head over-filled. One may be so overwhelmed that the only way to get out of the grief might just be to yell out and cry to God.

Black people have been hated and humiliated for a very long time that too many of them have regressed, are still regressing, and some of them are crying out for justice as they near their graves. Once again, why do you think that so many black people are crying joyfully at the current opportunity of Barack Obama of becoming the first black president of the United States, a chance afforded him by many, loving white voters? Many blacks cannot comprehend that these white people are actually voting for the black Barack and thus for them. Voting for Barack is a form of legitimization of them (the black race) as human beings and citizens of the United States. You will see that the countenance and words of people like Rev. Wright will change for the better with the election of Barack Obama.

Jeremiah Wright is not selfish. He is not hateful. He is hurting. He is crying out for his people. There are many of them like that. Just slip into select black churches on Sundays. It is usually a time to comfort the oppressed. The only problem is that many of them, because of the polarization of past sufferings and the lingering of hate that still exists, fail to see that things are getting better. You will see that all of them will line up behind President Barack Obama who will now lead them into the new era of loving white people, cherishing white people, and stopping the second-guessing of white people.

If you are a white person, please stop criticizing people like Rev. Jeremiah Wright too much. See if you can approach them and do your best to love them, hug them, and pat their chests. They are very loving people, but they are hurting very badly for the oppressed everywhere because they know the meaning of oppression very much. The average white person will not understand the meaning of "*Unashamedly Black* and *Unapolo-getically Christian*." Mitt Romney does not have to say "Unashamedly white and unapologetically Christian." That will be very foolish and psychotically troublesome. This is why. Mitt Romney is white and he is of the white majority race. He is fully accepted by everybody. He has never gone through series of degradation and years of oppression, suppression, beatings, humiliation, and being taunted as less-than-human. His race has never been killed, mutilated, and hung on the trees. He has never been bullied, directly and indirectly, with all kinds of means into seeing his ancestral continent or nation as something more like monkeys' domain and less than human hemisphere.

Therefore, Mr. Ronald Kessler and people like him may need to look a little better before they jump. Few strong-hearted and oppressed people might get their heads out of the raging rivers of oppression and demolition. However, most usually don't. People like Rev. Wright ends up being born or made because of it. Rev. Wright's church and similar ones are actually God's Therapeutic Hospitals for many black people in search of identity, who are ashamed of their original continent of Africa, who are ashamed of their color, and who are ashamed of their wonderful values as black people. Do you know how much crime is being caused just because someone does not know his identity, a perfect source of poor self-esteem? An Italian American has no problem being proud of his color, proud of being of Italian origin, and proud to be an American. So are other nationalities in the USA except the black race. Those people of other nationalities have not been bulldozed, squashed, and psychologically maimed by the majority race as black people have. Some black people in America may be proud to be American, but are not proud to be black or to be of African descent, hence the motto, "*Unashamedly African*."

My dear wonderful white folks, Can you see the prognosis now? I hope you do. You must help to build up the dignity of black people again. Guess what. You are already doing it. Pat yourself on the back and do not be deterred to continue until the end. You are doing 'good' for God not for man. Rewards come from God only. Golden rule is God's natural law. If anyone follows it closely, that person cannot help but to be blessed in many ways without any sorrow attached to it both here and hereafter. For as long as they are part of the USA system, hurting black people is hurting oneself. We are all interdependent, part of the same body, and should be working toward the same goal—together as a family—The Untied States of America.

Is Obama Elitist?

Elitism is a belief in the rule of or domination by intellectuals or those who are full of knowledge. Is Obama elitist? No! The man is the most down-to-earth among those who accuse him of being elitist. In fact, even those accusers know that he is not. They have to say what they have to say in order to win votes and deny the working class the chance to elect the friend that the working class can ever ask for today—Barack Obama. Is the man well educated? Yes! Unfortunately, most people who claim to be educated are not smart at all. In other words, they may be partially educated in one part of their heads, but the rest of their heads and their hearts need a serious hyssop and water of education. *Half education is a disease*. Most people who claim to be leaders in most parts of the world and even in the United States are half-educated. It's like eating food that is half-cooked. It will make you sick. Millions of people and citizens of many nations are sick today because they are being led by half-educated folks like Robert Mugabe in Zimbabwe and many others in our midst.

What is your education if you don't have love? Love is the application of education. If one is fully educated, one will love to love others, all people. One will be forced to work in such ways that will get the less fortunate to be at least as fortunate as he or she is. That's Barack Obama. He believes in people not elitism. The poor and the working class better not get cheated this time!

The Experience Thing

By now, you must have learned that incumbency without fruit or beef is worse than a new recruit's resume. Many people spend years in a position but what they have to show for it are years of unethical behavior, years of lame-dock exercises, years of backwardness instead of forwardness, years of nothing worth of having experience in. So when someone talks about experience, just look closely to see if he is talking about experience in good or experience in evil. As Al Gore, the former Vice president of the United States said in endorsing Obama:

> He said Republican candidate John McCain deserves respect for all he has done for this country and for his willingness to debate his party on climate change and other critical issues. But he said the 71-year-old McCain's "age and experience" aren't the same as Obama's judgment, noting the Democrat's early opposition to the Iraq war. He said Republicans criticized President Kennedy for being too young and inexperienced to be president as well, but Kennedy noted that Thomas Jefferson, George Washington and Christopher Columbus all accomplished great things before they reached their mid-40s. (Pickler 2008).

Some American Presidents who were supposed to have had so-called extended experience before they were elected ended up messing up. Experience is not the IT. The IT is the worth of the experience. Experience backed by worthless judgments spells disaster. Let the way that the candidates ran their campaigns so far show you what experience and judgment are worth. If I have to assign grades among campaign management of Hillary Clinton, John McCain, and Barack Obama, the scores will be 50 percent, 57 percent, and 98 percent, respectively.

Hillary Clinton, with all advantages of money, fame, and people to her side, messed up her primary campaign with poor planning, organizing, staffing, directing, and controlling. It was a campaign of problems, crises, and mismanagement. John McCain is not actually managing his campaign; it is more like chance outcomes. That's a very dangerous approach to management. He leads his campaign with an atmosphere of confusion and a wave of non-clarity of goals and objectives and non-clarity of strategy. This is super dangerous to have someone like that as the President and CEO of the United States of America. Some people think that Bush messed things up, which I beg to differ because the good man actually worked hard to hold America together, following the worst terrorist killings of September 11, 2001 in the nation. He should hold his head high. However, if you dare think that Bush is bad, McCain will be much, much worse because of his huge inadequacy in management.

What can we say about Obama's management approach? We have said enough. The man is more than experienced to be the President and CEO of USA. If President Lincoln can do it as good as he did, then Obama will do even better. Obama has more experience or exactly the same experience as Lincoln and both of them have love for the common people.

Is Obama Flip-Flopping?

He is really not. The man is actually being who he is. I mean he is a man that follows reason. He sees other's points of views, weigh them with whatever he used to believe, and may or may not change his mind to reflect current analysis. I have known this since the first time I took serious notice of Obama. I knew that he is not a 100-percent bible-believing Christian; but I know that if one engages him in a conversation and makes a serious argument that strikes down his own reasoning, he will make a change. That's being a man. He is not a flip-flopper. It would have been better for King Harod to rescind his promise to his stepdaughter than beheading an innocent man (John the Baptist) in order to please the girl, her mother, and to keep his word to the masses. He had promised the lad whatever she asked even to the half of his kingdom if the girl danced for him. Harod would have reasoned, swallowed his pride, and chose the right decision at the time, which was not to murder an innocent man. (Read the Holy Bible Matthew 14:1-10).

The Democratic Party is often referred to as being too soft, too emotional, and excessively compassionate to the point of being wickedly too liberal. I certainly agree with some of these criticisms, for the party has written and supported some of the worst laws that are wrecking American marriages and families today. Referring to what the DEMS used to be and wondering whether Obama is a flip flopper or just a tough fellow, Charles Hurt wrote:

> THE Democratic Party has long been mocked as the Mommy Party for its soft, nurturing, governing style and its paralyzing patience for listening to dissent from every quarter, no matter how small or irrelevant. The Republican Party is the Daddy Party - always tough, determined and willing to do whatever dirty work is necessary to get the job done. Democrats want Oprah Winfrey. Republicans want Jack Bauer. But now that Barack Obama has taken over the Democratic Party, he's bending these "genderizations." He's taking Mommy out of the Mommy Party. Now, it's the party that strides past a female reporter and calls her "sweetie" to dismiss her silly little question. And if you're wondering who's in charge, don't. Within days of winning the nomination, Obama moved party headquarters to his home town of Chicago and started pushing party heads around, telling them they can't raise money from PACs and Washington lobbyists. Yet when it comes to raising his own money, he tossed overboard his campaign promises to participate in the public financing system so he can maintain his massive cash advantage over the Republicans. And in the ultimate display of testosterone, Obama unsheathed a

> new campaign emblem that looked remarkably like the presidential seal. He has since dropped it. (New York Post, June 27, 2008).

The article indicated a possible lamentation by GOP that this Obama is now moving toward the center from arguably being the pentagon's most liberal senator. The author wondered if the Democrats are now the party of states' rights, gun rights and the death penalty. These questions are rising because Barack condemned the recent Supreme Court decisions against death penalty for raping a child and did not really condemn the court's decision for gun rights. If one closely looks at Obama's argument for decisions on each of the issues, including his change-of-mind against using public financing for his national campaign, you may tend to agree with him. After seeing the relatively poor fund-raising efforts of the Democratic party, understanding that the republicans can do just about anything (including getting money from anywhere) to pursue a win, and knowing that he cannot trust Senator John McCain to stop the GOP's independent supporters from spending huge cash on throwing negative TV ads against him, Obama made a good choice. At least there is a possibility that he would raise more money from over 1.7 million electrified and mostly low-income supporters.

Let me tell you this. The little people who are supporting Obama actually enjoy giving the money and may have been disappointed had Obama decided to take the public funding. A better choice would have been to take the public funding ($85 billion) and educate his donors to give to the Democratic National Committee if the DNC will agree for Obama to exercise full influence on the way the money will be spent without violating any law. My take was that the campaign had weighed the contingencies surrounding all options and chose to abandon the public financing system.

What about the gun rights? It is good for people to have guns for hunting and for some other rightful purposes; it is good for such ownership of guns to be carefully regulated or monitored by the government. Many people have used and are still using their guns to commit murders. Obama is right in his thoughts concerning gun ownership. Nevertheless, I must "scold" Senator Barack Obama to really get serious and spend a lot of time arguing and passing laws that favor traditional marriage and strong family system, which produce strong and well-raised children and adults who do not have to misuse guns. I strongly urge the Senator to take a serious look at Figure 1: *A General Model of Societal Building and Destruction*. The model shows American society in a glance. Is the figure right or wrong? I will be happy to join the Senator and the next president in discussing the model. It is the state of today's America. Once America's God is cut off, the rest goes haywire.

Obama and the Press

I agree with the writer on *Slate* which argued that the press is not in the tank with Obama (Shafer 2008). He proved that the press actually exposed all that needs to be exposed and Hillary Clinton threw knives, kitchen sink, and every other armour, but they just do not stick on Obama. He creditied the Senator for the way he portrayed or positioned himself from the beginning and it is hard to change that perception of or positioning of the candidate Obama within the electorate. Jack Scheafer wrote:

> Obama's poise and discipline allow him to resist whatever bait the press and politicians dangle in front of him. When he does address scandalous material, he generally does so to his advantage. In June, when the Web and cable news advanced false rumors that Michelle Obama had called white people "whitey" on a videotape, Obama squelched the gossip with a denial and, as Ben Smith of Politico reported, put the press on notice by questioning the appropriateness of the question. Smears undermine a politician only when they appeal to voters' pre-existing idea of what sort of person a politician is. Seeing as the pre-existing idea of Obama is so positive, the Obama-haters have had trouble portraying him either as a literal bomb thrower, like William Ayers, or a figurative one, like the Rev. Wright. When the smear artists dress him up as a radical or as "madrassa"-educated, the ploys only backfire. (Shafer 2008).

In a Good *Morning America* interview of George Stephanopoulos by Diane Sawyer, Diane wondered if the media was generally easier on Senator Obama than they were on Senator Hillary Clinton. After playing a clip of a *Saturday Night Live* sketch that mocked reporters for jollying with Senator Barack Obama, Stephanopoulos responded, "I do think, though, Senator Clinton has a point. She's being treated like the front-runner, even though she's still is, as Jake pointed out, she's the underdog in this race right now." (Whitlock 2008, NewsBurster). Now look at the counter punch of a serious blogger to my distant friend, Stephanopoulos:

> "I *do think, though, Senator Clinton has a point. She's being treated like the front-runner, even though she's still is, as Jake pointed out, she's the underdog in this race right now.*"
>
> Simply delusional, Stephie. If she's being treated like the front runner, it's only because she's acting like she's entitled to be the front runner. She is routinely getting her a** handed to her in primaries, caucuses and debates, her campaign is self-destructing and they're being exposed not just for being nasty and dishonest, but also for being incompetent. A non-complicit media would not have indulged any other campaign in this state of disrepair. You would think that the Clintonoids would learn not to repeatedly hang themselves with the endless supply of rope the media has provided them. Unfortunately, for them, they're simply not that smart. McCain's only hope is if this Clintonoid circus somehow manages to steal the nomination in Denver...she's damaged goods. (February 27, 2008 - 14:46 ET by fitzfong).

> *Would they still be seriously discussing his candidacy or would the race be dismissed as over? One could argue that jour-nalists have kept Clinton in the race.*

Interesting point, Scott. And you're not the only one who's brought that notion up...MoDo dangled the same theory out there in her column today. (February 27, 2008 - 14:46 ET by fitzfong).

Is the press lenient to Obama? May be or may be not. This blogger is serious, and I know I admire my friend, George. I think I support both of them to some extent. I will say that the press looks for what will make news and what people are mostly interested in now. The press consists of bunch of business people too. There is so much inspiration coming from Barack Obama, surrounding Obama, and infecting everybody, and the press simply does not wish to quench it. If Hillary were Obama, the press would have done the same for her too. If McCain were Obama, the press will also treat him likewise.

Obama's trip overseas was joined by the three anchorpersons of America's major TV stations, but they didn't do the same during Senator McCain's. Whose fault? It's not the press. It is the strategy and the level of excitement that the campaigns draw. Barack Obama's invention is drawing huge, huge crowds everywhere and people are extremely interested in seeing him and hearing what he has to say. Besides, he is new. Part of the reason is what Rush Limbaugh said:

> "My prediction is that the coverage of Obama on this trip will be oriented toward countering the notion he has no idea what he is talking about on foreign policy and defense issues...McCain, on the other hand, is a known quantity on these issues and his position does not excite nor fit the mainstream media's narrative on Iraq and Afghanistan, so they simply ignore it and him." (Bauder, David July 10, 2008).

The press is a business entity. Either you report on what people want to see or hear, or you are alone with an empty purse, poor rating, and weak advertising dollars. Obama is lively. He is providing a breathing atmosphere from what the press, young people, and bunch of other people in today's USA is seeing as a troubled situation in America and President George W. Bush's policies. After looking at the other candidates, it looks as if the press and the rest of the people do not want to mess up a gift to solving America's problems or even a chance to electing the first black American President.

Electing first black president is a seriously new invention in America. Many whites are excited and many whites, especially in the southern USA, are under great test. New invention attracts news. Furthermore, when the new invention is also smart in policies and new approaches to solving problems, it certainly draws crowds. Americans are so frustrated with the current state of things in America that both the press and the people are against anyone that looks more like Bush third term. Hillary Clinton is clearly seen as divisive and more of the same than Obama. McCain is seen as not as smart as Barack Obama in handling the affairs of the country; the perception is that he would be continuing Bush third term instead of something new.

The press will certainly pounce on Obama if the press has good reason to do so. The press pounced on him on Jeremiah Wright and on the small-town gaffe. People wanted to hear those. The only blame for the press not continuing with Obama long enough on these criticisms can be traced to Obama's opponents who seemed to produce more drama than Obama. By the time Obama's trouble is lasting for about a week or so, the opponent (Hillary Clinton or John McCain) seemed to get into one trouble or the other, causing the press to forget about Obama's problem and to rush after the more current and sometimes more serious one. Recall that as Rev. Wright's issue was hitting up, Hillary came up with the repeated lies about the sniper fire in Bosnia. The TV footage of what really happened dampened the Wright's issue. The oratorical skill and the excellent race-speech by Obama added salt to the injured Hillary while helping to dampen further the Wright's ravager.

Therefore, someone ought to give credit to Barack Obama on his handling of the press. The press likes something good. The innovative management of his campaign and his rhetoric on issues make the press and many people feel good about things. He became the favorite candidate for the people and the press. A political candidate has to find a way to deal with the press to his or her advantage. Doing things right and innovatively can win the favor of the press. Furthermore, the press is human and can be inspired too. The press is part of the United States of America. America has suffered for a long time and a new face found in Obama, and backed by some serious substance, is making people listen, including the press.

People love to read and buy something associated with Obama. What do you then want the press to do? Remember, the press is in business too. In order for them to sell, the press, just like other businesses, will give the people what the people want. Think about it. Tangible products like T-shirts, books, cups, and others associated with Obama produce millions of dollars for vendors while those of competitors produce thousands, hundreds or less. Which candidate will you prefer as a business partner--one that will make you millions or one that will make you few dollars? No one wants to be poor. The right choice is Barack Obama.

The key is to position your argument and sell your product as the best to solve the problems the people have. If majority of the people and members of the press buy it, you may get some favors. What you are selling, the total package of your product, determines your success, not the press. The characteristics of the candidate are part of the product package. The press follows what you do or say. Obama happens to win the press to his side. The people of the press are being inspired too. They are smart, and they may be for Obama too. Is it good to be biased in news reporting? No, it's not good. Is the press biased in its reporting so far? Not really. The product and the general condition of affairs, including the sentiment of the voters, drive the press.

Who Is Right—Obama Or Dobson?

Barack Obama and James Dobson got into it few weeks ago concerning Obama's interpretation of the Bible. This is very important. Obama messed up here, and it is really frightening or annoying. I strongly wonder what he has learned at Trinity United Church of Christ if what is quoted here about him is right. Furhtermore, and as it was rumored, if the Trinity United Church of Christ is encouraging and not preaching against gay lifestyle, then I must let people know that the church may not be teaching serious Christian doctrine and it may have affected Obama's watered-down, devilish interpretation of the Bible here. According to Alexander Mooney of CNN:

> A top U.S. evangelical leader is accusing Sen. Barack Obama of deliberately distorting the Bible and taking a "fruitcake interpretation" of the U.S. Constitution. In comments aired on his radio show Tuesday, Focus on the Family founder James Dobson criticized the presumptive Democratic presidential nominee for comments he made in a June 2006 speech to the liberal Christian group *Call To Renewal*. In the speech, Obama suggested that it would be impractical to govern based solely on the word of the Bible, noting that some passages suggest slavery is permissible and eating shellfish is disgraceful. "Which passages of scripture should guide our public policy?"
>
> Obama asked in the speech. "Should we go with Leviticus, which suggests slavery is OK and that eating shellfish is an abomination? Or we could go with Deuteronomy, which suggests stoning your child if he strays from the faith? Or should we just stick to the Sermon on the Mount? "So before we get carried away, let's read our Bible now," Obama said, to cheers. "Folks haven't been reading their Bible." He also called Jesus' Sermon on the Mount "a passage that is so radical that it's doubtful that our Defense Department would survive its application."...Dobson said Obama should not be referencing antiquated dietary codes and passages from the Old Testament that are no longer relevant to the teachings of the New Testament. "I think he's deliberately distorting the traditional understanding of the Bible to fit his own world view, his own confused theology," Dobson said, adding that Obama is "dragging biblical understanding through the gutter."
>
> Responding to Dobson's comments Tuesday evening, Obama sharply disputed the suggestion he was distorting the Bible. Someone would be pretty hard pressed to make that argument," he told reporters aboard his campaign plane. "It is a speech that affirms the role of faith not just in my life but in the life of the American people, that suggests that we make a mistake by trying to push faith out of the public square." "I do make the argument that it's important for folks like me, who think faith is important, that we try to translate some of our concerns into universal language so we can have open and vigorous debate rather than having religion divide us," Obama said. "And I do suggest that the

separation of church and state is important. But there's no, no theological work being done in that speech in terms of the Bible."...

Dobson also takes aim at Obama for suggesting in the speech that those motivated by religion should attempt to appeal to broader segments of the population by not just framing their arguments around religious precepts. "Democracy demands that the religiously motivated translate their concerns into universal rather than religion-specific values," Obama said. "It requires their proposals be subject to argument and amenable to reason." Dobson said the suggestion is an attempt to lead by the "lowest common denominator of morality."

"Am I required in a democracy to conform my efforts in the political arena to his bloody notion of what is right with regard to the lives of tiny babies?" he asked. "What he's trying to say here is, unless everybody agrees, we have no right to fight for what we believe."What the senator is saying there, in essence, is that 'I can't seek to pass legislation, for example, that bans partial-birth abortion, because there are people in the culture who don't see that as a moral issue,' " Dobson said. "And if I can't get everyone to agree with me, than it is undemocratic to try to pass legislation that I find offensive to the Scripture. Now, that is a fruitcake interpretation of the Constitution." (Mooney 2008, CNN June 24).

You can tell very much that I have supported Barack Obama enthusiastically until at this point. First, let me pass the judgment about who is right and who is wrong between Obama and James Dobson, and then I will pick some statements by Obama and address them.

<u>JUDGMENT</u>: James Dobson is right and Obama is flat-out wrong! Not only that he is wrong, he may be blaspheming God or may not really be a moderate Christian as I thought he is. He is a smart fellow. If he actually made the statement below, then we must seriously ask if he is an atheist, a humanist, a bold politician, or a misguided Christian of Trinity United Church of Christ. I am trying my best to give him the benefit of a doubt. If he continues to sound as if he has really read the whole bible and then sticks with this wicked conclusion, then something is terribly wrong with him! He needs to be asked some serious questions to help determine what he really means. That is, if he continues to insist on that interpretation.

I am repeating part of the quotation above, for that is where my major problem lies. I now address Barack Obama directly. *<u>Dear Sir</u>*, it is important to be a Christian and then to understand what you are talking about. I believe you when you said that you are a Christian. However, I also believe that you are not informed Christian. If you have been attending Trinity United Church of Christ for 20 years, I must wonder whether you attended Sunday school well, whether the preachers really preached or taught the word of God right, or you may be trying to create your own version of the Bible.

> According to Obama: In the speech, Obama suggested that it would be impractical to govern based solely on the word of the Bible, noting that some passages suggest slavery is permissible and eating shellfish is disgraceful. "Which passages of scripture should guide our public policy?"
>
> Obama asked in the speech. "Should we go with Leviticus, which suggests slavery is OK and that eating shellfish is an abomination? Or we could go with Deuteronomy, which suggests stoning your child if he strays from the faith? Or should we just stick to the Sermon on the Mount? He also called Jesus' Sermon on the Mount "a passage that is so radical that it's doubtful that our Defense Department would survive its application...."

I am now assuming that you are not informed Christian. For this reason, I must beg you to stop speaking as if you understand the Holy Bible. I am also assuming that you made the statements in the above quotation. **IF** you continue to insist on the above statements and continue to enjoy the cheers and laughs from similar minded, liberal Christians, then it is important that we need to know who you are and where you really stand. You must not use the word of God to play games unless you have a very different agenda that we do not know about, hence Rev. Dobson's fear that you are watering the gospel to fit your level. Whatever it is, and for the mere fact that millions of loving people have dedicated themselves to support you, you will be caught in God's net and you will be caught very well if you do not stop watering down God's word or knowingly twisting it.

Number one, I wonder what you mean by, *"So before we get carried away, let's read our Bible no; Folks haven't been reading their Bible."* Somewhere in the middle of that, you enjoyed the cheers and laughs, actually messing up yourself before God. Are you telling them to read their Bible so they can see that what you are saying is right or so they can see that the Bible is wrong and should be abandoned based on your interpretation? I think you need to offer some serious explanation here otherwise, you must agree that you are not a serious Christ at all and must quit lecturing on the word of God. If you throw away the Holy Bible, you throw away Christianity.

You said that Jesus Sermon on the Mount is "a passage that is so radical that it's doubtful our Defense Department would survive its application." Now, is the Defense Department a yardstick or benchmark upon which righteousness can be based? Does Jesus have to check with the Defense Department before He says what is righteous and what is evil? Sir, can you see the kind of religion or "No Religion at all" that you are spreading? If you do not repent from this statement or at least make it clear that you may not have a complete understanding of the scriptures, then the office of USA presidency, if you get it, might be a thorn in your flesh instead of a blessing if this is what you can use your podium to do.

Sir, do you know what you have really done? You are calling Jesus a liar or that He is telling us to do something that can't be done. Sir, the fact that you cannot handle it does not mean that someone else who trusts and gives himself or herself wholly to Him cannot do it. The fact that you cannot discipline your flesh and do it does not mean that some others cannot do it. You cannot be fornicating, saying demonic things, associa-ting with evil lifestyle, and doing as you like and expect God to function perfectly in your life or even function at all! Brother, God does not play games with His word. He is DEADLY and LOVINGLY serious!

I remember when I was relatively very holy, fasting, praying, and living right as Jesus Christ told us to do, according to the Holy Bible. I was so pure that God can show me what would happen before it happened, whatever I was interested in. I had so much confidence that I even told some of my friends that nothing evil would happen to them without God first showing it to me. Guess what. When God showed any of such things to me, I prayed and cancelled it. Then came a time in about 1994 (I forgot the exact year) when a wonderful lady of our church, Mrs. Lisa Russell of Port Gibson, Mississippi, died without God showing me before it happened. I was sad and disappointed with my God. I questioned Him.

Listen carefully now. About one month before that woman died, I had humbly called my wife and told her, "*Nne Nne, whatever you see in a dream or vision within 30 days, let me know immediately. Our house is holy and something is about to happen.*" On this quiet and gloomy morning, I received a call from a lady in Port Gibson telling me that Lisa Russell was killed by an 18-wheeler (semi-truck) in front of her house on Highway 61. I was uncharacteristically very quiet, saying nothing. After checking myself and discovered that God showed me nothing, I asked the lady, "Did God show any of you anything concerning her death? Did God talk to the Pastor in any manner?" She said "No," for she may have already talked to Pastor Randy. That was when I became very sad and annoyed toward my God.

My wife, who was sitting about 7 feet away from me, feeding one of our babies or giving her a bath, asked me what was wrong. She saw my grief, standing motionless with the phone on my ear, the other lady crying, and I was saying nothing, just angry and dismayed! I told her what happened. "Lisa died." Suddenly she said to me, "*Nnaa, about thirty days ago I saw in a dream where 18-wheeler killed Mrs. Lisa Russell. So I later called her on the phone and asked her 'Is everything OK?' and she said that everything is OK.*" Do you know what I did after she told me that? I was a very happy man. I mean I was happy, thanking my God for not letting me down. After that, I turned to my wife and asked her, "Why didn't you tell me, for I seriously told you to let me know of anything you see within 30 days." She said that she called Lisa and she replied that everything was OK. That's the problem…

God did not disappoint me at all. My wife did. She disappointed me heavily! She did not do what I said for her to do. The devil killed Lisa, the wonderful woman. I was forever sure that I would have prayed and stopped the mishap. I called my pastor and the lady who contacted me and let them know that God did not disappoint me. I was happy. There is nothing to dying. What I care about is God and I enjoying talks.

Dear Barack Obama, there are many examples that I can give you. In fact, since you may be too intellectually inclined, with little clue about the Holy Bible, let me tell you five more events which I will title: Mosella Carpent—No Heart Attack, God of Dr. Osag, God of Fayette-MS, God of Port Gibson Building, and General Sani Abacha of Nigeria.

Mosella Carpent—No Heart Attack

I forgot the year, but it may be about 1996. I was a resident at the campus of Alcorn State University. I received a call from Port Gibson that Mossella Carpent suffered a heart attack and was carried to the University Medical Center, Jackson, Mississippi. I learned about this after the old lady (about 68 years old) had been in the hospital for about 7 days. I was highly grieved. I immediately called my wife and my little children for about a 75-mile drive to Jackson. My unspoken intention was to undo the heart attack.

We got to Jackson and I told my wife that we better go to Wal-mart and buy Mossella some flowers because Americans love flowers. We stopped at Wal-Mart on Ellis. We picked some flower basket and happily matched to the checkout counter. I brought my check to pay for the cashier and discovered there was no unused stub in my checkbook and my wife had no money. Suddenly the Lord God spoke to me right there at the checkout counter, "Son, forget the flower. As soon as your feet get into the hospital, darkness will flee and Mrs. Mossella Carpent will no longer have heart attack." This is exactly what God told me. I told my wife quietly that we should forget the flower; I also let her know what God said. When we stepped outside, my wife told me that God just gave her John 1:1-5. I did not know what was in there. I consume the Bible, but I am not good at quickly locating chapter and verse of particular scriptures. I just know what is in the Bible. Well, she opened John 1:1-5 and read to me:

> In the beginning was the Word, and the Word was with God, and the Word was God. He was in the beginning with God. All things were made through Him, and without Him nothing was made that were made. 4-5: In Him was life, and the life was the light of men. And the light shines in darkness, and the darkness did not comprehend it. (Holy Bible, John 1:1-5).

Do you see what I saw? I was amazed and in total jubilation. I quickly explained to my family what just happened—a perfect confirm-ation of what God told me inside Wal-Mart by the cashier. My wife's main citation was really verses 4 to 5, telling us that we are light (Jesus Juniors) and as soon as you match into the hospital, darkness will run away, light will take over, and Mrs. Mossella Carpent would no longer have heart attack. In other words—whatever the doctors saw about heart attack, the doctors would not see again, as if it never happened.

By now, I was bragging and matching like a soldier toward the entrance into the University Medical Center. I usually make my tiny children match too. We got into Mosella Carpent's room and sat down. After we greeted, I quickly told Mosella Carpent, "You had no heart attack." She replied, "No, I had a heart attack." I said again, "You had no heart attack." She replied again, "No, I had a heart attack. The doctors took X-ray and confirmed it." I said again, "You had no heart attack. Mrs. Carpent." She would have taught I was a little crazy if she did not know that I could be like that sometimes because I kept telling her she did not have any heart attack. We stayed about an hour. Just when we were about to stand up and leave, some doctor came in with bunch of X-rays they had taken over the week. The doctor had no clue what Mossella and I had been arguing about. He declared, "Mrs. Carpent, you have no heart attack." Now, think about that! That was and still is my *USUAL* Man, JESUS! Do not forget to meditate on John 1:1-3. It will help you understand the whole Bible. Feel free to call me for explanation. I will be much obliged to do it as if my life depends on it.

God of Dr. Osag

It happened one winter season. Again, I forgot the year. It may be 1995. During this time my wife and I were on a 21-day fasting and praying. I just finished teaching my 5:30 p.m. Strategic Management class and was in my Toyota Van, getting ready to go home (back to Port Gibson, MS) at about 8:30 p.m. I had relocated from Alcorn State University Campus to a nearby town, Port Gibson, where I had a building, which I bought from Mrs. Mosella Carpent. As I was making a U-turn to head for Port Gibson, God spoke to me, "Son, go to that house and asked them what they want." I reversed my Van and headed straight for the house of my colleague, Dr. Osag. I asked Mrs. Osag, "What do you want?" She said, "I want children." Then I asked the husband, "Dr. Osag, what do you want?" He said, "Brother Festus, I want children like you have children."

Then I said, "Let's kneel down." They knelt down. As the man was kneeling down, he confessed something very serious to me, which I had already suspected. I cannot state it here; it is too personal. [At this juncture, I must say that as someone is about to pray for you and you have a confession, go ahead and make that confession]. Now guess what happened. As I was about to kneel down, white smoke filled the whole house. I saw it but they did not see it. I knew beyond the shadow of a doubt that the request has been granted. I just got back up and told them to get up. Then I said to them:

> We do not need to pray. God has answered the prayer. In exactly 9 months, you will have a champion baby. In fact, Dr.

> Osag, you will be rich. … (God showed me other serious things that I told the man which I could not state here).

What do you think happened? Nine months "is" nine months. On the next day, about 8:00 o'clock, Mrs. Osag called my wife and told her that she was ovulating. The same egg that showed up was fertilized the same month. Mrs. Osag became pregnant after many years of searching for a baby. Glory be to God! In the middle of the pregnancy, she called me because she was having problems and scared that she might lose the baby. I told her that nothing would happen and she must have the baby at the end of nine-month pregnancy. That was all she wrote folks! In exactly nine months, Dr. and Mrs. Osag gave birth to a huge baby boy who is now my God son. They decided to add one every year. I think they have three or four now. Isn't Jesus good? YES HE IS! That's my man!

God of Fayette-MS

I also refer to this event as *God of my wife*. I never forget this date. It was the evening of July 2, 1992. God very clearly told me about three times not to go to Natchez, Mississippi to collect some pictures that I was supposed to use in my first book, *Valentine Love.* This time I was living on campus of Alcorn State University. Well, I disobeyed God, jumped into my brand new Toyota Camry, taking my daughter, Anna, with me. Anna was about 3.5 years old then. I found myself on Hwy 61 in Fayette, accel-erating at about 60 miles an hour, a little over the speed limit for that blind and hilly place.

As soon as I came up the hill, here was a little red car, stopped just in front of me, waiting to make a left turn. On the left lane was a monstrous 18-wheeler log truck coming. Remember that I was still at full speed. If I go to the right, I will plunge into a ditch. If I go forward, I will slam on the little car and its driver. I found myself automatically going to the left with this mountainous semi-truck (18-wheeler) coming upon me. With my right hand, I was holding my daughter who was sitting on the front passenger seat. With the left, I was holding the steering.

In a split second, before my Camry and the truck rammed, I thought about my poor wife and then said in my head, "God will help her." Then the next thought was "Death, heaven." The next thing was the slamming jam between my car and the truck. A second after the jam, and I was alive, God told me, "Your wife just had a dream." A middle-aged woman came to us first and the only thing in my heart was to prove to the woman that God is and to help her become strong in the Lord Jesus. All I could think about was "What dream did my wife had?" If God told me this, it must be very relevant to what just happened." I was not even thinking about the accident at all. This was just about 30 seconds after the jam, and my car was totaled.

I quickly told the woman before she got a chance to say anything to me. "Take me back to Alcorn State right now. My wife just had a dream. When we get there, do not tell her what happened. Just ask her if she had a dream right now." The ambulance came to pick my daughter and me up. I told them that we do not need an ambulance and that I was not going to give the devil any glory, for we were not hurt at all. We left the wrecked car and the gathering crowd for my residence at Alcorn State University. On our way, we stopped at Fayette Hospital and conducted check up. Nothing was wrong. My daughter and I were in perfect health.

We drove off for Alcorn State. As soon as we got to the door, the middle-aged woman knocked on the door. My wife opened the door and the woman did exactly as I told her. She asked my wife, "Mom, did you just have a dream?" My wife said, with little nervousness, "YES!" Then she started telling the dreadful dream:

> About 4:00 p.m., after my husband left for Natchez, I lay down to get a nap. In my sleep, I had a dream. I saw a huge wall very tall and very wide, separating my husband and me. I knew that it is something very bad, so I started praying and rebuking it. I said, "In the name of Jesus I destroy this wall." I cursed the wall many times by the blood of Jesus. It was scary.

Can you see that, fellows? My wife did not even know what happened yet. My dear brother, Barack Obama: First, that was a perfect confirmation of what God told me just about a millisecond after my car slammed head-on with the 18-wheeler lug-truck. I knew God was telling me something, and whatever God was saying is HUGELY IMPORTANT! The woman was astonished. She reaffirmed her faith in Jesus Christ our Lord. If my wife had not challenged that death-wall in the spirit, I would have been dead since July 2, 1992, guaranteed! Do you know what else God told me immediately after He told me that my wife just had a dream? He said, "*Live for your wife.*" That is a perfect message to me, considering my sorrows of many years concerning my poor wife then.

That's what happened when you have good connection with God. God takes care of you and carries out what you say—for as long as you stay committed to Him, not playing fake and engaging in harlotry. Barack, your half-way (or even worse than that) doesn't cut it AT ALL! Once again, I strongly warn you to stop talking about something you do not really know or fully understand unless you have a secrete agenda. The Holy Bible and God in Christ are VERY REAL! You have not really sought God the way you should. Your little education and your voice, both gifts from God, are moving your head for now. However, your upbringing is helping you to want to work to help people, and I support that. If you really want to help people the right way and BIG TIME, just get serious and hook up with J-E-S-U-S completely. I know what I am talking about. That's how to be both cool and hot at the same time! One leg in the bush and another leg on the road can never make it with God in Christ, our God. God can simply choose to use you to accomplish a particular mission of His.

God can choose and use anybody He wants. He even chooses and uses the devil a lot and still has hell cut out for him. I strongly believe that you are God's instrument of great blessing to America and the rest of the world at this time. Work to please Him!!!

God of Port Gibson Building

I bought this building from Mosella Carpent. It was a very tall, old building, on Main Street of Port Gibson, Mississippi. The only taller building was the courthouse. Everyone, including the banker, worked hard to discourage me from buying the building, for they thought it was not good for the price I was paying for it. Unfortunately for my flesh and against what those people were saying to me, I strongly felt in my heart that God wanted me to buy the building at the relatively high price. I only had $1000 in the bank at the time. I finally borrowed the money and paid Mrs. Mosella Carpent for the building, saving her from continually paying 36 percent interest on a mortgage with Tower Loan.

This occurred about 1993; I was still residing at Alcorn State University campus housing. Since I was a little boy up to now, I always have a place of prayer. It grew from a small corner in my parents' house in Nigeria to the largest room in my house now, which I call, "*The Altar*." Jesus and I have been 'buddies' for a long time. My names, *Festus Sunday AkaOlisa Oguhebe-Strongblood,* mean so much to me:

> Festus – a Latin name, meaning 'celebration,' I suppose. [Just think good of yourself]
> Sunday – I was born on Sunday. My parents just named me 'Sunday,' the Lord's Day.
> AkaOlisa – Literally translated "Hand of God" and I am. I cannot help it, and I cannot run from it.
> Oguhebe – my grandfather's name, my last name, may mean, "Struggle never ends"
> Strongblood – Following a lengthy and lock-in fasting and praying in Joel's Place of New Christian Fellowship Port Gibson, God gave me the last-last name, "Obala Jesu" meaning blood of Jesus or Strongblood.

The devil has thrown munster-duty nuclear bombs at me, but I am still standing because of faith in my God and the names He gave me. This is enough to help many people. With these names and continued relationship with my God, I am always expecting something from Him. It is impossible to catch me not expecting something good from my God, the Lord Jesus. So, when I purchased this building, which my flesh and other people may rightly refer to as "no good," I was trusting God to do something good out of it. The building was not quite habitable, and many parts of the rugged roof were leaking. When it rains, you just have to expect buckets of water in the building.

One day I was sitting in my altar, just enjoying myself. Suddenly, the Spirit of the Living God spoke to me, "Tell God to tear the roof of Port Gibson building down and Insurance will give you the money to fix the whole roof." I just could not believe it. Furthermore, I felt a little awkward doing it because I had my insurance with a very good Caucasian man who is a Minister and a serious role model to many people. How can I tell him that God and I tore down his roof? [Guess what. The picture of the man and his family was what I was going to pick up from Natchez, MS when I had the July 2, 1992 accident].

As soon as I heard the Holy Spirit tell me to do the honor, for nothing will happen until it is first prophesied (Amos 3:7), I just wanted to brag first. I called my wife and Reverend Bennie Wade, an Alcorn student that was just visiting with us for few minutes. I told them exactly what the Holy Spirit wanted me to do. We were all seated. With some good bragging voice I said, "God, I want you to tear that roof down so the Insurance Company can give me the money to fix the roof." As soon as I said that, Rev. Bennie Wade interrupted, "God please don't tear the part where I was staying." I had forgotten that I let him use the room right next to the bathroom. This made me change the prayer, which was really charting with my God. I said, "All right God, tear the roof down but do not touch the roof that is covering where Bennie was staying."

Isn't that beautiful? This was a very tall, 9000 square-feet building, about 100 ft high from ground to the tip of the highly steeped, metal roof. Old style, tough and strong! I actually forgot that I had prayed. Exactly 7 days later, Bennie Wade called me from Port Gibson and said, "The sky!" I did not know what he was talking about. As I was wondering he said, "Festus, God tore the roof down. I just stepped out of my room to go to the bathroom and it was the sky!" Immediately I remembered. Listen now: the space between the bathroom and the room where the brother was staying was just 2.5 ft to 3 ft wide, a very narrow hallway.

Spectacular! No wind. No drama. My God sent His angels and they sculptured the roof as I told God to do. Well, as He told me to tell Him to do—that's how He works. The angels folded the thick metals where I told God to do the job and left just the room, Bennie's room, untouched! That's what I am talking about. That's the kind of God I serve. Unfortunately, you only get this kind through Jesus Christ. You must live holy through Him and Him alone. One leg in immoral vagina and corruptions and another on righteous pretense will never do it. That one person cannot do it does not mean that others can't. **Shout**: Jesus! Jesus!! Jesus!!! Jesus!!!! --- **Reply**: Power! Power!! Power!!! Power!!!!

General Sani Abacha of Nigeria

I have been scared of telling anybody this one until about three years ago. God took the fear out of my eyes and head. You may go and search the history books or read the encyclopedias. You will not see anything good about Genera Sani Abacha of Nigeria. He might be as good as Hitler or worse, at least to his own people, the people of Nigeria whom he was supposed to be leading. This man was not a leader but a bully, a destroyer, and a national thief and looter. We suffered to our teeth. We cried bitterly because of this wicked man. Everyone in Nigeria was in grave fear and danger. You are dead and gone if you dare say anything against him, for he was indeed a perfect criminal and a head gangster of evil. If he had stayed alive, Nigeria would have kissed religious freedom bye - bye and say welcome to criminals and 419s of all kinds. This man's evils still smell in Nigeria right now. From Wikipadia Encyclopedia, you might read:

> Abacha took over power from the caretaker government of Chief Ernest Shonekan, which was put into place by General Ibrahim Babangida after his annulment of the 12 June 1993 elections (won by Moshood Kashimawo Olawale Abiola) caused a massive popular uproar. Abacha's government was accused of human rights abuses, especially after the hanging of Ogoni activist Ken Saro-Wiwa by the Auta tribunal (only one of several cases against Ogoni activists opposed to the exploitation of Nigerian land by multinational oil companies); Abiola and Olusegun Obasanjo were jailed for treason, and Wole Soyinka charged in absentia with treason.
>
> His regime suffered stiff opposition internally and externally by pro-democracy activists who made the regime unpopular, and responded by banning political activity in general and by controlling the press in particular; a significant fraction of the military was fired, and Abacha surrounded himself with approximately 3,000 armed men loyal to himself. His foreign policy was inconsistent. He supported the Economic Community of West African States and sent Nigerian troops to Liberia and Sierra Leone to restore democracy to that country while denying it at home…
>
> The government of Obasanjo has implicated the deceased general and his family in a wholesale looting of Nigeria's coffers. The extent of his venality seems to have surpassed even that of more notorious African rulers, such as the late Mobutu Sese Seko. According to post-Abacha governmental sources, some \$3 or \$4 billion USD in foreign assets have been traced to Abacha, his family and their representatives, \$2.1 billion of which the Nigerian government tentatively came to an agreement with the Abacha family to return, with the *quid pro quo* being that the Abachas would be allowed to keep the rest of the money. Although this proposal caused a massive outcry at the time for seeming to reward the theft of public funds, it was subsequently rejected by the late dictator's son, Mohammed Abacha, who continues to maintain that all the assets in question were legitimately acquired.
>
> Although in 2002, Abacha's family accepted to return \$1.2 billion that was taken from the central bank. Abacha was listed as the world's fourth most corrupt leader in recent history by Transparency International in 2004. Abacha had also literally laughed in the face of any possible sanctions by the United States against his government, arguing that the Americans would not do that on account that the oil companies are taking care of the Republicans and the Congressional Black Caucus takes care of the Democrats, and that all American blacks have a dual loyalty to African leaders.

> The names of Sani Abacha and his widow, Maryam, are often used in 419 scams; he is "identified" in scam letters as the source for "money" that does not exist. General Abacha served during the controversial execution of Ken Saro-Wiwa. On 10 November 1995, Saro-Wiwa was hanged by Abacha, resulting in the immediate suspension of Nigeria from the Commonwealth of Nations...Abacha's death has been a subject of controversy, it was reported that he died of a cardiac arrest after an orgy with 4 prostitutes, 2 Indian, and 2 Nigerian. (Wikipadia Encyclopedia, Sani Abacha).

Now let me tell you exactly how this wicked man and grave oppressor died. On June 8, 1998 afternoon or mild evening in my living room of the Port Gibson building that you just finished reading about, I suddenly found myself disoriented and in a trance. Whenever I feel like that I just know that God is about to speak to me. I immediately motioned with my hand to my wife and children to be quiet and that God is about to speak to me. Lo and behold, God spoke to me. He said, "Son, kneel down and ask Me to kill Abacha." That was all. I was very happy. I quickly told my wife what God told me, because I love to brag whenever He shows up like that. I knelt down and asked Him, "God please kill General Sani Abacha." That was all. I had wanted Him to kill more than He told me to ask Him. I had prayed for Him to kill more than Abacha. But he knew not to do it. He knew that the wicked man was the instigator and producer of others who were working for him.

So what happened? I forgot about the prayer until I went to school the next day. On checking my email, the first mail read, "Abacha died of heart attack yesterday"—at exactly the time I asked God to do the job as He told me to ask Him. God is incredible, and He can do everything for us if we can humble ourselves and do whatever He tells us to do without reasoning or sounding stupidly smart or intelligent. I am knowledgeable in the books of the world, but I am smart enough to recognize God and to take my hat off for Him. Glory is to our God! Justifying ourselves when we cannot obey has been man's ultimate hindrance from letting God help him. I never justify myself. My problem is fear or fear of that, producing my inability to move quickly and obey when He tells me to do something.

My dear Barack Obama, my dear distant friend and yet not distant in my heart, there are other events that I can tell you, but a word is enough for the wise. I trust you have've it. Now let me turn to briefly teaching you how the Old Testament connects to the New Testament and how the Bible is completely one and sending the same message to you and me.

God is God of perfection in holiness and peace! He knows that we can be as holy and pure as He is; that is why He told us to be holy like Him (Holy Bible, 1 Peater 2). He created the world; everything was very peaceful for man and beast until man, out of lust and pride, decided to sin (Holy Bible, Genesis 1-3). Hells began to break loose since that time. The first man Adam had messed up. Man, because of sin, has separated himself from God. Sins, sickness, and troubles are everywhere. God has rendered His judgment upon all humanity in Genesis 3.

The Old Testament showed us how impossible it is to please God by ourselves without Christ in our lives. The Ten Commandments were given, including the do's and don'ts you referred to in your speech to the Liberal Christian group. You may need to re-read the parts of the Bible where you think that slavery was permitted to learn of the condition under which such permission was granted. Was it under condition of war, when defeated people were captured and made slaves instead of killing them off? Was it under a time when a family may have to give up a child or two to serve a creditor until an appointed time-period? Alternatively, was it just under no provocation? You will see that God did not really permit slavery as you thought. In some instances, Israelites turned their captors into slaves instead of killing all of them as God commanded. Sometimes God may allow the option of keeping defeated people as slaves.

Then I will say, "Sir, only God has the right to do so because he is perfectly righteous and all-knowing." The same God can reveal to the top leadership of a nation or society that he or she may have to fight and kill certain people (Check the Holy Bible Judges, Kings, etc). God is all-knowing and He knows His reasons for doing whatever He does, including giving instructions. When God asked me to kneel down and ask Him to kill Abacha, I was startled at first. Then the Spirit of God encouraged me. If a leader goes to war and kill without God permitting him to do so, that leader is in great trouble with God. If you read the scriptures, you will see where God killed such leaders and their families for disobeying Him (Holy Bible Judges, Kings, and Chronicles). So, my dear friend, Barack, you better learn to pray and to seek the face of God, and He will let you know what to do even if it involves attacking a nation. If you read Judges and Kings, you will learn how God gives permission to leaders about attacking a nation.

God dealt directly with human beings during the Old Testament times. That was why you read about thousands being killed at the same time for sin or disobedience. To avoid wiping out man and sending all to hell, second Adam has to come. No man was holy and pure enough to bear the burden and sins of the world, causing God to have to do it by Himself. He sent His son in human flesh to be punished for our sins, to reconcile us back to God, and to show us how to live righteous life, for sin must be punished.

> In the beginning was the word, and the word was with God, and the word was God, … and the word became flesh and dwelt among us, and we beheld his glory, the glory as the only begotten of the Father, <u>full of grace</u> and truth (Holy Bible, John 1:1-14).

Jesus arrival into the scene changes all things. You now go by the New Testament. The tooth for tooth and eye for eye in the Old Testament showed us that sin must not go unpunished. Every sin has serious and painful consequences.

It helps us understand the value of Jesus Christ who came and died for our sins. Whoever received Him will be forgiven; who rejects Him will be damned. If somebody does something against you and asks for forgiveness, then you must forgive and forsake tooth for tooth. In fact, in most instances you may have to place everything in the hand of God because of Jesus even when that offender fails to ask for forgiveness. God will deal with him or her.

According to the Law of Moses (Old Testament), you can take revenge against your enemy. According to New Testament (Jesus Time), you will have to forgive, especially when one asks you for forgiveness (Holy Bible, Luke 17:1-4). This must be part of Jesus' Sermon on the Mount, which gives you headache. Another one similar to it is about turning the other cheek when your enemy slaps you on one of the two. This does not mean that you let someone or some nation maltreat the people you are leading or protecting after you have humbly pleaded with that person or nation to cool it or stop it, but they continued. Again, the key is to be in tune with God to be able to know when He says strike or do not strike.

As a leader of a nation or state, God can tell you to commit some habitual offender to some strict punishment, including death penalty. As a leader of a nation, God can tell you to respond in a certain way to a hostile nation. Again, the key is to be humble to God and His directives. (Read 1 and 2 Kings carefully). Even in the New Testament, Peter, the leader of the apostles, in responding to God, had to be instrumental to the death sentence of a husband and wife who lied to God (Holy Bible Acts 5:1-5). In the New Testament, God Himself told everyone to submit to authorities, for those authorities do not have the sword (judgment gavel, key to prison, power to punish) in vain. The same applies to any nation who may continue to misuse you or hurt you after your humble pleas to that nation. The word says:

> Let every soul be subject to the governing authorities, for there is no auhtority except from God, and the authorities that exist are appointed by God. Therefore, whoever resists the authority resists the ordinance of God, and those who resist will bring judgment on themselves. For rulers are not a terror to good works, but to evil. Do you want to be unafraid of the authority? Do what is good and you will have praise from the same. For he is God's Minister to you for good. However, if you do evil, be afraid; for he does not bear the sword in vain; for he is God's Minister, an avenger to execute wrath on him who practices evil. Therefore, you must be subject, not only because of wrath but also for conscience sake. For because of this you also pay taxes, for they are God's Ministers attending to this very thing. (New Testament, Romans 13:1-6).

My dear brother Barack, do you see that? That is in the New Testament, well practiced by good (righteous) Israeli Kings and Judges in the Old Testament. This is not talking about leaders like Robert Mugabe who needs to be ousted out of office by any nation or people that are strong enough to do it. He is a bad leader and a terror to good works, murdering innocent people before our eyes. God did not appoint him to abuse his people like that. He cheats, lies, and deceives. Jesus Himself reveolted against bad leaders, and so were His apostles after Him. Good citizens cannot remain dumb while some immoral leader messes up the society. Nevertheless, you can see that God allows the leader to discipline troubling citizens and to defend nation's citizens against outside trouble-makers. Once again, the key is to be holy and be in-step with your God. Hallelujah! It is critical that a leader has a serious Minister by his or her side.

You see, my brother, this is why it is good to read the whole Bible and to possess THE HOLY GHOST that will help you to hear from God. You cannot understand the word of God until you become humble to it like a baby. I strongly suggest that you have a humble Minister of the Gospel as one of your advisers, someone who relates to God not someone who talks or says he does. If your heart longs for one, God will give you a good one. Real God Ministers are very few. They are usually sober-minded and very modest. They may not even be any person you have seen on the Television. They fast and pray a lot. They really fear God. People, despite my criticism here, I still urge you to vote for Barack. God will use him mightily. I know it.

Obama On Securing USA

Barack Obama is educated, and any intruder or any nation that may try to waylay the United States of America cannot fool him. He is a global thinker, meaning that he has high conceptual skill, enabling him to see necessary forces and their interative influences before they hit home. He will therefore make appropriate decisions to deal with the forces. As someone who is very competitive, he will not like to be seen as a loser or weak in protecting the nation he swears to protect. As Chipman and Goldman reported on Barack:

> The first year Barack Obama joined his fellow Illinois state senators for their annual golf game, he was less than impressive. ``He just wasn't good," said State Senator Donne Trotter of Chicago, adding that the yearly golf outing of the legislature's black caucus is a social-networking rite of passage, particularly for politically ambitious newcomers. In 1998, the following year, Obama showed up and surprised colleagues by hitting the longest ball, according to Trotter, a onetime political foe who now backs Obama, a U.S. senator from Illinois and presumptive Democratic presidential nominee.
>
> ``He took lessons during the winter," said Trotter, 58. ``That's the same way he addresses the more important things in life -- always preparing himself for the next level." Obama, who grew up in laid-back Hawaii, cultivates an image of cool. Yet friends and colleagues said his unflappable demeanor masks a competitive streak that fueled his ascent from average student to Harvard Law Review president to state lawmaker to Congress and possibly the White House…
>
> He wasn't the strongest player at Honolulu's prestigious Punahou School, though he was one of the most determined, according to former teammate Alan Lum. On a scale of one to 10, Obama is a clear ``10" when it comes to

> competitiveness, Lum said, adding that he didn't shy away from calling out his teammates when they weren't pulling their weight.
>
> ``He wasn't going to let anybody get away with anything -- that was his game," Lum said. Senator Bob Casey, a Pennsylvania Democrat, got a taste of Obama's competitiveness while helping him campaign in his state's primary in March. The two played each other in several early- morning games.
>
> ``Unfortunately for me, he's more than competitive," said Casey, 48. Obama's drive doesn't only extend to fellow senators. In Indiana last month, he was challenged to play basketball by a 14- year-old boy, Aaron Villicana. The two played PIG, a game of elimination in which a player earns a letter for failing to make a basket. `Finish You Off'. ``I'm going to finish you off right here," Obama said during the prolonged game, right before missing a basket. He ultimately won... `Competitive Spirit'
>
> ``Barack does not like to lose," Valerie Jarrett, a senior adviser and friend, said in an April interview. ``He's really competitive, he has a fierce competitive spirit." (Chipman and Goldman 2008)

What you just read is a lesson on how Barack Obama will approach economic and security issues for the United States of America. A serious assurance will come from the analysis that he is competitive to both young and old. Will you ever think that such a person will allow Iran or any other nation to waylay him and his nation? It cannot happen. He cannot let his legacy to be in the defeated column. This man will work everyday to grease and improve the wheel of progress of his presidency. Since he hates to lose and loves to win well, Barack Obama's presidency will back every decision with documented methodology that leads to correct inferences. The best thing about it is that he will use the best minds available to assist him.

Being unflappable is great for security purposes. When the leader shakes at every wind, the nation shakes at every wind. The spirit of the leader covers the nation and really determines what happens or does not happen to that nation. This characteristic of being calm and still have the mind to think things through will help to lower anxiety level of the nation as a whole and readies everyone for any action that can be taken to solve a particular problem.

I am glad Barack Obama supported Foreign Intelligence Surveillance Act (FISA). I would have been very surprised if he did not. Secret eavesdropping and surveillance are needed to help identify and catch those who desire to harm this nation. A serious Commander In Chief should see how serious it is now otherwise America may one day experience 9/11 times 1000. Such catastrophe will spell the end of America. Therefore, FISA is more than critical for the survival of America. Americans should really thank our President, George W. Bush Jr. for pushing for the law. Democratic Party should be careful about whom they listen to. Excessive liberty is not freedom. Furthermore, be careful to know who is sponsoring the push against laws like FISA. America's enemies may have a hand in it, taking advantage of America's free speech. Changing times call for changing strategies. Like the President said:

> Bush said the 9/11 attack "changed our country forever" and taught the intelligence community that it must know who America's enemies are talking to and what they are saying. "In the aftermath of 9/11," Bush said, "few would have imagined that we would be standing here seven years later without another attack on American soil. The fact that the terrorists have failed to strike our shores again does not mean that our enemies have given up." Even before Bush signed the legislation, the American Civil Liberties Union said it would challenge the new law in court. The president said the bill gives the government anti-terror tools it needs without compromising Americans' civil liberties.

The American Civil Liberties Union and their supporters who are against this kind of law should understand that they would have no liberty after the terrorists wipe out America. From the prairie of Pennsylvania to trade towers of New York, where is the freedom of all those people who died on the plane bombings of September 11, 2001? What about their relatives who are sorrowing now? Are any of them supporting ACLU in this FISA drama? Why or why not? I am sure they are not supporting ACLU and other groups' lawsuits against FISA because they know the value first hand.

I sometimes wonder who the members of ACLU really are or who is sponsoring their lawsuits. What you are doing is good, but do not overdo it to the point that you start committing suicide and not even know it. You must be careful about who is pushing you from behind; America's enemies can take advantage of America's "too-much-freedom." Where will be your freedom if your enemies who are certainly determined to destroy you wipe you and your USA off the face of the earth? FISA assures you freedom for now as long as it is not misused. Do you really love your country? Since you are very weak on trusting God, you had better do something like FISA.

Criticism by Dick Morris

During the Democratic primary contest, dick Morris was all over Hillary Clinton and in favor of Obama. Now he is all over Obama in this article of June 25, 2008, now that the nomination belongs to Obama, and the November election is between Barack Obama and GOP Senator John McCain. Did somebody get to dick Morris? What happened? The purpose here is not to answer these questions but to react to the article. Since I respect Dick Morris, I will look at the criticisms one by one and then assist him to criticize Obama where necessary. Obama should be smart to know that if any proposal in his platform is significantly off the good mark, he should be wise enough to change it.

On June 25, 2008, Dick Morris wrote an article titled, *The Debate McCain Must Force*, published by RealClearPolitics. I will address the tough allegations against Barack Obama and let the chips fall wherever they are due.

Number 1. Dick Morris argued that is now welcoming controversies between him and the conservatives in order to avoid the real issues. What is his reason? Read:

> Obama and the conservative right are mutually trying to keep the debate about his candidacy on the existential level -- is he the hope for America's future or a Manchurian Candidate, a kind of sleeper agent sent to destroy our democracy? That debate, which pits Obama's rhetoric against the Rev. Wright's ranting, is a contest that could go on all day, and Obama would win it. It is simply a bridge too far to believe that Obama is that evil and invidious. But the more the debate covers such fundamental questions, the more it ignores the details -- details which could bring Obama down. Quite simply, Obama would rather address his religious views and his optimism about America and his embrace of diversity than talk about his plans to raise taxes, let gasoline prices soar and socialize healthcare. (Morris, 2008, RealClearPolitics June 25)

Dick Morris is off here. He may have run out of how to start this article and just decided to spit out what he himself should know is still in the mind of voters. Republicans and their supporters are working hard through the net to smear Barack Obama, referring to him as a Muslim instead of a Christian that he really is. The candidate has no choice but to keep letting people know how much of a Christian he is by going to churches, preaching sermons, and debating with Christian conservatives. He may not be a deeply Bible reading Christian, but he is a Christian, and has been for over 20 years. Barack Obama has the right to keep defending himself for as long as there are some people who continue to perpetrate lies against him. Dick Morris is wrong here.

Number 2. Dick Morris reasoned that Obama would impose a 60 percent tax on upper income Americans, thereby killing all initiative and innovation. He gave some reasoning for his 60 percent, which sounds more political than facts. I only brought this criticism up to show you why America has been drifting downwards. Most inventions and innovations have always originated at and by the middle-income, working class Americans and students. Since when has the tiny percentage of the upper class, Morris is referring to, become the czar for inventions and innovations? It must have been since the trickle down theory squeezed the massive working class and the students to the corner of having to work double jobs to meet their necessities. Mr. Dick Morris, the working class and many forgotten Americans need to be rescued so inventions and innovation can thrive again. Is somebody asking you to do this? Stop making empty and confusing statements.

Number 3. Dick Morris stated that Obama would like to cover 12 million illegal immigrants with federally subsidized health insurance, driving up costs and forcing federal rationing of healthcare. If this is true, then somebody needs to talk sense into Barack Obama. However, the problem is that it seems Dick Morris is twisting what Obama is standing for. Is Obama talking about the children of the illegal immigrants born into this country or the illegal immigrants themselves?

Barack has been advocating not punishing the children but to punish their illegal parents. Immigration issue is something that the Republicans and the Democrats must sit their "butts" down and agree on a strict law that will protect America from invasion of unauthorized people. America does not want to be like Canada where every Dick and Harry can be admitted to the eventual terrorizing and destruction of the nation. America must look at America's values and admit people that can help strengthen such values or are open-minded. America: Stop playing politics with your borders!

Number 4. Now this criticism may have some bite to it if it is not dealt with. Dick Morris wrote, "He (Barack Obama) proposes requiring Homeland Security operatives to notify terror suspects that they are under investigation within seven days of starting the investigation. He says that unless they can establish that there is "probable cause to believe that a certain individual is linked to a specific terrorist group," Homeland Security cannot seize his documents and search his business. The current standard is only that the search be "relevant" to a terror investigation." (Morris 2008).

I believe that RELEVANCY should have, as part of its explanation, the establish-ment of probable cause. Now, this is where I have problem with Senator Obama and he should make a revision of the stand if Dick's criticism is correct. Dear America, you must wake up and know that the terrorist threat against America is HUGE, MULTIPLE, AND REAL. The threat from radical, Islamic funda-mentalist is REAL and almost permanent. Those who hate America and vowed to destroy her are recruiting many American citizens who have been raised by weak families and are controlled by drug-infested cerebellum and cerebral cortex.

EmancipationUSA.org
ChampionSociety.com

I called these American terrorist recruits, the *American Talibans*, just like the Caucasian John Walker Lindh, who fought with Al Qaeda against Americans in Afghanistan. The worst that is taking place now is that some America Muslim parents are sending their children to be trained in Islamic Madrassa schools in Pakistan and other places. Take this as a serious warning America; these kids are potential sources of terrorist recruits and destruction of America if such practice does not flatly terminate now!

Therefore, Mr. Barack Obama, you must be very careful about being liberal with terrorist investigation. Once the TRUSTED American Bureau of Terrorist Investigation has a strong inclination that someone may be a terrorist, the bureau needs to investigate that person. The bureau does not have to link the individual to any terrorist organization before the suspect's documents may be checked. There has to be another and minimal probable cause that needs to be established before documents are seized and searched. Things have changed, and tighter security is a *sine qua non.*

At first strong inclination, documents may be searched in the presence of the suspect and released if nothing was found. Now, how silly will that be to notify a potential terrorist that he is being investigated within 7 days or within 700 days after the investigation began? Oh my God! What kind of policy will that be? It sounds more like the policy the terrorists themselves will fund and create in America. I can understand the fear about the bureau of investigation violating human rights--but that's where America must make sure that the officers are men and women of integrity. However, to notify a potential mass-murder suspect that he or she is being investigated automatically foils any chance of finding anything and spells the end of the investigation whether the officers still investigate or not. Remember that terrorists are very intelligent people. They cannot sit down and wait for you to catch them. They can change plans and personnel.

Obama should be seriously reprimanded if he actually tried to propose a bill regarding this 7-day or any-day notification as Dick Morris claimed. It is ridiculous. Nevertheless, I doubt if Dick Morris was stating the facts right. I called the campaign on July 17, 2008 and had some discussions. They denied this criticism and others by Dick Morris as a smear. Besides, when you look at other homeland security propositions by Barack Obama, such as providing government and tougher security for our chemical and nuclear plants, one would agree that Obama is smartly serious about fighting terrorism at home and abroad toward protecting USA interests. According to Barack Obama's website, President Bush has been very slow at tackling this domestic security issue, ignoring the fact that a hit at one of those plants can kill about a million people.

You may need to go to BarackObama.com for help about what a smear is and what it is not. In fact, at a first glance of Dick Morris criticisms, I felt that someone might have gotten to him with some big 'buck' or something. It flashed my mind that some Democrat may be sabotaging Obama or that GOP has slipped something in the fire through Dick and company. Whatever it is, something smells, and it is not your favorite meal.

People, tough talk does not make a man look strong. The quiet demeanor of Barack Obama, with the smartness of treating every leader equal and giving all so-called enemies the benefit of doubts, spell strength. When an enemy proves to be enemy in-deed, just as Mahmoud Ahmadnejad continues to yell and portray in the name of Islam about destroying Istrael, then you can see the resolve of someone like Barack Obama. It is impossible for Barack Obama to let Iran secure a nuclear weapon because he knows and everyone knows that Iran must use it wrongly and at any time.

The statement Barack made to one Israeli group will let you know that he cannot espouse in his right mind what Dick Morris was implying. Barack Obama said in a speech to a conference of the American Israel Public Affairs Committee, a pro-Israel lobby group:

> The Iranian regime supports violent extremists and challenges us across the region. It pursues a nuclear capability that could spark a dangerous arms race and raise the prospect of a transfer of nuclear know-how to terrorists. Its President denies the Holocaust and threatens to wipe Israel off the map…I will do everything in my power to prevent Iran from obtaining a nuclear weapon--everything in my power to prevent Iran from obtaining a nuclear weapon--everything. That starts with aggressive principled tough diplomacy without self-defeating preconditions but with a clear-eyed understanding of our interests.
>
> We have no time to waste. We cannot unconditionally rule out an approach that could prevent Iran from obtaining a nuclear weapon. We have tried limited piecemeal talks while we outsource the sustained work to our European allies. It has not worked; it is time for the United States to lead. […] And contrary to the claims of some, I have no interest in sitting down with our adversary just for the sake of talking. But as President of the United States I would be willing to lead tough and principled diplomacy with the appropriate Iranian leaders at a time and place of my choosing if--and only if it can advance the interests of the United States. (Pierre 2008, About.com June 4).

Dear American citizens and Israel, do not be scared. Do not be scared at all as Barack Obama's opponents will like you to be. This man is serious and loving at the same time. He will fight for this country with every ounce of his being. Infact, if you like Abraham Lincoln, John F. Kennedy, and Ronald Reagan, then you should love Barack Obama. No one will mess with America with Barrack as America's CEO. Iran or any other nation will not have nuclear weapon if Barack has anything to do with it. Period! Go and put these words in the bank. The only difference with his opponents is that Obama cannot talk to other nations in an unruly manner; he will exhaust every diplomatic route with the right approach before taking any military action.

Is Obama a Liberal?

Is Obama liberal? Is he once liberal and now moving to the center? Is he really the center person at heart but takes up liberalism for political reasons? What is or who is Barack Obama in this area? Obama does not really wish to be classified as liberal or conservative. He may wish to be categorized as someone who looks at a problem and decides for a solution that fits the situation. As I have argued earlier, Obama at heart is more centrist than liberal. The man is not liberal at all. I may be wrong, but I tend to believe that he may have taken extreme liberal stance at the beginning for votes or because of pressures from the majority of Democratic Party liberal supporters. Alternatively, may be he is actually rethinking some issues as he analyzes circumstances. I still think that the former reasoning is more of the situation than the latter.

I strongly believe that Barack Obama is in the middle and of the middle personality. He is very compassionate and may adopt some programs that may seem liberal, but not without serious reasoning behind the adoptions. He is not an "*It's OK, Mama gives you whatever you want*" type of person. He is more of a paternalistic nature than of a softy-softy Mama which has messed up Democratic Party and programs for years. Therefore, I will not be surprise:

- To see Barack Obama support gun possession by those who can handle guns safely and responsibly and to curtail possession by others. If research can prove the type of people that misuses guns, Obama will support a law against such people in possessing guns. In fact, after witnessing the number of the mass murders that that gun-owners commit every year, the government and national Rifle Association need to engage in research to determine categories of violators and to ban them from owning guns.
- To see Barack always support welfare reform that promotes work and dignity.
- To see Barack speak with USA enemies face to face, following good preparations. To be in a position of godly strength before adopting a war option, it is good to use all diplomacies, including face-to-face talks.
- To always support laws like Foreign Intelligence Surveillance Act (FISA). This is the only strategic choice available in times like this when America's enemies are seeking to destroy her. Those liberals who are against it may really have to re-evaluate themselves and their love for USA as a whole. Changing times require changing strategies. FISA is critical for USA now.
- To consider the circumstances on the ground and the advice of the military before deciding how to pull US forces out of Iraq. It is perfectly safe to say that his ultimate strategic vision concerning Iraq is how to pull out within a year or 16 months or sooner. However, he will not do it erratically without complete analysis. He will certainly force the Iraqi's to wake up and quicken the process of pulling out while Senator McCain might slow the process down.
- That Barack Obama will govern from the center and by the center. This is his nature. Anything else will upset his cognitive mindset and causes him severe inadequacy and psychological imbalance.

However, many serious Christians like me are worried that Barack Obama, out of his tendency to stay committed to the far-left liberals, when in fact he is an analyst and centrist, may force him to nominate liberally skewed, Supreme Court judges. That will not be acceptable to the God of America and of the whole creation who is giving Barack the mantle to work for Him and Him alone. At a meeting of Evangelical Christians, the attendees worried and stated:

> ...they must support McCain regardless because an Obama presidency would mean passage of highly liberal policies that would probably allow "same-sex marriage," severely hurt religious freedom and ensure the appointment of only judges who would keep abortion on demand as the law of the land. Rick

> Scarborough, founder and president of Vision America, predicted that laws would be passed that would essentially criminalize basic Christian beliefs. (Charisma Magazine 2008).

Nevertheless, I like the tears of these Evangelical Christians and the so-called Jesus' lovers who have sat back for decades and decades, watching and cheering the devil as he eats up the poor, hardworking people, who have been left behind by the American ship for far too long. Another terrible thing is that some of the *supposed-to-be* Jesus followers worship hatred, racism, and injustices in their hearts for years, covering such devilish value system as subtly as Satan can. They cling to abortion issue and gay marriage, but they slaughter millions of people per year by their hatreds, injustices, racism, and inaction! Their dark values and behaviors destroy the society and kill more people than what the appointment of liberal judges can ever accomplish. The worst thing for us Christian conservatives is that God knows it.

Who are we then to judge or question Barack Obama when in fact the Senator may even have a lot more love than most of us (so-called conservative Christians) are? We need to repent, fellows! We need to repent! It is much more wicked to be calling on the name of Jesus and hating your brother than not to know Jesus and be working to alleviate the pains of a neighbor. What did God say? "Let every one that 'nameth' the name of Jesus Christ depart from iniquity" (Holy Bible, 2 Timothy 2:19). "Let love be without dissimulation or hypocrisy" (Holy Bible, Romans 12:9). What do we have among Evangelical America or or among those who attended that Colorado meeting? Some of them may be old, stiff-necked, pretentious Christians. The open-minded and loving young Christians are opening the closed minds of these stiff-necked conservatives. As Charisma Magazine pointed out:

> Various speakers lamented the lack of a unified strategy that had evangelicals supporting various primary candidates and the fact that their message does not seem to resonate with younger voters, African-Americans or Hispanics in the same way Sen. Barack Obama's does. More than an hour was spent listening to younger leaders tell the group that religious conservatives must be perceived "to care" about social issues and the environment to appeal to young people who are voting for the first time. (Charisma Magazine, July 14, 2008).

Everything about Jesus centers on love and social issues. God has let us know what true religion is about. Talk without action spells non-sense and empty gong (Holy Bible, 1 Corinthians 13). To all of us Christians, and for us to get our wishes fully, God is saying to us:

> Is this not the fast that I have chosen: to loose the bonds of wickedness, to undo the heavy burdens, to let the oppressed go free, and that you

> break every yoke? Is it not to share your bread with the hungry, and that you bring to your house the poor who are cast out; when you see the naked that you cover him and not hide yourself from your own flesh? THEN your light shall break forth like the morning, your HEALING shall spring forth speedily, and your righteousness shall GO BEFORE YOU, and the LORD shall be your rearguard. (Holy Bible, Isaiah 58:6-8).

Can you see that, fellow Christians? Is this not what Barack is standing for? That's the way it has to work with God. We have scared away too many people due to lack of love and pretense on our own parts. Love goes out first. Love is the condition that causes God to work for us, bringing healing to our homes and society. When love is in effect, your prayers become effective. That's how to reach out to the people you have not been able to reach. Genuine, not fake love is the key! God will then do the rest.

The above quotation is an Old Testament passage, and Barack Obama can learn from there that God does not support slavery or oppression as Barack fumbled before his liberal friends. Slavery (not oppression) only occurs under the conditions that I explained earlier. Even under those conditions, there are limitations as to what the victor would do to the captives.

Now to all people and to Senator Barack Obama, this is a prophecy: If Barack succumbs to the pressure of anything-goes people and makes this horrible mistake of appointing liberally skewed judges, I prophecy today that God will destroy or humiliate Barack Obama to the point that he will be crawling and yelling to the whole nation in repentance. He will spend the rest of his life letting America know that he has walloped the nation and everybody else. The only way he will get some sort of sleep at night is by turning an avid warrior against choices like that in the United States of America and against those who made him do it. He might even switch parties or strive to get the Democratic Party to wake up.

Nevertheless, I believe that Barack Obama will not appoint skewed judges. He will appoint serious men and women that truly love America and must be independent enough to evaluate every case in the eyes of America's constitution and laws. He cannot go against his analytical conscience and the country that loves him.

Obama and McCain on Military Service

This is another area where Americans really mess up in elections. They vote for the wrong person and forget the real issues just because the person served in the military. Senator McCain forgot that work is divided. No one can do everything, and everybody's work is critical to national security and development. McCain forgot that he joined the military because that was what God was calling him to do at the time just as God called other Americans to do other jobs that McCain could not do while serving in the military. Those other people in other jobs served McCain and everybody else. The job of a janitor in a restaurant is critically as important to national security as the job of Mr. McCain flying a warplane. The key is to flow where God leads you.

Can you imagine what will happen if God decides to call off all janitors, or if the janitors decide to half-clean their areas of work? The result will be an explosion of nuclear bombs of diseases and deaths all over USA. McCain's army commanders in the pentagon and McCain's wife and children can be among the dead. What kind of morale or news would that have been for McCain and other soldiers to receive in the war zone? First with the death of the top minds and the President of the United States, the army will have to start from the beginning after fleeing from or being slaughtered by their enemies. If McCain happens to be alive still, what must he do then? Three things may happen: (1) McCain may get too sorrowful and commit suicide, (2) McCain may be busy worrying about what the janitors did and the deaths of his relatives that he become bludgeoned into the hands of an enemy machine guns, or (3) McCain may just retire from the military, get back to the country and learn how to be a janitor, a very important patriotic job!

Senator McCain had criticized Obama for not serving in a military service and some ill-informed voters are actually buying it. This criticism is an insult to Abraham Lincoln, Ronal Reagan, and other great American Presidents who did not serve in the military but worked hard in their respective, God-assigned areas of services at home. Who would have done the entertaining films that Reagan did if he had gone off into the military? Didn't McCain and his relatives enjoy any movie or TV show? Who would have fought for the nation's poor, the working class, and the oppressed had Lincoln took off for the military?

Fellows, all areas of work or endeavor, which benefit the society, are as important as serving in the military. Such services also benefited the military and everyone else, including the soldier McCain and his loved ones. Any person performing in any of those areas of work is being patriotic. They are highly patriotic if they are doing excellent jobs in their assigned positions. Therefore, ladies and gentlemen, McCain's criticism of Obama for not joining the military is an insult to all American citizens--

1. Who patriotically work hard as nurses and medical doctors, taking care of the health of Senator McCain's relatives and keeping the whole nation healthy as McCain was off to war.
2. Who patriotically work in post-office counters and as post-masters, making sure McCain's relives get their mails and that mails flow well among America's people. They also make sure McCain got his letters while serving in the military.
3. Who patriotically work to build new roads and maintain our highways for the safety of McCain and everybody else.

4. Who patriotically work and maintain the economy so the nation can be healthy for McCain and everybody else, paying McCain's salaries and benefits and furnishing the military with all they need.
5. Who patriotically work as secretaries and office workers to make sure that the nation is not in chaos and managers are not confused to the managing and smooth running of USA.
6. Who patriotically work in restaurants as servers and pizza deliverers, making money for their companies as they and the companies pay taxes to serve McCain as McCain serves them.
7. Who patriotically work as missionaries or in foreign nations, promoting the good side of America and blessing other people.
8. Who patriotically work as leaders in their various positions as parents, babysitters, school teachers, and political leaders, building up citizens like John McCain and Janitor Joseph who will serve America in the future as doctors, lawyers, community organizers, soldiers, janitors, presidents, and so on.
9. Who patriotically work hard as firefighters and neighborhood watchers who make sure the nation is protected from fires and criminals for the benefit of McCain, his loved ones, and everyone else.
10. Who patriotically go to school and take up other professions like management, finance, accounting, marketing, humanity, and medicine instead of the military so the nation can be balanced, progressive, and secure.
11. Who patriotically floated in the hands of God in the cultivation process of being White American, Kenya-African, Indonesian, and the United Nation, enduring and learning through it all for America's benefit.
12. Who patriotically take up jobs as community organizers instead of corporate lawyers or executives, making over 90 percent less than they should have made just for the love of using their talents to help beautify the nation.
13. Who patriotically worked to become Illinois State Senator and now a US Senator for Illinois.
14. Who is now patriotically working hard to win the opportunity to serve America as her President so he can truly bring America's love and blessings to all Americans. He is the champion of America's working class and a steady friend to all Americans, who will serve as a no-drama, contingency oriented, and system-understanding CEO of USA.

Can you now clearly see that you are very important in the USA just as any soldier? Can you now see that if you do your job well that you are as patriotic as a soldier who does his job well? Can you now see that people like John McCain, who may try to criticize you that you are less qualified to be president just because you did not serve in the military, cannot intimidate you? I know you see now. As you see, it is also important to honor those soldiers as you will like to be honored. In fact, you must love them and cherish them for such expectant love and cherishing are part and parcel of what they must get from you.

Your love for them and your cherishing of them are part of military benefits to our soldiers. Many times I pay for their meals when I see any of them and their families at restaurants. I deliberately go to post office and issue refund cash to families sending packages to their loved ones (soldiers) overseas. Soldiers are our soldiers. I cherish them. However, you must be wise to know that being a soldier does not mean knowing how to be CEO and President of a nation. You need serious schooling, smart head, and proven judgment for such a position as I have analyzed in this book. Stop being fooled America! Now, is Senator McCain qualified to be president? Yes. Is his military service important in him being President? Yes. However, in general, McCain is far less qualified than Senator Barack Obama as already analyzed here. We must stop wasting our votes by looking at one or two factors only. Look at all attributes and then make a wise choice.

The Silliness of Not Drilling In America

Does it mean that other countries are silly for drilling in their own lands and supplying America? If these nations get to see what America is doing and dare work more cohesively, prices of crude oil might go beyond the roof or they may just decide to keep the price at a level just enough to prevent America from exlporing and drilling in America. We understand environmental problems. However, it has come to a point where the cost of living outweighs the cost of preserving some environment.

This is my own criticism of Barack Obama. It is such a silly thing for the Democrats not to know that the time has long passed for America to explore and drill for crude oil wherever they can get it in the USA until she discovers other alternatives. Again, I really believe that Barack is agreeing against the calling of his heart on this issue. His argument against McCain that the exploration and drilling will take 7 years to produce any oil does not sound like the rest of rational Barack Obama that I and many people know. It is better to start now to explore and drill than to start later. If you do not start now, then you will not have any significant domestic supply of oil seven years from now. The nation will then get into worse slammer-hammer seven years later, in worse hole than today!

It is sheer stupidity and silly to not explore and drill oil in the USA when the price of oil is skyrocketing and when America's enemies like Iran are using oil to harass the United States of America. This useless stand on not exploring and drilling as much oil as possible in America may cost Barack Obama the election if the price of oil stays above $3 per gallon of unleaded gasoline at the pump. It is now at an average of about $4 per gallon nationally. This can be deadly for the Obama campaign. I have a feeling that Barack will try to convince his leftists' supporters and then switch his position after he gets into office. However, it is critical that he switches right now, as McCain did, otherwise he may lose the election just for this reason. I have written Barack Obama campaign about this.

In fact, I tend to believe that Obama is under serious pressure with this issue because I do not think he actually shared in this static, nonstrategic view with the party and the environmentalists. I tend to believe that Barack Obama will certainly call for drilling offshore and any other place if the oil price continues to rise. Nevertheless, it is critical that he summons the muscle to let the electorate know right now that everything is on the table. The environmentalists' stance on oil exploration and drilling in the United States is no longer viable today as the economy keeps tittering. Such stance is threatening to and is wounding America's security and her economy. Iran is currently using oil as a weapon against the United States. America should have every possibility on the table when it comes to energy policy. I'm glad that Barack is gradually changing his mind few days after I wrote the campaign.

The Foreign Language Thing

Once again this is what I am saying when I stated that Barack Obama may be the best candidate or one of the top 3 percent of good candidates that America has ever fielded for a general election for the presidency of the United States. He is strategic, and he is telling America the truth and nothing but the truth. My first few years in America produced frustration and a concern for America. Almost all Americans have problems with accents. They keep saying, "Pardon, pardon, and pardon" to repeated attempts to get them to hear you. Oh poor Americans!

Dear America, do you know why you have such trouble hearing foreigners' English accents? It is because you do not have accent-ear. Your ear is not diversified. Compared to most nations of the world, you are less competitive in this area. I cannot imagine that the GOP will criticize Barack Obama for stating that Americans needs to learn to speak foreign languages. Shame to Republicans! That includes me because I am more of a Republican than a Democrat. Today the United States is diminishing in her national security, trade competitiveness, and global competition in employment because America's children and adults are dumb to foreign languages and possess uni-dimensional ears. Part of the reason is that most Americans do not have to travel to other nations to live and find food. Hwever, to be a serious world power and to compete in today's world, America needs to take advantage of her diverse population to learn other languages.

When I heard that the Republicans and conservatives are criticizing Obama for telling this important truth to Americans, I decided to write Barack to encourage him to yell some more:

Dear Barack Obama:

Your statement of America having the need to learn foreign language is a very good thing. It is strategic and of great help in national security and international competition for Americans to learn foreign languages. That is one area that foreign nations are also ahead of today's USA.

Learning foreign language actually forces one to meditate on the culture of the nation whose language one is learning. The person not only learns the language but he also develops his/her ear to understanding English spoken with different accents. This is critical for America's security, foreign relations, and excellence in trade. With America attracting many foreigners and the war on terrorism growing, billions of dollars can be saved by having a patriotic population that can serve as watchdogs against foreign-language discussions of terror-activities. Fluency in one or two foreign languages can eliminate employing risky foreigners in certain military or national security operations. Besides, look at how much job opportunities that will be available to Americans if they can speak more than English. Think about how Americans can talk better with Iranians and the Arab nations if Americans can speak Arabic, Farsi, Pashto, etc. Understanding other people's languages creates inroads in trade, relationship, and waterproof national security.

Therefore, Senator Obama, dismissing any criticism without serious explanation will cost you some votes, and you do not want to lose one vote that you can hold on. Let the American public understand the benefit of learning foreign languages. They will appreciate it. Explaining it right will give you votes. Go ahead and explain it.

Sincerely,

Festus S. Oguhebe (Strongblood)

Americans tend to see the Republicans as the whiz on issues like this, but Barack Obama is ahead of them at this time. GOP does not have patent on patriotism, national security, and some other things as the Republican Party may want voters to believe. Let this tell the average voter that Barack Obama is not GOP or Democrat. He is a strategic American presidential candidate who happens to identify with the Democratic Party. Learning foreign language is strategic and critical to Americans at this time. Please wake up America. China is coming and it will not be pretty for the rest of the world with China as the leading economic power and military power. China will not share. China will not care. China will look to develop dynasties and dominations through wars and intimidations. The world will kiss human and civil rights bye bye! Speaking foreign languages and developing accent-ears will improve America's security and innovation in every category of environmental forces.

Being Commander In Chief

An ABC News report on July 14, 2008 stated that a poll conducted by ABC News and Washington Post found 72 percent of Americans indicating that Senator McCain would be a good Commander In Chief and 25 percent saying he would not. The same poll recorded that 48 percent of Americans said that Senator Barack Obama would be a good Commander In Chief and 48 percent saying he would not (Langer 2008, ABC News). Senator Hillary Clinton had criticized Senator Obama on this subject, but Obama clearly proved that he would be a much better Commander In Chief than the former first lady would. Now here we go again with Senator McCain who actually has similar characteristics with Senator Clinton:

- McCain is relatively not as steady or calm as Obama, but has a tendency to be much more trigger-happy than Obama would ever get close to being.
- McCain is not as conceptual and analytical as Obama
- McCain is not as system-oriented as Obama
- McCain is not as management process oriented as Obama

I am beginning to think that American people may not have a clue as to what Commander In Chief really means. If they know, the results of the above poll should be in reverse. Barack Obama will be a better Commander In Chief than Senator McCain by most measures. You cannot be a good Chief Executive Officer without being a good Commander In Chief. All these functions or their makeups are interdependent. Obama is genuinely more system and contingency oriented than Senator McCain and may be as competitive as or better than McCain. He will therefore make a much better leader at both CEO level and at Commander In Chief definition.

Let us look at the roles of a good President. By the constitution and laws of the United States, a US President performs seven roles: (1) chief executive, (2) commander in chief, (3) foreign policy director, (4) legislative leader, (5) party head, (6) popular leader, and (7) chief of state (World Book Encyclopedia and Learning Resources 2008).

(1) Chief executive – The president has the power to enforce federal laws, treaties, and federal court rulings; to develop federal policies; to prepare the national budget; and to appoint federal officials.

(2) Commander in chief -- The president is to defend the country during wartime and to keep it strong during peacetime. The chief executive appoints all the nation's highest military officers and helps determine the size of the armed forces. Only the president can decide whether to use nuclear weapons.

(3) Foreign policy director -- The president is to appoint ambassadors, make treaties, and receive foreign diplomats. The chief executive may refuse to recognize a newly formed foreign government. The president also proposes legislation dealing with foreign aid and other international activities.

(4) Legislative leader -- The president greatly influences the development of many laws passed by Congress. At the beginning of each session of Congress, the chief executive delivers a State of the Union address to the lawmakers. In this message, the president discusses the major problems facing the nation and recommends a legislative program to solve them. The president also gives Congress detailed plans for new legislation at other times during the year.

(5) Party head -- The president helps form the party's positions on all important issues. The president hopes these positions will help elect enough party members to Congress to give the party a majority in both the House and the Senate. Such a strong party makes it easier to pass the president's legislative program.

(6) Popular leader -- The people rely on the chief executive to serve the interests of the entire nation ahead of those of any state or citizen. In turn, the president depends on public support to help push programs through Congress. The president seeks such support by explaining the issues and by showing the confidence and determination to deal with problems.

(7) Chief of state -- As the foremost representative of the U.S. government, the president is expected to show pride in American achievements and traditions. In this role, the president attends historical celebrations, dedicates new buildings and national parks, and may throw out the first ball of the professional baseball season. The president also presents awards to war heroes and invites distinguished Americans to the White House. (World Book Encyclopedia and Learning Resources 2008).

Can you see how all the roles are fused together? A mistake in one can cause domino effects on the rest and catastrophe upon the nation. People, let me strongly tell you that following serious analysis, our current President is better than John McCain in Commander-In-Chief test. He may understand the interconnectedness of things better than McCain, yet he made one serious mistake. [Let me also tell you that I am not a fan in criticizing our current President because the man has worked hard to hold this nation from collapsing.

Besides, I just like him as a brother and I mean it, but he made a serious mistake.] He failed to see the delicate but dangerous link of his war strategies to the economic wellbeing of America and how to strategize to safeguard what is happening to America today.

If you think that the *Honorable* George W. Bush Jr. is a one-track-mind person, McCain will be gross! That is not being a good Commander In Chief, at least when you compare Senator McCain to Senator Barack Obama. It is like night and day! America, you need to wake up, smell the coffee, and then move toward the direction of the aroma to find the coffee. If you have a bad nose or keeps ignoring the right smell for one wrong reason or the other, you must always have yourself to blame. Be truly patriotic for a change. Stop going by emotion or by one attribute-voting mindset. Since a picture is worth more than a thousand words, please take a close look at *Figure 1: The Head of the President of the United States of America.* That is exactly what is going on in the head of America's president, and that is why most of them get old faster while in office. However, some of them are more ordained to navigate through all the necessary channels and deal with the constant puzzles that affect the presidency and arrive at the ONLY RIGHT SOLUTION better and faster than others.
Who do you think will navigate through the maze better? Who do you think will deal with the problems better and let you worry about other things concerning your household? Who do you think is strongly minded enough to do the interwoven mathematics and calculus involved to get to the correct decision, a decision that will guarantee defeat of the enemy WITHOUT CONFUSION, strengthening of the economy, and maintaining a healthy international, domestic and foreign-relations balance? Who has the appropriate GRAY MATTER AND THE ACUMEN to intellectually and psychologically read and understand the maze of things and make decisions that really bless the nation (not bringing one benefit and taking away 1000, or bringing one dollar profit but creating a million dollar costs)? The only answer to these questions, given the choices that we have and based on the analysis up to this moment, is cleanly Senator Barack Obama for the next President of the United States.

What is acumen? It is QUICKNESS AND ACCURACY OF JUDGMENT. Good schooling and drills through life contribute heavily to acumen. A person that has gone from bottom up is expected to have better acumen than someone who is stationed only at either extreme. Barack Obama has gone from bottom, through in-betweens, to the top, and then he decides to live and reside in the middle. I hope you understand this characteristic because it is critical to understanding the rich, the poor, the middle class, the black, the white, the Indonesian, the Middle-Eastern, the Africans, and the United Nations.

The humble fellow just finished paying off his school loans recently; he became rich two or three years ago because of God's light upon him. He understands all classes and knows that someone has to fight for the poor and the working class while still loving the rich. He wants people to have the opportunity to be like him or better. That is the kind of person you should

FIGURE 1: THE <u>HEAD</u> OF THE PRESIDENT OF THE UNITED STATES OF AMERICA

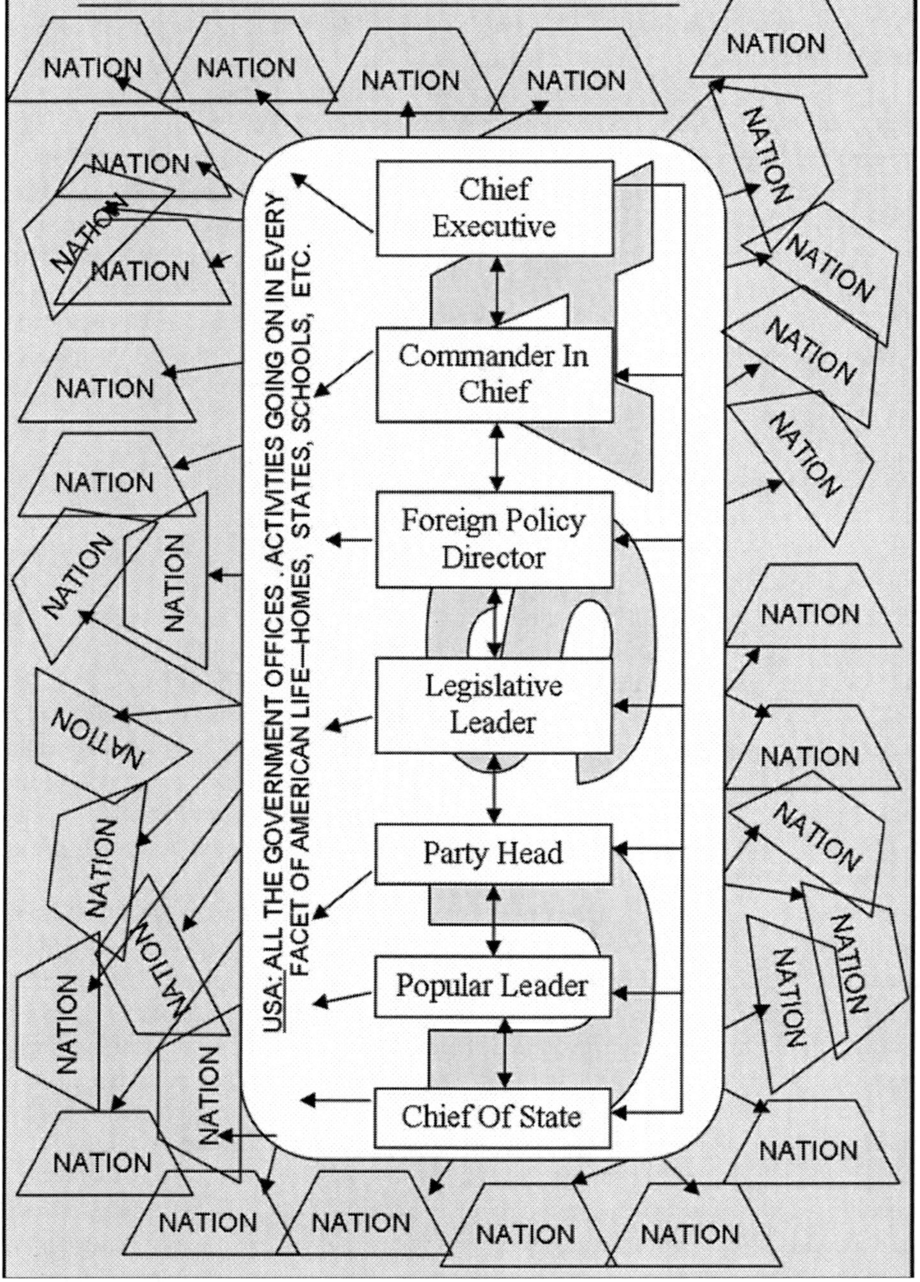

want to be a covering for America. Being a covering is the ultimate spiritual function of the President and CEO of a nation. You do not want an immoral person to be at the helm of any ship. The rest of the ship will be polluted worse and worse. As far as God is concerned, Barack Obama is a plus to USA considering what has been going on with the America's top office for years.

Now see this. Acumen—the quickness and accuracy of judgment -- cannot thrive without a relatively challenged, viable, and healthy grey matter. What is gray matter? It is a major component of the central nervous system, consisting of nerve cell bodies called neurons, glial cells, capillaries, and short nerve cell extensions and processes called axons and dendrites. Its function is to route sensory or motor stimulus to interneurons of the CNS in order to create a response to the stimulus through chemical synapse activity. Gray matter structures process information originating in the sensory organs or in other gray matter regions. This information is conveyed via specialized nerve cell extensions, which form the bulk of the cerebral, cerebella, and spinal white matter. (Wikipadia Encyclopedia).

Now let us come down to earth. All these cells or tissues of the gray matter, which occupy the head and the spinal cord, carry messages and conduct impulses. They are instrumental to your reasoning ability, the extent to which you may be confused and how much you can handle (depending on training). If they are dead, weak, or old, such functions can be mitigated or interfered with, especially in strenuous circumstances. If one is an angry person or does not have the ability to control himself or herself, some parts of the grey matter will be controlling him instead of him controlling the grey matter. If one has not been trained in education and serious problem-solving processes, the roads in this grey matter and the rest of the head can be jammed up easily. Think about what is involved in being America's CEO:

(1) As the person performs the functions of the Chief executive, he will always be worrying and analyzing in his head how whatever he does in this function affects the nuances of commander in chief intricacies—past, present, and future; foreign policy director intricacies—past, present, and future; legislative leader intricacies—past, present, and future; party head intricacies—past, present, and future; popular leader intricacies—past, present, and future, and chief of state intricacies—past, present, and future.

(2) As the person performs the functions of the Commander in chief, he will always be worrying and analyzing in his head how whatever he does in this function affects the nuances of foreign policy director intricacies—past, present, and future; legislative leader intricacies—past, present, and future; party head intricacies—past, present, and future; popular leader intricacies—past, present, and future, and chief of state intricacies—past, present, and future.

(3) As the person performs the functions of the foreign policy director, he will always be worrying and analyzing in his head how whatever he does in this function affects the nuances of commander in chief intricacies—past, present, and future; present, and future; legislative leader intricacies—past, present, and future; party head intricacies—past, present, and future; popular leader intricacies—past, present, and future, and chief of state intricacies—past, present, and future.

(4) As the person performs the functions of the legislative leader, he will always be worrying and analyzing in his head how whatever he does in this function affects the nuances of commander in chief intricacies—past, present, and future; foreign policy director intricacies—past, present, and future; party head intricacies—past, present, and future; popular leader intricacies—past, present, and future, and chief of state intricacies—past, present, and future.

(5) As the person performs the functions of the party head, he will always be worrying and analyzing in his head how whatever he does in this function affects the nuances of commander in chief intricacies—past, present, and future; foreign policy director intricacies—past, present, and future; legislative leader intricacies—past, present, and future; popular leader intricacies—past, present, and future, and chief of state intricacies—past, present, and future.

(6) As the person performs the functions of the popular leader, he will always be worrying and analyzing in his head how whatever he does in this function affects the nuances of commander in chief intricacies—past, present, and future; foreign policy director intricacies—past, present, and future; legislative leader intricacies—past, present, and future; intricacies—past, present, and future; intricacies—past, present, and future; party head intricacies—past, present, and future; and chief of state intricacies—past, present, and future.

(7) As the person performs the functions of the chief of state, he will always be worrying and analyzing in his head how whatever he does in this function affects the nuances of commander in chief intricacies—past, present, and future; foreign policy director intricacies—past, present, and future; legislative leader intricacies—past, present, and future; intricacies—past, present, and future; intricacies—past, present, and future; party head intricacies—past, present, and future; and popular leader intricacies—past, present, and future.

The President's head is full all the time, and he must be a type of person that loves and enjoys challenges and solving complex problems. A quick-tempered person cannot handle it at all. A person who is not well schooled cannot handle it well. A person with anxiety will have a serious problem. As the President performs any of the above roles, he must always be considering how each action in any of them interactively affects each other—on every facet of

USA and on each of the nation of the world. Your head will be clear to be the president of the United States of America if the individual actually wants to do the job right and not for the name!

Once again, America, "Rise up and smell the coffee right or you will find yourself forced into drinking mud water instead of coffee." Do you know that some things may smell like and look like orange when in fact it is not orange? All that glitter is never gold. By my own analysis, President George W. Bush Jr. is not adequately diverse in his brain-ability to handle complex problems. He is too single-minded and would suffer serious headache if he faces multiple tasks at a time. He did fairly, but Senator John McCain will be relatively worse. Again, the honorable President, Brother George is better than McCain. Senator Obama will be much, much better than both of them. Obama already knew and he is frustrated by both Senator McCain's and the President's single-minded and open-end approach to handling Iraq (Bohan 2008, Reuters). Strategically, given all circumstances, it is not wise. Setting a timetable and bringing the troops home and refocusing constitute better strategic choice now. It will force Iraqi government to strengthen up.

When you are asked to pick gold and you have a choice between gold and silver, please choose gold. When you are faced with a less-than-desired situation where you have to choose gold, but you only have "X" with 50 percent gold and "Y" with 95 percent gold, then you had better choose "Y" or you will be playing roller coaster and other problems with your life and the life of the nation. In addition, this is no period to be shaking America too much. America is very fragile now and does not need too much drama at all. Senator Obama is a clear 95 percent in CEO and Commander In Chief tests for the United States of America for such a time as this in American and world history. The *honorable* Senator McCain is about 50 percent. Obama is the better choice. He is the much better qualified person to not only deal with the domestic problems and normal international relations, but what you have just read qualifies him as more capable to respond well to international crises on behalf of USA than his opponent will.

Now how hard or effective are the candidates, McCain and Obama, working to convince voters to vote for them? Is it any measure of the candidates' strategy or motivation? Does it have anything to do with what will happen in the oval office once a candidate is elected? The answer may be indirectly YES to any of these questions. It speaks more on strategy, which McCain people may have realized and started making some reshuffles in personnel.

A Los Angeles Times report showed how voters rated Senator McCain' and Senator Obama's campaigns (July 17, 2008). The paper indicated that the finding has to do with measuring how the candidates are making the sale. Even McCain's supporters rated him much lower than Obama's supporters did for Senator Obama. According to Pew Research:

> A solid majority (56%) give the Obama campaign letter grades of A or B for the job he is doing to convince the American public to vote for him, while only 32%

say the same of the McCain campaign. More than a third (35%) offer a grade of C to McCain's campaign so far, and nearly as many (30%) say the campaign has earned a D or F.

The grades voters give to the Obama campaign for the job it is doing convincing them to vote for him are the highest measured for any candidate over the past four election cycles. In June 2004, for example, just 39% gave Bush's efforts an A or B; even fewer gave high grades to Kerry's campaign (31%). In contrast, McCain's middling grades are slightly lower than those awarded to Bush in both 2000 and 2004. McCain's campaign does garner higher grades than the 1996 Dole campaign, which only 22% graded highly.

In this regard, the 2008 campaign has the largest disparity in high grades for the Democratic and Republican candidates over the past four election cycles (24 points). The gap between the grades for Obama and McCain is even larger than for Bill Clinton and Bob Dole in July 1996; at that time, 37% gave Clinton an A or B, while just 22% gave top grades to Dole. The differences in the ratings of the two presidential campaigns are reflected in the opinions of their partisans. Nearly eight-in-ten Democratic voters (79%) give the Obama campaign letter grades of A or B for the job he is doing to convince the American public to vote for him, and a smaller majority of Republican voters (54%) give high marks to the McCain campaign. More independents give A or B grades to the Obama campaign than to the McCain campaign (49% v. 31%). In addition, while more than a third of Republicans (35%) give high grades to Obama, just 16% of Democrats give high grades to McCain. (Los Angeles Times, July 17, 2008).

Is Barack Obama Arrogant?

You may have heard some people, the GOP surrogates or just some bloggers, state or suggest that Obama is arrogant. The great trouble with people like these is that they never justify such statement with anything. They just throw it in there. Such behavior strikes me gravely as either jealousy or the annoyance that some black, bold, and confident candidate is just being himself—calm, smart in presentation of materials, and enjoying himself at the same time.

Some of them argued that he was acting as if he is Mr. President already, and therefore he must be arrogant. Is this not silly? The man is campaigning to be President; the best way to prove that he can be a good president is to begin to show now that he is capable. Part of this capability measurement is to start now to act like it. Barack is being an extraordinary example to all people of all creed and race. He is showing all so-called little folks that once you work hard and get your facts together, then be bold and refuse to be intimidated by anybody. The problem is that most of these arrogant critics are actually offended that Barack Obama is not acting like a cotton-picking, timid slave. Barack is showing us that America is different now and for the better. The time of timidity by any race has passed. It is now and truly, *The United States of America.*

Dear voters, recall that the McCain campaign had criticized Barack Obama for not traveling overseas as many times as McCain did. I have argued that it is not how many times one traveled overseas but how qualitative the travels were. All right, Obama made the right round to visit with key trouble areas and with the major allies of the United States of America. The personality, the candor, and the warmth that Barack Obama portrayed created atmosphere of comradeship between him and each head of state that he met. They were heavily excited to meet him, to talk with him, and to tell him that they would love to work with him. Now, the McCain campaign become jealous and begins to define him as being a mere celebrity and not a leader.

Fellows, you have learned from this book that Barack Obama is at every wit a no-nonsense leader. Nobody has to explain this to you any longer. What the McCain campaign is also failing to comprehend is that the President of any nation is the biggest celebrity that exists in that nation. Obama is a celebrity and so is McCain. It just happens that Obama is a more popular one. Ladies and gentlemen, the Obama July-2008 trip overseas showed America one major lesson—Obama can work with world leaders, there is no friction between his persona and any of those leaders. They can get together, drink coffee or tea and just delve into solving world's problems without any personal barrier. Dear America, seize the moment! Our best choice is Barack Obama as the next President of USA.

Slavery Reparations Or No Reparations

My dear fellow black people of America, please lend me your ears. What can reparations do? Reparation always sounds like paying back for the sins of slavery. Can all the money in the Central Banks of every nation put together ever be able to pay for what many of you are asking? Dear black leaders, don't you have something else to work on? Are there not too many things to do? Why are you touching something and trying to make money off of something that is BEYOND, BEYOND, AND BEYOND MONEY!!! Why do we always have to mess up this way?

My dear people, please forget about slavery reparation completely, completely! God is dealing with it and He is doing it well. He has done it. Years and years of this kind of slavery is not what any reparation can wipe away. Only God can wipe it away and it is being wiped away both to your advantage and to all of America's advantage. Please stop putting people in bondage, especially the many white people (the Lincoln's, the Kennedy's, etc.) who have repented, who were part of the fight for stopping slavery, and who have sacrificed their lives during slavery and after slavery. Any black leader that is talking about this kind of reparation is a very divisive person, hateful, and may be worse. This is not money issue. This is far, far, far, and far beyond money or any material thing that can never be paid! Why are you trying to attach One penny to something that is worth heaven, earth, and all planets put together?

The devastation that man did to himself is too much that it cannot be paid for by anything man can come up with. That's why God Himself has to come up with Himself (through Jesus) to clean the mess and unite us back to Himself.

Very similarly, only Jesus Christ fits the bill that many of you are asking for. Why are you asking for $1 bill for what will take *$forever-bills* to take care of? I want all of you to see the problem of slavery as completely solved! Let God, the Lord Jesus be your portion (Holy Bible). Please stop putting the white people in psychological bondage. Many of them have cried and repented. Stop reminding them, for God does not like it all. Stop putting them in psychological slavery, for God seriously warned those who have suffered slavery never to attempt to enslave anyone! Before the eyes of the righteous God, you are also bruising and hurting the black race worse and worse by sticking to such selfish and anti-divine demands. God is our $Bill! It has been paid in full.

PLEASE STOP! You are not being a leader but a destroyer by instigating these so-called reparations. JESUS is our every reparation in all slavery cases! "O God, on behalf of all black people, I forgive all white people and any person who may have involved in enslaving and maltreating any black person; I ask you, God, to bless all those people and to bless us, the black people, too. May God bless all of us together, and may God forgive us, black people, who have been invoking the slavery thing in subtle, devilish ways, causing unnecessary psychological uneasiness to any white person or persons. JESUS, you are our reparation and you are the blessed of America. These I ask in Jesus name, Aaaamen!"

Again, fellow black people, JESUS is our reparation! Our job is to forgive, forgive, and really forgive and then start loving all people. That is our best and only choice investment in a problem like this. Any other thing we do besides this only choice takes our God, the "*In God We Trust*," out of the equation and messes us up, including the country that we are part of and cherish, the USA. Dear black people, you had better listen to the voice of God as I have clearly stated here. You had better listen to Barack Obama, for he is telling you the truth. Get away from selfish politics and selfish leaders. There are too many of them among black race. Many a time, the devil uses them to cause confusions so they can get what they want, pleasing their flesh instead of God. Stop trying to put words, wrong words into Barack Obama's mouth and better listen to him. I wish you'd listen to me too.

I want to let you know that although I was not in America during the civil rights movement and did not suffer like most of you, I understand. I do. In fact, after Jesus Christ, Rev. Martin Luther King Jr. is my role model. I have fought against racism for the little part I have been in this country; my building may have been set on fire by some racists. I have cried and lamented for black people like you cannot imagine. I have lamented to the point of being ill and being unable to tackle other problems of life. I meditate on black issues a lot, almost every second.

You may visit EmancipationUSA.org or ChampionSociety.com to get some information concerning the black race, some issues we must deal with. I put together a Martin Luther King Jr. album, sang the songs with my tiny children, doing my best to let black people know what our problem truly is and what the heart of the Honorable Martin Luther King Jr. is. My dear, beautiful and fellow black folks of America, the heart of the Reverend Martin Luther King Jr. is not far-fetched at all. Selfish black leaders may tell you otherwise. My role model wants us to forgive and to love all white folks, all green folks, all yellow folks, and one another. He also wants us to forget the foolishness of reparations, for our reparations are all in Christ Jesus, Our Lord and Savior.

Reparations cannot be paid for our slavery. Only God is equal to the bill, and He is our bill! Anything short of this is wickedness, selfishness, and anti American that my role model, the honorable Martin Luther King Jr. fought for. If we have ears, then we had better hear and do. The government can do something to help the black race rise up to a level of equal competition, but that must not include paying any money to anybody for being enslaved. All members of the black race were enslaved and God represents and fits the bill that no human being and central banks can ever pay. Let us now love and care for one another in One-USA as Barack Obama continually stated and stands for.

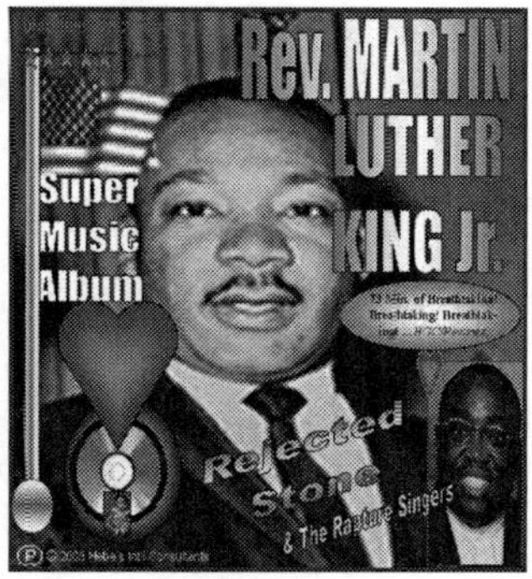

Author's Martin Luther King Jr. album. Serious message to black folks. EmancipationUSA.org or ChampionSociety.Com

Be Careful About Any Attack Book Like "Obama Nation"

Once agin, be careful about any attack book like the Obama Nation. Listen carefully. Books and many articles are quickly coming out to discredit Barack Obama's quest for the presidency of the United States of America. This quest is not of man, but of God. You must be careful not to be derailed by such books and articles. The book called *The Obama Nation* and any other like it do not have to attract your hard-earned money. This is why. Any of such books is written with the sole purpose of disliking Obama as a person and his race as "No good for President." They do not focus on criticizing his strategies for helping the USA. Such evil motivation has been part of what is derailing America behind the scenes. Anytime someone is doing anything that goes against God, that thing is contributing to the destruction of a system of which it is a part, regardless of how good the thing might seem at the moment. Be very careful! You must always remember…What you vote for is what you get! Stop looking in the outward appearance. Look to the heart.

Again, be very careful. When something is done out of wrong motive, the 'something' either backfires or becomes a cancer that will help eat the nation to death eventually. Do not be tricked into buying what such books and writings say. Ask yourself a serious race question. If Barack Obama were a white person, will you vote for him? If you will, then just close your eyes, obey your God and vote for Barack Obama. You are doing it for God not for Mr. Obama. The key is to build America and help lives. Do not let built-up fear steal your vote away. Such incident causes deep regrets in the future. Show fear and negative campaigns that you are much smarter than they portray you to be.

Barack Obama is a very fine individual, a dedicated, strategic-oriented, family man. You can never expect him to get into scandals but only love for, admiration of, and fighting for all people of USA. Do not let fear mongers and racists scare you. Your God knows no fear. You are children of your God. You will also know no fear. Act boldly and give this nation, the lovely USA, a positive and life-building atmosphere that she really needs right now. Again, be careful about the so-called swift-boating technique. It is a political phrase that simply means, "*Lying to get what you want.*" They did it before and it worked for them. They are doing it again. If you vote based on lies, then you are a supporter of lies and you are part of whatever happens to the nation when the lies catch fire in the future. Be very careful!!! What you sow is what you must reap. Don't blame anybody if you vote wrongly.

CHAPTER 14

SUGGESTION TO BARACK AND BUILDING THE AMERICAN BASE

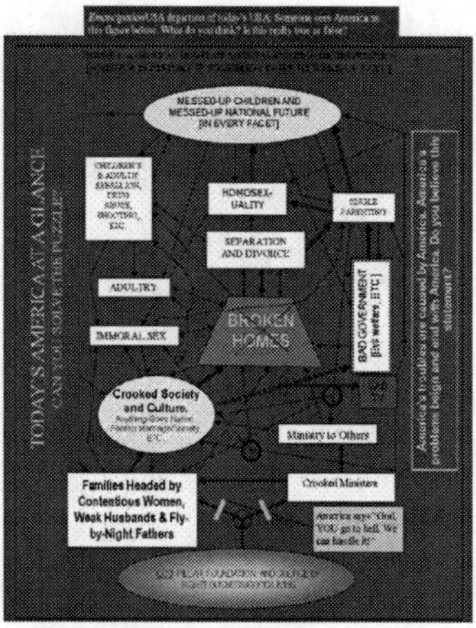

Leadership is not pleasing every Dick, Harry, and Sussy. Leadership is doing what you know is right and mobilizing others to follow based on your presentation of the pro-blems and the true, not symptom-atic, solutions to those pro-blems. Killing the cancer cells is solving the problem. Striving to plant a lost hair is wasting time on solving symptoms, although it may look good.

Dear Barack Obama, take a close look at our Figure 1 again on the next page—*the making or destruction of a society*. Your messages must center on that. Why am I still supporting Barack Obama although I strongly dislike his unqualified comments about the Holy Bible? It is because:

(1) I believe has not really read the Bible as well as he professes to have done.
(2) He has not been taught the Bible right or may not have attended church and Sunday school regularly.
(3) He still needs to learn the word of God and he is open to learn; and
(4) He is the only presidential candidate in many years who, more than others are, may feel freer to discuss the messages that I am suggesting below once he is convinced.

I still like Barack for that number 4, for the other reasons that I stated earlier, and the fact that his election will free many minds and hearts from past bondage, especially the black race. God's honor for Barack's presidency depends on the following messages, otherwise he will experience

*Emancipation*USA depiction of today's USA: Someone sees America as this figure below. What do you think? Is this really true or false?

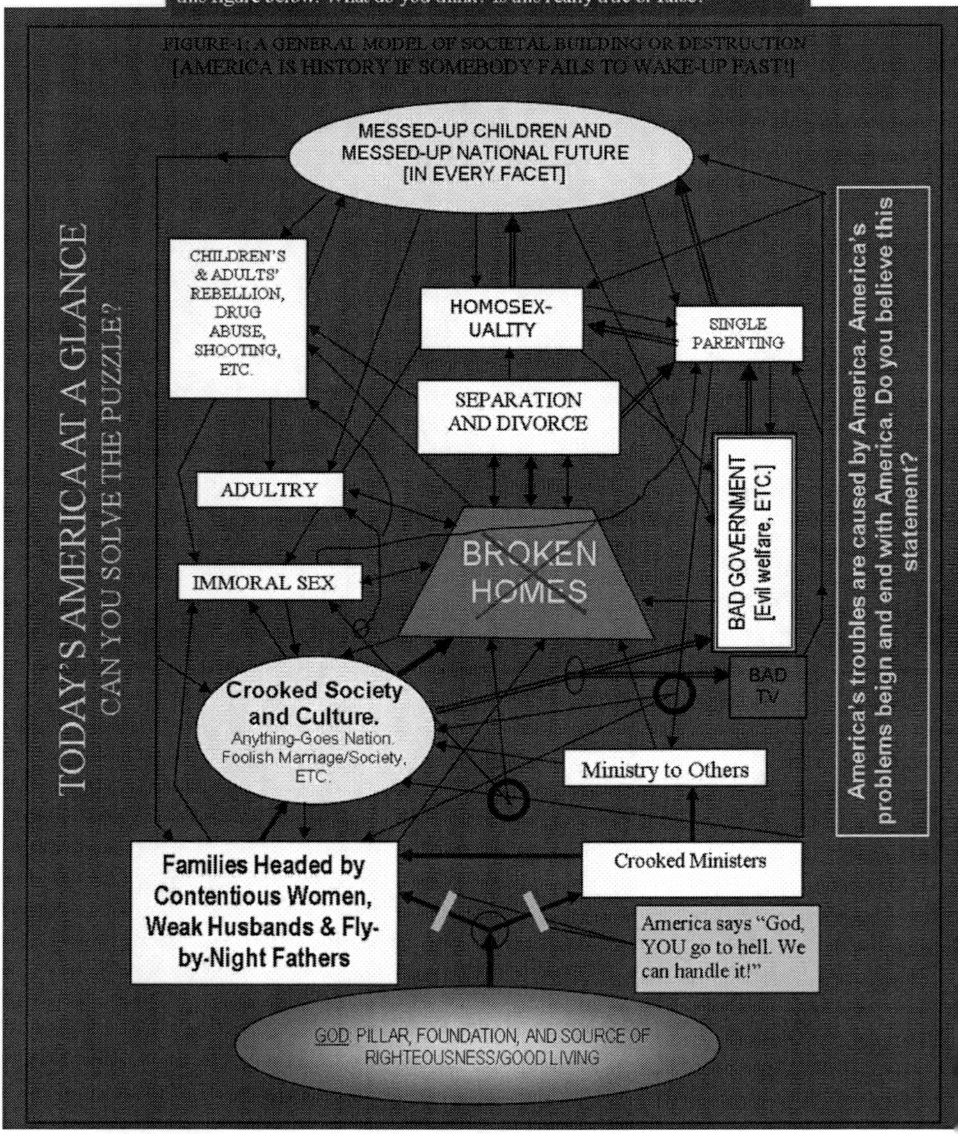

There must be a standard of behavior for one to be disciplined enough to act consistently toward achieving society-building goals with society-building strategies. That's today's America.

some fiery and unwelcome curved balls the devil will strike into his presidential tenure; such demonic balls will mess up Obama's history. To Barack, I say: "Do what.God says do, and God will do His part for you." Below, I will try to enumerate what Barack needs to say to various groups of the United States of America for their own benefit and for the benefit of the nation as a whole.

When there is no wholesome or moral standard of action, chaos and anything-goes become the order of the day for that society. Such is deadly. "Anything-goes" has become the emblem of today's America because America has forsaken her God, the moral compass of life. Hells are breaking loose in and on America because of this error. It will take a serious and humble leader to rise up to the challenge of blowing the trumpet aright! Why not let it be you, President Barack Obama? Do you have enough testosterone to do it? Hold onto your God and He will give you all the guts you need to do the job right. People are perishing. People are suffering. God is choosing you because you can be bold enough to tell the people their problems and offer the true solution, refusing any kind of bribery or enticement that will sway you from the truth!

Your Message To The Black Race

You need to let the black race know that not only that they can do it, but that they have done it. They must speak faith and godly reality now. They have indeed done it. It is no longer that "*We Shall Overcome*" but that "*We Have Overcome*!" It is high time we flushed into the toilet the victim and slave mentalities. God is waiting for the leaders of black race to learn this necessary principle and for all black people to be saying it, believing it, and striving to live it so God can kick in and boost the black race and all races 'big time.'

The time to blame anybody has passed. We must stop blaming the white folks and instead love them and thank them for whatever good parts they have played in black history. Stop remembering the bad things; but if you do, let it be a time of testimony, jumping up with the white race and all races in the praising of God. Remember that many white people also participated and fought for the freedom and civil rights of black people in America. Let the black race remember that millions of white people also fasted and prayed quietly in their homes that God would intervene, and God intervened.

It is now time to keep kissing, hugging, loving, and blessing one another in righteousness until our numbers are called or till Jesus comes. Let them know that the white people, although they may not jump as high as their brothers and sisters (the black folks), are just as beautiful as the same brothers and sisters (the black folks). Let them also know there may be some things that their white brothers and sisters can do better than they will. Nevertheless, when we come together, loving one another, and working together toward the achievement of common (USA) goals, we can do all things much, much, much better than when we are divided, cynical, and complaining. Let God be God!

Now, you must let all black people know that many of our (black) fingers must be pointed to us as the cause of most of our problems today. In fact, let them know that as we cause ourselves all these problems, we are really helping to destroy our nation and everybody else. You must trumpet these necessary problems and solutions at the top of your voice and be ready to lambaste any so-called black leader who might challenge you:

- ✓ How can the black race and the nation it is part of survive with their black men and women fornicating like animals from East to West and North to South without shame and embarrassment just like mindless children and adults who have received no training? That is right! They have received no training at all! They have become sexually sensitized into oblivion!

- ✓ How can the black race and the nation it is part of survive with their black men and boys committing adulteries and fornicating like animals from East to West and North to South without shame and embarrassment? They mindlessly get mindless black women and girls pregnant, making *Welfare* babies, babies that are never loved and raised, babies that grow tall to become wasted and into psychologically destroyed so-called adults. Can black leaders feel ashamed for a change?

- ✓ How can the black race and the nation it is part of survive with their black men and women fornicating like animals from East to West and North to South without shame and embarrassment? They make babies just for the devil, for crimes, and for prisons, because the lazy so-called Mom and so-called Dad used them to get *food stamps* and other wicked and un-scrutinized government so-called benefits. Are these benefits or are they really marriage and family destroyers?

- ✓ How can the black race and the nation it is part of survive with their black women having ungodly-warranted babies here and there and then getting rid of their husbands for love of alimony dollars, child-support dollars, government welfare; the poor husbands and biological fathers are left in the dust, psychologically destroyed, maimed, crime-bound, and jail-bound? How can a race and a nation survive with such wicked women?

- ✓ How can the black race and the nation it is part of survive with their black women having ungodly-warranted babies here and there and hopping from man to man for the sake of immoral dollars, immoral government welfare, and immoral sex acts? The mindless men and boys who fell into their traps become more mindless and totally destroyed as they ravage in crimes, prisons, gangs, and deaths!

- ✓ How can the black race and the nation it is part of survive with their black men and boys not knowing how to be real men and boys because they are mostly hen-raised, acting confused as they are battered with lady-like and whatever-like demons and values? Their own mothers have knocked out and messed up their biological fathers or the so-called fathers were actually badly mama-raised minds who have no clue on how to be fathers, resorting to messing up themselves.

- ✓ How can the black race and the nation it is part of survive with their black men not being no-nonsense fathers and examples to their wives and children? Most of them are scared of their wives; most of them are just ceremonial husbands and fathers; and a lot of them have no love of God. They are fornicators and adulterers, hopping from woman to woman, being the foolish Mandingo. What nonsense is this? What atrocity and murderous act this is? My heart is broken.

- ✓ How can the black race and the nation it is part of survive with too many of their black Ministers rattling the words but not walking the walk? Many of them are too much into white bashing and collecting all kinds of money during all kinds of days (pastor's day, that day, this day), but hardly serve their flock. Their congregations serve and worship them like kings, but they are not humble enough to be like Christ whom they profess to serve. Black Ministers are the number one destroyers of their own race (check out audio from *EmancipationUSA.org* or *ChampionSociety.com*). Enough is enough! They are very wicked people, not Ministers. How can you give birth to what you do not have in your belly? How can an immoral so-called preacher give birth to moral congregation? So many black people go to church and trust their Ministers to help them; but what they get is extremely deplorable, messed up home and people! It is a shame!

- ✓ How can the black race and the nation it is part of survive with too many of their black leaders being as selfish as selfishness can be? They deceive the black race, get their votes, and then serve themselves, betraying the people who supported them. Many of these leaders are too money and self-loving that they do not mind suffocating their subjects and enslaving them for as long as they serve their personal bellies. These leaders have become emblems of mismanagement and corruption in the USA.

- ✓ How can the black race and the nation it is part of survive with members of this race hardly wanting to help each other excel, having deep jealousy and contempt among each other, with the haves oppressing instead of helping the have-nots?

✓ What about the unchallenging schools and school systems, prisons without punishment and correction--more like free motels and a place for long vacations? What about the wicked musical lyrics, hip-hop nonsense, the baggy pants, men and boys behaving like sissies, and so on? If singing means perpetrating crimes and immoral lifestyles that are destroying a race and the nation, then the society needs to do away with such an art. Shame to you, black folks!

My dear brother, President Barack Obama: You have your hand full, but the God of America can do all things through you if you humbly let Him. Among other things, *The* Almighty God is giving you a platform to deal with this mess among the black race. If you refuse to address these issues vehemently and convincingly to God's liking, you yourself will be in a terrible mess, suffering the wrath of God. Your conscience will always let you know if you are doing it right or not. God knows who you are before He plucked you up to be the President and CEO of USA. He knows that you can do it. You must please Him or else! You must not be any kind of President. You must be God's President. That is how America can be blessed. You may check my website, EmancipationUSA.org or ChampionSociety.com to get some resources you may need.

Black Leaders and The Jesse Jackson Factor

I wrote a little information book in 2002 titled *Jesse Jackson: A Menace Or Some Trouble Maker?* (EmancipationUSA.org). I am not going to discuss what is in there. The reader is welcome to visit the site and get a copy. Right now, I am stating that Jesse Jackson and the like must mellow down and humbly turn the touch over to Barack Obama and the new minds of Jesse Jackson Junior. It's time for *The Johua Generation*.

Old picture of Jesse Jackson. Wikipedia

We thank God for what Jesse Jackson Sr. has contributed to the blessing of the black race and all races in the USA. It is not easy by a long, long shot. May God bless him! He should comfort himself in God by knowing that without him, Martin Luther King Jr., Al Sharpton, and numerous other black people and white people who have been fighting injustices and crying out for the black race, there will be no President Barack Obama today.

Therefore, Jesse Senior, "Stop letting jealousy cause you to be saying nonsensical things about Obama." Everybody knows you love Obama, but many people also know that it is hard on you to accept his popularity. Encourage yourself as I have explained and be happy. You are of Moses generation. God has blessed you; He will continue to bless you and comfort you. Now God is putting together the Joshua generation to help clean the minds and bellies of black people off slave mentality and victim mentality as He begins a new era in American and world history.

Dear Jesse: I dare you to throw a BBQ party, invite me, invite Barack, invite Eddy Young, Sharpton, and many others; let us do a hand-the-torch ceremony. You can cry if you want to. We will cry with you too. In fact, all of us will pretend crying with you, including Barack. Therefore, it does not matter what you called Barack (Associated Press July 9, 2008) or how many of his "*you-know-what*" you and I might cut off, others and I know that you love Barack and you fought for him. So, stop apologizing and killing yourself, for we know your heart. We know you are just a little jealous. As Clarence Page of the Chicago Tribune wrote:

> No, I suspect Jackson's objection is less to what Obama said than to who was saying it. Jackson misses that national spotlight that he has not held in recent years. Deep down, his anger suggests that Jackson wanted the world—and Obama—to know the depth of his anger. His objections sent a message that sounds more personal than political: He will not be ignored. He got his wish, although not with the sort of publicity he would like to have had. Even his son Rep. Jesse Jackson Jr., an Obama campaign co-chair, instantly issued a statement that scolded his father with the strongest rebuke that a loving son could give. (Chicago Tribune13, 2008 July).

God actually used that unforeseen statement of jealousy to humble you. He loves us and I love you. You know your son, Jesse Junior, loves you a lot. Hey Jesse Jackson, I am almost glad I found someone who can be as jealous as I can. We just need God to help us. Many of us can be jealous like that. So, quit crying! However, we must remember: Barack Obama is the President of the United States of America, not just the President of black folks. Barack loves black, white, Hispanic, Italian, whatever, whatever American, and that is what it should be—*The* United States of America!

Dear Jesse Jackson, notice that in the above statements I did not really address your criticism of Barack Obama. According to you, "Barack is talking down on black people by stressing the importance of fathers being real fathers instead of talking about jail population, etc." You even employed derogatory and jealous-rage attitude to make the statements. The so-called criticism of yours is not the problem. The problem is jealousy, which I have addressed. Besides jealousy, dear Jesse Jackson Sr., your behavior also exposed the self-interest that has been hindering black leaders from helping black people over many years. I hope you can learn from this attitude of yours and call on other black leaders to get serious and evaluate themselves. Selfishness does not give birth to anything good.

Now you know for sure that Barack Obama is not talking down on any body. He is simply telling the black people the truth that you should have told them many times and years ago; that is where you and many other black leaders committed serious misleading. Family is number one. When you mess up in the family, you mess up in all. Barack is right by letting fathers know that they must be real fathers, not to be flying off the coup after they make babies. Yes, real man is not having the ability to make babies but having the guts to raise them right. The only thing is that Barack also needs to address the atrocities of black women too, as I addressed earlier. Black children and so-called adults fill up the jails because of poor black family management. Stop blaming white folks for a change.

It is time for black leaders to lead. As Al Sharpton, Jesse Jackson, and others like them continue to work as God called them, they must release the rest of the black leaders to line up behind Barack Obama and learn something serious. It is high time that excessive "blackism" was thrown out the window so the United States of America can take over completely. The past is past! We must now move forward in the new direction and with the new USA of togetherness, love, and being there for all Americans. We Have Overcome! YES, WE CAN! That is "Change We Can Believe In!" Aaaaaaaaaaaamen!

Your Message To The White Race and All Races

Thank them for voting for you. Thank them for trusting you. Thank them for looking beyond race, being example to the rest of the world, and making America better. It takes boldness and the tenacity of an avid inventor like Thomas Edison and others to walk past what used to be the usual behavior and to match into change. Thank them for being great Americans. Thank those that did not vote for you. Let them know that they voted their conscience and that is being great American too. Let them know you love them and that you will prove to them that you are the President of the United States of America:

- ✓ America where Race-A + Race-B + Race-C + Race-whatever = 1 Race called the *United States of America.*
- ✓ America where the rich, the middle class, the working class, and the poor will thrive together toward victory and love for one another.
- ✓ America where the nation's know-how can be mobilized and wisely deployed to catalyze the fittest and still reach out and grab the laggards, quickening the left-behinds of the Indian Reservations, the Appalachia, the south, the north, the west, the east, and from sea to shining sea, matching together into the promise that America's God

has for America. No one should be left behind—that goes to every adult and to every child.

- ✓ America of "*In God We Trust*" where our God has to be respected and worshipped so He can help us out of the pit that we have bludgeoned ourselves and badly need a rescuer. That rescuer is our God if we can humble ourselves to trust Him, to obey Him, to get our acts right, to get serious with strong family values and impeccable child-rearing system that promotes the principles of our God.
- ✓ Our beloved America where men should be men again, being of high moral integrity, and women should be women again--not being a piece of sexual meat and promiscuous immoralities, which madly provoke our God and destroy our homes and societies. Such immoralities hinder our promotion of demo-cracies abroad as nations hate to embrace America's demo-cracy with America's cancer of family demolitions.
- ✓ Our beloved America where children, boys, and girls can be true Americans and God lovers again by submitting to their parents, respecting authorities, and challenging their minds in schools. They can no longer be children, boys, and girls who consume sexual immoralities and snub authorities. Such are behaviors that madly provoke our God and have brought massive curses upon America in the form of (1) teenage pregnancies and all the economic wastes and huge crimes associated with them, (2) single-parenting and all the economic wastes and huge crimes associated with it, (3) useless marriages and all the economic wastes and huge crimes associated with them, (4) sickness and diseases and all the economic wastes and huge crimes associated with them, and so on.
- ✓ Our beloved nation where divorce, legalized prostitution, and glorified harlotry can no longer reign. Such immoralities emit poisons into America's atmosphere that once again provoke our God and cause us irreparable harms, culturally, politically, educationally, economically, and competitively. When people have a habit of divorcing and remarrying, divorcing and remarrying, divorcing and remarrying, and our broken system cheers them on—that's legalized prostitution and glorified harlotry.
- ✓ Our beloved America where prisons will be prisons in-deed and not a place to just eat, sleep, play, watch TV (including XXX shows), get more criminalized, and get lazier than before. That is why America's prisons are overflowing. Prison has become a business to many so-called correctional officers and their sponsors.
- ✓ Our beloved nation where, when we get our acts together and put our houses in order, then our God will fight and subdue our enemies for us.

Al Queda is a tiny enemy. Iran cannot measure up. That is if, and only if, we get our acts together and put our homes in order to the pleasing of our God and our motto, "*In God We Trust*." Let us not kid ourselves. Truth may hurt. However, the truth is the only thing that can set us free! America, please love yourself!

To Specific Humanity

The podium of presidency is a podium of grandiose ministry. No today's Evangelist is greater than any president in terms of reach, especially the President of USA. Many people believe what you say or at least take time to listen and be influenced. You are the ultimate role model for the nation and for the world. It is therefore important that Mr. or Madam President use this podium wisely. What must President Barack Obama say to men and boys, women and girls, Gays and Lesbians, parents, young people, American leaders, citizens and immigrants?

To Men and Boys

To Men, you may have to be blunt and let them know that they have messed up. You may need to consult my book or audio-discussion titled, *GOD'S NUMBER 1 PROBLEM IN THIS WORLD: From the So-Called Men To the So-Called Husbands, Not the Women* (EmancipationUSA.org). Men have betrayed God who trusted them to be examples. They have let God down, they have let women and children down, and they have let the society down. A man or boy with uncontrollable penis is no man; he is worse than a sissy. A man that cannot love his wife and children, provide for them, and be godly example to them needs to know that he is not really a man but anything-goes. He is an impostor of a man.

Anything-goes man or boy is worse than 'nothing.' Why? It is because 'nothing' is created to be 'nothing' and it is being 'nothing.' However, the man or boy that is created to be a man or boy is worse than 'nothing' when he acts anything less than a man or boy. Real men should also stop encouraging promiscuity and misusing of women; they should stop sponsoring immoral movies, shows, and magazines, polluting the society and the world. What kind of man would like his daughter's vagina to be misused and be spreading in magazines and wicked shows? Only men who are hen-dominated, sissy-raised, drug-raised, immorally raised, and demonically deceived can do something like that.

To Women and Girls

To women and girls, you have no choice but to say the truth. Contentions and strife in a home kill the home and destroy the product of that home. The products (children and adults) of that home never measure up with the products that come out of loving and well-structured homes. You must let them know that being a strong woman is not subduing your husband, not letting him be a real man of the home, fighting him day and night, and not submitting to his leadership. It is better for any woman not to be married than to marry a man that she cannot trust to lead her, help her, love her, and be willing to die for her. You cannot therefore marry any foolish man because he is tall, macho, rich, and all the other nonsense. That kind of woman is no woman in the first place but a demonic female impostor, looking for whom to devour.

A serious girl or lady who wants to have and maintain a good home should live a God-fearing life so God can give her a God-fearing man who will love her till death, protect her till death, provide for her till death, raise his children with the lovely wife's help, and makes the family godly and lovely. A *fly-by-night* woman or girl will be getting into marriage and be plotting for divorce at the same time, bringing curses to herself and to her own children.

It is good to have feminist movement for as long as it is fighting against injustices directed against women such as equal pay for equal work. However, do not use feminism to try to promote divorce, killing children in the womb, family instability, and destroying anything that God has established, such as family structure and traditional family system. Any wise woman will know that by fighting against God who loves her and knows what is right for her, she is actually fighting against her own well-being.

I will also like the feminist movement to really rise up and fight against people like the so-called Music artist Madonna, the naked-body actresses, and the porn women who are polluting America and the rest of the world by shamelessly spreading their legs, exposing their bodies, and fornicating for the world in movies, shows, and videos. Is this not a total misuse of a woman? Do you not see that such behavior not only displeases the Almighty God of holiness, but it is also destroying the whole population of America and the rest of the world? Millions of people have become sexually sensitized into demons of rapes, school dropouts, immoral brains, and family destructions.

People are working hard to resist the devil, but these women have become instruments of the devil for destroying the society. This is lack of patriotism at the highest degree. Millions of children and adults are sky-high sexually sensitized that millions start having sex by age 8; rapes, divorces, adultery, and countless immoralities stem from these demonic so-called singers and actresses? People like Monica Lewinsky, whose mind was messed up from childhood, can mindlessly commit adultery with the President of the United States, whose mind was also messed up as a child by immoral TV and other shows.

Do you know what this Lewinsky woman has done to Mrs. Hillary Clinton and her daughter? What about others like her? What about people like Bill Clinton? Feminist movement needs to wake up and fight this crude and immoral behavior and the misuse of women bodies. Do you like your girls to grow up and be acting like these wicked girls and women? Shame to you,

America! That's one of the major reasons why so many nations reject you and your democracy. Feminist movement should also rise up and start fighting against adultery and divorce if the movement really claims to have an ounce of love for any child. The movement should start fighting for family stability and not family break-ups.

I really thank God for Hillary Clinton for staying with her husband and forgiving him many times. Men should do it a lot more for their wives who offend in any way. That is the word of God. Hillary has every right to divorce Bill Clinton, but she did not. That's what I call 'strong woman.' Taking the easy road is weakness. May God reward her and continue to comfort her. It is not easy at all for her to keep enduring. Love never fails (Holy Bible, 1 Corinthians 13). Serving God is not easy for as long as the flesh is alive.

Your Message To Gays and Lesbians

God hates homosexuality. He considers it a grave sin. This practice is stated all over the Holy Bible as evil, and God has seriously dealt with people who are involved in such a thing. While you sympathize with their situation, it is necessary that you let them know that gay and lesbian lifestyles are not right according to the Holy Bible. They can stop. It is a sin. Many people like the popular gospel singer, Donnie McClurkin, who used to practice homosexuality have stopped through the help of Jesus Christ. Like my brother, Donnie McClurkin, and Jesus Christ, I am saying:

> Homosexuality is a choice. Gay and lesbian lifestyle are evil practice in the sight of God. It is a damnable behavior. One thing is to be committing a sin. The worst thing is to justify the sin as right. I love gay people just as I love any other people who are sinning. However, gay people need to recognize that they are sinning and need to repent. Homosexuality is not a disease. It is a choice that God can clean up just as God can clean up a liar.

Homosexuality is a grave sin just like lying, cheating, fornication, etc. I use to be a liar, and it was difficult to stop, especially when you are faced with punishment. God helped me stop because I strongly desired to stop. I prayed and cried to Him for years and He helped me. A homosexual or a fornicator can do the same thing as I did. You are not supposed to use government money to support such immorality. It is like using the same money to pay people to lie or cheat. Both the Old Testament and the New Testament seriously condemn homosexuality. You should also condemn it or at least not support it.

Your Message To Parents

Bad parenting begins with bad marriage. Having children out of wedlock is bad and a sinful act. Single parenting is damaging to the children and the society. Single parents have to get serious resources they can use to help raise their children. Marrying the father or mother of the children is very important. Big trouble exists when you have a woman who has babies by different men. It is a mess here. The ultimate advice is to run to a serious Christian church where she can get help with teachings on morality and raising the children at the same time.

There has to be structure in a home so the children will learn submission and obedience to authority. Like a good organization, which runs smoothly and effectively because of a viable structural authority, a good family with a godly flow of authority produces wise, intelligent, moral, and stable children. A family of strife and confusion is the graveyard and factory for emotionally wounded children and adults. Parents must be examples to their children according to set standard of life. Fornication-laden parents will produce fornication-laden children and adults, whether the children see you do it or not. As the spiritual covering for your children, your thoughts and actions perfectly affect your children through spiritual wiring.

Anything-goes parents (especially where the man is ceremonial and/or spiritually weak) produce anything-goes children and adults. A good man must be careful of marrying any kind of woman. Marrying a woman because she is physically beautiful can be the worst mistake a man will ever make. That woman can create all sorts of havoc in the home and prevents him from fulfilling his God-appointed duty of raising spiritual children. There are millions of men in the streets, in prisons, and in some lonely places right now; their so-called beautiful wives kicked them out of their homes and skinned them to half-death, denying them everything, especially the right to raise the poor, beautiful, and unaware children. These men are living in terrible paranoia today, wishing for God to take their lives. Marrying for beauty may spell torturous suicide.

One African man who has suffered so much cruelty in the hands of his beloved African wife, whom he married for wrong reason, once cried out, "I have married death!" The same thing goes for a good woman who dares to marry a person because he looks handsome or has money. Many women have married to their graves and to sleepless nights like that. These men can go out, fornicate with one or more women, and then come home to you with a million roses. They can commit adultery on Saturday night and then go to church with you on Sunday morning, wrapping his hands on your shoulder in "love"—love from hell.

What kind of children will come out of a relationship like this? Answer: demonically oppressed children, who cannot help it but to grow and be acting like the spiritual atmosphere of the home in which they are raised. That is the major tumult in today's America. What you do in the so-called secret and what you do elsewhere affect the children you are raising. Raise your children by example. As the head of your home, it is critical that you confess and repent of any sin so that sin (evil) cannot be your family's covering. Can you imagine the devil (unconfessed sin) being the head of a home? That is trouble! Everyone in the home may look like they are progressing, but time will tell. The children and adults out of that home are spiritual time bombs, unless God intervened somewhere along the way. Parents must be godly examples to their children, striving to raise them in holy and modest lifestyle.

Your Message To Young People

Young people must submit to their parents' leadership and obey authorities. They should know that they are America's future. They must learn responsibility. They must have their priorities right, desist from immoral behavior, and engage serious subjects in schools, making excellent grades.

Unfortunately, today's American children are super arrogant and disrespectful to everybody. This behavior is a function of the parent, parents, and the spiritual atmosphere from where they come. Since their parents have messed up, leaders should know how to renovate children to be able to go back to their homes and alter the evil atmosphere. I just recalled how I picked up one of my former students who made an "A" in one of my classes. I saw him one day patrolling aimlessly on a street in downtown Jackson, Mississippi. I just knew that something was terribly wrong. His mind was off.

The first time I saw him I was on a one-way street and could not make a U-turn. I prayed to God to show him to me again. Another day I saw him and flagged him down. I could tell that his mind was not in order. I felt so much compassion because he worked hard in my class and was one of the few students who made an "A" in my Principles of Management class about three years before that encounter. I was expecting him to be successful in the world. Well, I convinced him and took him to my house. Thank God, I was then a bachelor. After I checked where he was living with his people and determined that it was the source of the trouble, I just let him stay in my house for several days so I could influence him. It worked fairly.

Many a time it will take loving and no-nonsense outsiders to rehabilitate a child or adult who has been messed up in a home. That child can go back to that home and help set things in order. When I was accused of child abuse for spanking my boy too much (which I did, out of anger), I refused to defend myself. Besides, I strongly believed that God wanted me to go to jail for Him and to help some young people. My colleagues and my boss just could not believe it. God made it where I must have to go to prison. I really had no other choice. Guess what. About 16 years ago I had told one of my Caucasian friends that we need to contact the City of Jackson Sheriff to insert us in jails so we can live and minister to inmates. My friend said, "Heck No!" When the child-abuse thing came up, I strongly felt in my heart that God wanted me to go to jail for Him and to learn some lessons for myself too.

I was sent to prison for two years. I did not know what to expect, but I humbly followed my God wherever He sent me. It was very sobering. I cried in my heart as soon as I went into the place they call, Tank, with many criminals, waiting to be dispatched. I was extremely naïve, not knowing a thing about criminal life. To almost all those tough men and boys, I was acting like something they just did not have a word to describe. "This one does not belong in jail," some stated. After looking at twelve of them with me, on a concrete floor, very cold area, I felt compassion in my heart. All I could do was pray. I never felt hungry. Since there was no privacy, and I had no other place, I just made the place and any other place they took me my home. I always knelt down for prayer.

Soon I started calling on all of them to teach them how to pray. First I told them that we need to repent our sins and that I should start. They just could not believe that I was doing it. I confessed my sins before them, and then got them one by one to confess theirs. This was hard for me to write because I am crying and shaking as I write this portion, for I could not believe I did all that I did. I really did not know when I did them. God did all. Well, they all confessed their sins. After the last person, the Spirit of God showed me that some of them were hiding murders that they committed. Immediately I laid hand on each of them and confessed murders in their behalf. We prayed and sang after the confession. They had no clue how to pray nor did they know a single song. I taught them. They were very happy and encouraged.

To cut everything short, my prison life transformed about 400 prisoners. God used me to break some gang, to snatch some people out of gangs. Some gangsters hated me, plotted to do something to me, but their plot was spoiled because they held their meeting close to the bed of a Caucasian young man, Mr. Tim, for whose reason and others I strongly believed God sent me to prison. See, Tim had become my sidekick; I was mentoring him in prison. All we did was studied the Bible and prayed. In a dream, God placed a baby Tim in my hand and said, “This is your son, give birth to him.” They had taught that Tim was sleeping. After they had finished and gone, Tim came and told me their plot.

I forced the scary Tim to get them to me or I will go after them. Later on, Tim and I talked to the head of the gang, and the only language I knew is the language of God. Again, to cut the story short, the head of the gang and the gang became my friends and started going to church with me. Sometimes it was me against bunch of them. I stopped some of them from smoking marijuana; whenever I smelled it I got sad and began to look for who was doing it so I could scold at him, minister to him, and help their parents who were not their.

They started calling me a snitch because I let the officers know when they were doing some evil thing. After they had talked to me many times and learned that I could not help it but serve my God, or may be that I just did not know a thing about prison lifestyle, some of them started protecting me even without me knowing it. Many of them changed their lives and repented from their sins. Some of them fasted with me for 3 days, 7 days, 21 days, and 40 days. The whole prison began to change. Some inmates were so fired up that they called their parents, ministered to them, and got them crying and repenting. How do I know? Well, they sometimes put me to the phone to talk to their parents or they shared testimonies during our bible studies.

I have always believed that prisoners are gold mines of God. Those so-called criminals are victims of bad marriages, bad parenting, and wicked

American welfare system. Almost all the people in prison, especially the black people, are products of divorce, broken homes, single parenting, and welfare menace. However, I know, and I have confirmed that these so-called criminals can be changed to go back and change their parents and relatives who raised them. They can be truly overhauled so they themselves can be role models in the society.

If someone like me can get all kinds of money that American government has been throwing away on useless programs, I can use that money to empty most American prisons, perfectly rehabilitating over one-third of the inmates; I can turn the inmates into golden men and women for renewing and rebuilding American society. They can go from being criminals to being the cream of God's crops. God works with the love that is on the inside of His man or woman to help the subjects that the lover is focusing on. Where there is no love, there is no God. When love is there, God uses that love to go to work. Love is the antenna of God through which one can reach God, for God is love. Just as cellular-phone companies give their customers the phones with appropriate built-in antennas so their customers can connect to their towers or satellites, so God gives love to those that seek Him so they can use that love to call Him and reach Him anytime for undertaking a project or projects.

Your Message To America's Leaders

They need to be leaders, for the world is looking at them. Many people are running and being elected into America's political offices that have no business being there. A lot of them are Democrats, with addictive lifestyles of immoralities and anything-goes personalities, which can only contribute to wounding and destroying America. Many Republican candidates, although they are good in some areas, tend to harbor unnecessary hate or deep dislike against certain segments of the American society; such attitude makes it difficult for them to love and lead. In both cases, God is seriously handicapped.

God always excuses Himself from anything immoral. He seems to have natural hate for someone who is yellow but has been deceiving people into believing he is black or green. We need America to be strong. The true and sustainable strength of America can only come from building America's house on the sure foundation of strong, traditional family system with sound (holy) standard of behavior. America must get back to the wishes of her founding fathers.

Leaders must be example. They must be people of high integrity, with fear of God and submission to righteousness and holiness. American leaders must do something about their marriage with fornication and adultery, selling their souls and the American people to bribery and corruption through special interests and lobbyists, divisiveness on party lines instead of unity in representing USA all the time, seeking for votes by succumbing to demands by any segment of the electorate even when that demand is truly unpatriotic and destructive to the nation, etc. American leaders should take strict control of America's borders and allow America's God back into every facet of America's life.

True American leaders must cry out, clean themselves in repentance, and call on America's God to intervene in the affairs of USA, for America is going downhill. Today's America is worshipping vagina instead of America's God—the ONE in "IN GOD WE TRUST." Today's America is badly confused because the citizens have been living in immorality for too long and have been trying so hard to psych themselves into believing that good is bad and bad is good, and that whatever seems pleasing to the flesh is god. Yet, after the psychotic drug or exercise wears out, the real hole in the center of their hearts that only real GOD can satisfy continues to yearn for help and mercy. The stiff-necked generation knows they should fill this hole appropriately but the commitment to another god, sexual immorality, is always in the way.

Who can bail this filthy cat? Only serious leaders who are dedicated to God and righteousness and are ready to fight, live or die for the same can do it! America's welfare system and select laws are wicked (against God) and unpatriotic (against the nation). The welfare system and such laws weaken strong and traditional family system by encouraging a wide range of absurdities; they encourage divorces, single parenting, teenage pregnancies, hatred and disobedience to parents and authorities, dangerous schools and school systems, co-ed abomination, demonic television shows and movies, and prisons without correction. They stuff America's atmosphere with Satan's number one weapon of mass destruction called immoral sex and promiscuity. Real American leaders need to rise up and fight against these laws. Total revolution is needed!

Your Message To Citizens and Immigrants

Citizens need to be patriotic citizens not haters of their own country. Most Americans think they love America, but in action, they hate America. Anytime you find yourself doing something that is harming instead of helping your nation, you hate that nation not loving it. Examples of people who hate America are those committing adulteries and destroying their marriages and homes, lazy Americans, tax cheaters, cheaters in schools, weak and lazy teachers and workers, selfish employers, selfish leaders, disobedient children, producers of immoral TV shows and movies, citizens helping outsiders to kill and hurt Americans, haters of God and righteousness, bad parents, etc. Americans need to love America the right way for a change! They need to embrace their God and righteousness; they need to act as that value system of righteousness directs them.

As for immigrants and visitors, it is a simple message—"love America, help America, or just please go back to your country, for America has enough problems of her own." How can immigrants love America? Wish America well in all your thoughts and prayers. Cry to God for Him to intervene in America's affairs and correct things. Do not terrorize America; expose any hater of America that wishes to destroy her if you cannot correct the person. Pay your taxes. Love American citizens and criticize them constructively; do not close your mouth. Thank God and America for helping you in any way so they can have strength to keep helping you and many others.

Do not take evil advantage of America's freedom and love of human rights to try to hurt the nation in any way. GOD ALMIGHTY MUST EXPOSE YOU AND HURT YOU BACK IN RETURN! Remember that so many little people and little nations would never have the guts to exist today if America had not intervened or had kept quiet like many other nations usually do. Do you now witness the murders, the humiliation and the treatment of Zimbabwean citizens by their so-called leader? When America humbly rose up to intervene, Russia and China vetoed the move with the general reason of 'it is not good to intervene in other nations' domestic affairs.' (Bone and Robertson, 2008, Times Online). Imagine yourself or your own children naked, their bellies ballooning due to malnutrition and injustice, and you are killed when you speak up. Imagine your parents and your loved ones under such a regime where thugs and police are used to slaughter oppositions or intimidate voters. Imagine yourself and your loved ones being raped and killed daily by wicked tyrants.

Now, do you think Russian and Chinese leaders would love for any nation or all nations to intervene for their help if they switch places with the Zimbabweans who are suffocating in the hands of Robert Mugabe, the Sudanese Darfur people who are being raped daily and murdered off the face of the earth by their Muslim leaders, or the Bosnian Muslims who once faced extermination by the Serbs? They won't do it! They will never like themselves and their loved ones to be constantly raped, suffer millions of deaths with no end in sight, and looking helpless like hungry and dying babies. They will even attack you for trying to get them to imagine it or reason empathetically.

Can you now see the wickedness of the two nations? China supplies weapons to the government of the two African nations. "Almighty God, please have mercy on America; cleanse her, and stand behind America again!" Do you know that there are nations where the only available job is to join the military or the rebels because all they know is war; they have been fighting for years and years? (Nessman, Ravi 2008). Criminals, selfish warlords, and corrupt politicians usually orchestrate these wars. Left to America alone, she would have intervened to help the innocent people in Myamnar and toher places. The world will become a semi-hell without strong America in it, ceteris paribus.

America is one nation that does well for her enemies and everybody else when catastrophes strike. Sometimes she actually gets no "thank you" but more insults from those she helped. If some natural disaster hits Iran right now, American citizens and government will be in the lead to pull Mahmoud Ahmadnejad out of the rubble and pour billions of dollars in aid to help all Iranians even though America is suffering massive Balance of Trade deficit and general economic hardship. China, which is making most of the money now, may or may not help at all.

Why is America like that? America still loves her God in that respect. I have learned immeasurable and priceless virtues from America and Americans that I must employ to help and treat fellow citizens of Nigeria, Africa, and all people. Therefore, my dear immigrants and visitors, please love and treat America nice. She may just, on one or two occasions, act like a pain in a bad place, but she is still the best loving nation in the world by millions of miles. I just cry with deep cry that she will get her family system back in order and avoids the worship of vagina. Those are the only cancers that will kill her sooner or later.

God, please help America. The world needs her. I need her. You, the reader, need her too if you think about it. The worst that can happen is for wicked people to take over America or for her economic strength to wane badly. Unwise leadership gradually destroys strong nations. God can use Barack Obama to help, but he must be careful not to be liberal to the point of promoting laziness and stifling innovation. I believe he will not do that. America's welfare system needs to be eradicated or acutely revised and monitored. The system is a major instrument of Satan and his demons in destroying the American family and everything else. It is the major producer of many crimes in the United States of today. When you break homes and become an instrument for breeding lazy and immoral people, the results are a society filled with criminals and overpopulated prisons.

Wise Perception. Good Decision

This is 'congratulation' to Barack Obama. It is not because of how well he is doing on the campaign trail. It is because of the perception and the decision he made concerning his children's appearance on the television for such interviews. Many Americans may not understand it. Even Barack may not pinpoint a finger to why it is dangerous and destructive to the children; it just clicked in him that the exposure and treatment might not be good for the children.

America--that is a good decision by the presidential candidate, Barack Obama, and the one that all parents must learn. Millions and millions of American children are out-of control, just to say the least. Part of the reason is the way they are being treated like highly, mature adults when their brains are just fluid and needed to be first grounded on guiding, moral principles or values. Getting them unmonitored boy friends or girl friends, treating them independently of parents on TVs, and failure to rebuke them as hard as possible when they start doing wrong or when their heads start getting bigger than their bodies are some of the subtle destroyers. You must plant all that need to be planted while they are still at raising-age.

Once you expose your kids or children to the wide accolades of the public and, especially, to the Western or Amrican television without very tight control, you have ruined those children morally. You have planted a destruction-wage or antenna that will continually destroy that child like cancer, negatively affecting everything he or she does. It is a very subtle demon. Only very few, loving aprents may see it. Be careful about planting unwarranted pride in your child!

Once a person is morally destroyed, everything in him or her is ruined until he she gets back that moral connection to authority—understanding that someone is over him or her, spiritually and physically. Such knowledge shall cause him or her to weigh whatever him or her does before doing any. Millions of American children who turn out to be millions of America's so-called adults have lost such moral guidance or authority. They are very confused, continually looking for wrong love or anything to fill the vacuum (of control); they are finally being destroyed if God fails to intervene somewhere along the way. Early exposure of children to public accolades is destructive, especially in material-driven USA. That's just part of the problem with Britney Spears, Madona, so-called child stars, and the rest of them.

Quick Lesson On Culture and Sustaining America

Culture is everything. The base upon which a culture is standing defines the stability of the culture. A culture may prefer to stand on a pillar of pleasing the flesh and doing whatever feels good, while another may stand on the pillar of God's righteousness and directions. Only time tells which is which. When the wind blows, the chicken's anus is exposed and seen. The wind is blowing heavily on America today.

Sometimes I hear Americans say, "Your attitude determines your altitude." That statement is perfectly right. However, the real trouble is "what kind of attitude did you portray that got you to the top?" Is it an attitude that gets you to that top just to have you destroyed eventually or the one that gets you to that top to keep you and to bless you without sorrows and nightly tears? Is it the kind of attitude that gets you to the top to make a classic fool and a showcase of your selfishness or the one that gets you up there to promote the nation and everyone else?

Every good and perfect gift comes from God (Holy Bible, James 1:17). God blesses you and adds no sorrow to it (Holy Bible, Proverbs 10:22). What can you say about a so-called actress who messed-up her body and fornicated her way up to where she is now? Is she really on top or is she really at the bottom of some trash? Think about it very deeply. It will not take long for the trash on top of her to turn into maggots and scorpions, attracting snakes and other unwanted beings, eating her alive and destroying others with her. That is what is happening to America today from Marylyn Monroe and Madonna to their supporters and to the whole nation. From bunch of fornication-laden so-called stars to bunch of adulterous men in American homes and political offices, America is burning! It's a pollution! It's in the atmosphere! American TV is it's ocean of distribution.

It can only take a seriously stubborn, righteous-minded, and true-love president to lead the way toward cleaning America. Yes, people will rebel and lament, but it will take a tough leader and some serious members of the American society to yell, "Enough is enough!" They must be ready to fight and die for cleaning this mess toward truly emancipating America and reclaiming her dreams. If you fail to fight now, demons and their possessors will take over America completely. You cannot do much then but sit and wallow in endless tears, running and hiding from demons and their possessors. Wake up America or else!

Culture defines everything else. Get the culture right to get beliefs right, to get attitudes right, to get intentions right, and to get behaviors right. Culture is strictly values that typify a group of people or a nation. The behaviors of a society are manifestations of the culture of that society. Behaviors and their precedents are offspring of value system. They easily manifest in the society's politics, economics, education, technology, competitiveness, international relations, etc. The real difference between the wheat and the chaff, where the rubber really meets the road, is "which culture sustains a society on top steadily and unflappably" Demonic culture can only go so far, but "*In God We Trust*" culture defines a steady progress and a steady hand. America, you are safe only with your God! You are "in good hands with your God only!" You cannot reason it away. You cannot run away from it.

Dear beloved America: You are going down into the Bermuda Triangle at a geometric pace because your current culture is a demonic mess. America, you better listen to me or perish! You must change! Get back to your God! God called me to give you this message, and I am doing my best, although I am frustrated. You may go to *Emancipation*USA.org or ChampionSociety.com to get a copy of my audio or video presentation, "*THE ULTIMATE AUDACITY OF HOPE FOR TODAY'S USA: Emancipating America and Her Dreams and Where Barack Obama Really Missed It.*" The next page contains some of my books or audio-CDs and *Music Albums* that can help rebuild America's culture.

Just visit EmancipationUSA.org or Championsociety.com

CHAPTER 15

STATEMENTS OF ENDORSEMENT

A good name is better than many riches. What you get anytime in life is a function of what you inputted in your life days and the lives you touched or hurt. What you give is what you get. If you sow the wind, you will reap the whirlwind. If you sow 'good,' you'll reap many goodies. So, do 'good!'

Barack Obama, as a Harvard Law School student, was the first black president of the Harvard Law Review. (Photo courtesy Obama campaign)

Is George W. Bush Jr. a mistake? Some people, all-right—millions of people tend to believe that George W. Bush Jr. may have been a mistake or even a punishment to USA. You may need to *Think Again*. You do not know God completely, and He works in ways that we may never figure out no matter how hard we try. Are you saying that someone else would have handled the blow of September 11, 2001 better than George W. Bush did? When he was coming into office he did not know, and nobody else knew that September 11 2001 would be a horrible day of what Al Queda did. Al Queda had been planning for the attack in years. It would have happened to any person o rmay be not. We just do not know.

EmancipationUSA.org, ChampionSociety.com

Let me tell you. What happened to America on September 11 was enough to derail or dismantle America. The man, our President, really tried to hold America together. He deserves someone to quit criticizing him too much and may be give him some hug and a smile. Some other person may have panicked too much that the whole nation would also be in hyper-panic mode. May the Almighty God bless and comfort George W. Bush Jr. As I said earlier, I was tired of the criticisms and insults he was getting that I created what I believe are beautiful Music albums for him and for his champion wife, Laura.

September 11, 2001 attack changed everything about America and only somebody called George W. Bush Jr. may have been able to not only absorb the greatest blow of that terrorist hit, but only him may have been in a position to help America cope and to curtail some freedom in order to close in on terrorists among us. Another person as the President of America during this period may not have been able to handle the situation. We just don't know. No one could ever imagine the pressure and pains he endured. Thanks to the ever comforting and nurturing hands of his wife who continues to stand strong by his side. Only God knows what he is doing and how he is holding on. Some people may argue that if Al-Gore were the winner of the presidency that Al Queda may not have struck or that something would have been better. That may be a lie or a wrong assumption.

These terrorists have been plotting and training for over three years before September 11, 2001 to use those airplanes as bombs against world-trade center, the white house, the pentagon, and other places. They did not know who would be the leader of the USA and they do not care. Guess who knew all the plans from the beginning. God. Do you think that God chose George Jr. to be president because of the Al Queda event and other factors He may have considered? May be or may be not. We do not know. Nevertheless, I am sure of one thing that has been proven in the Holy Bible many times. Enthroning a person who really fears God and leads a holy lifestyle will cause God to abort or expose evil actions like Al Qaeda's September 11 before they hatch (Holy Bible 1 kings, 2 Kings, 2 Chronicles). God is a warrior and a protector for a nation whose leader portrays holiness and urges the people to live a holy life. That is the only situation that may cause Al Qaeda to fail on achieving the results of September 11, 2001.m Unfortunately, most American Presidents to date do not fight against immorality in the nation.

If you believe that a mistake was made in electing George W. Bush Jr. as President, then this your chance again to cast your vote for the next President of the United States. Stop blaming Bush Jr. too much and look to God too. The President has truly worked hard and made tough decisions to keep America safe during America's darkest hour and trying times. Some President called George W. Bush Jr. may have to come before the calling of President Barack H. Obama Jr. This is now your chance to vote, not based on anything else but on ability to perform. This is the time to cast your vote so you don't have to chew your tongue tomorrow. Look very closely at the two candidates we have and you will discover that the right person for the job is handily Barack Obama. Can you vote for him? Let's make history together. There are areas you may not agree with him, but it is important that you look at all areas before you vote. ALL AREAS!

Make your best decision now so you don't have to worry afterwards. Let these endorsements remind you why there is Obama fever in today's USA.

Edward M. Kennedy's Endorsement of Obama

Sen. Edward Kennedy
Wikipedia

Rep. Patrick Kennedy
Wikipedia

Caroline Kennedy
BarackObama.com

This is the most powerful and very significant endorsement for Barack Obama. Coming from the American icon, Senator Edward (Teddy) M. Kennedy, it is like getting an endorsement from mountains of years of experience in American government, receiving an endorsement from the late and assassinated presidential candidate, Robert Kennedy, and from the late and assassinated president, John f. Kenney—all combined. In fact, it is like receiving an endorsement from half of the nation. For decades, Ted Kennedy has been on one side and the GOP on the other side. Teddy, Patrick (his son), and Caroline (the daughter of President John f. Kennedy) and many members of the family are supporters of Barack Obama for the next president of the United States.

Whenever Teddy finishes his course in this world and dies, I want him to know that God's mercy is with him in a big way. "So, my dear friend and loving brother, Teddy: Do not fear death. Let it come when God allows it, for the devil has no control over you. Death is a friend to a child of God. You are a child of God. You will rest in peace, my friend. *God has heard your heart cries and talks to Him*. I repeat, "*God has heard your heart cries and talks to Him*." Don't worry about the brain tumor or whatever tumor that you have. God may or may not take it out. We will continue to pray. However, be rest assured that you will rest in piece and your soul will be with the Almighty God. You and your family have been permanent examples to me and to many other people in the service of unselfishness. I'm still learning."*...Festus.*

Ted Kennedy may be better referred to as *Mr. Democratic Party*. In spite of my disagreement with him on certain issues, I like him and I love the Kennedy family as a whole. They may be what the pundits negatively call liberal, but they may also be what Jesus Christ positively calls *love for the common man, the less fortunate, and the left-behinds*. They have sacrificed, fought, and died for social justice. They are America. I hope that Barack Obama won't let them down on

behalf of all Americans. Satisfying them must require Barack to pay attention to the messages in the previous chapter.

On that faithful day at the American University, Caroline Kennedy endorsed Barack Obama, saying, "Over the years, I've been deeply moved by the people who've told me they wish they could feel inspired and hopeful about America the way people did when my father was president. This longing is even more profound today. Fortunately, there is one candidate who offers that same sense of hope and inspiration and I am proud to endorse Senator Barack Obama for President…" (Mike on January 28, 2008 BlogforPresidents.us). Then Senator Kennedy followed, after being introduced by Caroline:

> "Thank you, Caroline. Thank you for that wonderful introduction and for your courage and bold vision, for your insight and understanding, and for the power and reach of your words. Like you, we too "want a president who appeals to the hopes of those who still believe in the American Dream, and those around the world who still believe in the American ideal; and who can lift our spirits, and make us believe again." Thank you, Caroline. Your mother and father would be so proud today.
>
> Thank you, Patrick, for your leadership in Congress and for being here to celebrate and support a leader who truly has the power to inspire and make America good again, "from sea to shining sea." Thank you, American University.
>
> I feel change in the air. Every time I've been asked over the past year who I would support in the Democratic Primary, my answer has always been the same: I'll support the candidate who inspires me, who inspires all of us, who can lift our vision and summon our hopes and renew our belief that our country's best days are still to come.
>
> I've found that candidate. And it looks to me like you have too. But first, let me say how much I respect the strength, the work and dedication of two other Democrats still in the race, Hillary Clinton and John Edwards. They are my friends; they have been my colleagues in the Senate. John Edwards has been a powerful advocate for economic and social justice. And Hillary Clinton has been in the forefront on issues ranging from health care to the rights of women around the world. Whoever is our nominee will have my enthusiastic support.
>
> Let there be no doubt: We are all committed to seeing a Democratic President in 2008. But I believe there is one candidate who has extraordinary gifts of leadership and character, matched to the extraordinary demands of this moment in history. He understands what Dr. Martin Luther King, Jr. called the "fierce urgency of now..."
>
> ..Now, with Barack Obama, there is a new national leader who has given America a different kind of campaign—a campaign not just about himself, but about all of us. A campaign about the country we will become, if we can rise

above the old politics that parses us into separate groups and puts us at odds with one another...

And in Barack Obama, I see not just the audacity, but the possibility of hope for the America that is yet to be. What counts in our leadership is not the length of years in Washington, but the reach of our vision, the strength of our beliefs, and that rare quality of mind and spirit that can call forth the best in our country and our people.

With Barack Obama, we will turn the page on the old politics of misrepresentation and distortion. With Barack Obama, we will close the book on the old politics of race against race, gender against gender, ethnic group against ethnic group, and straight against gay. With Barack Obama, we will close the door on the old economics that has written off the poor and left the middle class poorer and less secure.

He offers a strategy for prosperity—so that America will once again lead the world in better standards of life. With Barack Obama, we will break the old gridlock and finally make health care what it should be in America—a fundamental right for all, not just an expensive privilege for the few... Barack Obama is the one person running for President who can bring us that change. Barack Obama is the one person running for President who can be that change.

I love this country. I believe in the bright light of hope and possibility. I always have, even in the darkest hours. I know what America can achieve. I've seen it. I've lived it—and with Barack Obama, we can do it again. I know that he's ready to be President on day one. And when he raises his hand on Inauguration Day, at that very moment, we will lift the spirits of our nation and begin to restore America's standing in the world.

There was another time, when another young candidate was running for President and challenging America to cross a New Frontier. He faced public criticism from the preceding Democratic President, who was widely respected in the party. Harry Truman said we needed "someone with greater experience"—and added: "May I urge you to be patient." And John Kennedy replied: "The world is changing. The old ways will not do…It is time for a new generation of leadership."

So it is with Barack Obama. He has lit a spark of hope amid the fierce urgency of now. I believe that a wave of change is moving across America. If we do not turn aside, if we dare to set our course for the shores of hope, we together will go beyond the divisions of the past and find our place to build the America of the future. My friends, I ask you to join in this historic journey -- to have the courage to choose change. It is time again for a new generation of leadership. It is time now for Barack Obama." – and "the glow from that fire can truly light the world." (Mike on January 28, 2008; BlogforPresidents.us).

Other Selections From Obama's Endorsements

The excitement for Barack Obama becoming the next President of the United States is like fireworks on America's Fourth of July all over the world. Read this excerpt from Bob Cesca, a common man endorsement of Barack Obama:

> ...after seven years in this Dark Age, I've almost forgotten what it was like to have a real president occupying the White House: a president who, even if I dis-
>
> agreed with his policies and ideology, dignified the office with a stature that symbolized the awesomeness of America...
>
> American history is inextricably tied to the presidency. It's how we mentally assemble the chronology of our past. For going on eight years, we've endured a chief executive who never should have ascended to this post. Consequently, this decade has been an aberration; a time when Americans somehow championed an illegitimate, Orwellian hooplehead and, naturally, we suffered for our lack of vision. This is how most of the first decade of this century will be remembered.
>
> Yet our generation is being offered another chance here -- an opportunity to set things straight and elect a president who not only illustrates the historical qualities of the office, but who also defines an energetic new approach. The next president has to be Senator Barack Obama.
>
> Senator Obama's intelligence, passion and quality of character can inspire us to recapture our own potential for greatness. And after all these years of darkness, there is no alternative other than to correct our trajectory with someone who can elevate our common goals -- the American Dream. For the American Dream to survive, this era demands a new president who will include all of us in the debate over our future, whether or not we agree on every issue.
>
> And I'm proud to say that I don't agree with the senator on everything. But it doesn't matter because this campaign is about much more than individuals and their pet issues. This is about the reacquisition of an ideal -- of a benevolent greatness, which has been stolen away from us. I see in Senator Obama an historic character who fits within my persnickety and idealistic template for the presidency -- and this time around, it happens that my idealistic choice has a realistic chance to win. So this isn't necessarily an endorsement based on ideology, but an endorsement based on that which is required from an historical perspective. (Cesca 2007, The Huffington Post).

Pat Hogue, 53, a physician assistant, said that she hasn't seen such excitement in her 35 years of voting. "There's a passion, a fever," she said. Yet when it comes to the candidate, "I just like the fact that he has a calm spirit. We've had the cowboy." (Zaborney 2008). Mr. Ogletree, Obama's Harvard professor, is highly impressed about Obama then and now. In just about everywhere Obama has functioned, people who worked with him or went to school with him has only good memories of him. Truly, it is remarkable how this man has maintained such an incredible record of innocence, integrity, and love of people everywhere he has been. I am ashamed of myself. Obama is truly a serious, no drama Obama. According to an interview:

> A Harvard law professor who taught presidential candidate Barack Obama - and his wife, Michelle - spoke for nearly two hours yesterday about the man who first impressed him as a law student. "I'm so excited about this candidacy that I just can't tell you. I'm just overfull with joy," Professor Charles Ogletree said to

> 35 mostly African-American professionals gathered at the faculty club in the Hilton Hotel Toledo on the University of Toledo Health Science Campus, the former Medical College of Ohio…"If you take a step back and take a look at his background, you wouldn't expect him to be where he is today," he said. Yet, he
>
> said Mr. Obama has remembered his background by helping others. Mr. Ogletree cited Mr. Obama's rejection of an all-but-certain clerkship with a federal judge to become a community organizer in Chicago. "That was unthinkable for anyone, certainly [for] an African-American to avoid the trappings of success," he said.
>
> The candidate and his wife have "always impressed me as people who put the community first," he said. "They lift as they climb. As they take a step up, they take someone with them." Mr. Ogletree spoke of Mr. Obama's stances on issues from health care to education to energy-efficient cars... (Zaborney 2008).

Zbigniew Brzezinski is a counselor and trustee at the Center for Strategic and International Studies. He cochairs the CSIS Advisory Board. He is the Robert E. Osgood Professor of American Foreign Policy at the School of Advanced International Studies, Johns Hopkins University, in Washington, D.C., a cochair of the American Committee for Peace in the Caucasus, and a former Chairman of the American-Ukrainian Advisory Committee. Zbigniew Brzezinski was also a member of the Policy Planning Council of the Department of State from 1966 to 1968, Chairman of the Humphrey Foreign Policy Task Force in the 1968 presidential campaign, director of the Trilateral Commission from 1973 to 1976, and principal foreign policy adviser to Jimmy Carter in the 1976 presidential campaign. From 1977 to 1981, Dr. Brzezinski was national security adviser to President Carter. This is what he has to say about Barack Obama:

> … thus far in Hillary Clinton's campaign, she is demonstrating a disturbing trend towards incrementalism and continuity of Bush administration policies that she should cease.
>
> This is a "discontinuous moment" in American history in which it's highly dangerous to American interests to plot tomorrow's course by what one did yesterday. There are no easy patterns or templates for the time we are in. America may be slipping from being a globally recognized, earth-sprawling hegemon to something that looks like just another great power -- well, perhaps not just any great power, a big one with great assets -- but that slippage has real costs….
>
> … "Obama recognizes that the challenge is a new face, a new sense of direction, a new definition of America's role in the world." … "Obama is clearly more effective and has the upper hand," Brzezinski, who was President Jimmy Carter's national security adviser, said. "He has a sense of what is historically relevant, and what is needed from the United States in relationship to the world." …

> Cinton's foreign-policy approach is "very conventional,"...don't think the country needs to go back to what we had eight years ago." "There is a need for a fundamental rethinking of how we conduct world affairs," he added. "And Obama seems to me to have both the guts and the intelligence to address that issue and to change the nature of America's relationship with the world."...
> Barack Obama has a practical, near term policy approach on Cuba that clearly differs with the Bush administration and is in American interests, but Hillary Clinton said that she supports the Bush administration's tough embargo policy and a travel ban that is more restrictive and punitive than when she and her husband occupied the White House. (Clemons 2007, Washington Note).

Gazette-Journal of Reno, Nevada stated that Obama's "back-ground and experience have given him the insight needed to deal with the world in a different way. He knows how to listen and to respond appropriately to questions, propositions and opinions, regardless of whether he agrees." A Presidential candidate "must be someone who can unify the nation on domestic issues, successfully uphold its democratic ideals and restore its reputation as a global force." (January 17, 2008). Florida's *St. Peteresburg Times* endorsed Obama:

> ... like many voters who have cast ballots so far, we find Obama to be a more promising choice and a more inspiring voice in these troubled times. His message of hope and change has resonated with voters, including independents and young people. He speaks of the kind of change many Americans yearn for in their politics and their government - not just turning the page on George W. Bush's presidency but changing something more fundamental in Washington.
>
> What separates these two candidates (Hillary Clinton and Obama) are not the issues, where their differences are minimal, but the values and vision they would bring to the presidency and the kind of political character they have displayed so far. In Clinton, we see the past; in Obama, we see a fresh start. Clinton is a divisive political figure; Obama's appeal transcends racial and party lines. She exudes competence; he radiates optimism. She came to the campaign with a sense of entitlement; he came to it with a sense of possibilities. She can be evasive, even misleading; he can be refreshingly candid about his own shortcomings and his political mistakes. She represents business as usual in politics; he at least offers the hope of something better. ..
>
> Clinton, a former first lady now serving her second term as a U.S. senator from New York, would bring conventional political experience to the Oval Office. Obama offers a different kind of experience - his "life experience" as the son of a white woman from Kansas and a black father from Kenya, as a Harvard law graduate who passed up a U.S. Supreme Court clerkship to work as a community organizer in Chicago's poor neighborhoods, as a state senator and since 2005 as a U.S. senator from Illinois.
>
> Another Illinois politician was elected president with even less experience than Obama. He was a former state legislator and one-term congressman named Abraham Lincoln. We don't suggest that Obama is a Lincoln, only that Washington experience should not be the only standard for measuring a candidate's qualifications to be president. (St. Peteresburg Times, Jan. 20, 2008)

The Star Ledger and *The Times* endorsed Obama, saying, "At a time when our country is mired in a disastrous war of choice, and when the disaster of the aftermath of Hurricane Katrina has revealed the failures of our federal government, we desperately need change in America. That is why I am enthusia-

stically supporting the candidacy of Sen. Barack Obama for president of the United States. We need a president who had the judgment and courage to oppose the war in Iraq from the beginning. We need a president who has demonstrated a willingness, time and time again, to take on powerful special interests and work and fight for change. We need a president who can unify the country around a forward-looking agenda." (February 3, 2008).

Yale Unniversity Daily News, after bragging about Bill Clinton, Hillary Clinton, George W. Bush Jr, and his daddy H. W. Bush, all alumni of Yale, declared that it has to skip Hillary at this time and recommend Barack Obama as the next President of the United States. The Yale editors wrote:

> ...Still lingering, though, is the question of substance. Too often asserted is the notion that one should run for the presidency with a crystal-clear, unchanging slate of party-line policy initiatives. With Obama's candidacy, however, comes an opportunity to correct this flawed conception of the chief executive as a glorified policy wonk. Our legislative system, after all, is designed to encourage compromise and cooperation. Overwhelming majorities for a single party are rare enough that a combative, polarizing politics that insists on a fixed agenda is self-defeating. Solid policy planks, then, are only half of the battle. What we must know — and do know in Obama's case — is which philosophy a candidate would bring to the West Wing. And we are impressed by his deep-rooted belief in one nation, not two.
>
> But we do have a dose of humble advice for Obama: Reveal your potential cabinet now. Part of the reason we are endorsing you is that we have confidence in your ability to surround yourself with good people and great statesmen. As Obama said in last night's debate, explaining his ability to attract droves of young supporters: "Part of the task ... of leadership is the hard nuts and bolts of getting legislation passed and managing the bureaucracy, but part of it is also being able to call on the American people to reach higher."
>
> Nothing more aptly sums up the spirit of youth. And as Obama rises, so, too, does our generation, once called leaderless, amorphous, solipsistic and uninterested. Forty-eight years ago, John F. Kennedy, whose daughter endorsed Obama this week as "a president like my father," visited the New Haven Green in the hours before the election. Thousands came. Hope filled a depressed town.
>
> Electing Barack Obama — another candidate who could surely fill the Green — would reclaim part of that era. But it would achieve more. An Obama presidency promises a reassertion of the natural, American optimism for which JFK stood, but also new reforms of which he could only have dreamt. Let us not let this moment slip away. (Yale Daily News, Friday, February 1, 2008).

The endorsement of Barack Obama is extensive. It ties the feelings of many voters in the USA. It reflects the enthusiasm in the nation and outside the United States about Obama's candidacy for the President of United States of America. The LA Times wrote:

...We urge voters to make the most of this historic moment by choosing the Democrat

most focused on steering the nation toward constructive change: We strongly endorse Barack Obama. The U.S. senator from Illinois distinguishes himself as an inspiring leader who cuts through typical internecine campaign bickering and appeals to Americans long weary of divisive and destructive politics. He electrifies young voters, not because he is young but because he embodies the desire to move to the next chapter of the American story. He brings with him deep knowledge of foreign relations and of this nation's particular struggles with identity and opportunity. His flair for expression, both in print and on the stump, too easily leads observers to forget that Obama is a man not just of style but of substance. He's a thoughtful student of the Constitution and an experienced lawmaker in his home state and, for the last three years, in the Senate.

On policy, Obama and his rival Democratic candidate, Sen. Hillary Rodham Clinton of New York, are a hairsbreadth apart. Both vow to pull troops from Iraq. Both are committed to healthcare reform. Both offer candid critiques of the failed George W. Bush presidency, its blustering adventurism, its alienating stance toward other countries and its cavalier disregard for sacred American values such as individual liberty and due process of law.

With two candidates so closely aligned on the issues, we look to their abilities and potential as leaders, and their record of action in service of their stated ideals. Clinton is an accomplished public servant whose election would provide familiarity and, most important, competence in the White House, when for seven years it has been lacking. But experience has value only if it is accompanied by courage and leads to judgment.

Nowhere was that judgment more needed than in 2003, when Congress was called upon to accept or reject the disastrous Iraq invasion. Clinton faced a test and failed, joining the stampede as Congress voted to authorize war. At last week's debate and in previous such sessions, Clinton blamed Bush for abusing the authority she helped to give him, and she has made much of the fact that Obama was not yet in the Senate and didn't face the same test. But Obama was in public life, saw the danger of the invasion and the consequences of occupation, and he said so. He was right.

Obama demonstrates as well that he is open-eyed about the terrorist threat posed to the nation, and would not shrink from military action where it is warranted. He does not oppose all wars, he has famously stated, but rather "dumb wars." He also has the edge in economic policy, less because of particular planks in his platform than because of his understanding that some liberal orthodoxies developed during the last 40 years have been overtaken by history. He offers leadership on education, technology policy and environmental protection unfettered by the positions of previous administrations.

By contrast, Clinton's return to the White House that she occupied for eight years as first lady would resurrect some of the triumph and argument of that era.

Yes, Bill Clinton's presidency was a period of growth and opportunity, and Democrats are justly nostalgic for it. But it also was a time of withering political fire, as the former president's recent comments on the campaign trail reminded the nation. Hillary Clinton's election also would drag into a third decade the post-Reagan political duel between two families, the Bushes and the Clintons. Obama is correct: It is time to turn the page.

An Obama presidency would present, as a distinctly American face, a man of African descent, born in the nation's youngest state, with a childhood spent partly in Asia, among Muslims. No public relations campaign could do more than Obama's mere presence in the White House to defuse anti-American passion around the world, nor could any political experience surpass Obama's life story in preparing a president to understand the American character. His candidacy offers Democrats the best hope of leading America into the future, and gives Californians the opportunity to cast their most exciting and consequential ballot in a generation.

In the language of metaphor, Clinton is an essay, solid and reasoned; Obama is a poem, lyric and filled with possibility. Clinton would be a valuable and competent executive, but Obama matches her in substance and adds something that the nation has been missing far too long -- a sense of aspiration. (Los Angeles Times, Friday, February 1, 2008).

Why is it necessary to bring some of these endorsements together? It is so you can be be able to read them and visualize a common theme in what very intelligent people and voters like you are saying. Their words are coming from deep down in their bellies, and some of the people make the endorsements even when such an open support of a black man may cost them heavily. They simply do not care, for they unanimously keep crying and seem to be saying, "The time is now, let's cease the moment, we better not miss this opportunity." Does this not say something serious to you? Let me tell you again, "This is of God, not of man."

America is about to be blessed. America is about to be resurrected. God will do it by the mere presence of the man, Barack Hussein Obama, in the White House. As a serious Christian, a lover of Jesus Christ--take it from me. It is a plan God may have put together years ago. It is left to us to cast our votes by faith. Read the following excerpt from US Representative Joseph Andrew, a super delegate who switched from supporting Senator Hillary Clinton to Senator Obama:

I have been inspired. Today I am announcing my support for Senator Barack Obama for President of the United States of America. I am changing my support from Senator Clinton to Senator Obama, and calling for my fellow Democrats across my home State of Indiana, and my fellow super delegates across the nation, to heal the rift in our Party and unite behind Barack Obama…

Here is my message, explained in this lengthy letter that I hope is perceived as a thoughtful analysis of how to save America from four more years of the misguided polices of the past: …we should focus our efforts on those who are truly on the opposite side: those who want to continue the failed policies of the last eight years, rather than bring real change to Washington. Let us come together right now behind an inspiring leader who not only has the audacity to challenge the old divisive politics, but the audacity to make us all hope for a better America.

Barack Obama is the Right Candidate for Right Now…I recognize that this is a difficult decision for super delegates like me, who owe so much to President Bill Clinton. It is right to be loyal, to be grateful and to be consistent. But it is also right to acknowledge the inevitability of change, right to dare to dream for a better world, and right to know what in your heart is the right thing for the future even if your friends and family disagree. ..

What is best for our Party and our country is not blind loyalty, but passionate support for the candidate who can best correct the misguided policies of the last eight years. We need a candidate who will re-invigorate the economy and keep good jobs here in America. We need a candidate who will end the war in Iraq. We need a candidate who will provide health coverage for our 45 million uninsured neighbors. We need a candidate who will end our addiction to high-priced foreign oil by investing in renewable energy here at home.That candidate is Barack Obama.

Let's seize the opportunity… and vote for someone who was against the war from the beginning, and who brings a new energy, a new excitement, and a new politics to our country. Let's put things right. As Democrats, however, we risk letting this moment slip through our fingers.

A New Era of Politics: My endorsement of Senator Obama will not be welcome news to my friends and family at the Clinton campaign. If the campaign's surrogates called Governor Bill Richardson, a respected former member of President Clinton's cabinet, a "Judas" for endorsing Senator Obama, we can all imagine how they will treat somebody like me. They are the best practitioners of the old politics, so they will no doubt call me a traitor, an opportunist and a hypocrite. I will be branded as disloyal, power-hungry, but most importantly, *they will use the exact words that Republicans used to attack me when I was defending President Clinton.*

When they use the same attacks made on me when I was defending them, they prove the callow hypocrisy of the old politics first perfected by Republicans. I am an expert on this because these were the exact tools that I mastered as a campaign volunteer, a campaign manager, a State Party Chair and the National Chair of our Party. I learned the lessons of the tough, right-wing Republicans all too well. I can speak with authority on how to spar with everyone from Lee Atwater to Karl Rove. I understand that, while wrong and pernicious, shallow victory can be achieved through division by semantics and obfuscation. Like many, I succumbed to the addiction of old politics because they are so easy.

Innuendo is easy. The truth is hard. Sound bites are easy. Solutions are hard. Spin is simple and easy. Struggling with facts is complicated and hard. I have learned the hard way that you can love the candidate and hate the campaign. My stomach churns when I think how my old friends in the Clinton campaign will just pick up the old silly Republican play book and call in the same old artificial attacks and bombardments we have all heard before.

Yet, despite the simple and overwhelming pressure to do anything and everything to win, Barack Obama has risen above it all and demanded a new brand of politics. People flock to Senator Obama because they are rejecting the hyperbole of the old politics. The past eight years of George Bush have witnessed a retreat from substance, science, and reason in favor of spin, cronyism and ideology. Barack Obama has dared not only to criticize it, as all Democrats do, but to actually reject playing the same old game. And in doing so, he has shown us a new path to victory.

We must reject the notion that we have to beat the Republicans at their own game -- or even that the game has to be played at all. It is so easy for all of us involved -- candidates, campaigns and the media -- to focus on the process and the horse race that we forget why we got into it in the first place. Barack Obama has had the courage to talk about real issues, real problems and real people. Let's pause for a second in the midst of the cacophony of the campaign circus and listen.

In 1992, I was inspired by Bill Clinton because he promised, and delivered, a framework for addressing America's problems. President Clinton ended a long-running left-right debate in our Party, and inspired millions. He drew giant crowds and spoke passionately for a generation of Americans who often disenfranchised and rarely participated in governing. Today, Barack Obama does the same thing. Winners redefine the game. Winners connect with the American people and not only feel their pain, but inspire them to take action to heal the underlying cause. Barack Obama is that kind of candidate and that kind of leader, which is why he will win in November.

My speech ended with these words, which are even more relevant today: The difference between the Republican Party and the Democratic Party is that you are always welcome in the Democratic Party. Because Democrats don't care if you are black or white or brown or a nice shade of green, you are welcome in the Democratic Party. We don't care if you pray in a church or a synagogue or a temple or a mosque, or just before math tests, you are welcome in the Democratic Party. We don't care if you are young or old, or just don't want to tell your age, you are welcome in the Democratic Party.

We don't care what gender you are, or what gender you want to hold hands with; as long as you want to hold hands, you are welcome in the Democratic Party. We don't care about the size of your bank account, just the size of your heart; and we don't care where you are today, just where you dream you want to be tomorrow. That is your Democratic Party. That is Barack Obama's Democratic Party. That's the Party that will win in November. (Huffington Post, May 1, 2008).

This is a powerful endorsement. There are many others like this such as those of Governor Bill Richardson of New Mexico and the former Vice President, Al Gore of Tennessee. You read where Representative Andrew referenced Bill Richardson and the criticism and dislike he received for abandoning his former boss, the former President Bill Clinton and his wife. Governor Richardson was the first or one of the very first two or three Democrats to make the bold move of getting away from the clutches of Bill Clinton and his wife to support a candidate of their heart.

Governor Richardson practically rebuk-ed Bill Clinton and his wife for acting as if the party and the country are entitled to them only, and as if somebody owed them something. America needs more leaders like Bill Richardson. In fact, the governor came at the perfect time for Barack Obama, right at the height of Rev. Jeremiah Wright TV clips and uproar. The Clinton Campaign was happy and eagerly watching Barack Obama to be derailed. I consider Bill Richardson's endorsement a major lifesaver for Barack's campaign, ranking up there with Senator Edward Kennedy's.

After the spectacular race speech, Richardson came up with his surprising, highly coveted endorsement, a bold endorsement that really helped get Obama out of the water of Rev. Wright's controversy. This governor showed up when a lot of other potential supporters or those who had already pledged to Barack Obama may have been scratching their heads about what to do. Governor Richardson said:

Governor Bill Richardson of New Mexico. Wikipedia

> My friends, Earlier this week, an extraordinary American gave a historic speech. Senator Barack Obama addressed the issue of race with the eloquence and sincerity and decency and optimism we have come to expect of him. He did not seek to evade tough issues or to soothe us with comforting half-truths. Rather, he inspired us by reminding us of the awesome potential residing in our own responsibility. Senator Obama could have given a safer speech. He is, after all, well ahead in the delegate count for our party's nomination.
>
> He could have just waited for the controversy over the deplorable remarks of Reverend Wright to subside, as it surely would have. Instead, Senator Obama showed us once again what kind of leader he is. He spoke to us as adults. He asked us to ponder the weight of our racially-divided past, to rise above it, and to seize the opportunity to carry forward the work of many patriots of all races, who struggled and died to bring us together.
>
> Senator Obama reminded us that cynicism is not realism, and that hope is not folly.
>
> He called upon us not just to dream about a less racially-divided America, but also to do the hard work needed to build such an America. He asked every American to see the reality and the pain of other Americans, so that together we can rise above that which has divided us. He appealed to the best in us.
>
> As a Hispanic, I was particularly touched by his words. I have been troubled by the demonization of immigrants--specifically Hispanics-- by too many in this country. Hate crimes against Hispanics are rising as a direct result and now, in tough economic times, people look for scapegoats and I fear that people will continue to exploit our racial differences—and place blame on others not like them.
>
> We all know the real culprit -- the disastrous economic policies of the Bush administration! Senator Obama has started a discussion in this country long overdue and rejects the politics of pitting race against race. He understands

clearly that only by bringing people together, only by bridging our differences can we all succeed together as Americans. His words are those of a courageous, thoughtful and inspiring leader, who understands that a house divided against itself cannot stand.

And, after 8 years of George W. Bush, we will desperately need such a leader. Our national security and our global standing have been gravely

damaged by the divisive partisanship of recent years. We need a President who can bring us together as a nation so that we can face urgent global challenges and repair the damage done in the last 7 years. Barack Obama will make the historic and vital investments into renewable energy, to help create clean energy jobs and fight global warming.

Barack knows that the safety and future of every American child requires that we restore our shared sense of national purpose, so that we can then set about the hard work of rebuilding our alliances and rehabilitating our image in a dangerous world. By uniting our nation, we can reverse America's global decline. We need a realistic, principled, and bipartisan foreign policy again.

We must restore our international reputation, our influence and our capacity to lead others. America must become the beacon for the world again. We need a foreign policy based upon American ideals, and not upon the mere ideology of a President. A foreign policy of diplomacy and respect for international human rights.

We prospered and prevailed in the Cold War because both our friends and our enemies knew that containment of the Soviet Union and the promotion of democratic values was not a Democratic or a Republican policy – it was an American policy--the very essence of what America was. Senator Obama understands the importance of realism, principle, and bipartisanship in foreign policy.

He opposed the Iraq war from the beginning because he knew that, despite what the Administration claimed, this war would not be easy. He also opposed the war because he saw President Bush's rush to employ military force, and to do so without the support of most of our allies, as dangerous and unwarranted. And he saw the war also for what it so quickly became – a terrible source of partisan political division -- and a catastrophic distraction from the war that had united us against the real threat posed by Al Qaeda.

Now, I trust him to do what is so long overdue—End the Iraq war and bring our troops home!! I know Senator Obama well. I first got to know him when I chaired the last Democratic National Convention, where he gave that wonderful keynote address. And then, last year, as we campaigned against each other for the Presidency, I came to fully appreciate his steadfast patriotism and remarkable talents.

I also felt a kinship with him because we both had one foreign-born parent and we both lived abroad as children. In part because of these experiences, Barack and I share a deep sense of our nation's special responsibilities in the world. Barack Obama, you are an extraordinary leader who has shown courage, sound judgment and wisdom throughout your career.

You understand the security challenges of the 21st century, and you will be an outstanding Commander in Chief. Above all, you will be a President who brings this nation together and restores American global leadership. You will make every American proud to be an American, and I am very proud indeed to endorse your candidacy. Before concluding my remarks, I would like to say that we are blessed to have two great American leaders and great Democrats running for President.

My great affection and admiration for Hillary Clinton and President Bill Clinton will never waver. It is time, however, for Democrats to stop fighting amongst ourselves and to prepare for the tough fight we will face against John McCain in the Fall. The 1990's were a decade of peace and prosperity because of the competent and enlightened leadership of the Clinton administration, but it is now time for a new generation of leadership to lead America forward.

Barack Obama will be a historic and a great President, who can bring us the change we so desperately need by bringing us together as a nation here at home and with our allies abroad. I know that all Democrats will work tirelessly to get him elected. It is my distinct honor and privilege to introduce to you the next President of the United States, my friend, Barack Obama. (New York Times, March 21, 2008).

Here comes an online media from Richardson's state, the Tribune of Albuquerque, New Mexico. It is recommending Barack Obama for the presidency of the United States. Noting that Barack Obama's campaign has caught fire, they added fuel to the blaze by calling on New Mexico voters to rise up for Barack. This is a fiery endorsement.

We have a dream. In it, a new, young president inspires all Americans to rise above partisan politics, gender, race, religion, region, money, ideology and economic philosophy to make this nation all that it can be. That young president of vision and promise is the charismatic Barack Obama....

The Tribune believes Obama has reawakened the imagination, work ethic and hope of Americans coast to coast and across the political spectrum — particularly among the nation's youngest voters who finally seem engaged in their country and their future. In this dream, he wins the nomination of his party, prevails in November and leads America back to the progressive promised land.

There, a united America walks its democratic talk. There, its Constitution — in particular its Bill of Rights — once again reigns supreme. There, Americans stand shoulder to shoulder against any and all foes, not as conservatives or liberals, Republicans or Democrats, not as men or women, black, white, Hispanic or American Indian, but as Americans. It's not that Obama's resilient rival, New York Sen. Hillary Clinton, would not be a good president. She could be. Indeed, she has been tested and has dedicated virtually her entire adult life to American public service. But in the tumultuous life that is competitive politics, Obama offers true change — a different and unique vision with purpose, determination and outstretched hands.

From Iraq to health care, both candidates hold similar positions on major issues. But Obama has a far better chance of unifying the country by refusing to play the standard political game. Pick your metaphor, but he rises above ordinary politics, does an end run around the old guard and challenges every

American to step up and make a difference. In spite of his relative youth and inexperience — which have drawn barbs from Clinton and her husband, Bill, the former president — Obama's candidacy most recently gained impressive traction among all categories of voters — women, men, black, white, brown, rich, poor, red, blue.

Yet there also have been incredible endorsements from some of the most potent and legendary Democratic voices of our time, including the brother and daughter of President Kennedy. Like John F. Kennedy, who asked his "fellow Americans" to come to the aid of their country, Obama makes it plain that each of us can do something to make America great — together. In doing so, we can achieve America's global destiny as the mother of all democracies.

It has been a very long time since America had the leadership of someone who could disarm us of our pessimism, remind us of our roots and heritage and insist that we can solve America's enormous problems together. Instead of an impassable American mountain, Obama sees a team of American mountaineers plodding toward the summit.

There, law rules, not men. There, every citizen is equally free and accountable. There, opportunity, ability and hard work determine our individual and collective dreams. Not since the 1960s have we been so touched by someone who espouses the hopes and strengths of a nation. Some will find a reason not to vote for Obama. He is too young, too inexperienced. Too liberal. Too conservative. Too black. Too white. Too soft. Too religious. Too secular. Too naive. Too full of himself.

But we see in him a vibrant American leader who understands that leadership begins first and foremost with the people and a respect for — not manipulation of — them. Obama seeks to leapfrog Washington's harsh political rhetoric and gridlock for all the right reasons. While some might ask why him, why now, we ask: Why not?

We enthusiastically endorse the presidential aspirations of Obama as the candidate in the New Mexico Democratic caucus most capable and willing to lead this country by challenging each and every one of its citizens to do what needs doing — achieve the American dream, rooted in those famous words: life, liberty and the pursuit of happiness. (Tribune, February 4, 2008).

This book's purpose is to help you see the light on how to choose a president. More critically is what is at stake for America now come November 2008. These endorsements are uniquely different. They are priceless, emanating from the hearts of people who know that America needs change and her people need to believe in her leadership again. The endorsements are supposed to help you make a choice and cement that choice all the way into the voting booth. Your future is in your vote. The previous endorsement is just heartfelt and fierily excellent. Another hearty endorsement from Saint Louis Today of Missouri stated:

...Thus did Barack Obama, in his campaign book "The Audacity of Hope," touch on a fundamental problem in today's American politics: It's too much about yesterday's American politics. In too many ways, it's still about Vietnam. It's still about hardhats and hippies. It's about Watergate and Iran-contra and Whitewater. It's about the past. Barack Obama is aware of yesterday, but he is about today and tomorrow and next year. In a strong field of Democratic presidential contenders, he offers the best hope of transforming the debate and moving on to

what America can be in the 21st century. He is unlikely in many ways: He is young, only 46. He is the junior United States senator from Illinois, only a little more than three years out of the Illinois state Senate — as unlikely a forest for presidential timber as ever was. His middle name is Hussein. He spent his boyhood in Indonesia and Hawaii. His mother was a Kansan; his father was a Kenyan. Did we mention he is black?

If America can get past all that, if America can unload its baggage and get on with the trip, there is no telling far and how fast it can go. It's true that Mr. Obama's legislative portfolio is slim, although he has been strong on ethics reform and the disclosure of lobbyist influences. He's never managed any organization larger than his Senate staff, and he admits a weakness when it comes to paperwork and organization. The nice thing is that a president has people to do those things, and Mr. Obama has surrounded himself with a cadre of seasoned professionals. Mr. Obama can do things that better managers can't.

The toughest part of any president's job is to inspire and to lead. Think of Franklin Roosevelt and fear itself, of John F. Kennedy challenging America to go to the moon "because it is hard," or Ronald Reagan after the Challenger disaster. Mr. Obama, by virtue of his life story and his compelling gift for oratory, has that kind of capacity.Already he has energized thousands of voters who had written off politics or never bothered to get involved.

It's exciting to think of what that might mean...Comets don't come around that often. In January of 1961, Ann Dunham Obama was six weeks pregnant with Barack Obama Sr.'s child when President Kennedy said at his inauguration that "the torch has been passed to a new generation." It's that time again. (ST Louis Today, January 27, 2008).

Just like many foreign news media and foreigners in general, London Financial Times is understandably excited and does not want to see the Democrats and America blow it this time. They enthusiastically endorsed Obama.

...Mr Obama has fought a brilliant campaign, out-organising his opponent, raising more money, and convincing undecided Democrats as well as the country at large that he was more likeable, more straightforward and more worthy of trust. On form, he is a spell-binding orator and holds arena-sized audiences in thrall. He is given to airy exhortations, it is true, but genuinely seeks consensus and has cross-party appeal. Mrs Clinton's campaign, in contrast, has been a shambles.

She and her team expected to have it all sewn up long ago; they made no plans for a long struggle, ran short of money and had to reorganise on the run.

Her speaking style is pedestrian, when it is not actually grating. Those who dislike her tend to do so with a passion: her disapproval ratings started high and after months of campaigning are climbing still. It is a tribute to her tenacity and to the loyalty she commands in the party that her fate was not sealed weeks ago.

How much the way that a campaign is run tells you about a candidate's fitness to be president is debatable - but it does tell you something, especially if the candidate with the misfiring strategy is running on a claim of management expertise.

In fact, the campaigns have underlined the contenders' respective strengths and weaknesses. Mr Obama's consistent and relaxed demeanour attested to his coolness (in both senses, his swooning young admirers would add); it seemed to affirm his authenticity. In contrast, Mrs Clinton's hyperactive advisers dressed her in a new personality each day, sometimes several in the course of an interview.

They wheeled out Bill Clinton, to remind people of the 1990s, then reeled him back, to help them forget. Too many course corrections, not enough course. Mr Obama has had some travails - over his association with Jeremiah Wright, the ranting demagogue pastor, and most recently over condescending remarks about small-town Democratic politics.In the first case, he responded with a masterly speech about race that may even have improved his standing. In the second, he was evasive and unconvincing - yet the public seems to have given him the benefit of the doubt...The Democratic Party has waited an awfully long time for a politician like Barack Obama. Enough already. (London Financial Times, Monday, April 21, 2008).

Barack Obama's clinching of the number of delegates needed to secure the Democratic Pary's nomination for President caused a cry of joy both in the USA and across the the nations. A Newspaper in London has a front-page title that says, "NOW BRING McCAIN." Senator John McCain, as we know, is the Republican presumptive nominee for the president of the United States.

In Mexico City, hairdresser Susan Mendoza's eyes lit up when she learned Obama had clinched the nomination. "Bush was for the elite. Obama is of the people," she said. The German government's coordinator on U.S. relations, Karsten Voigt, said many Germans "find (Obama's) mixture of Martin Luther King and John F. Kennedy very attractive."

In an editorial, the *Times* newspaper of London said Obama's campaign "has rekindled America's faith in its prodigious powers of reinvention — and the world's admiration for America." Obama opposed the invasion of Iraq and has called for an early troop withdrawal. He also has shown willingness to engage in dialogue with Iran, North Korea and Cuba — nations long isolated by the policies of Bush. "He seems to be a peace lover," said Ngo Van Hung, a Vietnamese real-estate salesman. "He would have a better understanding of how to treat people of different nationalities and different countries." (USA Today/AP, June 4, 2008).

Content Analysis of Endorsements

The above endorsements are representative of the enthusiasm surrounding Barack Obama's candidacy for the president of the United States. Individual endorsements from millions of little, big, young, old, rich, poor, and all kinds of people in the blogs constitute mountains of excitement and expectancy of something new and good for America. Bunch of the little people, most of them on minimum wage, are part of Obama's 1,700,000-donor list. They give five dollars and 10 dollars, and so on. In fact, they feel like they own Obama and the campaign. They are very excited.

All the endorsements that compared Senator Hillary Clinton's campaign problems to Obama's well-managed campaign reflect what are being said now with Senator McCain's campaign relative Obama's. At the back of the heads of those analysts, if the skill of managing a campaign is a measure of Presidential success, McCain ought to lose the election to Senator Barack Obama as Hillary Clinton lost to him in the Democratic primary. Senator McCain's campaign has been grossly criticized for lack of purpose, lack of objectives, lack of known strategy, and full of problems—literally filled with lobbyists, turnovers, and some financing secrecy (Gilgoff 2007, CNN Ploitics.Com 2008, Malkin 2008, Shear and Birnbaum 2008).

Barack has been seriously commended on how he manages his senate office and personnel, his calmness in dealing with people regardless of how much the fire is burning, and his understanding of problems and coming up with innovative solutions. Since we have not been with these presidential contenders in their homes and offices to monitor and record how they manage and lead their subsystems, the only thing we have and that all of us can see must count. The planning, organizing, staffing, directing, and controlling of their campaigns are important factors in the equation of how they can run the presidency. The presidency of the United States is the worst place to do things by whimsical thinking and erratic leadership. That will result to catastrophes after catastrophes.

If America really wants a highly qualified, serious and knowledge-eable mind, and and calm spirit to be a true and credible CEO and Commander In Chief, America better give Barack Obama their votes. He is by far the better choice in this year's presidential election. In a picture, what do all the endorsements mean? What are the endorsements saying for Obama's presidency? Let us try to categorize their points to help people see what choice they have in Barack Obama as the next president of the United States.

Category 1: President of the whole people. The endorsements see Barack as one who will make a perfect president for the haves and have-nots. The common man will have a say. They really see him as one that will run the government of the people, for the people, by the people. They are seeing him as a would-be All-Hands-On-Deck President.

Category 2: A unifier President. They see in Barack one who will be a true unifier of all factions in the nation that has been polarized for too many years. He is the quartz or the linking pin that unites all people into one true United States of America. There is therefore love in the air among the citizens of the country. There is also healing of hearts in the air.

Category 3: International bridge-builder and healer of rifts. They truly see Barack as the one God can use to amend fences they believe the Bush administration has destroyed, and to bring healing in the perceived crumbling America's international connectedness with the rest of the world, especially with America's allies.

Category 4: Intelligent and Analytical President. They see Barack Obama as one president that will not be shy of analyzing a nation's problem and comes up with careful solution. He is not shy to delve into the mathematical equations needed to do things right instead of shying away from reasoning and adopting a messy decisional option that will injure everyone with time.

Category 5: Steady and Sure President. They see in Barack a man of no drama, calmness, and without anxiety, and yet masters what he is doing. They just have so much confidence that he will bring the same skills into the White House, transmitting stability and quiet atmosphere to the whole nation even in the presence of facing serious problems. In other words, they see this Obama as one who can pilot a nation through boisterous winds or noisome waves with the nation still intact and getting better.

Category 6: Intelligent Commander In Chief of America's Armed Forces. Gradually but surely, you can just hear the hearts and minds of American people and read between the lines that they certainly know Barack is TOUGH but loving and peaceful. He is wise and smart, but down-to earth. He knows America's military might, but cannot put it up-front as a way of intimidation of opponents. He knows how to employ the weapons when the push dares come to shove. You can see in the air that they believe the man will employ strategic management principles and processes in dealing with the nation's military, avoiding wars and saving lives as much as possible. They believe he can fiercely go after America's determined enemies but according to pre-determined strategies not whimsical maneuvers.

Category 7: A CEO President. The tone of the endorsements and the substance show that the people seriously believe Barack Obama may be one of the best Presidents America has ever produced, for he will smartly make executive decisions that will positively sift and expunge a lot of the nation's problems and strengthen her cultural, economic, and political atmospheres. Policies will be based on sound problem-solving methodologies, intelligent reasoning, and critical processes but not on whimsical value system and special interests' infestations. America will really come first.

Category 8: An Inspirational President. They have compared him to late President John F. Kennedy and his brother, Robert Kennedy, but they seem to believe that this man is even better. The flame of inspiration is sweeping every age group, every race, and every creed. People cannot function well and right if they are not fired up and ready to go. Without inspiration, there will be no motivation, and without motivation, the people can't perform or dare to get the ability to perform, and without inspiration of the masses, the leader is really on his own, and if the leader is on his own, there goes the nation. This brings us to the next category.

Category 9: An Institutional leader. They truly see Barack Obama as an institutional leader in the sense that this man, quite unlike most politicians they have seen, is seeking power not for personal gain but to be able to mobilize the country toward the achievement of the critical national goals and objectives, educationally, politically, economically, technologically, and internationally. The man is not seen as a selfish man but a man of the people, all people—not just for black folks but for all *U-N-I-T-E-D S-T-A-T-E-S O-F A-M-E-R-I-C-A.,* one nation under God!

Category 10: A Trustworthy President. They see a man they can trust to help lift them up. They see a man they can depend on. They see a decent man that is strong enough not to let them down.

See if you can read the heart of this blogger, Anthony Retford. He represents a segment of the common folks who are rooting for Barack Obama. He was making a statement about what he would have done to help the Obama campaign if he were in his home state of Kentucky:

> …I would have said to them that the time for voting (participation) and then forgetting about it and going around doing what the government says … can end with Obama. I would have told them that if they vote for Obama that would not be the end of their responsibility. Millions of people like me have accepted that this country cannot change unless we the people make it change. Obama intends to do exactly that and that challenge and exciting participation is why we should all vote for Obama. **Posted by: anthonyretford.**

Dear America, can you imagine what will happen if all Americans get it as this blogger got it? Inspired by Obama's campaign, this American has come to an intrinsic conviction that America cannot just be good by itself just by letting the government doing what it wants or doing it alone while everyone else lays dead; America will blossom if everyone continues to work for America after they have voted. Now that is INSPIRATION! That's what a leader needs to help him lead! America, you have a good choice in Barack Obama as your next able CEO and Commander In Chief! Seize the moment! This is your moment!

Senator Joe Biden: The Able Running Mate

I certainly congratualate Barack Obama and reaffirm my endorsement for him based on another wise decision. On Saturday, August 23, 2008, Barack Obama ushered in his running mate as the Honorable Senator, Joe Biden of Delaware. This is another great plus in his judgment for most other candidates usually choose running mates on the bases of whether or not the choice will help win his or her state. You can tell that Barack chose Biden for his qualification, independent thought process, and dedication to work and nation. Barack is not looking for Yes-Man. He searches and chooses the best for the job. He continues to show acumen in this area of staffing as we have exemplified earlier.

Barack Obama and Senator Joe Biden of Delaware. – BarackObama.com

Ladies and gentlemen, Barack Obama is into this race not for any selfish gain, pride, or name. He is into it because of a calling in his heart to do so for the benefit of the United States of America. His choice in Biden and other reasons in this book continue to qualify my assertions. McCain and the GOP criticize Barack Obama as '*The One*.' Well, they forgot that every person in this world is '*The One*' in something. Some are the '*The One*' for doing good and others are '*The One*' for evil. Many Americans see John McCain as '*The One*' in carrying out President Bush Junior's third term and the politics of secrecy, whimsical decision-making, fumbling foreign policy, sobbing social system, and epileptic economy. Obama is seen by many as '*The One*' to change this wrong part and to move America toward a new direction of strategic thinking, 24-hour presidency, One-USA, and no-drama domestic and foreign policies. Yes, Barack is the one for this change, and the Honorable Senator McCain seems to recognize that. Thanks to America for recognizing and rooting for a good thing.

Fellows, Barack and Joe will provide sound leadership for USA. These two men are not into scandals. They are men of integrity and hard work. Barack has made an excellent choice in a running mate. Together they will work to heal America and nourish USA, domestically and internationally. Vote for Barack and Joe, and then watch America be blessed highly. God bless America! God bless the USA.

CHAPTER 16

CONCLUSION: PATRIOTISM IMPERATIVE!

The most patriotic act of any person is to put God first. Who is God?—love, peace, holy lifestyle. Such produces the greatest and enduring blessing for a nation. Fellows, it begins with your home. Do you love your spouse and children as God commands? Start now! It's not too late for you.Barack will do it for USA. Charity begins at home. He will fight for America as he will fight for those three people.

From a family to a community to a town to a state to a nation to the world. We are interconnected. Love is the only binding factor. A citizen of the world is a perfect amalgam of various cultures of the world to the benefit and acclaim of the nation to which the person belongs. To lead a nation is to understand the nuances of the world surrounding that nation and uses the knowledge to bring blessings to that nation while maintaining good relationship with the rest of the world system, understanding that we are all interdependent. Love of people is true patriotism, and one cannot love people without loving the righteous God. It's more of action than talks.

Defining Patriotism

Senator John McCain defines patriotism as putting the counry first. In addition, the Senator said, "the gift we can give back to our country is a patriotism that requires us to be good citizens in public office or in the community spaces where government is absent… It is the willing acceptance of Americans, both those whose roots here extend back over generations and those who arrived only yesterday, to try to make a nation in which all people share in the promise and responsibilities of freedom… To love one's country is to love one's countrymen. And if we are to replicate the spirit of our founding age, if we are to be genuine patriots, we must remember also that we are patriots because we love the countrymen we will never know, who will be born after we are gone." (Parade.com July 3, 2008). Beautiful!

Barack Obama stated that, "As with most Americans, patriotism starts for me as a gut instinct, a loyalty and love for my country that's rooted in my earliest memories…true patriotism also means a willingness to sacrifice for our common good… That is the community we strive to build—one in which we recognize we share common hopes and dreams, one in which we continue to insist that there is nothing we cannot do when we put our minds to it, and one in which we see ourselves as part of a larger story, our own fates wrapped up in the fates of all who share allegiance to America's singular creed. " (Parade.com July 3, 2008).

These responses, which are just excerpts from many other things they said, are beautiful recognition of patriotism. The ability to be a strong or unwavering patriot stems from who your Commander or role model is and whether that Commander is with you always and rewards you for being patriotic. That is why you witness serious religious people not cheating on their taxes, volunteering to help others, working hard for their employers, and not cheating on their spouses. All of the activities are patriotic behaviors. So is exercising your right to vote wisely.

Just look at the description of patriotism by the two Senators. They let you know that whatever you do that harms your fellow citizen is unpatriotic. Whatever you do that hurts the common good of the nation is unpatriotic. For instance, committing adultery destroys your spouse and your children, leads to divorce, and causes other numerous and cyclical havocs for the victims and for the whole nation. So is committing fornication, which leads to teenage pregnancies, murders, single parenting, explosion in government welfare spending, etc. I just want to make sure these Senators know what they are talking about. That's why I also like my definition which says, "Putting God first, and that God stands for love, peace, and holy lifestyle." When you put God first--as your role model, as the one that directs your actions, and as your 'rewarder,' it will be extremely hard for you to mistreat another person. It will be hard for you not to put the common good first. At least you will always find yourself repenting when you violate it, which is good.

For instance, there is one election that I really did not like the person I was supposed to vote for just because I thought he was a racist, but I have no proof. To make matters worse, God told me to go and vote for that person. For fear of God, for His love and friendship to me, which are immeasurably important to me, I just got up almost grudgingly and drove about 70 miles to cast my vote for the person. After I voted, my flesh was somewhat wishing for the other fellow to win, but the person that received my vote won by a slim margin. You see, if I had no boss who is holy, righteous, and loving enough to direct me, I would have failed to be patriotic by not voting as directed. Similarly, without the same guiding principle, I would have been unpatriotic by fornicating with girls and women who are supposed to be other people's wives some day, causingg cyclical turmoils by such act. That's ideal patriotism.

However, voting is a much more popular knowledge as a patriotic issue than what I just presented; it is one of those items that commonly comes to mind when we speak of patriotism. Can you vote patriotically? Can you vote for America? Do you belive that some people can actually vote selfishly and others patriotically? When you look at all the needs of the nation and prioritize them, you may be able to vote patriotically instead of voting on what concerns you the most as an individual. Can you imagine how beautiful the country will be if people actually vote patriotically? It is not easy to vote patriotically when the flesh is ticking.

America: Behold Your Institutional Leader

He is the man that can harness America's talents and gifts, can take all Americans together toward the achievement of America's goals. He can not only work with you to set goals, determine strategies, implement those strategies, evaluate and make appropriate corrections, but he will also work through you. You see, someone may try to work with you even though you are hurting very badly by that person's undeserved dictatorial actions and disregard to your emotions. Here is a man, Barack Obama, who will go at length to prove that he is trustworthy and honest enough that you yourself will be convinced that he is doing all for the common interest not for selfish ends or for pleasing special interests.

Barack Obama
richmonddemocrat.blog spot.com

Your heart will not be injured as you work with him. That's working through you. As the President of EmancipationUSA and Cham-pionSociety organizations, I humbly recommend to you, Senator Barack Obama as the next President of the United States of America. You have everything to gain in this man. To be the President and CEO of USA is not a child's play or some hide and seek activity. People, it is serious. It is especially important now that America is at the crossroads of many routes, not knowing which way to go. You can let this man lead you. Let's do it. Barack Obama has weighed very well on the balances of management process scale, production process scale, management-approach scale, the marketing scale, the domestic policy scale, the foreign policy scale, and the strategic management scale. Those weights are necessary in defining a true CEO and Commander In Chief of a nation like the USA.

Like many Newspapers and individual endorsements, and consid-ering the emotions and tearful supports of millions of the haves and the have-nots of the blogs who are rooting for this man, I candidly encourage you to consider making this Barack Obama our next president. God, through him, will do us good. The man, Barack Obama

- Is consumed with America from birth until now, understanding the need to admire the rich and the dire need to lift up the poor and the working class to experience the American dream too.
- Is a man of Love whose heart and mind are set on helping the people and less on selfish purpose.
- Is equipped with High Contingency Oriented ability, capable of knowing when and how to switch leadership styles to fit appropriate situations from decisions associated with domestic policy to decisions associated with foreign policy.
- Is equipped with High Internalized System's Make-Up that naturally makes him to see everyone as essential, to think about everyone, and to avoid decisions that will lift one and harm the other. Decisions can only be made that will bless the USA together.
- Is a Moderate Moral Man. He is doing his best to serve God the best he knows. He will improve as he learns. All of us are the same way.
- Is a Unique Motivational and Inspirational type of person who knows how to get us to be fired up and ready to go from grass level to the top, with one dollar to millions of dollars, with everyone feeling as Mr. President or Madam President.
- Is endowed with or possesses Intrinsic Gauge for Societal Achievement. The man is for us, not for himself. When "Us" achieve then 'he' and each of us also achieve. He possesses a clock within him that lets him know how to adjust the ship continually to remain on the right course of societal building. In other words, the man's personal achievement is only measured in terms of what you and I achieve.
- Is Mr. Reconciliation and OnenessUSA, a long overdue achievement. He thinks One-America not Faction-America.
- Is Abraham Lincoln, John Kennedy, Ronald Reagan, and some humble dove combined. Meditate on this.
- Is God's Nobel Prize Trophy to America for such a time as this. He is an evidence of America's charity to the rest of the world all these years. He is also an evidence of what God is about to do for America again.

Patriotism and Casting Your Vote

In his article of June 29, 2008, George, Stephenapoulos, ABC News Chief Washington Corresspondent, teaches Americans how to vote (Parade.com). To be a better voter, Stephenapoulos explained that voters should look at the following factors or tests:

1) Know What Matters to You: Determine what matters to you and then see where the candidates stand on that list you made. The least can be the character of the candidates, your values, beliefs, etc. Then think about what the candidates will make their priorities when they get into office.

2) Use the Godfather Test: Choose a candidate that will provide and protect your children. "The decisions made by the next President will help determine whether your children will have to fight in wars, how dependent they'll be on foreign oil, and whether Medicare and Social Security will be there when they retire. Vote for the candidate who has the competence and character to guide your child and the country."

3) Find Out What Your Friends and Family Really Think: What your friends and loved ones think might help you make the right decision.

4) During the Debates, Focus on What the Candidates Say—and Do: look at how they respond to questions, the verbal and nonverbal behaviors, how they handle pressures, the kind of answers they give to questions and the ease of answering such questions. Remember that some candidates may do better on the camera and some do not. So, you may use multiple ways to evaluate the candidates.

5) Balance It All Out: This is a very important advice to you. George Stephenapoulos writes--

> (Look at)Where the candidates have come from, what positions they take on the issues, whom they listen to, and how they make decisions all matter. No one quality is the key to success. Take experience, for example. It's hard to imagine a President coming to the White House with a more stellar resumé than James Buchanan, who had been a Congressman, a Senator, an ambassador, and Secretary of State. But he failed miserably as President—passive in the face of a looming Civil War.
>
> Nor can a candidate who promises change necessarily achieve it. Jimmy Carter came in after Watergate promising "a government as good as the American people," but he ended up not having the political skill to deliver one. Experience, judgment, and competence all have to be weighed in equal measure.
>
> And think hard before disqualifying a candidate for being a flip-flopper. Flip-flopping can be the most devastating criticism—and deservedly so, if the candidate shifts with the political winds. But history also is full of Presidents who changed their minds for the right reasons. The Louisiana

Purchase was the kind of power-grab that ran against Thomas Jefferson's deepest principles, but he came to see it as a wise investment in America's future, and supporting it turned out to be one of the best Presidential decisions ever. Abe Lincoln promised the South that he wouldn't abolish slavery. Thank goodness he changed his mind." (Parade.Com, June 29. 2008).

6) Always Remember That Your Vote Counts: Failing to vote may cost your favorite candidate the election. It has happened many times. If all the people who favored Al Gore in 2000 had voted, President George W. Bush Jr. would not have been President. Al Gore lost by a very slim margin of 537 votes in Florida which gave the presidency to George instead of Al, following a Supreme Court decision in favor of George.

Voting is a serious personal and patriotic act that you cannot miss. Your future, your children's future, your relatives' future, and the state of the whole nation depend on it. If after reading this book you still feel strongly about voting for someone else other than Barack Obama, then feel free to do so. It is important that you cast your vote for the love of the nation as a whole. After you weigh the points that matter to you as George Stephenapoulos just finished teaching, then consider the points that matter to everyone else or that is MOST IMPORTANT to the nation as a whole. Remember that the presidential candidate is running for the President of the whole nation not just for you. That is voting patriotically.

Nevertheless, I am requesting of you to consider seriously voting for Barack Obama (1) because of the analysis in this book and (2) because I encouraged you to do so. I believe that God is calling the man to this job. Now take it from me—if he dares not put you (America) first and do the best for the nation as God directs him, God Himself will strike him down and hard. When God calls a one, and that one does whatever he pleases without listening to the God who called him, the same God explodes on that person to humiliation.

Fortunately for us, Barack does not have the ability or the strength to think of letting you down. He cannot stomach it! It cannot happen! This country has blessed and loved him over his head; that is why he left the corporate money for grassroots' work with common people. His struggles and background are counter disappointment at this post. He desires in his gut to pay back and to help you. He is ready to die or live fighting for you, protecting and strengthening America, domestically and internationally in every category of environmental forces. He is ready to be President and CEO of USA starting from Day-1! He will be a 24-hour President and Commander In Chief of the United States of America.

Since you now know that God is in charge, go ahead and vote for him by faith. God will honor your faith. This is a special period in American and world history. I believe God has something good up His sleeves for USA, which He can do by using the man, Mr. Barack Hussein Obama of USA and of the world. Only in America will the story be possible; America is about to be highly blossomed because of the prayers of her concerned citizens and for her years of charity and sacrifices that have received little or no thanks from many parts of the world! Bob Cesca wrote:

> …after seven years in this Dark Age, I've almost forgotten what it was like to have a real president occupying the White House: a president who, even if I disagreed with his policies and ideology, dignified the office with a stature that symbolized the awesomeness of America…
>
> …President Bush was never a hero in the first place and only grew more ridiculous with each subsequent crime against the Constitution, against human decency and against democracy itself. If there's any justice left in this nation, history will record that President Bush was an entirely inadequate tool; a bungling villain whose early popularity grew out of a traumatic and patriotic need to support the office regardless of who occupied it.
>
> And when the flood waters literally rose up and washed away the disguise, the slack-jawed poseur was revealed -- the "bore" who had always been there, but who had been previously and cynically costumed in cowboy drag. Some of us recognized the charade from the beginning, but it required a second national tragedy, this time in New Orleans, to alert the media and the rest of America to his (Bush Jr.) criminal incompetence.
>
> American history is inextricably tied to the presidency. It's how we mentally assemble the chronology of our past. For going on eight years, we've endured a chief executive who never should have ascended to this post. Consequently, this decade has been an aberration; a time when Americans somehow championed an illegitimate, Orwellian hooplehead and, naturally, we suffered for our lack of vision. This is how most of the first decade of this century will be remembered. Yet our generation is being offered another chance here -- an opportunity to set things straight and elect a president who not only illustrates the historical qualities of the office, but who also defines an energetic new approach. The next president has to be Senator Barack Obama.
>
> Senator Obama's intelligence, passion and quality of character can inspire us to recapture our own potential for greatness. And after all these years of darkness, there is no alternative other than to correct our trajectory with someone who can elevate our common goals -- the American Dream. For the American Dream to survive, this era demands a new president who will include all of us in the debate over our future, whether or not we agree on every issue.
>
> And I'm proud to say that I don't agree with the senator on everything. But it doesn't matter because this campaign is about much more than individuals and their pet issues. This is about the reacquisition of an ideal -- of a benevolent greatness, which has been stolen away from us. I see in Senator Obama an historic character who fits within my persnickety and idealistic template for the presidency -- and this time around, it happens that my idealistic choice has a realistic chance to win. So this isn't necessarily an endorsement based on ideology, but an endorsement based on that which is required from a historical perspective.

> The alternatives on either side of this campaign are ultimately redundant to what we have now. On the Republican side, each frontrunner represents a rage-inducing aspect of the present Bush regime. The Romney Unit represents the Paris Hilton fiscal policy of the Bush administration; Giuliani is the unstable, crazy-ass hubristic gunslinger; and Mike Huckabee is the cross-bearing fundamentalist who floats in the same fantasy world as Kirk Cameron and Ray Comfort. ..
>
> On the Democratic side (he tore Senator John Edwards apart). Senator Clinton, meanwhile, is certainly more intelligent and centrist than President Bush, but there's a secretive, calculating DLC side to the senator which drifts too dangerously close to the universe of Dick Cheney than the fresh approach her husband, President Clinton, offered in 1992. … for now he's the historical antidote to the darkness and division we've endured for too many years. He's our best hope to restore the national equilibrium and to fulfill both the expectation of greatness the presidency deserves and, thusly, the greatness of America. (Cesca 2007, The Huffington Post).

Once Again, Don't Forget the Overall CEO Test

If you have forgotten, then read this analysis again. Otherwise, you may skip this section. It is that important to help you not to forget. An ABC News report on July 14, 2008 stated that a poll conducted by ABC News and Washington Post found 72 percent of Americans indicating that Senator McCain would be a good Commander In Chief and 25 percent saying he would not. The same poll recorded that 48 percent of Americans said that Senator Barack Obama would be a good Commander In Chief and 48 percent saying he would not (Langer 2008, ABC News). Senator Hillary Clinton had criticized Senator Obama on this subject, but Obama clearly proved that he would be a much better Commander In Chief than the former first lady would. Now here we go again with Senator McCain who actually has similar characteristics with Senator Clinton:

- McCain is relatively not as steady or calm as Obama, but has a tendency to be much more trigger-happy than Obama would ever get close to being.
- McCain is not as conceptual and analytical as Obama
- McCain is not as system-oriented as Obama
- McCain is not as management process oriented as Obama

I am beginning to think that American people may not have a clue as to what Commander In Chief really means. If they know, the results of the above poll should be in reverse. Barack Obama will be a better Commander In Chief than Senator McCain by most measures. You cannot be a good Chief Executive Officer without being a good Commander In Chief. All these functions or their makeups are interdependent. Obama is genuinely more system and contingency oriented than Senator McCain and may be as competitive as or better than McCain. He will therefore make a much better leader at both CEO level and at Commander In Chief definition.

Let us look at the roles of a good President. By the constitution and laws of the United States, a US President performs seven roles: (1) chief executive, (2) commander in chief, (3) foreign policy director, (4) legislative leader, (5) party head, (6) popular leader, and (7) chief of state (World Book Encyclopedia and Learning Resources 2008).

(8) Chief executive – The president has the power to enforce federal laws, treaties, and federal court rulings; to develop federal policies; to prepare the national budget; and to appoint federal officials.

(9) Commander in chief -- The president is to defend the country during wartime and to keep it strong during peacetime. The chief executive appoints all the nation's highest military officers and helps determine the size of the armed forces. Only the president can decide whether to use nuclear weapons.

(10) Foreign policy director -- The president is to appoint ambassadors, make treaties, and receive foreign diplomats. The chief executive may refuse to recognize a newly formed foreign government. The president also proposes legislation dealing with foreign aid and other international activities.

(11) Legislative leader -- The president greatly influences the development of many laws passed by Congress. At the beginning of each session of Congress, the chief executive delivers a State of the Union address to the lawmakers. In this message, the president discusses the major problems facing the nation and recommends a legislative program to solve them. The president also gives Congress detailed plans for new legislation at other times during the year.

(12) Party head -- The president helps form the party's positions on all important issues. The president hopes these positions will help elect enough party members to Congress to give the party a majority in both the House and the Senate. Such a strong party makes it easier to pass the president's legislative program.

(13) Popular leader -- The people rely on the chief executive to serve the interests of the entire nation ahead of those of any state or citizen. In turn, the president depends on public support to help push programs through Congress. The president seeks such support by explaining the issues and by showing the confidence and determination to deal with problems.

(14) Chief of state -- As the foremost representative of the U.S. government, the president is expected to show pride in American achievements and traditions. In this role, the president attends historical celebrations, dedicates new buildings and national parks, and may

> throw out the first ball of the professional baseball season. The president also presents awards to war heroes and invites distinguished Americans to the White House. (World Book Encyclopedia and Learning Resources 2008).

Can you see how all the roles are fused together? A mistake in one can cause domino effects on the rest and catastrophe upon the nation. People, let me strongly tell you that following serious analysis, our current President is better than John McCain in Commander-In-Chief test. He may understand the interconnectedness of things better than McCain, yet he made one serious mistake. [Let me also tell you that I am not a fan in criticizing our current President because the man has worked hard to hold this nation from collapsing. Besides, I just like him as a brother and I mean it, but he made a serious mistake.] He failed to see the delicate but dangerous link of his war strategies to the economic wellbeing of America and how to strategize to safeguard what is happening to America today.

If you think that the *Honorable* George W. Bush Jr. is a one-track-mind person, McCain will be gross! That is not being a good Commander In Chief, at least when you compare Senator McCain to Senator Barack Obama. It is like night and day! America, you need to wake up, smell the coffee, and then move toward the direction of the aroma to find the coffee. If you have a bad nose or keeps ignoring the right smell for one wrong reason or the other, you must always have yourself to blame. Be truly patriotic for a change. Stop going by emotion or by one attribute-voting mindset.

Since a picture is worth more than a thousand words, please take a close look at *Figure 1: The Head of the President of the United States of America.* That is exactly what is going on in the head of America's president, and that is why most of them get old faster while in office. However, some of them are more ordained to navigate through all the necessary channels and deal with the constant puzzles that affect the presidency and arrive at the ONLY RIGHT SOLUTION better and faster than others. Who do you think will navigate through the maze better? Who do you think will deal with the problems better and let you worry about other things concerning your household?

Who do you think is strongly minded enough to do the interwoven mathematics and calculus involved to get to the correct decision, a decision that will guarantee defeat of the enemy WITHOUT CONFUSION, strengthening of the economy, and maintaining a healthy international domestic and foreign-relations balance? Who has the appropriate GRAY MATTER AND THE ACUMEN to intellectually and psychologically read and understand the maze of things and make decisions that really bless the nation (not bringing one benefit and taking away 1000, or bringing one dollar profit but creating a million dollar costs)?

FIGURE 1: THE <u>HEAD</u> OF THE PRESIDENT OF THE UNITED STATES OF AMERICA

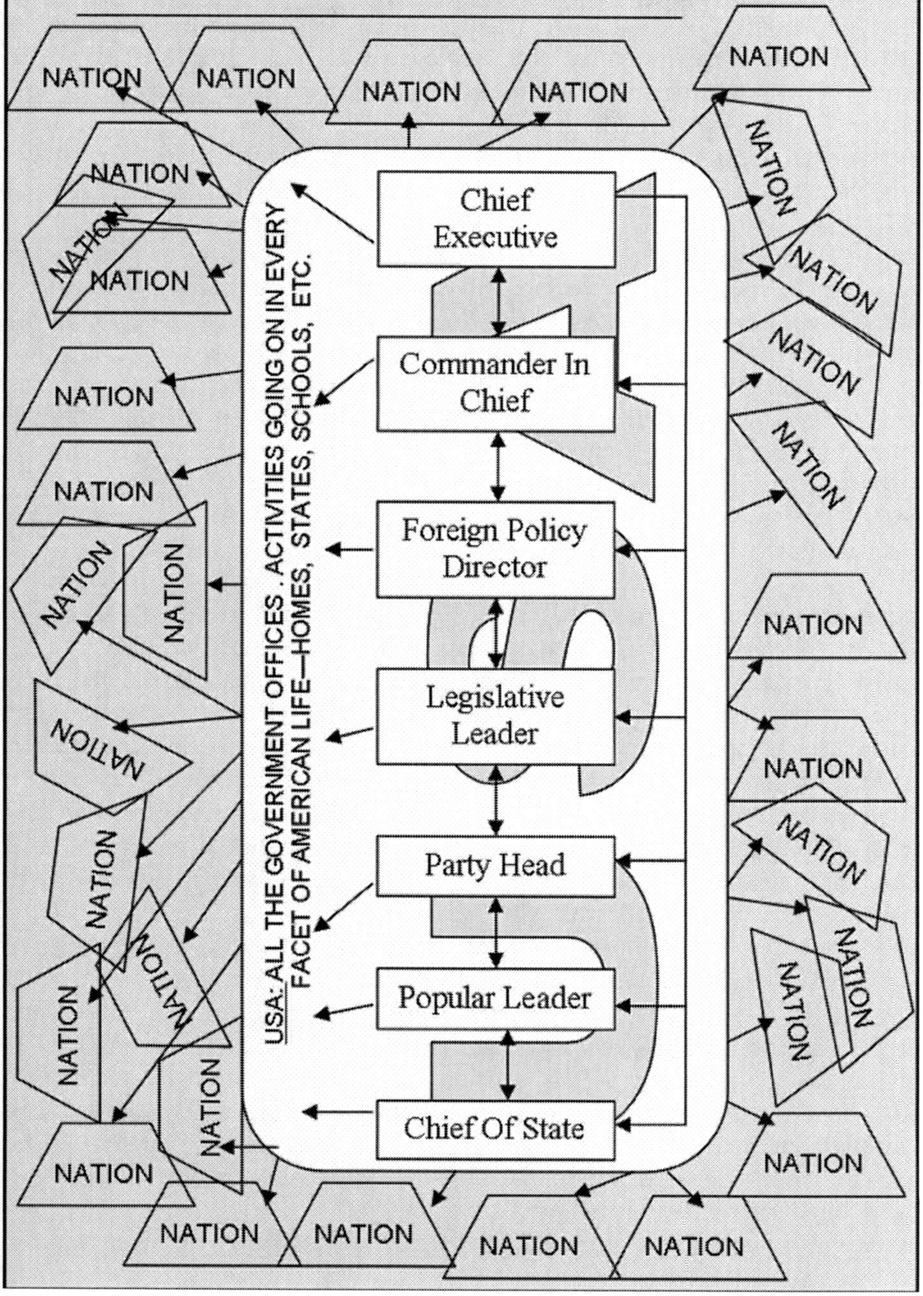

The only answer to the above questions, given the choices that we have and based on the analysis up to this moment, is cleanly Senator Barack Obama for the next President of the United States. What is acumen? It is QUICKNESS AND ACCURACY OF JUDGMENT. Good schooling and drills through life contribute heavily to acumen. A person that has gone from bottom to up is expected to have better acumen than someone who is stationed only at either extreme. Barack Obama has gone from bottom, through in-betweens, to the top, and then he decides to live and reside in the middle. I hope you understand this characteristic because it is critical to understanding the rich, the poor, the middle class, the black, the white, the Indonesian, the Middle-Eastern, the Africans, and the United Nations.

The humble fellow just finished paying off his school loans recently; he became rich two or three years ago because of God's light upon him and his books. He understands all classes and knows that someone has to fight for the poor and the working class while still loving the rich. Obama wants people to have the opportunity to be like him or better. That's the kind of person you must want to be a covering for America. Being a covering is the ultimate spiritual function of the President and CEO of a nation. You do not want an immoral person to be at the helm of any ship. The rest of the ship will be polluted worse and worse. As far as God is concerned, Barack Obama is a plus to USA considering what has been going on with the America's top office for years.

Now see this. Acumen—the quickness and accuracy of judgment -- cannot thrive without a relatively challenged, viable, and healthy grey matter. What is gray matter? It is a major component of the central nervous system, consisting of nerve cell bodies called neurons, glial cells, capillaries, and short nerve cell extensions and processes called axons and dendrites. It's function is to route sensory or motor stimulus to interneurons of the CNS in order to create a response to the stimulus through chemical synapse activity. Gray matter structures process information originating in the sensory organs or in other gray matter regions. This information is conveyed via specialized nerve cell extensions, which form the bulk of the cerebral, cerebella, and spinal white matter. (Wikipadia Encyclopedia).

Now let us come down to earth. All these cells or tissues of the gray matter, which occupy the head and the spinal cord, carry messages and conduct impulses. They are instrumental to your reasoning ability, the extent to which you may be confused and how much you can handle (depending on training). If they are dead, weak, or old, such functions can be mitigated or interfered with, especially in strenuous circumstances. If one is an angry person or does not have the ability to control himself or herself, some parts of the grey matter will be controlling him instead of him controlling the grey matter. If one has not been trained in education and serious problem-solving processes, the roads in this grey matter and the rest of the head can be jammed up easily. Think about what is involved in being America's CEO:

(1) As the person performs the functions of the Chief executive, he will always be worrying and analyzing in his head how whatever he does in this function affects the nuances of commander in chief intricacies—past, present, and future; foreign policy director intricacies—past, present, and future; legislative leader intricacies—past, present, and future; party head intricacies—past, present, and future; popular leader intricacies—past, present, and future, and chief of state intricacies—past, present, and future.

(2) As the person performs the functions of the Commander in chief, he will always be worrying and analyzing in his head how whatever he does in this function affects the nuances of foreign policy director intricacies—past, present, and future; legislative leader intricacies—past, present, and future; party head intricacies—past, present, and future; popular leader intricacies—past, present, and future, and chief of state intricacies—past, present, and future.

(3) As the person performs the functions of the foreign policy director, he will always be worrying and analyzing in his head how whatever he does in this function affects the nuances of commander in chief intricacies—past, present, and future; present, and future; legislative leader intricacies—past, present, and future; party head intricacies—past, present, and future; popular leader intricacies—past, present, and future, and chief of state intricacies—past, present, and future.

(4) As the person performs the functions of the legislative leader, he will always be worrying and analyzing in his head how whatever he does in this function affects the nuances of commander in chief intricacies—past, present, and future; foreign policy director intricacies—past, present, and future; party head intricacies—past, present, and future; popular leader intricacies—past, present, and future, and chief of state intricacies—past, present, and future.

(5) As the person performs the functions of the party head, he will always be worrying and analyzing in his head how whatever he does in this function affects the nuances of commander in chief intricacies—past, present, and future; foreign policy director intricacies—past, present, and future; legislative leader intricacies—past, present, and future; popular leader intricacies—past, present, and future, and chief of state intricacies—past, present, and future.

(6) As the person performs the functions of the popular leader, he will always be worrying and analyzing in his head how whatever he does in this function affects the nuances of commander in chief intricacies—past, present, and future; foreign policy director intricacies—past, present, and future; legislative leader intricacies—past, present, and future; intricacies—past, present, and future; intricacies—past, present, and future; party head intricacies—past, present, and future; and chief of state intricacies—past, present, and future.

(7) As the person performs the functions of the chief of state, he will always be worrying and analyzing in his head how whatever he does in this function affects the nuances of commander in chief intricacies—past, present, and future; foreign policy director intricacies—past, present, and future; legislative leader intricacies—past, present, and future; intricacies—past, present, and future; intricacies—past, present, and future; party head intricacies—past, present, and future; and popular leader intricacies—past, present, and future.

The President's head is full all the time, and he must be a type of person that loves and enjoys challenges and solving complex problems. A quick-tempered person cannot handle it at all. A person who is not well schooled cannot handle it well. A person with anxiety will have a serious problem. As the President performs any of the above roles, he must always be considering how each action in any of them interactively affects each other—on every facet of USA and on each of the nation of the world. Your head will be clear to be the president of the United States of America if the individual actually wants to do the job right and not for the name!

Once again, America, "Rise up and smell the coffee <u>right</u> or you will find yourself forced into drinking mud water instead of coffee." Do you know that some things may smell like and look like orange when in fact it is not orange? All that glitter is never gold. By my own analysis, President George W. Bush Jr. is not adequately diverse in his brain-ability to handle complex problems. He is too single-minded and would suffer serious headache if he faces multiple tasks at a time. He did fairly, but Senator John McCain will be relatively worse. Again, the honorable President, Brother George is better than McCain. Senator Obama will be much, much better than both of them. Obama already knew and he is frustrated by both Senator McCain's and the President's single-minded and open-end approach to handling Iraq (Bohan 2008, Reuters). Strategically, given all circumstances, it is not wise. Setting a timetable and bringing the troops home and <u>refocusing</u> constitute better strategic choice now. It will force Iraqi government to strengthen up.

When you are asked to pick gold and you have a choice between gold and silver, please choose gold. When you are faced with a less-than-desired situation where you have to choose gold, but you only have "X" with 50 percent gold and "Y" with 95 percent gold, then you had better choose "Y" or you will be playing roller coaster and other problems with your life and the life of the nation. In addition, this is no period to be shaking America too much. America is very fragile now and does not need too much drama at all. Senator Obama is a clear 95 percent in CEO and Commander In Chief tests for the United States of America for such a time as this in American and world history. The *honorable* Senator McCain is about 50 percent. Obama is the better choice. He is the much better qualified person to not only deal with the domestic problems and normal international relations, but what you have just read qualifies him as more capable to respond well to international crises on behalf of USA than his opponent will.

Now consider the multiple, reported problems that John McCain is having in putting a strategy together against Obama (Vogel 2008). It's all over the tabloids, most reported by the Republicans. He doesn't have a steady strategy. He may start with one and end with another, and then back to the one he started with, and may vacillate to other areas; he and his advisers are confused is part of the summary of McCain's campaign strategy or problems. If they take these troubles into the White House, America will sink into deeper waters. How can one manage today's America if one cannot run the intricacies of a campaign?

God Bless America. God Bless the USA!

Dear God, you are holy, and you desire us to be holy too. Unfortu-nately, we have failed you in many ways, leaning to our own understand-ding and doing what feels good to our flesh instead of listening to what you say. Please forgive us and start helping us again. Remember this nation's charity all over the world. Remember the billions of dollars in taxes that they have used to alleviate sufferings in people's lives around the globe. Remember the incredible Catholic charities, the evangelism and sacrificial mission lifestyles of many congregations, and the relatively great love of America's average citizen. Because of these people, their unmatched love, and for the prayers of many young and old, please bless America again. Bless the USA again! Help us to live right. Fight our enemies, and heal our domestic and international sicknesses.

This is a critical period in America's life and in the world as a whole. The one we choose as a leader is critical to our wellbeing. I believe that your hand is upon Barack Obama. Now help us to vote him into leadership, and help him to lead according to your guidance without fear or favor. I pray in the name of your darling son, Jesus Christ. Amen.

> "No public relations campaign could do more than Obama's mere presence in the White House to defuse anti-American passion around the world, nor could any political experience surpass Obama's life story in preparing a president to understand the American character. His candidacy offers Democrats the best hope of leading America into the future, and gives Californians the opportunity to cast their most exciting and consequential ballot in a generation."
>
> ………………… *LA Times, Feb. 1, 2008*

> "Obama's campaign has rekindled America's faith in its prodigious powers of reinvention - and the world's admiration for America."
>
> ………………………………*The Times Newspaper of London*

> "I think he feels it. He feels it just like Bobby did. He has the passion in his heart. He's not selling you. It's just him."…………….….*Ethel Kennedy, widow of Assassinated Presidential Candidate, Robert F. Kennedy*

REFERENCES AND BIBLIOGRAPHY

Associated Press "VIDEOS: Obama Shrugs off Jesse Jackson Comments" Originally published (July 9, 2008)

Bone, James and Robertson (2008) "West Suffers Historic Defeat as China and Russia Veto Zimbabwe Sanctions" Times Online July 12.

Cesca, Bob (2007) "Obama For President." The Huffington Post, December 19.

Charisma Magazine (2008) "Evangelical Leaders Meet and Decide to Back Sen. John McCain," July 14.

CNN (2008). "Analysis: Lack of Message Led to McCain Staff Shake-Up," CNN Ploitics.Com, Thursday, July 3.

Chipman, Kim and Goldman, Julianna (2008) "Obama's Cool Masks `Fierce' Competitiveness in Politics, Sports" Bloomberg, Friday, June 27

Clift, Eliano (2008), "Mappin a Win: Inside Obama's 50-State Strategy" NewsWeek, June 27.

Espo, David and Rising, David (2008), "Obama Addresses Huge, Adoring Crowd in Berlin," Associated Press July 24.

Gilgoff, Dan (2007), "Fired McCain Campaign Aides Sound Off," US News and World Report May 31.

Johnson, Sasha (2008) "Obama Uses Berlin Symbolism to Reunite Old Allies," CNN, July 24

Joshi, Vijay (2008) "Iranian president says no war with US, Israel" Associates Press July 8

Kessler, Ronald (2008) "Barack Obama's Racist Church" *Newsmax.com* Monday, January 7.

Kmiec, Doug (2008) "Endorsing Obama" www.slate.com, March 23.

Kuhn, David Paul (2008) "McCain Game Plan Worries Insiders," Politico.Com, July 1.

Langer, Gary (2008),"McCain Tops Obama in Commander-in-Chief Test; Stays Competitive on Iraq." ABC News July 14.

London Finacial Times (2008), "Democrats Must Choose Obama." April 21.

Los Angeles Times (2008) **"**Barack Obama for Democratic Nominee,**"** Friday, February 1.

Loven, Jennifer (2008) Bush signs new rules on government wiretapping" Associated Press July 11.

Malkin, Michelle (2008) "Open borders + campaign finance hypocrisy + eco-radicalism = McCain's billionaire national finance co-chair Jerry Perenchio," Michelle Malkin, January 28.

McCain, John (2008) "On Patriotism: Putting The Country First" Published: July 6, 2008 <u>in July 3, Parade.com</u>

Mooney, Alexander (2008) "Evangelist Accuses Obama of 'Distorting' Bible." CNN, June 24.

Morris, Dick (2008) "The Debate McCain Must Force" RealClearPolitics. June 25

Murphy, Josh (2008) "Why Barack Obama Should Be President," *The Minaret Online Edition*, (University of Tampa, Florida, May 22).

Nessman, Ravi (2008) "War is only job available in Sri Lankan village" Associates Press, 7/15/08.

New York Times (2008), "Richardson's Endorsement of Obama." March 21.

Obama, Barack (2008) "On Patriotism: Faith In One Another As Americans…" Published: July 6, in July 3, 2008 Parade.com

Oguhebe, Festus S. (2008) *THE ULTIMATE AUDACITY OF HOPE FOR TODAY'S USA: Emancipating America and Her Dreams* (Hebe's Global Consultants/ *Emancipation*USA.Org or ChampionSociety.Com).

______ (2002) *Valentine Love, How To Find the Right Spouse*, (Hebe's International Consultants, Jackson, Mississippi)

_______(2008) *WHITE HOUSE 101: How to Choose Whom to Vote for As President Or CEO of USA--Now who Is More Qualified—Hillary Clinton, Barack Obama, or John McCain?* (Hebe's Global Consultants/ChamioSociety.Com/EmancipationUSA.Org)

Page, Clarence (2008), "Rev. Jackson's 'Obama trauma'" Chicago Tribune July 13.

Reed, Betsy (2008) "Hillary Clinton: Race to the Bottom," The Nation May 3.

Robbins, Stephen P. and Judge, Tim (2006) *Organizational Behavior* 12/E (Prentice Hall).

Scafidi, Ben (2008), "Divorce, Out-Of-Wedlock Child-Bearing Cost U.S. Taxpayers More than $112 Billion A Year," Associates Press, April 15.

Shear, Michael D. and Birnbaum, Jeffrey H. (2008), "The Anti-Lobbyist, Advised by Lobbyists"

Smith, Ben (2008), "Bush Backer Pens Pro-Obama Book" Politico, Monday, June 16.

Sonner, Scott (2008) "Quayle Res*pects Obama, McCain Has Uphill B*attle*"* Associates Press July 01.

Song, Jaymes (2008) "Obama Finds Refuge, Identity In Basketball," (Associate Press)

St. Peteresburg Times (2008) "Endorsment of Obama" Sunday, January 20.

Stephanopoulos, George (2008), "How To Be A Better Voter" Published: June 29, 2008 in Parade.com Thursday, July 3, 2008.

Stirland, Sarah Lai (2008) "Obama: I'm Not a Muslim! Forward This to Everyone You Know" Wired, January 01.

Tristam, Pierre (2008), "Barack Obama's AIPAC Speech, June 4, 2008: The Full Text," About.com: Middle East Issues.

Tribune Staff (2008) "The Trib Endorses Barack Obama in Tuesday's N.M. DemocraticPresidential Caucus." Albuquerque, NM. Tribune February 4.

USA Today/AP (2008) "World Welcomes Obama Win" June 4.

Vogel, Kenneth P. (2008), "McCain's cacophonous Cabinet," Politico, Wednesday July 30.

Washington Note (2007), "Brzezinski Endorses Obama; Calls Hillary Clinton's Foreign Policy 'Very Conventional' Friday, Aug 24, 2:59PM.

WashingtonTimes, The (2008) "Obama's Associations May haunt Bid" Sunday, June 8.

Webb, Jim (2008) "What It Means To Be a Leader" Published: May 18, *Adapted from* A Time to Fight © *Jim Webb (Broadway Books, 2008).* In Parade.Com.

Wheelen, Thomas L. and Hunger, David L. (2008) *Strategic Management and Business Policy*, 11/E (Prentice Hall).

Whitlock, Scott (2008) "Stephanopoulos Attacks Media Bias Against Hillary." February 27.

Wikipadia Online Encyclopedia--Barack Obama, Michelle Obama.Wikipedia Encyclopedia: Sani Abach.

Wolffe, Richard and Thomas, Evan (2008) "Sit Back, Relax, Get Ready to Rumble" News Week, May 19, Issue

Yahoo News/AP (2008), "Israeli paper publishes Obama Western Wall prayer" July 25.

Zaborney, Mark (2008) "Obama Impressed Harvard Law Professor." Toledblade.com, Sunday, March 2.

APPENDIX 1

IRAQ WAR COSTS

Studies: Iraq war will cost $12 billion a month

Copyright 2008 The Associated Press

Economists project a much higher 'burn rate' than government estimates

updated 9:26 p.m. CT, Sun., March. 9, 2008

The flow of blood may be ebbing, but the flood of money into the Iraq war is steadily rising, new analyses show.
In 2008, its sixth year, the war will cost approximately $12 billion a month, triple the "burn" rate of its earliest years, Nobel Prize-winning economist Joseph E. Stiglitz and co-author Linda J. Bilmes report in a new book.
Beyond 2008, working with "best-case" and "realistic-moderate" scenarios, they project the Iraq and Afghan wars, including long-term U.S. military occupations of those countries, will cost the U.S. budget between $1.7 trillion and $2.7 trillion — or more — by 2017.
Interest on money borrowed to pay those costs could alone add $816 billion to that bottom line, they say.
The nonpartisan Congressional Budget Office (CBO) has done its own projections and comes in lower, forecasting a cumulative cost by 2017 of $1.2 trillion to $1.7 trillion for the two wars, with Iraq generally accounting for three-quarters of the costs…..

[NOTE—the figure amount does not include costs to other nations and numerous damges, etc. You cannot even put any price to the loss of the many lives.
To read the article and for explanation of these figures go to AP website with the above topic.

==

COST OF IRAQ WAR AND NATION BUILDING
From ZFacts.Com

"If we don't stop extending our troops all around the world in nation-building missions, then we're going to have a serious problem." — George W. Bush, Jan. 2001.

As of July 17, 2008 at 7: 50 p.m. CT. $556,832,839,551 AND COUNTING
Free Clock

The US budget for Iraq in FY 2007 came to $4,988/Iraqi. This is triple Iraq's per-person GDP. It's like spending $121,000 per person ($484,000 per family of 4) in the US. Why not just bribe the whole country? See spreadsheet for details.

Before the war, White House economic adviser Lawrence Lindsay estimated the cost at $100 to $200 billion. So the White House got rid of him and "re-estimated" the cost at $50 to $60 billion. It's now over $500 billion.

The neocons, Rumsfeld, Cheney, Wolfowitz, etc. were just totally unrealistic. "We are dealing with a country that can really **finance its own reconstruction,** and relatively soon." – Wolfowitz, March 28, 2003.

Go to Zfacts.com to see current figures.

By us, this change will not happen. Divided, we are bound to fail. But the life of a tall, gangly, self-made Springfield lawyer tells us that a different future is possible. He tells us that there is power in words. He tells us that there is power in conviction. That beneath all the differences of race and region, faith and station, we are one people. He tells us that there is power in hope. As Lincoln organized the forces arrayed against slavery, he was heard to say: "Of strange, discordant, and even hostile elements, we gathered from the four winds, and formed and fought to battle through." That is our purpose here today. That's why I'm in this race. Not just to hold an office, but to gather with you to transform a nation. I want to win that next battle – for justice and opportunity. I want to win that next battle – for better schools, and better jobs, and health care for all. I want us to take up the unfinished business of perfecting our union, and building a better America. And if you will join me in this improbable quest, if you feel destiny calling, and see as I see, a future of endless possibility stretching before us; if you sense, as I sense, that the time is now to shake off our slumber, and slough off our fear, and make good on the debt we owe past and future generations, then I'm ready to take up the cause, and march with you, and work with you. Together, starting today, let us finish the work that needs to be done, and usher in a new birth of freedom on this Earth. ....Barack Obama. 2/7/07

YES WE CAN!

OTHER BOOKS, AUDIOS, AND/OR VIDEOS BY THIS AUTHOR
c/o EmancipationUSA.org or ChampionSociety.com

THE ULTIMATE AUDACITY OF HOPE FOR TODAY'S USA: Emancipating America and Her Dreams And Where Barack Obama Really Missed It.

WHITE HOUSE 101: How to Choose Whom to Vote for As President Or CEO of USA [Now who Is More Qualified—Hillary Clinton, Barack Obama, or John McCain?[

PRESIDENT BARACK OBAMA OF USA: The Atmosphere of America and the Rest of the World With Barack As America's CEO.

PENTAGON GROUND ZERO: Job Expectation Of America's Leaders and the Verdict of a Wise Electorate.

WHITE HOUSE BILL CLINTON: The Real Truth About the Contribution of Bill Clinton's Presidency to the United States of America and his New Call to Life.

MADE IN AFRICA: The Real It Takes a Village To Raise a Child and Where Hillary Rodham Clinton May Have Missed It!

THE COMMON DENOMINATOR: The Primary Reason Why American Children and Adults Are Freaking Out and Going Haywire!

BEWARE OF OPRAH WINFREY?: Be Wise To Know When To Run Or Else!

THE PARTY OF GOD—DEMS OR GOP?: Which Part Will God Join If He Were In Person?

TIME BOMB KIDS AND THE AMERICAN NIGHTMARE: What's In Your Child's Head and What Must You Do?

I SEE YOUR HEART: The Great Soul of Senator Edward Kennedy of USA and What We Must Learn From Him.

THE DEATH OF USA: Do Something Now Or Kiss America "Bye Bye"

WHY DO THEY REALLY, REALLY HATE US?—The Right Answer to the Tough American Question [Surprise! Surprise! Surprise!]

REVEREND JESSE JACKSON: A Menace Or Some Trouble Maker?

GOD'S VERDICT ON McCAIN & OBAMA PASTORS: Are Jeremiah Wright, John Hagee, and Rod Parsley Trouble Makers Or What?

PASTOR JOHN OSTEEN: A Fake, A Serious Minister Of the Gospel, Or What?
BEHOLD VAGINA WORSHIPPERS!—Most Probably You Are One of them.

DIAGNOSIS WOMAN PRESIDENT: Is a Woman Capable To Lead the United States Of America?

PRESIDENT HUCKABEE 101: How Evangelicals and Folks Like Huckabee Can Win the Presidency of the United States Without Much Sweat!

STRONG WOMAN 101: The Only Way To Know If You Are a Strong Woman Or a Weak Woman! The Only Way!

GOD'S NUMBER ONE PROBLEM IN THIS WORLD: From the So-Called Men to the So-Called Husbands. Not the Women!

HEN-RAISED HUSBAND DISORDER AND A SOCIETY'S DEAD END: The Trouble With Female-Raised Children and Husbands.

FACT-Z: How To Know If You Are Really In Love Or Not! [THO ONLY WAY!!!]

WHO HAS THE FINAL SAY: The Husband Or the Wife In the Home? [The Answer Might Surprise You!]

SILENT KILLERS: How Bad Wives Abuse Their Husbands Silly and the Society Plays Deaf Ears.

BLACK WOMAN DISEASE: BWD and the Death of Black Race in USA.

DIAGNOSIS-1>HOW WHITE FOLKS MUST TREAT BLACK FOLKS IN AMERICA AND SIMILAR AREAS OR ELSE.

DIAGNOSIS-2>HOW BLACK FOLKS MUST TREAT WHITE FOLKS IN AMERICA AND SIMILAR AREAS OR ELSE!

THE AMERICAN TALIBAN?>Bullet Hole In the American Flag. The Reason for His Treason, and Why You May be Blamed for His Actions Also.

BITCHLESS 101: How To Avoid Marrying a Bitch Woman and Save Yourself Tons of Headaches, Heartaches, Sleepless Nights, and Death!

PENISLESS MAN 1000: How To Avoid Marrying a Stupid Man for a Husband and Save Yourself Tons of Headaches, Heartaches, Sleepless Nights, and Death!

DIVORCE DECISION 101: When Will I Divorce Him Or Her! See Your Final Answer!

HOW TO LOVE YOUR SPOUSE: The Only Way!

BETRAYAL 101: How To Survive the Ultimate Crime of Adultery. Can this Nuclear Bomb Leave Any Survival?

REAL FATHER 101: How to Be a Real Father For a Change. The Only Right Way!

REAL MOTHER 101: How To Be a Real Mother For a Change. The Only Right Way!

GOOD CHILD 101: How To Be a Good Boy Or Girl To Your Parents From Age Zero Till Death. The Only Way!

BEST-FRIEND IMPERATIVE: How To Know If Your Best Friend Is Really Your Best Friend Or Else!

IN-LAWS 101: How To Deal With Your In-laws In this Day and Age Or Else! How To Be a Good In-Law.

FRIENDSHIP 101A: How To Love Your Girl Friend. The Only Way!

FRIENDSHIP 101B: How To Love Your Boy Friend. The Only Way!

SUPER SEX 1000: The Best and the Worst Sex You Will Ever Have! [My O My!]

TEACHING GROUND ZERO: How To Be a Real Classroom Teacher In This Day and Age!

WOES OF USA STUDENTS: Why American Students Must Continue To Lag Behind Most foreign Counterparts and the Only Solution!

THE BOTTOM-LINE CAUSE OF DIVORCE ANYTIME: Forget Lack Of Communication, Financial Problem, and the Like.

THE BOTTOM-LINE THEORY OF FAMILY MANAGEMENT: Any Other Way Smells and Spells Trouble Anytime!

STRATEGIC MANAGEMENT PRINCIPLES OF LIFE IN GENERAL: A Critical Knowledge That Separates the Champs, the Average, and the Rest of the Stories!

OFF THE MAP<>ConspiracyUSA — Exposing the Ultimate Plot of America's Enemies. Let America Beware!

TODAY'S JEWS & ISRAEL 101: Protect Them, Kill them, Or Live Them Alone?

THE Da CODEINE AND THE HEFTY GREEN: The Real Code Behind the Da Vinci Code.

BLACK RACE SABOTAGE GROUND ZERO: Black Ministers And Leaders As Number One Destroyers of their Own Race!

DIAGNOSIS "PRINCE OF AMERICA"— The Ultimate Demonic Secret On Why Britney Spears and the Like Are In Shambles and May Keep On Suffering and Dying!

MR. WELFARE: The Husband Of American Women, the Father Of American Children, and the Death of USA.

SOUND CHRISTIAN DOCTRINE—STOP THE CONFUSION: How to Know Which Church to Join Or Which Preacher to Follow Or Risk Destroying Yourself and Loved Ones!

TO SPANK OR NOT TO SPANK: Fly-by-Night Doctors, Time-Bomb Parenting, and Your Loving Child.

GOD BLESS AMERICA: Why America May Still Be the Best Country in the World of Today Despite Her Follies.

GOD BLESS THE USA: Continuing Testament Concerning the Neighborly Spirit of America and Her Love Poems.

AMERICA AS THE POSTER CHILD: What Other Nations Need to Copy From America So God Can Bless Them Too.

DEAR GOD KEEP BLESSING AMERICA: How All Citizens, Immigrants, Visitors, and the Like Must Think and Treat the USA.

MY DEAR DARLING USA: God's Love Letter to America.

REMEMBER SEPTEMBER 11, 2001 IN THE USA: What Really Happened? Message To You, Message To America, Message To the World.

ISLAM EX-EXPOSED: The Truth and Nothing But the Truth At Last

BABY ON THE LOOSE: Columbine, the Rest of the Stories, and Why Children and Babies Go On a Shooting Rampage In the USA and Spreading.

PULPIT IN HELL FIRE: Are God's Ministers Thieves Or Tricksters Or...

IN SATAN'S NEST: Making Love With the Devil and Don't Even Know It [Most People Are Victims of this Love-Making].

EXTRA ROUGH 101: How To Be a No-Nonsense Single Parent Or Else!

VALENTINE LOVE: How to Find and Marry a Peaceful and Lasting Spouse for a Change.

BEYOND THE HONEYMOON: Dealing With America's Real Danger

MARRIAGE AND LOVE STORIES 101: Super Help In Dealing With Your Current Or Your Existing Marriage

WORLD LEADERSHIP MANIFESTO: If You Can't Rule This Way, Then Don't Assume Leadership In Your Nation.

CHILD ABUSE 101: The Ultimate Causes of Child Abuse In America-Like Environment.

UNIVERSITY OF THE VALLEY: Where God Is the Only Professor & the Making of God's Gold--Remember What You Do Not See!

THE RESTORATION OF MANHOOD: How a Man Must Think and Behave In This Day and Age. Period!

THE RESTORATION OF WOMANHOOD: How a Woman Must Think and Behave In This Day and Age. Period!

BEAUTY GROUND ZERO: How to Tell Whether You Are Really Beautiful, Really Handsome, Or Really Ugly!

TOTALLY BLIND GOVERNMENT & SUICIDE-GENOCIDE USA: How America Murders Her Children and Adults and Cripples Her Society Toward Oblivion

BLACK VOTES FOR GOP-1000: How Republicans Can Get Black Votes In American Elections

GOP AND DOWNHILL USA: The Woes Of America's Republican Party and How It may be Contributing To America's Destruction!

DEMS AND SUICIDE USA: The Woes Of America's Democratic Party and It's Possible Contribution To Destroying the USA!

TEENAGE PREGNANCY CAN BE STOPPED. A Grass-Root Approach to Dealing With a Formidable Menace!

Diagnosis FEMINISM> Is Feminism God's Blessing Or Devil's Demon?

GAYS AND LESBIANS 123— A Menace Or What? Kill Them Or Keep Them? Support AIDS Research Or Sabotage It?

DEPARTMENT OF CORRECTIONS OR DEPARTMENT OF DESTRUCTIONS! How America Destroys Instead of Corrects Her Prisoners. The Reason for High Relapse.

DIAGNOSIS TERRIBLE CANCER: The Masked Woes of Pentecostal and Apostolic Churches In the USA and Spreading!

THE REAL MONICA LEWINSKY—Misplacement, Misnomer, Misogamy, Misogyny, Or Sex Symbol. Her Score In Hillary Clinton's Book!!!

TRIPP THE TIPPER: Why Linda Tripp Should Be the Celebrity Instead of Monica Lewinsky.

A TRIBUTE TO GRACIOUS WHITE FOLKS IN AMERICA: Black People Do Say "Thanks A Million" To You!

MOTIVATION IMPERATIVE: How To Motivate Your Child to Good Performance and Success In Today's World . The Only Way to Do It!

A-Z SELF ESTEEM: The Only Right Way to Build STANDING Self Esteem In Your Child.

CATHOLICISM AND THE CATHOLIC CHURCH: Good For You Or Bad for You?

MORMONISM: The Church Of Jesus Christ Of Latter Day Saints. Is this Organization Evil?

JEHOVAH'S WITNESSES: Are They Any Good Or Just Bad?

GUARANTEED LOVE: The ONLY WAY To Know If Your Spouse Truly loves You Or Not, May Cheat On You Or Not.

Trouble-USA: Supreme Court Under Siege Spells Catastrophe Death-America
[Are They For America?]

THE ARMY, THE MARINES, THE AIR-FORCE: How Americans and Many Foreigners Must Learn To Treat Their Soldiers On a Daily Basis!

DARWINISM THE FINAL VERDICT: Darwin and the Origin of People. Is He Right Or Lunatic? Why Must people Believe Him?

BRITNEY SPEARS101: The Ultimate Reason Behind the So-Called Mental Illness of Britney Spears and Numerous American Children and Adults and the Only Solution!

SPOUSE KILLERS 101: Why Wives Or Husbands Kill their Mates In America-Like Cultures and the Only Way Out Or Else!

PARENT KILLERS 101: Why Children Have Little Or No Problem In Killing Their Parents In America-Like Environments and the Only Way to Stop the Mess!

DeToGoBa DISEASE: One of the Most Wicked Enemies Against Marriage and Other Necessary Commitments.

DOES GOD REALLY EXIST OR ARE THEY FOOLING US ALL? Why Do Some People Suffer and So Many Enjoy Life? Search No More!

STRESS AND ANXIETY DISORDER! The Only Way To Deal With Stress and Anxiety Without Those Pills and Other Empty Talks

THE WEAPONS OF JEZEBEL AND HOW TO WITHSTAND THEM: What Husbands and Men Must Do To Help Them Please God not a Snake Woman.

GOD AND OUR FLESH: Why Did the All-Smart God Place Us in This Flesh Since He Knows the Flesh Is Weak? Is He Crazy?

THANK GOD FOR MUSLIMS: Why Should Christians Thank God for Islam?

GOVERNMENT AGAINST ADULTERY: 23 Things Governments Must Do In Order to Disarm Adultery In America-Like Cultures

SELF ENEMY 101: See Why You Are Your Own Worst Enemy and What You Must Do To Free Yourself From Yourself!

Diagnosis ME! Why I Seem To Always Make The Same Mistake Over and Over Again!

EDUCATION MINUS JESUS IS DEVIL TO THE HIGHEST DEGREE! What the Crap Is This? Are They Really Serious Or Stupid?

ILLUSION 101—HUSBANDS BEWARE! The Deadly Trick of the Devil in a World Ruled by Rebellious Wives and Children.

PRESIDENT GEORGE W. BUSH Junior: Is He a Monster, an Angel, Or an Ass-Hole?

SURPRISE 101 BILL CLINTON AND GEORGE W. BUSH: Who Really is the Better President?

UNDERSTANDING JOHN McCAIN: A Rare Analysis

THE AUDACITY OF HOPE FOR AFRICA: The Only way To Bail this Cat Or else!

REV. JEREMIAH WRIGHT: GOOD OR BAD FOR AMERICA? GOD'S MESS OR GOD'S MESSANGER?

REV. ROD PARSELY: GOOD OR BAD FOR AMERICA? A POISON OR A PASTOR?

REV. JOHN HAGEE: GOOD OR BAD FOR AMERICA? A POISON OR A PASTOR?

AMERICAN SEX SCANDALS: Celebrities, Politicians, and Clergies In the Killing of USA—A Compilation and the Only solution.

PRESIDENT BARACK OBAMA *Of USA*

Dr. Festus Sunday AkaOlisa Oguhebe-'Strongblood' is a Nigerian immigrant who is very concerned about the depleting condition of the United States of America. He was a professor of Strategic Management and International Business for over 16 years, an uncompromising role model to students both inside and outside the classroom. A dedicated Christian conservative, Dr. Oguhebe-'Strongblood' once served as the President of African Christian Fellowship, south region, United States. He has sponsored and advised several Christian student organizations. Valentine Love Conference [now called Marriage Enrichment Conference], which the Lord helped the professor start in 1996 is still going strong every year. He has writte and/or presented several books or topics on solving societal problems [ChampionSociety.com Dr. Oguhebe is currently the President of *Emancipation*USA, an organization dedicated to expos ing and helping to solve America's problems. America is her own worst enemy; she is goin downhill at a geometric pace. Something has to be done and quickly. After examining the cand dates for 2008 USA presidential election, the professor has no choice but to write an analytic endorsement for Senator Barack H. Obama from Illinois. That's what this book is about. Read and learn how to make a true patriotic choice for the President of the United States of Americ <u>OR</u> see whether you made the right choice with your vote and be ready for next time!

"This is a serious piece of work, both an admonition to Americ and great love for America. Yet it educates you systematicall on why Barack is the best choice for America at this period i American and world history. Guard your loins"……*Hebe's Int Consultan*

"Whether you voted for Barack Obama or someone els whether we are before or after November general election, think you need to read this book to discover what a brillia choice you have helped make or to re-evaluate your vote f … w to choose a leader ar … ous book!"…*Min. Keith Purry, MS, US*

… oted for him or not., … SA"……………….*EUSA*

…tionUSA.org
…Society.com